DISCOVERING INDIGENOUS LANDS

Discovering Indigenous Lands

The Doctrine of Discovery in the English Colonies

ROBERT J. MILLER, JACINTA RURU, LARISSA
BEHRENDT, AND TRACEY LINDBERG

OXFORD
UNIVERSITY PRESS

OXFORD
UNIVERSITY PRESS

Great Clarendon Street, Oxford OX2 6DP
United Kingdom
Oxford University Press is a department of the University of Oxford.
It furthers the University's objective of excellence in research, scholarship,
and education by publishing worldwide. Oxford is a registered trade mark of
Oxford University Press in the UK and in certain other countries

First published 2010
First published in paperback 2012
Reprinted 2012

Crown copyright material is reproduced under Class Licence
Number C01P0000148 with the permission of OPSI
and the Queen's Printer for Scotland

British Library Cataloguing in Publication Data
Data available

Library of Congress Cataloging in Publication Data
Data available

ISBN 978-0-19-965185-6

Foreword

How can Canada claim to own Indigenous peoples' lands and resources? My grandfather asked me questions like this when I was still in grade school. My mother echoed these questions throughout my childhood. Neither was legally trained, but both spent their formative years on the Cape Croker Indian Reserve in southern Ontario. They knew from experience, and that of their community, that something was not right about how Canada purported to take our homelands. Their questions about Canada's claims were a natural and common part of my young everyday life. They wanted answers, and they would ask anyone for help in their quest, including their children.

For generations these same questions have been circulating within Indigenous communities throughout the world. Thus it should come as no surprise that these concerns followed Indigenous people when they entered law school. And it should be noted that, by most measures, Indigenous people have really only entered law school for the first time over the past thirty years. After gaining important initial experiences in diverse fields of legal practice or securing advanced degrees, the first generation of Indigenous law professors are now making their presence known in the wider world. Their voices are being heard beyond their communities, offices, and lecture halls. This book denotes the expansion of this work and signals the persistence of their ancestors' inquiries.

In *Discovering Indigenous Lands* you will encounter the voices of four distinguished Indigenous academics from the United States, Australia, New Zealand, and Canada. They ask and answer questions posed to me by my grandfather and mother. They show that when Indigenous lands were claimed by other countries there was no persuasive justification for this act. The 'doctrine of discovery', which supposedly undergirds the taking of Indigenous lands, is fully discredited by the authors of this book. They show how it is contrary to International and Indigenous legal orders. They demonstrate how the doctrine of discovery is inconsistent with domestic legal regimes that aspire to incorporate broader human rights concerns.

Professor Robert Miller is the first to write in this collection. An enrolled citizen of Oklahoma's Eastern Shawnee Tribe, he writes with authority and concision. His previous book demonstrated how Thomas Jefferson deployed the doctrine of discovery against American Indians and their governments. That work, entitled *Native America, Discovered and Conquered: Thomas Jefferson, Lewis and Clark, and Manifest Destiny*, marked the arrival of a sharp new scholar in American legal history. In the present book Professor Miller builds on his previous work to detail the doctrine of discovery's development from medieval times to the present. He shows how American colonies and US Presidents, legislatures, and courts have problematically relied upon this doctrine to dispossess the country's first peoples. He demonstrates how this doctrine relies on the assumed superiority of Euro-American religions, cultures, and 'race' to the detriment of Native American peoples.

Professor Tracey Lindberg's chapters about Canadian law are the next to appear in this book. She is a gifted scholar who incorporates Neheyiwak (Cree) principles throughout the body of her work. I was first introduced to Tracey's writing through a graduate thesis she wrote at Harvard Law School wherein she skillfully critiqued the stereotyping of Indigenous women in Canadian political and legal thought. Dr Lindberg's award-winning doctoral thesis is also a groundbreaking academic work. In *Discovering Indigenous Lands* Professor Lindberg demonstrates how Canadian law applies the doctrine of discovery despite its pretence to be following higher principles. The thesis of her contribution is that '[t]he Doctrine of Discovery in Canada may not be as evident on the face of the law as in other countries, but the assumption of authority under Discovery indisputably informs the development of policy and legislation' in that country. She writes with grace, power, and clarity.

Professor Larissa Behrendt is the third of four authors to write in this book. She is an Eualeyai/Kamillaroi woman, and one of Australia's most prominent Aboriginal intellectuals. She has published two acclaimed novels and numerous books and articles on Indigenous life and law. When I first met Larissa she had just finished a doctorate at Harvard Law School and was working with Harold Cardinal, who was perhaps Canada's most influential Aboriginal political writer of the twentieth century. After successfully working with Canadian First Nations, Larissa moved home to become a Professor of Law and Director of Research at the Jumbunna Indigenous House of Learning at the University of Technology, Sydney. This is where she still teaches. Professor Behrendt's thesis in this book is that the doctrine of discovery continues to contribute to the erosion of Aboriginal peoples' participation in public life. She shows how the assumption of inferiority that underlies the doctrine still allows contemporary Australian governments to override Aboriginal rights. The doctrine of discovery justifies suspending protection against racial discrimination by denying them meaningful community governance and violating their human rights. Her insights in this book are profound.

Professor Jacinta Ruru, a Maori Ngati Raukawa/Ngai te Rangi author, is the final scholar to have contributed to this book. Her work accomplishes what all the chapters in the book successfully achieve. She gives us a concise yet insightful overview of the main contours of law dealing with Indigenous peoples in the state she is examining, while at the same time demonstrating how the doctrine of discovery continues to permeate every aspect of their relationship with these states. She expertly takes us through the Treaty of Waitangi and the leading cases and statutes interpreting its provisions, and she does this without getting lost in the details. She succinctly summarizes the main contours of *Symonds*, the 1860s

Native Acts, *Wi Parata, Nireaha Tamaki, Te Heuheu Tukino, Te Wheehi*, the Lands Case of 1987, Lord Cooke's contributions in the mid-1990s, the *Ngati Apa* case, and the foreshore and seabed controversy of recent years. Professor Ruru's chapters demonstrate why she is one of New Zealand's most accomplished Maori law professors. In two short chapters she has written a complete, though concise, statement of law dealing with Māori people in Aotearoa New Zealand. Her work is simply brilliant.

When Chief Justice John Marshall of the US Supreme Court was writing about the doctrine of discovery in the 1830s he called it an 'absurd and extravagant idea'. However, this conclusion did not cause him to abandon the doctrine in his decisions. In contrast, the four authors of this book argue that the doctrine should be overruled. They show why it should be abandoned. Thus, this book accomplishes what I could not do when, as a young boy, I was asked how Canada could claim Indigenous lands and resources in ways that were contrary to our laws. *Discovering Indigenous Lands* details why the doctrine of discovery should no longer form a part of any country's legal framework. I believe my grandfather would have been happy to read this work. He would have finally received an answer to his question that made sense. Canada's claims to our lands do not make sense.

John Borrows
Robina Chair in Law and Public Policy
University of Minnesota Law School & Law
Foundation Chair in Aboriginal Justice
Faculty of Law, University of Victoria

Acknowledgements

All four of us would like to acknowledge our relations who passed before us and who put their feet down, held their heads high, stood on (and before) our territories, and who were sometimes forced off of our territories, and those who put pens to paper in order for us to be able to do the work that we do.

We thank the Elders, women, youth, and community leaders who continue to meaningfully pursue anti-colonial agendas and who work to inform all peoples about the impact of colonization on Indigenous territories, relations, and futures.

Importantly, we thank our families and communities for creating climates of curiosity and opportunities for intellectual growth. As each moment with this manuscript was time away from them, thanks goes to them particularly.

Thank you, George Littlechild, for your lovely painting, *October 500 Years Ago*. It is the only image we talked about once we saw it and we feel fortunate to have it on the cover.

Finally, we dedicate this book to the next generation of Indigenous scholars. We are reliant on the renewed energy of our peoples to get the important work of anti-colonialism and the rejuvenation of our nations done.

All of which within and above, is written with good intent and spirits.

Contents

List of Contributors

Larissa Behrendt is Professor of Law and Director of Research at the Jumbunna Indigenous House of Learning, University of Technology, Sydney. She is a Eualeyai/Gamillaroi woman.

Tracey Lindberg is Professor of Law at the University of Ottawa and Professor of Indigenous Studies at Athabasca University. She is a member of the Saskatchewan bar. She is a Cree citizen (Neheyiwak) whose family is from the Kelly Lake Cree Nation.

Robert J. Miller is a Professor at Lewis & Clark Law School in Portland, Oregon United States. He serves as the chief justice for the Court of Appeals for the Grand Ronde Community of Oregon. He is an enrolled citizen of the Eastern Shawnee Tribe of Oklahoma.

Jacinta Ruru is a senior law lecturer at the University of Otago, New Zealand, and is of Ngati Raukawa (Waikato), Ngati Rangi and Pakeha descent.

Table of Cases

Table of Legislation and Analogous Documents

1

The Doctrine of Discovery

On 13 September 2007, the United Nations General Assembly adopted the long anticipated Declaration on the Rights of Indigenous Peoples by a vote of 143:4. The UN Declaration was drafted, negotiated, and advocated for by Indigenous peoples from dozens of countries for more than 20 years before it was finally adopted.[1]

The only four countries that voted against the Declaration were Australia, Canada, New Zealand, and the United States. The opposition by these four countries to the UN resolution on the rights of Indigenous peoples is perhaps surprising because they are allegedly 'liberal' countries that enforce the 'rule of law,' support individual rights, and are part of the English common law system where one might suppose that human rights and the rights of native peoples would be respected and protected. All four countries do, however, have large populations of Indigenous peoples and a history of ignoring and even actively expropriating the rights and assets of native peoples and nations. In fact, the histories and legal regimes of all four countries towards their Indigenous peoples and rights are remarkably similar. Their similar histories and laws are not surprising considering that all four countries stem primarily from common English legal, social, and cultural systems.

We argue in this book, however, that there is a more basic and invidious reason why these four countries voted against the Declaration on the Rights of Indigenous Peoples and came to have similar histories and laws that infringed and still infringe today on the rights and powers of native nations and peoples. We believe that the common legal and cultural heritage of these four former English colonies heavily influenced and still influences their treatment of Indigenous peoples and the rights and powers of Indigenous peoples and continues to control and mandate the modern day treatment of native peoples and nations. This common heritage is also primarily why these four countries opposed for 20 years and ultimately voted against the Declaration in the United Nations.

The primary legal precedent that still controls native affairs and rights in these four countries is an international law formulated in the fifteenth and sixteenth centuries that is currently known as the Doctrine of Discovery. We will examine

---

[1] Robert T Coulter, 'The U.N. Declaration on the Rights of Indigenous Peoples: A Historic Change in International Law' (2009) 45 Idaho L Rev 6.

that legal principle in depth in this book and will compare how our four countries applied and utilized the Doctrine and English legal thought to control and dominate the Indigenous peoples that already lived in and owned the lands that today comprise Australia, Canada, New Zealand, and the United States.

When England and English colonists set out to explore, exploit, and settle new lands outside of Europe in the fifteenth through the nineteenth centuries, they justified their claims to sovereignty and governmental and property rights over these territories and the Indigenous inhabitants with the Discovery Doctrine. This international law had been created and justified by religious and ethnocentric ideas of European superiority over the other cultures, religions, and races of the world. In essence, the Doctrine provided that newly arrived Europeans immediately and automatically acquired legally recognized property rights in native lands and also gained governmental, political, and commercial rights over the inhabitants without the knowledge or the consent of the Indigenous peoples. When English explorers and other Europeans planted their national flags and religious symbols in 'newly discovered' lands, as many paintings depict, they were not just thanking God for a safe voyage. Instead, they were undertaking a well-recognized legal procedure and ritual mandated by international law and designed to create their country's legal claim over the 'newly discovered' lands and peoples. Needless to say, Indigenous peoples objected to the application of this European devised international law to them, their governments, and their property rights. As already stated, the Doctrine is still international law today and is also the original and controlling legal precedent for Indigenous rights and affairs in Australia, Canada, New Zealand, and the United States. In fact, just in recent decades, the governments and courts of these four countries have struggled with questions regarding the Doctrine of Discovery, native ownership of land, and native rights and governance issues.[2]

In this book, we analyse the legal and historical evidence that demonstrates the common application of the Doctrine of Discovery against the Indigenous peoples and their governments and rights in our four countries. We will see that English explorers, colonial officials, colonists, and our modern day governments all utilized the Doctrine and its religiously, culturally, and racially based ideas of superiority and preeminence to stake legal claims to the lands and property and governmental rights of Indigenous peoples. Australia, Canada, New Zealand, and the United States were ultimately able to enforce the Doctrine against the native nations and almost totally swept these governments and peoples from their paths. Discovery is still the law today in these countries and is still being used

---

[2] *City of Sherrill v Oneida Indian Nation of NY* 544 US 197 (2005); *Delaware Nation v Commonwealth of Pennsylvania* 446 F 3d 410 (3rd Cir), *cert denied*, 549 US 1071 (2006); *Delgamuukw v British Columbia* 3 SCR 1010 [1997]; *Guerin v The Queen* 2 SCR 335 [1984]; *Attorney-General v Ngati Apa* [2003] 3 NZLR 643 (New Zealand Court of Appeals); *Mabo v Queensland* 107 ALR 1 (1992) (Australian High Court).

against their Indigenous peoples and governments. Thus were Indigenous lands in our four countries 'discovered'.

A. The Doctrine of Discovery

In the chapters to follow, we trace the legal and historical evidence that demonstrates the development and use of the Doctrine of Discovery against the Indigenous peoples in our four countries. We will see how the international legal principle of Discovery was used by England and by the governments, courts, politicians, and English settlers in Australia, Canada, New Zealand, and the United States to justify Crown and colonial control of the Indigenous peoples and ownership of the Indigenous lands within these countries. We will start by setting out the general definition and parameters of Discovery and what we consider to be its constituent elements so that readers will be better equipped to understand how the Doctrine was developed in Europe and England and, then, in Chapters 2 through 9, to see how our four countries specifically adopted and applied the Doctrine in their legal regimes and throughout their histories.

The US Supreme Court defined Discovery in the very influential case of *Johnson v M'Intosh* in 1823. This case set the standard and the baseline principle for how the United States would deal with American Indians and their lands, rights, and governments. The Court based much of its analysis on how England and its officials and colonists had always dealt with the native people of North America. This case was, and still is, a very influential and important precedent around the world because it has been heavily relied on by the governments and courts of Australia, Canada, New Zealand, and the United States in devising and developing their laws, policies, and opinions regarding Indigenous peoples.

We will examine the *Johnson* case in more detail in Chapter 2 but it is beneficial at this point to quickly state how the US Supreme Court defined the Doctrine of Discovery in 1823 when it held that Discovery had become American law after already being English colonial law. In a nutshell, the Supreme Court said that under this international law when a European, Christian nation discovered new lands it automatically gained sovereign and property rights over the non-Christian, non-European peoples even though Indigenous nations and peoples were already occupying and using the lands. According to the US Supreme Court, the property right that European countries and the English Crown had acquired in America was a future right in the discovered lands, a kind of limited fee simple title or ownership right. This right, sometimes referred to as European title, was the exclusive right to buy the newly discovered lands if and whenever natives consented. The property right held by the discovering European country was limited by the natives' right to continue to occupy and use their land, which ostensibly could last forever. In actuality, Europeans were considered to have acquired an exclusive option to buy American Indian lands if ever a Tribal nation chose to sell. This right was called preemption by many because the discovering European country had the power and property right to exclude or preempt any other European country from buying the discovered lands. And the discovering country was also considered to have automatically gained some limited governmental or sovereign powers over the Indigenous peoples and their governments because, allegedly, the native governments were now restricted in their international political and commercial relationships because they were now supposed to just deal with their discoverer. This transfer of political, commercial, and property rights was accomplished without the knowledge or the consent of the Indigenous peoples or their governments and without payment of any kind.[3]

It is worthwhile to quote some of the Supreme Court's statements that demonstrate its definition of Discovery. The *Johnson* Court stated:

> The United States...[and] its civilized inhabitants now hold this country. They hold, and assert in themselves, the title by which it was acquired. They maintain, as all others have maintained, that discovery gave an exclusive right to extinguish the Indian title of occupancy, either by purchase or by conquest; and gave also a right to such a degree of sovereignty, as the circumstances of the people would allow them to exercise... discovery gave title to the government by whose subjects, or by whose authority, it was made against all other European governments, which title might be consummated by possession.

Consequently, under this legal doctrine, a discovering European country gained exclusive property rights that were to be respected by other Europeans and which preempted other Europeans from the same rights.[4]

According to the Court and the Doctrine, the discovering European nation gained real property rights to native lands and sovereign powers over native peoples and governments merely by finding lands unknown to other Europeans and planting their flag in the soil. The Court defined this property right as being an 'absolute ultimate title... acquired by discovery'. But native rights, however, were 'in no instance, entirely disregarded; but were necessarily, to a considerable extent, impaired'. This was so because although Indigenous peoples and governments still held the legal right to possess, occupy, and use their lands as long as they wished, 'their rights to complete sovereignty, as independent nations, were necessarily diminished, and their power to dispose of the soil at their own will, to whomsoever they pleased, was denied by the original fundamental principle, that discovery gave exclusive title to those who made it'. This loss of property and sovereignty rights was justified, the Court said, by 'the character and religion of its inhabitants... the superior genius of Europe... [and] ample compensation to the [Indians] by bestowing on them civilization and Christianity, in exchange for unlimited independence'. Thus, 'superior' European civilizations and religions justified Discovery claims in Indigenous lands and the loss of rights

---

[3] *Johnson v M'Intosh* 21 US (8 Wheat) 543, 573–4, 584, 588, 592, 603 (1823).
[4] *Johnson* 21 US 573–5, 578–9.

for Indigenous peoples and their governments. The Court also explained how expansive these claims could be when it explained that England's Discovery claim crossed the entire North American continent 'from sea to sea' and that French claims were made to 'vast territories...on discovery...[even to] country not actually settled by Frenchmen'. Finally, the Court relied on the idea of *terra nullius*, that Indigenous lands in North America were empty, when it discussed the English 'title...to vacant lands'.[5]

In considering just the real estate or real property right, the US Supreme Court said that a discovering nation gained, among other rights, the right to preempt or preclude other European nations from buying the newly discovered Indian lands. In other words, the discoverer acquired an exclusive option to purchase tribal lands whenever tribes consented to sell. The discovering European country gained a current property right, a current 'title' in the lands of the native people; the exclusive right to buy the natives' occupancy and use rights in their lands at some later date. European countries could even sell or grant this interest in the property to others while the lands were still in the possession and use of the native peoples. European and American governments did this many times in North America and elsewhere. This European title, the power of preemption, limited the real property right of natives and their governments to freely sell their lands to whomever they wished and for whatever price they could negotiate because Discovery granted to the discovering European country the right of preemption. Obviously, preempting American Indian nations from selling their lands as they wished diminished the economic value of their land assets and greatly benefited European countries and settlers. Consequently, Indigenous real property rights and values were severely injured immediately and automatically upon their discovery by Europeans. Indigenous sovereign powers were also greatly affected because their national sovereignty and independence were allegedly diminished by Discovery since the doctrine confined their international diplomatic, commercial, and political activities to only their 'discovering' European country.[6]

On one esoteric level, Discovery was an international legal principle designed only to control the European nations. Clearly, however, as we will see, Indigenous peoples and nations have felt most heavily its onerous burdens. The political and economic aspects of the Doctrine were developed to serve the interests of European countries by attempting to control European exploration and conflicts. The Doctrine was motivated by greed and by the economic and political interests of European countries to share, to some extent, the lands and assets to be acquired in the New World instead of engaging in expensive wars fighting over

---

[5] *Johnson* 21 US 584, 587–8, 592, 596–7, 603.

[6] *Johnson* 21 US 573–4, 579, 584–5, 587–8, 592; Eric Kades, 'The Dark Side of Efficiency: Johnson v. M'Intosh and the Expropriation of American Indian Lands' (2000) 148 U Pa L Rev 1065, 1078, 1110–31; Terry L Anderson and Fred S McChesney, 'Raid or Trade? An Economic Model of Indian–White Relations' (1994) 37 J L Econ 39.

them. This is not to say that Europeans did not fight over land in the New World, but they did try to develop a legal principle to regulate exploration and colonization and make it as profitable for Europeans as possible. While they occasionally disagreed over the exact definition of the Doctrine, and sometimes fought over discoveries and power in the New World, one thing they never disagreed about was that Indigenous peoples lost significant property and governmental rights immediately upon their first discovery by a European country.

One US Supreme Court Justice from the *Johnson* case demonstrated his clear understanding of the advantages the Doctrine granted Europeans. Justice Joseph Story wrote that Discovery avoided conflicts for European countries and was a 'most flexible and convenient principle [because] the first discovery should confer upon the nation of the discoverer an exclusive right to the soil, for the purposes of sovereignty and settlement'.[7]

The Doctrine has been severely criticized as a fictional justification for the European colonization and subjugation of Indigenous peoples and lands around the world. A close look at the origins and development of this legal principle does leave one thinking more of the adage 'might makes right' than of the principled development of law in a singular society where all people share the same rights and obligations. In fact, one might conclude that the legalistic international law Doctrine of Discovery was nothing more than an attempt to put a patina of legality on the armed confiscation of the assets of Indigenous peoples. Chief Justice John Marshall, the author of *Johnson v M'Intosh*, and his colleague Justice Joseph Story both admitted that the 'rights' of discovery were required to be 'maintained and established ... by the sword' as 'the right of the strongest'.[8]

From the above quotations and the entire *Johnson* case, we discern that the US Supreme Court's definition of the Doctrine of Discovery contains ten elements. We state them here so the reader can follow their historical and legal development and application in Europe in the 1400s and to observe the adoption and use of Discovery and these elements by England, English colonial governments, and our four governments.[9]

1. *First discovery.* The first European country to discover lands unknown to other Europeans gained property and sovereign rights over the lands. First discovery alone, however, was often considered to create only an incomplete title to newly found lands.

---

[7] 'The History and Influence of the Puritans' in *The Miscellaneous Writings of Joseph Story* (Union, NJ: Reprint, Lawbook Exchange, 2000, William W Story (ed), 1852) 459.

[8] Vine Deloria Jr and David E Wilkins, *Tribes, Treaties, & Constitutional Tribulations* (Austin: University of Texas Press, 1999) 4; Henry Wheaton, *Elements of International Law* (Boston: Little, Brown, William B Lawrence (ed), 6th edn 1855) 219, 225–6; *Johnson* 21 US 588; Story, note 7, 460, 464–5.

[9] Robert J Miller, *Native America, Discovered and Conquered: Thomas Jefferson, Lewis and Clark, and Manifest Destiny* (Westport, CT and London: Praeger Publishers, 2006) 3–5.

2. *Actual occupancy and current possession.* We will see that Elizabeth I and her advisers added an element to the definition of Discovery that a European country had to actually occupy and possess newly found lands to turn a first discovery claim into a claim of complete title. This was usually accomplished by building a fort or settlement, for example, and leaving soldiers or settlers on the land. Physical possession had to occur within a reasonable length of time after the first discovery to create a complete title to the land for the discovering country.

3. *Preemption/European title.* Discovering European countries acquired a property right of preemption, that is, the sole power and authority to buy the land from the Indigenous peoples and governments. It is a valuable property right. The government that held the power of preemption thus prevented or preempted any other European government from buying the discovered land.

4. *Indian title or Native title.* After first discovery, Indigenous nations and peoples were considered by European legal systems to have lost the full property rights and ownership of their lands. They only retained the occupancy and use rights. Nevertheless, these rights could ostensibly last forever if Indigenous people never consented to sell. But if they ever did choose to sell, they could only sell to the government that held the power of preemption over their lands. Thus, Native title is considered to be a limited ownership right.

5. *Indigenous nations limited sovereign and commercial rights.* After first discovery, Indigenous nations and peoples were also considered to have lost some of their inherent sovereign powers and their rights to free trade and diplomatic relations on an international scale. Thereafter, they were only supposed to deal with the European government that first discovered them.

6. *Contiguity.* Dictionaries define this word to mean the state of being contiguous to, to have proximity to, or to be near to. This Discovery element provided that Europeans had a claim to a reasonable and significant amount of land contiguous to and surrounding their actual settlements and discovered lands. This element became very important when European countries had settlements somewhat close together. In that situation, each country was considered to have rights to the unoccupied lands between their settlements to a point half way between the settlements. Most importantly, contiguity held that discovering the mouth of a river gave a European country a claim over all the lands drained by that river; even if it was thousands of miles of territory such as the Louisiana Territory (defined by the Mississippi River) and the Oregon Country (defined by the Columbia River) in the United States and Canada.

7. *Terra nullius.* This term means a land or earth that is empty or null or void. The phrase *vacuum domicilium* was also sometimes used to describe this

Discovery element. It literally means an empty or vacant home or domicile. Under this element, lands that were not possessed or occupied by any person or nation, or were occupied by non-Europeans but not being used in a fashion that European legal systems understood and/or approved, were considered to be empty and waste and available to be claimed. Europeans were very liberal in applying this definition to the lands of Indigenous peoples. Europeans often considered lands that were actually owned, occupied, and being actively utilized by Indigenous peoples to be vacant and available for Discovery claims if they were not being properly used according to European laws and cultures.

8. *Christianity.* Religion was a significant aspect in the development and application of the Doctrine. Under Discovery, non-Christian peoples did not possess the same human and natural law rights to land, sovereignty, and self-determination as Christian peoples. Indigenous peoples were assumed to have lost many rights upon their discovery by Christians.

9. *Civilization.* The European definition of civilization was an important part of Discovery and the idea of European superiority. Europeans thought that God had directed them to bring civilization, education, and religion to Indigenous peoples and to exercise paternalism and guardianship powers over them.

10. *Conquest.* This element appears to have two different definitions. It definitely referred to the rights Europeans claimed to acquire by winning military victories over Indigenous peoples. We will see that definition reflected in Spanish, English, and American ideas of 'just wars' that allegedly justified the invasion, conquest, and acquisition of Indigenous lands in certain circumstances. But that is not the only meaning of this element. The element of 'conquest' was also used by the US Supreme Court as a 'term of art' or a word with a special meaning.

As defined in *Johnson v M'Intosh* by the US Supreme Court, conquest also described the property rights Europeans automatically gained over American Indian nations after a first discovery. In essence, the Court considered first discovery to be analogous to a military conquest because the European country claimed political, real property, and commercial rights over the Indigenous peoples just by discovering them. Under European law, however, actual conquest in a military victory did not impact the property rights of the ordinary inhabitants of a conquered country. Instead, the property rights of the individual people were not forfeited or affected and the people were ultimately expected to be absorbed into the culture and life of the conquering country. But the US Supreme Court said that this European theory of conquest could not be applied in America because of the different cultures, religions, and the 'savagery' of American Indians. Thus, the Court stated that American Indians and tribes lost some property rights automatically after their first discovery by Europeans as if they had been conquered in a just war. The Court claimed it had to develop this modified theory of the European principle because the Indian nations could not be left in complete ownership of the lands in America.

B. The Development of the International Law of Discovery

International law is the body of generally accepted legal principles that allegedly govern the conduct of nations vis-à-vis other nations. The Doctrine of Discovery is one of the earliest examples of international law. It was developed by European countries to control their own actions and potential conflicts over exploration, trade, and colonization in non-European countries. It was also used, as we will see, to justify the domination of non-Christian, non-European peoples and the confiscation of their lands and rights.[10]

Scholars have traced the Doctrine as far back as the fifth century AD when, they argue, the Roman Catholic Church and various popes began establishing the idea of a worldwide papal jurisdiction that placed responsibility on the Church to work for a universal Christian commonwealth. This papal responsibility, and especially the Crusades to recover the Holy Lands in 1096–1271, led to the idea of justified holy war by Christians against infidels to enforce the Church's vision of truth on all peoples.[11]

In particular, Pope Innocent IV's writings in 1240 influenced the famous sixteenth and seventeenth century legal writers Franciscus de Victoria and Hugo Grotius when they began writing about the Discovery Doctrine. Pope Innocent asked whether it was legitimate for crusading Christians to invade infidel lands. He answered yes because these actions were 'just' wars fought for the 'defense' of the Church. Innocent focused on the legal authority of Christians to dispossess non-Christians of their *dominium*, their governmental sovereignty and their property. The Pope answered that the non-Christians' natural law right to elect their own leaders and to own property were qualified by the papacy's divine mandate to care for the entire world. Since the Church and popes were entrusted with the spiritual health of all humans, that necessarily meant they had a voice in the affairs of all humans. It was a duty, then, for the Church and popes to intervene even in the secular affairs of infidels when they violated natural law. Natural law was, of course, defined by Europeans and the Church.[12]

---

[10] *Black's Law Dictionary* (St Paul, MN: West Publishing Co, 5th edn 1979) 733.

[11] Anthony Pagden, *Lords of all the World: Ideologies of Empire in Spain, Britain and France c. 1500–c. 1800* (New Haven: Yale University Press, 1995) 8, 24, 126; Robert A Williams, Jr, *The American Indian in Western Legal Thought: The Discourses of Conquest* (New Haven: Yale University Press, 1990) 13–18; 24, 28–32; *The Expansion of Europe* (Philadelphia: University of Pennsylvania Press, James Muldoon (ed), 1977); Carl Erdmann, *The Origin of the Idea of Crusade* (Princeton: Princeton University Press, Marshall W Baldwin and Walter Goffart trans, 1977) 155–6.

[12] Wheaton, note 8, 226–39; Williams, note 11, 13 and note 4, 14–17, 43–7, 49, 66.

The European and Church development of the principles of Discovery continued most significantly in the early 1400s in a controversy between Poland and the Teutonic Knights to control pagan Lithuania. This conflict again raised questions about the legality of the seizure of infidels' lands under papal sanction and the legitimacy of the argument that infidels lacked lawful *dominium*, sovereignty, and property rights. In the Council of Constance, held in 1414, the Teutonic Knights argued that their territorial and jurisdictional claims to Lithuania were authorized by papal proclamations dating from the time of the Crusades. They argued that these papal bulls, or edicts, allowed the outright confiscation of the property and sovereign rights of heathens. The Council, which was called to answer this question, disagreed and accepted Poland's argument and the interpretation of Pope Innocent IV's writings that infidels possessed the same natural law rights to sovereignty and property as Christians but that the pope did have the authority to order invasions to punish violations of natural law or to spread the gospel. Consequently, future crusades, discoveries of new lands, and conquests of heathens were supposed to proceed under the legal rule that pagans had natural rights, but that they had to comply with European concepts of natural law or else they risked a European 'just war' of conquest and subjugation. The Council of Constance in 1414 had now placed a formal definition on the Christian Doctrine of Discovery. The Church and secular Christian princes had to respect the natural rights of pagans but not if heathens deviated from the European definition of natural law. Commentators have argued that this meant that to be considered civilized a country had to be Christian because 'Christians simply refused to recognize the right of non-Christians to remain free of Christian dominion'.[13]

By the mid-1400s, the advances of Spanish and Portuguese exploration, trade, and conquest raised questions about the control of the island groups off the Iberian coast. The Church became involved and in 1434 Pope Eugenius IV issued a papal bull banning all Europeans from the Canary Islands to protect both the Christian and infidel Canary Islanders. In 1436, though, the King of Portugal appealed the ban on colonizing the Canary Islands. He argued that Portugal's explorations were actually conquests on behalf of Christianity. The king stated that converting the infidel natives was justified because, allegedly, they did not have a common religion or laws, lived like animals, and lacked normal social intercourse, money, metal, writing, and European style clothing. The king claimed that the Canary Islanders who had converted to Christianity had made themselves subjects of Portugal and had received the benefits of civil laws and organized society. Moreover, the king said that the pope's ban interfered with the advance of civilization and Christianity which the king had only undertaken out of the goodness of his heart: 'more indeed for the salvation of the souls of the

[13] Williams, note 11, 58–63, 65–7; James Muldoon, *Popes, Lawyers and Infidels* (Philadelphia: University of Pennsylvania Press, 1979) 109–19; Pagden, note 11, 24, 126; Steven T Newcomb, *Pagans in the Promised Land: Decoding the Doctrine of Christian Discovery* (Golden, CO: Fulcrum Publishing, 2008); *Johnson* 21 US 572–3.

pagans of the islands than for personal gain...'. The king appealed to the Pope to grant the Canary Islands to Portugal due to the Church's guardianship duties for infidels.[14]

This dialogue helped refine the European definition of the Doctrine of Discovery. This new argument for European and Christian domination of pagans and their lands was not based on the infidels' lack of dominion or natural rights but was instead based on Portuguese rights of discovery based on the perceived need to protect natives from the oppression of others and to lead them to civilization and religious conversion under papal guidance. Pope Eugenius IV and his legal advisors agreed that under the Roman law of nations (*jus gentium*) infidels had a right to *dominium* even though the papacy maintained an indirect jurisdiction over their secular activities. But based on Pope Innocent IV's writings in 1240, they also agreed that the Church had the authority to deprive pagans of their property and sovereignty if they failed to admit Christian missionaries or if they violated European defined natural law. Pope Eugenius agreed with this extension of papal and Discovery authority and he issued another bull in 1436, *Romanus Pontifex*, which authorized Portugal to convert the Canary Island natives and to manage and control the islands on behalf of the pope. This bull was reissued several times in the fifteenth century by different popes. Each new bull significantly extended Portugal's jurisdiction and geographical rights over Indigenous peoples and their lands down the west coast of Africa as Portugal extended the scope of its discoveries and travels. The bull of Pope Nicholas in 1455 was significantly more aggressive because it authorized Portugal 'to invade, search out, capture, vanquish, and subdue all Saracens and pagans' and to place them into perpetual slavery and to take their property. These papal bulls demonstrated the meaning of the Doctrine of Discovery at that time. They also recognized the Church's interest in bringing all humankind to the one 'true' religion and authorized Portugal's work for conversion and civilization while they also recognized Portugal's title and sovereignty over the lands of infidels 'which have already been acquired and which shall be acquired in the future'.[15]

Under the threat of excommunication if they violated these papal bulls, the Catholic monarchs of Spain had to look elsewhere for lands to explore and conquer. Consequently, Christopher Columbus' proposal for a westward voyage struck a resonant chord with the Spanish King Ferdinand and Queen Isabella. After studying the legal and scriptural authority for the mission, Spain dispatched Columbus under a contract that stated he would become the Admiral

[14] *Expansion of Europe*, note 11, 47–8, 54–6; Edgar Prestage, *The Portuguese Pioneers* (London: A & C Black, 1966) 8–9, 27, 38–41, 43–50, 54–9, 96–7, 100–2; Muldoon, note 13, 119–21; Williams, note 11, 69–71.

[15] *Church and State Through the Centuries* (New York: Biblo and Tannen, Sidney Z Ehler and John B Morrall (trans and eds), 1967) 146–53; Williams, note 11, 71–2; Muldoon, note 13, 126–7; *European Treaties Bearing on the History of the United States and Its Dependencies to 1648* (Washington: Carnegie Institution of Washington, Frances G Davenport (ed), 1917) 23.

of any lands he would 'discover and acquire'. Under the precedent of Discovery, the papal bulls, and his contract with the Spanish Crown, it is no surprise that he claimed that his discovery of already inhabited islands in the Caribbean meant that the islands had become Spanish possessions. Ferdinand and Isabella wasted no time in seeking papal ratification of the discoveries. They immediately asked the Pope to confirm Spain's title to the islands Columbus had discovered. In 1493, Pope Alexander VI issued three bulls confirming Spain's title. Specifically, in May 1493, he issued *Inter caetera divinai* which stated that the lands found by Columbus, since they had been 'undiscovered by others', now belonged to Ferdinand and Isabella. Pope Alexander also granted Spain any lands it might discover in the future provided that they were 'not previously possessed by any Christian owner'. Consequently, the Doctrine of Discovery was transported to the New World. The idea that the Doctrine granted European monarchs owner-ship rights in newly discovered lands and sovereign and commercial rights over Indigenous peoples due to first discovery by European Christians was now estab-lished international law, at least to Europeans.[16]

Spain and Portugal, though, became concerned about the geographical limits of their possibly conflicting papal bulls. So Spain requested another bull that would clearly delineate its ownership of the islands and lands that Columbus discovered or would discover in the New World. In 1493, Alexander VI again obliged and issued *Inter caetera II*. The Pope now drew a demarcation line from the north pole to the south pole, 100 leagues (about 300 miles) west of the Azore Islands off the coast of Europe, and granted Spain title under divine authority to all the lands discovered or to be discovered west of the line. This bull also assigned Spain this 'holy and laudable work' to contribute to 'the expansion of the Christian rule'. The pope had thus divided the world for Christian explor-ation and domination to be carried out by Spain and Portugal. In 1494, these two countries signed the Treaty of Tordesillas and moved the papally drawn line 370 leagues further west (about 1,100 miles) of the Cape Verde Islands. This new dividing line now gave Portugal Discovery rights in part of the New World. Thus, Portugal's right to colonize and control Brazil was recognized by Spain and Portugal because that land mass lies east of the line drawn by the Treaty of Tordesillas. Today, Portuguese is still the official language of Brazil as Spanish is for the remainder of South and Central America and Mexico.[17]

The Church's interest in expanding Christendom and adding to its wealth, and Spain's and Portugal's economic and political interests in acquiring new

[16] Williams, note 11, 74–8; 2 Samuel Eliot Morison, *The European Discovery of America: The Southern Voyages* (New York: Oxford University Press, 1974) 27–44; Samuel Eliot Morison, *Admiral of the Ocean Sea* (Boston: Little, Brown & Co, 1942) 105, 229; *European Treaties*, note 15, 9–13, 23, 53–6.

[17] *Church and State*, note 15, 156; Morison, *Admiral*, note 16, 368–73; *III Foundations of Colonial America: A Documentary History* (New York: Chelsea House, W Keith Kavenagh (ed), 1973) 1684; Pagden, note 11, 47; Williams, note 11, 80.

territories, assets, and colonies had solidified by 1493 under the canon and international law of the Doctrine of Discovery. According to commentators, the Doctrine was recognized to stand for four basic points: 1. the Church had the political and secular authority to grant Christian kings a form of title and ownership in the lands of infidels; 2. European exploration and colonization was designed to exercise the Church's guardianship duties over all the earthly flock, including infidels; 3. Spain and Portugal held exclusive rights over other European, Christian countries to explore and colonize the entire world; and, 4. the mere sighting and discovery of new lands by Spain or Portugal in their respective spheres of influence and the symbolic possession of these lands by undertaking the rituals and formalities of possession, such as planting flags or leaving objects to prove their presence, were sufficient to create rights in these lands. The law of Discovery, as it applied between Europeans, was thus well settled by the Church, Portugal, and Spain by 1493.[18]

Portugal and Spain long argued that their rights of Discovery arose from their explorers merely visiting the lands of non-Christians and performing the rituals of symbolic possession. Even as late as the 1790s, a Spanish expedition in North America used the traditional rituals of Discovery and the taking of symbolic possession of land by marking trees and engraving stones with the name of King Charles IV. These countries claimed that these rituals of possession were sufficient to establish their legal rights to newly found lands. Spain and Portugal were delighted with this argument because the papal bulls and first discovery gave them an almost exclusive right to explore and claim the entire non-Christian world. England and France, as we will see, thought differently, although even these countries also engaged in making Discovery claims based only upon first discovery and performing Discovery formalities and rituals.[19]

Notwithstanding these well-established principles of Discovery, a serious debate arose within Spanish legal and religious circles as to the authority for the Crown's rights against the Indigenous peoples of the New World. This dispute led the king to seek legal opinions on the legitimacy of papal authority as the sole basis for Spain's titles. He also convened a group to draft regulations to control future Spanish discoveries and conquests. The priest Franciscus de Victoria became involved in these discussions. He was the king's lead advisor, held the first chair in theology at the University of Salamanca for twenty years, and is considered to be one of the earliest writers in international law. In 1532, Victoria delivered a series of influential lectures entitled 'On the Indians Lately Discovered'. In the lectures, he accepted the idea that Indigenous peoples had natural rights and

---

[18] Pagden, note 11, 31–3; Muldoon, note 13, 139; Morison, *Admiral*, note 16, 368.

[19] Patricia Seed, *Ceremonies of Possession in Europe's Conquest of the New World, 1492–1640* (Cambridge: Cambridge University Press, 1995) 9 and note 19, 69–73, 101–2; James Simsarian, 'The Acquisition of Legal Title to Terra Nullius' (March 1938) 53 Pol Sci Q 111, 113–14, 117–18, 120–4; Friedrich August Freiherr von der Heydte, 'Discovery, Symbolic Annexation and Virtual Effectiveness in International Law' (1935) 29 Am J Int'l L 448, 450–2.

that title to their lands could not pass to Europeans by Discovery alone because Indians were free men and the true owners of the lands they possessed under their natural law rights. This principle led him to three conclusions regarding the Spanish explorations and claims in the New World. According to one professor, Victoria's conclusions were 'adopted essentially intact as the accepted European Law of Nations on American Indian rights and status'. First, Victoria said that the natives of the Americas possessed natural legal rights as free and rational people. Second, the Pope's grant of title to Spain to the lands in the Americas was invalid and could not affect the inherent rights of the Indigenous peoples. Third, any violations by the natives of the natural law principles of the Law of Nations (as defined by Europeans) might justify a Christian nation's conquest and empire in the New World.[20]

Victoria's first two conclusions sound treasonous because they rejected Spain's land titles in the New World if the titles were based solely on papal grants. It sounds as though Victoria was dismissing the Doctrine of Discovery. But what Victoria did actually strengthened Spain's claim to title, empire, and rights against other Europeans and against the Indigenous peoples in the New World. Victoria transferred Spain's claims from being based solely on papal authority to a firmer foundation based on the 'universal obligations of a Eurocentrically constructed natural law'. In fact, by applying European natural law to the New World and Indigenous peoples and nations, Victoria greatly benefited Spain. In essence, Victoria reasoned that natives were required to allow Spaniards to exercise their natural law rights in the New World. These rights included the right of Spanish explorers to travel to foreign lands, to engage in trade and commerce in native lands, and to take profits from items Indigenous peoples apparently held in common, like minerals. Native peoples also had to allow Spain to send missionaries to their territories to preach the gospel. Victoria's conclusion, which strengthened Spanish claims, was that if infidels prevented the Spanish from exercising any of their natural law rights then Spain could 'protect its rights' and 'defend the faith' by waging lawful and 'just wars' against Indigenous peoples. It is striking how similar this definition of Discovery is to the justifications put forth for the holy wars of the Crusades.[21]

Furthermore, while Victoria rejected the idea of papal sanction as the sole authority for Spain's title in the New World, he also created an enormous loophole for Spain. His reasoning that Indigenous peoples were bound by European definitions of the natural law rights of the Spanish was an ample excuse to dominate,

[20] Williams, note 11, 89–91, 97, 99–101; Franciscus de Victoria, *De Indis et de Iure Bellie Relectiones* (Washington: Carnegie Institution, Ernest Nys (ed) and John Pauley Bate (trans), 1917) 115, 123, 125–31, 135–9, 151, 153; Pagden, note 11, 46; Lewis Hanke, *The Spanish Struggle for Justice in the Conquest of America* (Philadelphia: University of Pennsylvania Press, 1949) 17–22, 113–32.
[21] Williams, note 11, 98, 101–3; Victoria, note 20, 54–5, 151–61; Arthur Nussbaum, *A Concise History of The Law of Nations* (New York: Macmillan Co, 1947) 61–2; Seed, note 19, 88–97; Pagden, note 11, 93, 97–8; Hanke, note 20, 133–46, 156–72.

defraud, and then engage in 'just wars' against any native nations that dared to stop the Spanish from doing whatever they wished. Consequently, Victoria limited the freedoms and the rights of the Indigenous peoples of the Americas by allowing Spain's natural law rights to trump native rights. The legal regime envisioned by Victoria was just as destructive to Indigenous sovereignty and property interests, if not more so, than the earlier definition of Spain's authority in the New World as being based solely on papal authority.

An interesting example of Spanish natural law rights in the New World was demonstrated by the regulations drafted by the group the king convened to consider future Spanish discoveries. The best known regulation this group drafted was the *Requerimiento*. This document informed New World natives that they must accept Spanish missionaries and sovereignty or they would be annihilated. Spanish explorers were required to read the document to Indigenous peoples and nations before hostilities and 'just war' could legally ensue. The *Requerimiento* informed the natives of their natural law obligations to hear the gospel and that their lands had been donated to Spain. If the natives refused to acknowledge the Christian Church, the Spanish King, and admit priests, then Spain was justified in waging 'just war' on them. Many conquistadors must have worried that this preposterous document would actually convince Indigenous peoples to change religions and accept Spanish rule and prevent the explorers from gaining conquests and riches because they took to reading the document aloud in the night to the trees or they read it to the land from their ships. They considered this adequate notice to the natives of the points in the *Requerimiento*. So much for legal formalism and the free will and natural law rights of New World Indigenous peoples.[22]

C. England and the Doctrine of Discovery

England became heavily involved in the development of the principles of Discovery after 1493, and that is the time period that we will focus on. But this does not mean that conquest and using law and legal principles to colonize foreigners was anything new to the English Crown. In fact, England had long used the imposition of its laws, legal system, and religious authority in an attempt to control and rule Ireland.

In 1155, Adrian IV, the only English pope, purportedly issued a papal bull or edict known as *Laudabiliter* granting King Henry II of England dominion and lordship over Ireland and the authority to invade the country to curb church excesses. The English invasion of Ireland then followed in 1167–1171 and Henry II claimed sovereignty due to papal authority. He ultimately received the

[22] Muldoon, note 13, 141–2; Seed, note 19, 69–73; Hanke, note 20, 33; *The Spanish Tradition in America* (New York: Harper & Row, Charles Gibson (ed), 1968) 59–60; Pagden, note 11, 91.

submission of the Irish kings in Dublin, Pope Alexander III ratified the grant of Ireland to Henry II in 1172, and the Irish bishops accepted that decision.[23]

Henry VIII's break with the Catholic Church in 1529–1535 led him to search for alternate grounds to claim Ireland rather than relying on papal authority. His advisors and various commentators claimed that conquest would justify England's dominion over Ireland so Henry reconquered some parts of Ireland and established permanent plantations of English settlers. On the other hand, his daughter Queen Mary, a Catholic, looked directly to the pope to ratify her ownership of Ireland. In 1555, Pope Paul IV issued a bull that named Mary the monarch of Ireland. Yet again, it was only natural that Mary's successor Elizabeth I, a Protestant, did not want to rely on papal orders or authority for her claim to Ireland. Between 1559 and 1561, the English Parliament re-established the Churches of England and Ireland and named Elizabeth as their 'Supreme Governor'. She thereafter commenced a war of conquest against Ireland that resulted in victory six days after her death in March 1603.[24]

It is important to note though that under papal authority, the invasion of 1171, English reconquest, and royal and parliamentary authority in the late sixteenth and early seventeenth centuries, England used its law in an attempt to supplant Irish law and to help effectuate the English domination of Ireland. As many scholars have noted, including William Blackstone in 1763, the Irish Brehon law system was purposely eclipsed by English law and legal systems after the invasion of 1171 and then almost totally replaced by English law in the seventeenth century as the Crown established control over Ireland. With this type of precedent, it is no surprise that English colonies, courts, and colonists also ignored Indigenous legal and property rights regimes around the world and worked to impose English law systems on native nations. In fact, one professor argues that Elizabethan England used its colonizing and legal efforts in Ireland to develop its expertise in empire and colonization and applied the same strategies in North America.[25]

---

[23] Williams, note 11, 136–7; Eleanor Hull, *A History of Ireland*, vol 1 (Dublin: Phoenix Publishing Co, 1931) 139–61; *Selected Documents in Irish History* (Armonk, NY: M E Sharpe, Inc, Josef Lewis Altholz (ed), 2000) 13–18; *Select Historical Documents of the Middle Ages* (London: George Bell and Sons, Ernest F Henderson (ed), 1910) 10–11. The authenticity of Adrian's bull has been questioned; but as is correctly pointed out, its existence is consistent with historical events, later papal decrees and documents that have never been disputed, and the decision was accepted by the Irish bishops in 1172. *Selected Documents in Irish History*, note 23, 13; Kate Norgate, 'The Bull Laudabiliter' (January 1893) The English Historical Rev 18–52; *Church and State*, note 15, 53–5.

[24] Hans S Pawlisch, 'Sir John Davies, the Ancient Constitution and Civil Law' (1980) 23 The Historical J 696–7 and n 47 (citing Henry's Chief Baron of the Exchequer from 1534, Edmund Borlase, and a 1534 bill drafted by Thomas Crowell to establish title to Ireland by conquest); Hans S Pawlisch, *Sir John Davies and the conquest of Ireland: A Study in Legal Imperialism* (Cambridge: Cambridge University Press, 1985) 34; Williams, note 11, 136–8.

[25] Pawlisch, The Historical J, note 24, 696–7; Pawlisch, *Sir John Davies and the Conquest of Ireland*, note 24, 3–14; William Blackstone, *Commentaries on the Law of England* (London: Dawsons of Pall Mall, 1966, reprint of 1765 edn) 99–100, 104–5; G J Hand, *English Law in Ireland, 1290–1324* (Cambridge: Cambridge University Press, 1967) 1–6, 26–9, 40–7, 135–77,

After developing a taste for foreign empire in Ireland, England became a strong advocate of the Doctrine of Discovery and began using that international law to claim the rights and powers of first discovery, conquest, and title in North America. England thereafter claimed for centuries that John Cabot's 1496–1498 explorations and discoveries along the coast of North America, from Newfoundland to Virginia perhaps, gave it priority over any other European country even including Spain's claims under the papal bulls and the first discovery of the New World via Columbus. In fact, one English author wrote in 1609 that James I's rights in America were based on a 'right of discovery'. England also later contested Dutch settlements and trading activities in the modern day American states of New York, New Jersey, and Pennsylvania based on England's claims of 'first discovery, occupation, and . . . possession' by its explorers and colonial settlements.[26]

England's claims to first discovery in North America did not go unchallenged, however. France claimed that its alleged first discoveries of parts of Canada and the United States established its overriding legal claim to ownership and sovereignty. In 1627, Louis XIII discussed France's 'newly discovered lands' in the New World, and detailed accounts of Jesuit activities in New France demonstrate the common understanding of the principles that first discovery and possession of territory inhabited only by non-Christians created legal claims for European kings to sovereignty, title, and jurisdiction. In 1670–1672, for example, Jesuits wrote that they had taken possession of land near the Great Lakes by 'observing all the forms customary on such occasions'. These priests had undertaken the accepted Discovery rituals to establish France's claim. Other Jesuits also argued that France had discovered and 'taken actual possession of all the country' years before the English arrived and thus France owned the area because 'no Christian had ever been [here] . . . [and] this hitherto unknown region [was] brought . . . under [French] jurisdiction'. France and England were unable to settle their Discovery claims and ultimately fought a 'world war' in 1754–1761, which is known in the United States as the French and Indian War and elsewhere as the Seven Years War, over conflicting rights in North America and elsewhere. In the treaty that ended the war in 1763, France transferred its Discovery claims in Canada and east of the Mississippi River in America to England, and granted its Discovery claims to lands west of the Mississippi River to Spain.[27]

214–18; Williams, note 11, 136–47; *Selected Documents in Irish History*, note 23, 36–9, 58–9; *The Voyages and Colonising Enterprises of Sir Humphrey Gilbert*, vol 1 (Liechtenstein: Kraus Reprint Ltd, David Beers Quinn (ed), 1967) 9–10, 12–20, 35–9, 49–52, 55–9, 90–1, 100–3, 118–28.

[26] Pagden, note 11, 90; Williams, note 11, 161, 170, 177–8; VII *Early American Indian Documents: Treaties and Laws, 1607–1789* (Washington: University Publications of America, Alden T Vaughan and Barbara Graymont (eds), 1998) 30–2.

[27] Pagden, note 11, 34; I Joseph Jouvency, *An Account of the Canadian Mission* (1710, reprinted in Rueben Gold Thwaites, *The Jesuit Relations and Allied Documents* (Cleveland, OH: Burrows Bros Co, 1896)) 179, 205; II *Travels and Explorations of the Jesuit Missionaries in New France* (New York: Pageant Book Co, Reuben Gold Thwaites (ed), 1959) 33, 127, 199, 203; ibid vol III, 33, 39, 41;

In addition to their conflicting Discovery claims in the New World, France and England also faced an additional problem regarding their exploratory and colonization interests. Both England and France were Catholic countries in 1493 and their monarchs were very concerned with infringing Spain's rights in the New World, violating Alexander VI's papal bulls, and running the risk of excommunication. But they were also anxious to get their share of these new territories and assets. Therefore, the legal scholars of England and France analysed canon law, the papal bulls, and history, and devised slightly new theories of Discovery that allowed their countries to explore and colonize the New World. Not surprisingly, Europeans were always very creative at interpreting Discovery in ways that benefitted their own situations and interests.

The new legal theory, primarily developed by English legal scholars, argued that the Catholic King Henry VII of England would not violate the 1493 papal bulls, which had divided the world for the Spanish and Portuguese, if English explorers confined themselves to claiming lands that had not yet been discovered by any other Christian prince. This new reading of Discovery was further refined by Elizabeth I and her legal advisers in the 1580s when they added a crucial new element to the international law. They argued that the Doctrine required that a European country had to actually occupy and possess non-Christian lands to perfect their Discovery title to discovered lands. This seemed logical because any country could falsely claim first discoveries, as European countries occasionally did. This type of problem, and the problems created for France and England from the papal bulls, were solved by the new requirement of actual occupation and possession. Under this element of Discovery, there should be no argument about who held the legal rights to non-Christian lands; it only came down to whether a European country was in actual possession of the territory at the time French and English explorers arrived.

It is interesting to consider why England and Elizabeth I worried at all about the papal bulls and complying with the international law of Discovery. Elizabeth was excommunicated in 1570 and seemingly had nothing to fear from violating the papal bulls of 1493 that divided the world for Spain and Portugal. But she and her government decided to comply as closely as possible with this law. It seems correct to conclude that Elizabeth was not worried about religion and the approval of the Pope. What she no doubt wanted was for England's Discovery claims in foreign lands to be recognized and respected by the international community of nations so she must have decided to comply with international law as far as possible.

ibid vol XXXIV 217–19; ibid vol LV 95–7, 105–15; ibid vol XLI, 245–7; ibid vol XLVII, 259–71; Fred Anderson, *Crucible of War: The Seven Years' War and the Fate of Empire in British North America, 1754–1766* (New York: Alfred A Knopf, 2000) xv, xix; Jack M Sosin, *Whitehall and the Wilderness: The Middle West in British Colonial Policy, 1760–1775* (Lincoln: University of Nebraska Press, 1961) 21–2, 73.

Consequently, Henry VII, his granddaughter Elizabeth I, and her successor James I, and other English monarchs repeatedly instructed their explorers to comply with the law of Discovery and to seek out, claim, and colonize lands 'unknown to all Christians' and 'not actually possessed of any Christian prince'. In the 1606 First Charter of Virginia and the 1620 Charter to the Council of New England, James I granted his colonists property rights in America because the lands were 'not now actually possessed by any *Christian* Prince or People' and 'there is noe other the Subjects of any Christian King or State...actually in Possession...whereby any Right, Claim, Interest, or Title, may...by that Meanes accrue'. English monarchs also invoked other elements of Discovery when they granted colonial charters in America because they ordered their colonists to take Christianity and civilization to American Indians for the purpose of 'propagating *Christian* Religion to those [who] as yet live in Darkness and miserable Ignorance of the true Knowledge and Worship of God, and [to] bring the Infidels and Savages, living in those Parts, to human civility, and to a settled and quiet Government...'. King James also recognized the contiguity element of Discovery, the extent of land that could be claimed by actual possession, when he granted the Virginia colonists the right to own the lands, woods, and rivers within 100 English miles around the sites where they actually built settlements.[28]

England and France thus added to the Doctrine the element of actual occupancy and possession as a requirement to establish European claims to title by Discovery and they applied this new element in their dealings with Spain and Portugal. For example, Elizabeth I wrote to the Spanish minister in 1553 that first discovery alone 'cannot confer property'. England repeatedly argued in 1580, 1587, 1600, and 1604 that it could colonize any lands where Europeans were not in possession. In addition, in the 1550s both England and France tried to negotiate treaties with Spain and Portugal to settle issues regarding discoveries in the New World. France insisted on a right to trade in the West Indies while Spain relied on its papal title and argued for monopoly rights to the entire region. The Spanish negotiators reported to their king that they could not convince the French to stay away from 'such places which are discovered by us, but are not actually subject to the King of Spain or Portugal. They are willing only to consent not to go to the territories actually possessed by your majesty or the King of Portugal.'[29]

---

[28] I *Foundations*, note 17, 18, 22–9; III *Foundations*, note 17, 1690–8; Williams, note 11, 126–225; Heydte, note 19, 450–4; *Select Charters and Other Documents Illustrative of American History 1606–1775* (London: The MacMillan Company, William MacDonald (ed), 1906, Reprint, Littleton, CO: Rothman & Co, 1993) 2–3, 18, 24–5, 37–9, 51–2, 59, 121–6, 184, 205; Samuel Smith, *History of New Jersey* (Burlington; James Parker, 1765; Reprint, Philadelphia: David Hall, 1890) 16.

[29] Heydte, note 19, 450–2, 458–9; Williams, note 11, 133; I Hyde, *Treatise on International Law* (Boston: Little, Brown & Co, 1922) 164; *European Treaties*, note 15, 219.

This debate over the exact definition of some of the elements of Discovery demonstrates that European countries often argued for the definition of Discovery that best fit their particular situations and interests. In fact, in contrast to their usual arguments, England, France, and Holland sometimes tried to claim new lands based only on first discovery and 'symbolic possession' established by performing the rituals of Discovery. For instance, in 1642 Holland ordered an explorer to take possession of new lands by planting posts and hanging plates to 'declare an intention...to establish a colony'. In 1758, a French explorer claimed Tahiti based on first discovery and by symbolic possession and the performance of Discovery rituals. In 1770, English King George III instructed Captain James Cook to find uninhabited lands and to 'take possession of it for His Majesty by setting up proper marks and inscriptions as first discoverers and possessors'. In 1774, Cook even erased Spanish marks of possession in Tahiti and made his own marks to prove English possession and 'ownership' of the island. Upon hearing of this action, Spain immediately dispatched explorers to re-establish Spain's claim by restoring its marks of symbolic possession. These almost comic episodes of trying to prove who 'owned' what had real world implications under the Doctrine of Discovery.[30]

In 1776–1778, Captain Cook also engaged in symbolic possession activities in today's British Columbia, Canada. He claimed to take possession of specific areas by performing Discovery rituals such as leaving English coins in buried bottles. Another example of this type of conduct and ritual is that at least three times France claimed symbolic possession of lands in America by burying inscribed lead plates. In 1742–1743, French explorers buried a lead plate at the mouth of the Bad River and some time before 1763 a combined Spanish and French mission ran a boundary line up the Sabine River and built a small fort and 'buried some leaden plates'. Also, in 1749, a French military force travelled throughout the Ohio country in America to renew France's 1643 Discovery claim to the territory. The French 'buried small lead plates..."as a monument"..."of the renewal of possession"'. The English noted this French effort and the Discovery claim: 'It appears by a leaden plate found by the Indians upon the River Ohio, in the year 1749, that the Crown of France assumes a Right to all the Territories lying upon that River.'[31]

---

[30] Heydte, note 19, 460–1; Pagden, note 11, 81.
[31] Anderson, note 27, 25–6; 'Journal of Captain Fitch's Journey to the Creeks' (May 1756), *Colonial Indian Documents Microfilm Collection*, *Instances of Encroachment made by the French upon the Rights of the Crown of Great Britain in America*, I Records of the British Colonial Office, Class 5: Westward Expansion 1700–1783, Reel I, vol 12, Frame 0158 (Randolph Boehm (ed), 1972); Thomas Maitland Marshall, *A History of the Western Boundary of the Louisiana Purchase, 1819–1841* (Berkeley: University California Press, 1914) 12; Donald Jackson, *Thomas Jefferson and the Stony Mountains* (Urbana and Chicago: University of Illinois Press, 1981) 3; *A Voyage Round the World: Which was Performed in 1785, 1786, 1787, and 1788, by M. De La Peyrouse* (Edinburgh: J Moir, 1798) 70–1.

The fact that European countries claimed lands by hanging and burying plates and coins, and painting signs and planting their crosses and flags in the soil is not a surprise. It was really the only option they had to claim ownership in situations where they were just passing through a new territory. Moreover, this type of conduct was a direct analogy to the feudal formalities used to transfer land ownership in the days before written deeds and title insurance offices. In fact, to demonstrate the sale of land in England up to the middle of the seventeenth century, a buyer and seller would engage in a ritual called livery of seisin. This was the process in which the possession and ownership of land was transferred and delivered to a new owner. It was accomplished by a ritual performed on the land itself and in the presence of neighbours and witnesses. The transfer of ownership was demonstrated by the former owner turning over some dirt with a shovel and handing a clod of dirt or a twig from the property to the new owner for the witnesses to observe. Europeans followed these same types of procedures when they utilized the analogous rituals of making Discovery claims to new lands.[32]

England also developed another element of Discovery to justify its alleged right to the lands of Indigenous peoples. This was the principle called *terra nullius* (a land or earth that is null or void), or *vacuum domicilium* (an empty, vacant, or unoccupied house or domicile). This element stated that lands that were not occupied by any person or nation, or which were actually occupied but were not being used in a manner that European legal systems approved, were considered to be available for Discovery claims. One scholar defined *terra nullius* as having two definitions: 'a country without a sovereign recognized by European authorities and a territory where nobody owns any land at all'. Another author stated that *terra nullius* defined areas that were populated by inhabitants who were not members of the family of nations and not subject to international law. Europeans did not recognize the sovereignty or property rights of such 'noncivilized' peoples to the lands they occupied. Needless to say, 'Europeans regarded North America as a vacant land that could be claimed by right of discovery'.[33]

England and France, for example, no doubt developed these additional elements of Discovery because they could not rely on papal grants to trump the rights of the native inhabitants to their lands in the New World. Consequently, England and France developed and relied on two new Discovery factors: first, land was available for their claims if other European countries were not in actual

---

[32] Cornelius J Moynihan and Sheldon Kurtz, *Introduction to the Law of Real Property* (St Paul: Thomson/West, 4th edn, 2005) 212–13.

[33] Henry Reynolds, *The Law of the Land* (New York: Viking Penguin, 1987) 173; Lynn Berat, *Walvis Bay: Decolonization and International Law* (New Haven: Yale University Press, 1990) 118; Colin G Calloway, *Crown and Calumet: British-Indian Relations, 1783–1815* (Norman: University of Oklahoma Press, 1987) 9; Alex C Castles, 'An Australian Legal History' in *Aboriginal Legal Issues, Commentary and Materials* (Holmes Beach, FL: Wm W Gaunt & Sons, H McRae et al (eds), 1991) 10, 63.

occupancy and possession when English or French explorers arrived, and second, land was available for taking from Indigenous peoples even if they were currently occupying and using the land if it was considered legally vacant, empty, or *terra nullius*. The development of these additional elements of Discovery demonstrated the creativity and adaptability that Europeans used to make the Doctrine work in favour of their particular situations.

In conclusion, it is obvious that England and all the European countries that engaged in exploration and colonization utilized the international law Doctrine of Discovery and its elements. The Doctrine was widely accepted and applied by Europeans as the legal authority for colonizing the lands of Indigenous peoples and for dominating the native inhabitants and governments. Europeans occasionally disagreed over the exact meaning of Discovery, and even sometimes violently disputed their divergent claims; but one principle they never disagreed about was that the Indigenous peoples and nations lost sovereign, commercial, and real property rights immediately upon their 'discovery' by Europeans.

* * *

In Chapter 2, we examine how the Discovery Doctrine was adopted into American colonial and state law, and then into the US Constitution, federal laws, executive branch, and finally by the US Supreme Court in *Johnson v. M'Intosh* in 1823.

Chapter 3 shows how throughout American history the US government, state governments, and US citizens relied on Discovery principles in claiming and acquiring the lands and rights of the native governments and peoples who occupied and owned the lands that now comprise the United States.

Chapter 4 begins by discussing Indigenous conceptualizations of land, legal orders, and governmental authorities. Addressing Indigenous land in the context of familial relationships, the chapter proceeds to address problems with the reconstruction of land history and the requirement of Indigenous inclusion in the dialogue. Interpreting the Doctrine of Discovery and European legal imperialism as antecedents to the construction of Canadian false understandings of Indigenous inhumanity, Chapter 4 provides readers with the opportunity to identify and examine colonial constructions of Indigeneity and the disregard for Indigenous land relationships, legal orders, and notions of sovereignty as precursors to settlement on Indigenous territories in the land that has become known as Canada. The chapter proceeds to examine Canadian constitutional doctrine, early treaties between First Peoples and settlers, Canadian legislation, and early case law in order to determine to what degree Canadian legal understanding about Indigenous peoples and Indigenous land relationships has been informed by the Doctrine of Discovery.

Chapter 5 looks at the Contemporary Resonance of the Imperial Doctrine. Reviewing contemporary documentation, including Canadian constitutional provisions, Canadian principles of treaty interpretation, Canadian case law, and the Canadian policies related to land claims and other Agreements, the work builds upon the previous chapter in assessing the Doctrine of Discovery prevalence and bases for the understandings reached by Canadian lawmakers, the judiciary and negotiators. Assessing the body of information to determine the nature and influence of Doctrinal presumptions and Doctrinal informed understandings of Canadian legal supremacy and rightfulness, the author addresses Indigenous legal and governmental authorities and orders to contextualize and ground the analysis and arrive at an understanding of the requirements of reconciliation in a pluralistic and contemporary context.

Chapter 6 explores the way in which the Doctrine of Discovery was used to justify the assertion of British sovereignty over Australia and continued to be used to justify its colonization. It looks particularly at the development of the legal fiction of *terra nullius*.

Chapter 7 explores the continual adoption of the principles of the Doctrine of Discovery into contemporary Australian law. It looks at the overturning of the *terra nullius* principle in 1992 but looks at the way in which the Doctrine of Discovery still leaves a legacy in Australian law whereby the rights of Indigenous people are unprotected.

Chapters 8 and 9 turn to focus on the assertion of the Doctrine of Discovery in the South Pacific country of Aotearoa New Zealand. First discovered by Māori, it had been their home for some hundreds of years before the British began to visit their shores and eventually claim sovereignty of the lands via a treaty of cession but with actions steeped in a Discovery mindset. Chapter 8 discusses the signing of the Treaty of Waitangi in 1840 and traverses the early case law. Chapter 9 explores how Discovery and its elements have continued to haunt contemporary legal and political reasoning in Aotearoa New Zealand. It focuses on case law post 1970, Treaty of Waitangi claim settlements concerning national parks and the foreshore and seabed, and the constitutional standing of the Treaty of Waitangi. These case studies highlight the still permeating influence of the Doctrine of Discovery in Aotearoa New Zealand.

Chapter 10 provides concluding remarks by drawing on comparative law to illustrate the combined pervading power of the Doctrine of Discovery in the English colonies of Australia, Canada, Aotearoa New Zealand, and the United States. The ten elements of Discovery outlined in Chapter 1 provide the perfect structure to better understand that while differences in application in these four countries occurred, the overall sentiment is very similar. Discovery is a dangerous fiction that if not tackled will continue to undermine attempts to create a better, reconciled Crown-Indigenous future.

* * *

We hope that by analysing the use of the Doctrine of Discovery by our four countries readers will more fully understand the histories and legal regimes of these four ex-English colonies and better appreciate the situations, conditions, and legal, political, and social rights of the Indigenous peoples and nations in those countries. We cannot ignore the modern day relevance of this ancient international law doctrine and the amazing fact that Discovery is still a major part of the law of our countries and the daily lives of Indigenous peoples and governments. Clearly, Discovery continues to play a very significant role in the law and policies of our four countries and restricts the property, governmental, and self-determination rights of the Indigenous peoples and nations.

The governments and citizens of Australia, Canada, New Zealand, and the United States need to carefully examine their continuing use of Discovery against their native citizens and nations. The cultural, racial, feudal, and religious justifications that created Discovery should not and cannot continue to be applied in modern day legal and political affairs with Indigenous peoples. The Doctrine of Discovery is not just an obscure relic of the histories of our countries. And it is not just a mistake of the past that cannot be corrected today. The Doctrine of Discovery needs to be addressed and eliminated from the modern day life and law of our four countries.

We are very encouraged by the recent actions of several churches in responding to requests by Indigenous peoples and others to reject Discovery. In July 2009, the Episcopal Church adopted a resolution entitled 'Repudiate the Doctrine of Discovery' at its 76th General Convention in California. The resolution states that Discovery creates 'destructive policies ... that lead to the colonizing dispossession of the lands of indigenous peoples and the disruption of their way of life ... '. The Church called on the United States to review its 'historical and contemporary policies that contribute to the continuing colonization of Indigenous Peoples' and for Queen Elizabeth II to 'disavow, and repudiate publicly, the claimed validity of the Christian Doctrine of Discovery ... '. Furthermore, in September 2009, a Quaker group disavowed the Doctrine and voiced its support for the United Nations Declaration on the Rights of Indigenous Peoples. The Indian Committee of Philadelphia Yearly Meeting of the Religious Society of Friends issued a resolution that 'renounces the Doctrine of Discovery, the doctrine at the foundation of the colonization of Indigenous lands, including the lands of Pennsylvania. We find this doctrine to be fundamentally inconsistent with the teaching of Jesus, with our understanding of the inherent rights that individuals and peoples have received from God, and inconsistent with Quaker testimonies of Peace, Equality, and Integrity.' And in December 2009, at the parliament of the World's Religions conference in Australia, delegates expressed their concerns about Discovery in a document that, among other things, called on Pope Benedict XVI to 'repudiate the papal decrees that legitimized ... the dehumanized Doctrine of Christian Discovery ... '.[34]

---

[34] Robert J Miller, 'Will others follow Episcopal Church's lead?', *Indian Country Today*, 12 August 2009, 5; Judy Harrison, 'Maine Episcopalians move to back tribes', *Bangor Daily News*,

We hope that other churches and governments all around the world will also take up this call to review the use of the Doctrine of Discovery in law and policies against Indigenous peoples and to take substantive actions to correct the egregious results of Discovery.

23 July 2009; Gale Courey Toensing, 'Quaker Indian Committee disavows Doctrine of Discovery, affirms Declaration', *Indian Country Today*, 14 December 2009, <http://www.indiancountryto-day.com/home/content/79059862.html>; Gale Courey Toensing, 'Indigenous delegates ask Pope to repudiate Doctrine of Discovery', *Indian Country Today*, 23 December 2009, at 1, <http://www.indiancountrytoday.com/home/content/79636552.html>.

2

The Legal Adoption of Discovery in the United States

The legal evidence of American history shows that the establishment of the 13 original English colonies and the 13 original American states and the creation and expansion of the United States thereafter was based on the Doctrine of Discovery. The American Founding Fathers were well aware of this international law and utilized it while they were part of the colonial English system. They then naturally continued to use Discovery as the law of the new United States. From Benjamin Franklin and Presidents George Washington and Thomas Jefferson onward, American leaders used Discovery to justify their claims of property rights and political dominance over the Indian nations and citizens. In particular, Thomas Jefferson had a working knowledge of Discovery and used it against the Indian nations within the original 13 states, in the trans-Appalachia area, the Louisiana Territory, and the Pacific Northwest. The United States used the elements of the Doctrine to argue to Russia, Spain, and England for four decades that the United States owned the Pacific Northwest under international law. The United States justified its claim on the first discovery of the Columbia River in the Northwest by the American Robert Gray in 1792, the first inland exploration and occupation of the territory by the Lewis and Clark expedition in 1805–1806, and then the building of the trading post of Astoria at the mouth of the Columbia in 1811, the first permanent non-Indian settlement in the Northwest.[1]

All the European countries that colonized North America imported the international law Doctrine of Discovery to justify their actions and relationships with the Indigenous nations and peoples. It is no surprise that the North American colonists and colonial governments also expressly adopted and applied Discovery to their interactions with American Indians and their governments. We will see that the English colonies, the 13 original American states, and then the various permutations of the US federal government all used the legal framework of Discovery to deal politically, diplomatically, and commercially with the American Indian nations.

---

[1] Robert J Miller, *Native America, Discovered and Conquered: Thomas Jefferson, Lewis and Clark, and Manifest Destiny* (Westport, CT and London: Praeger Publishers, 2006) 25–76, 121–7, 131–6.

A. American Colonial Law of Discovery

The Doctrine of Discovery was the international law under which America was explored and was the legal authority the English Crown used to establish colonies in America. Discovery allegedly passed 'title' to Indian lands to the Crown and preempted sales of these lands to any other European country or individual and granted sovereign and commercial rights over Indian nations to the Crown and its colonial governments. For example, a 1622 letter to the Virginia Company of London recounted that the colony was the King's property because it was 'first discouered' at the charge of Henry VII by John Cabot in 1497 who 'tooke possession thereof to the Kings vse [use]'. A Virginia legislative committee repeated this Discovery principle in a 1699 report. Additionally, a history of the state of New Jersey in 1765 defined English claims as being based on Cabot's voyage and discovery, subsequent English possession, and 'from the well known *Jus Gentium*, Law of Nations, that whatever waste or uncultivated country is discovered, it is the right of that prince who had been at the charge of the discovery'. This author also stated that discovery of such lands 'gives at least a right of preemption, and undoubtedly must be good against all but the Indian proprietors'. Moreover, Benjamin Franklin, one of America's most prominent Founding Fathers, stated at the Albany NY Congress in 1754 that 'his Majesty's title [in] America appears founded on the discovery thereof first made, and the possession thereof first taken, in 1497'. Consequently, American colonists in the 1600s, Benjamin Franklin in 1754, and an historian in 1765 all plainly relied on the elements of the Doctrine of Discovery to prove the English Crown's title to the lands in the 13 American colonies. The elements of Discovery, such as first discovery, *terra nullius*, possession, and the power of preemption were well known and applied by the colonists.[2]

1. Colonial statutory laws

The English colonists and their governments established political and diplomatic relationships with tribal governments and dealt with them as sovereign entities from the beginning of European settlement. The colonists assumed that the Crown legally held the Discovery power over tribes and that the colonies

---

[2] III *The Records of the Virginia Company of London* (Wilmington: Scholarly Resources, Susan Myra Kingsbury (ed), 1933) 541–3; IV *Early American Indian Documents: Treaties and Laws, 1607–1789* (Washington DC: University Publications of America, Alden T Vaughan and W Stitt Robinson (eds), 1983) 112; Samuel Smith, *The History of the Colony of New Jersey* (Burlington: James Parker, 1765; Trenton: Reprint, Philadelphia: William S Sharp, 1890) 7–8; V *The Papers of Benjamin Franklin* (New Haven: Yale University Press, William B Wilcox (ed), 1959–2008) 368; II *The Papers of George Mason* (Chapel Hill, NC: University of North Carolina Press, Robert A Rutland (ed), 1970) 751.

were authorized to conduct political affairs and property transactions with the Indian nations under the authority granted to the colonies in their royal charters. All 13 colonies enacted numerous laws exercising this delegated authority to purchase Indian lands, protect their exclusive right of preemption to buy Indian lands, exercise limited sovereignty over tribes, and to grant titles in Indian lands to others even while Indians were occupying and using their lands. A Pennsylvania state court demonstrated this thinking in 1813: 'The royal charter did indeed convey to *William Penn* an immediate and absolute estate in fee [over Indian lands].'[3]

The English colonies spent an enormous amount of time over more than 150 years in dealing with Indian affairs and enacted an enormous number of laws concerning Indians, their governments, and Discovery issues. We will only highlight a limited number of the colonial era laws to observe the use of Discovery and its elements by the English colonial governments and to trace the adoption of Discovery in American law.

The colonial laws regarding Discovery, Indians, and tribal governments fall into four general categories. First, each colony enacted multiple statutes exercising the preemption right to regulate sales of Indian lands. Second, the colonies tried to control all trade and commercial activities between Indians and colonists. Third, several colonies created trust relationships to allegedly benefit tribal nations because they apparently felt a responsibility to protect Indians and help them progress to a 'civilized' state. Finally, several colonies passed laws to exercise the sovereign authority they assumed Discovery had granted them over Indian nations.

In addition to the 1622 Virginia Company letter mentioned above, one of the earliest examples of an express claim to legal Discovery powers was demonstrated by the Maryland colony in 1638 when it enacted a law to control trade with Indians. The Act stated that its specific legal authority was based on the Crown's 'right of first discovery' whereby the King had 'became lord and possessor' of Maryland and had gained outright ownership of the land. This is an accurate statement of the legal and sovereign rights that the Doctrine purportedly passed to a discovering European country.[4]

---

[3] Robert J Miller, 'American Indian Influence on the U.S. Constitution and Its Framers' (1993) 18 Am Indian L Rev 135–8; *A Bibliography of the English Colonial Treaties with the American Indians* (Mansfield: Martino Publishing, Henry F De Puy (ed), 1917, reprinted 1999); *Thompson v Johnston* 6 Binn 68, 1813 WL 1243, at *2 (PA Sup Ct 1813); *Sacarusa & Longboard v William King's Heirs* 4 NC 336, 1816 WL 222, at *2 (NC Sup Ct 1816); Shaw Livermore, *Early American Land Companies: Their Influence on Corporate Development* (New York: The Commonwealth Fund, 1939) 20, 31; XV *Early American Indian Documents*, note 2, 47–8; ibid VIII, 576–7; ibid I, 57; Thomas L Purvis, *Colonial America to 1763* (New York: Facts on File, 1999) 188; I *Foundations of Colonial America: A Documentary History* (New York: Chelsea House, W Keith Kavenagh (ed), 1973) 96, 102; *Laws of the Colonial and State Governments Relating to Indians and Indian Affairs, From 1633 to 1831* (Washington DC: Thompson and Homans, 1832; Stanfordville: Reprint, Earl M Coleman Enterprises Inc, 1979) 41, 52, 133–4, 178.   [4] II *Foundations*, note 3, 1267.

The first category of Discovery-related laws concerned governmental attempts to exercise the preemption power to regulate Indian land sales. The fourth president of the United States, James Madison, recognized the importance of preemption to colonial governments. He wrote in 1783 and in 1784 to James Monroe, the fifth US president, that 'pre-emption...was the principal right formerly exerted by the Colonies with regard to the Indians [and] that it was a right asserted by the laws as well as the proceedings of all of them...'. This was undoubtedly true because all 13 colonies repeatedly enacted laws declaring preemption as their governmental prerogative. The colonies exercised preemption by requiring individuals to get licences or the permission of the legislative assembly or governor to buy, lease, or occupy Indian lands and the colonies declared all sales or leases of Indian lands without prior governmental approval to be null and void. Most colonies also imposed forfeitures and heavy fines on unapproved land purchases. Consequently, by enacting these laws over 15 decades, the colonial governments applied the Doctrine of Discovery and preemption to sales of Indian lands so that only the colonial government could buy or regulate the purchase of such lands. They were working to create a managed and orderly advance of their borders, maintaining a profitable and beneficial trade with Indians, keeping the peace with powerful tribes, and enforcing the power of Discovery against their own citizens, other colonies and countries, and against the Indian nations.[5]

The colonial governments also used the *terra nullius*, or vacant lands, element of Discovery. They did this even though much of the allegedly 'vacant land' was owned and utilized by Indian people. One chaplain for the Virginia Company even asked: 'By what right or warrant can we enter into the land of these Savages [and] take away their rightful inheritance...?' The stock answer was *terra nullius*. 'In order to justify the expropriation of indigenous populations, the British colonists came up with a distinctive rationalization, the convenient idea of '*terra nullius*', nobody's land.' The colonists helped themselves to as much land as they could because, as one early governor of Virginia stated, their first work was the 'expulsion of the Savage'. Similarly, the English philosopher John Locke said that if Indians resisted the expropriation of their lands they should 'be destroyed as

[5] VIII *The Papers of James Madison* (Charlottesville: University Press of Virginia, Robert A Rutland et al (eds), 1983) 156; ibid XIV, 442; I *Foundations*, note 3, 194, 413, 601; ibid II, 925–31, 1282; XV *Early American Indian Documents*, note 2, 46–8, 153–4, 259, 268; ibid XVI, 20–1, 170–1, 295–6, 406; ibid IV, 93–4; ibid XX, 597; II *Colony Laws of Virginia, 1619–1660* (Wilmington: M Glazier, John D Cushing, and William W Henning (eds), 1978) 467–8; *George Washington Writings* (New York: Literary Classics of the US, John Rhodehamel (ed), 1997) 779, 903, 919, 923; Jack M Sosin, *Whitehall and the Wilderness: The Middle West in British Colonial Policy, 1760–1775* (Lincoln: University of Nebraska Press, 1961) 108–9, 122; *The Earliest Acts and Laws of the Colony of Rhode Island and Providence Plantations: 1647–1719* (Wilmington: M Glazier, John D Cushing (ed), 1977) 139; *Acts and Laws of New Hampshire 1680–1726* (Wilmington: M Glazier, John D Cushing (ed), 1978) 142; *The Colony Laws of North America Series* (Wilmington: M Glazier, 1977) 35–6; *The World Turned Upside Down: Indian Voices from Early America* (Boston: St Martin's Press, Colin G Calloway (ed), 1994) 78; XXVII *The Writings of George Washington* (Washington DC: Gov't Print Office, John C Fitzpatrick (ed), 1931) 140.

a *Lyon* or a *Tyger*, one of those wild Savage Beasts, with whom Men can have no Society or Security'. We will see this analogy of Indians to animals repeated in President George Washington's statement calling Indians 'the Savage as the Wolf'. Thus, while relying on the Discovery legal principle of *terra nullius*, several colonies such as Virginia in 1676, 1688, and 1699 defined lands that they considered vacant to be available for colonial disposal while they ignored Indian rights.[6]

The second category of colonial laws regarding Indians demonstrated the colonies' assumption of sovereign and superior positions over tribal governments to control all commercial relationships between colonists and Indians. The colonies enacted dozens of statutes regarding Indian commercial issues including requiring licences for colonists who wanted to trade with Indians (a legal requirement that is still federal law to this day). The colonies hoped to control the trade of weapons and alcohol to Indians and to prevent fraudulent trade practices because these activities often caused friction and conflicts.[7]

In the third category of laws, many colonies established trust or fiduciary like relationships with tribes, ostensibly to protect tribal interests. This idea probably arose from English and French monarchs charging their colonists with responsibilities to civilize and Christianize North American Indians. Colonies might also have been attempting to keep the peace by treating Indian nations fairly. One suspects, however, that the real motivation was not a concern for Indian rights but to serve the Discovery idea that colonial governments had ultimate control over all dispositions of tribal lands, control over all tribal/colonial relationships, and a role in civilizing and converting Indians. It is also possible that these trust situations were actually shams and nothing more than another attempt to acquire tribal assets easily and cheaply. Many of these statutes, for example, allowed specifically named colonial citizens to control tribal property.[8]

Many colonies also enacted a fourth category of laws in which they read the Discovery Doctrine and the Crown's power very expansively to include Crown and colonial sovereignty over Indian tribes and individual Indians. In an extreme application of ethnocentrism, some colonies assumed that Indians had become

---

[6] XV *Early American Indian Documents*, note 2, 80–1; ibid IV, 92–3, 110–14; Peter S Onuf, *Jefferson's Empire: The Language of American Nationhood* (Charlottesville: University Press of Virginia, 2000) 81; Niall Ferguson, *Empire: The Rise and Demise of the British World Order and the Lessons for Global Power* (New York: Basic Books, 2002) 54–5.

[7] IV *Early American Indian Documents*, note 2, 51, 70–1; XII *The Writings of Thomas Jefferson* (Washington DC: Jefferson Memorial Assoc of the US, Andrew A Lipscomb and Albert Ellery Bergh (eds), 1903) 100; Francis Paul Prucha, *The Great Father: The United States Government and the American Indians* (Lincoln: University of Nebraska Press, 1995 edn) 116, 120.

[8] Anthony Pagden, *Lords of all the World: Ideologies of Empire in Spain, Britain and France c. 1500–c. 1800* (New Haven: Yale University Press, 1995) 34–5; *Select Charters and Other Documents Illustrative of American History 1606–1775* (London: MacMillan Company, William MacDonald (ed), 1906, Littleton: Reprint, Rothman & Co, 1993) 131; XVI *Early American Indian Documents*, note 2, 295–6; ibid XX, 597; *Laws of the Colonial and State Governments*, note 3, 12, 16–17, 22, 37, 45, 59, 136, 142, 146, 150, 154; *The Livingston Indian Records, 1666–1723* (Gettysburg, PA: The Pennsylvania Historical Assoc, Lawrence H Leder (ed), 1956; Stanfordville: Reprint, Earl M Coleman Publisher, 1979) 98.

subjects of England and that Indian nations had become the King's tributaries due to Discovery. In several instances, in a perverse twist on the preemption element, colonial laws even required tribes to apply to the Crown or colony for a deed to their own lands. Colonies maintained that they had the authority to grant tribes titles to land, to restrict the movements of individual Indians, and to force tribal chiefs to pledge loyalty to colonial governments.[9]

The sheer breadth of the subject matter and the hundreds of laws relating to Discovery issues that were enacted by the 13 colonies demonstrates the express and unanimous acceptance of the elements of Discovery such as first discovery, preemption and European title, Indian title, limited tribal sovereignty, *terra nullius*, and the alleged superiority of European civilizations and religions. The English colonies all adopted the idea that they held and could exercise the power of Discovery over the Indian nations. Discovery and its elements were so widespread and accepted in colonial times that Indian individuals and tribal nations were often aware of how their rights were defined by the colonists and by Discovery. Tribes often argued against these Eurocentric principles. Some tribes claimed the Discovery right of conquest themselves over the lands of other Indian nations, some Indian leaders argued that Europeans could not trade tribal property rights back and forth, and the Mohegan Nation even sued in colonial and Royal courts for over 100 years to stop the application of Discovery against its lands. Notwithstanding tribal views on property rights and their occupation of land for centuries, the colonial governments enacted hundreds of laws adopting the elements of Discovery.[10]

2. Colonial courts

There are only a few colonial era court cases that directly address Discovery issues. One commentator, however, reports that the second most important category of cases the colonial courts heard concerned the laws governing interactions with Indians that we have just discussed. The colonial courts, then, were actively involved in issues of Discovery and this further demonstrates the widespread understanding and use of the Doctrine by the colonial governments and colonists.[11]

[9] XV *Early American Indian Documents*, note 2, 40–1, 47–8, 153, 283, 306–7; ibid XVI, 46–8; ibid XIX, 30, 176–8, 406–12, 436, 525, 538–9; ibid IV, 70–1; *The Livingston Indian Records*, note 8, 65, 86, 89, 117, 182.
[10] *Bibliography of the English Colonial Treaties*, note 3, 17; *The Writings of Benjamin Franklin* (New York: Macmillan Co, Albert Henry Smyth (ed), 1907) 481–2, 488–9; XI *Early American Indian Documents*, note 2, 202; Joseph Henry Smith, *Appeals to the Privy Council from the American Plantations* (New York: Columbia University Press, 1950) 418–42; Vine Deloria Jr and David E Wilkins, *Tribes, Treaties, & Constitutional Tribulations* (Austin: University of Texas Press, 1999) 11.
[11] George Lewis Chumbley, *Colonial Justice in Virginia* (Richmond: Diety Press, 1971) 5; *County Court Records of Accomack-Northampton, Virginia 1632–1640* (Charlottesville: University Press of Virginia, Susie M Ames (ed), 1954, reprint 1975) lxi, lxv, 56–7; Smith, note 10, 165.

The most relevant English case of the era was *Calvin's Case* from 1608. Calvin, a Scotsman, petitioned an English court to restore his ownership of land that he claimed had been unjustly taken from him by an Englishman named Smith. Smith argued that Calvin was an alien, being a Scotsman, and since Calvin owed no allegiance to the King he did not even deserve an answer to the suit he brought in an English court. The Court reasoned that since infidels are the perpetual enemies of the King and all Christians, they are unfriendly aliens and cannot use the King's courts. The Court also inferred that military conquest of infidel lands gave a Christian king outright title to their lands whereas, in contrast, a similar conquest by one Christian king of another Christian domain did not alter the property rights of the conquered people. Consequently, this court defined the conquest element of Discovery in the same way we perceive it defined in the US Supreme Court case of *Johnson v M'Intosh* from 1823. This loss of title that infidels suffered from conquest was apparently first defined in English law in *Calvin's Case*.[12]

The element of conquest became an important issue in colonial courts and especially in a Connecticut colonial case that lasted from the 1640s to 1773. In this case, the Mohegan Indian Nation sued Connecticut over land rights for 130 years. The tribe won a court judgment in 1705 but finally lost the appeal to the King's Privy Council in 1773. The parties litigated issues concerning the ownership of Mohegan lands, the significance of the colony's military conquest of the neighbouring Pequot Tribe, the validity and meaning of Connecticut laws that prohibited purchases of tribal lands, and the significance of land conveyances by tribal chiefs to colonists. Over many decades, the parties argued in various courts the meaning of Discovery elements such as conquest, preemption, the right to purchase Indian lands, and the Connecticut laws that declared void individual purchases of Indian lands. This case was called by one attorney of the time 'the greatest cause that ever was heard at the Council Board'. Therefore, issues regarding the ownership of Indian lands and various elements of Discovery became well known and publicized by just this case alone. The US Supreme Court even mentioned this case in 1823 in *Johnson v M'Intosh*.[13]

Other colonies also litigated issues about the ownership of Indian lands and the impact of Discovery. Some colonies disputed their boundaries with each other on the basis of the validity of Indian titles and tribal land sales. Some Indians even used colonial courts to try to protect their property rights. Individual colonists also used Indian titles and land purchases from Indians to make claims against each other and against their colonial governments. In *Barkham's Case*, for example, in 1622, a colonist tried to affirm in London a title for lands in Virginia that had been granted him by the colonial governor and affirmed by an Indian

---

[12] 77 Eng Rep 377, 378, 397 (KB 1608); Robert A Williams, Jr, *The American Indian in Western Legal Thought: The Discourses of Conquest* (New Haven: Yale University Press, 1990) 199.

[13] Smith, note 10, 418–42; *Bibliography of the English Colonial Treaties*, note 3, 21; *Johnson v M'Intosh* 21 US (8 Wheat) 543, 598 (1823).

chief. The directors of the Virginia Company in London, sitting as a court with jurisdiction granted by the King, were troubled by the involvement of the chief and the question of the power of a tribe to grant titles. The Court reasoned that since Discovery had terminated tribal powers over their lands and limited their ability to sell land, then only the King's power could be used to grant titles in America. The Company's right to grant titles in Virginia came only from the King and could not be contingent on the approval of an Indian nation or chief. Accordingly, the Company court held Barkham's title invalid because it had not been issued by the King through the Company and because it recognized 'a Soveraignity in that heathen Infidell . . . and the Companies Title thereby much infringed'.[14]

The few colonial era cases available demonstrate that the elements of Discovery and the Crown's preemption power to grant titles in America was well understood by the colonial court systems.

3. Royal attempts to enforce Discovery

The English Crown could not afford or did not want to pay to colonize America and thus Elizabeth I in the late 1500s and James I in the early 1600s relied on private companies to enlist settlers, pay for the voyages, and take the risks. Sir Walter Raleigh was granted a charter in 1587 to explore and colonize America, to seek profits, and to obtain lands in fee simple ownership while at the same time he was also making claims of jurisdiction and sovereignty for Queen Elizabeth and paying her a percentage of the profits. Under James I, the Crown granted far ranging powers to individuals and named them the proprietors or owners of colonies and granted them vast tracts of land in America in fee simple ownership. Later, the Stuart line of English kings rescinded most of the colonial charters and made them into royal or Crown colonies and turned them into the king's property. Even so, the Crown still exercised very loose control over the colonies and the colonists became very independent. For example, the Crown appointed governors for the royal colonies but the individual colonists elected their own legislative assemblies. The King and Parliament did not begin taxing and regulating the colonies by statutes until the 1760s. Prior to that, Parliament had taken almost no steps to interfere with what was considered to be the King's private property in the New World.

The Seven Years War (started in North America in 1754 and ended by a treaty signed in Europe in 1763, called the French and Indian War in America) was in reality a world war that was largely caused by conflicting Discovery claims

---

[14] Smith, note 10, 115, 122, 124; IV *Early American Indian Documents*, note 2, 27–8, 62, 110–11, 114–15; ibid XIX, 506; II *The Records of the Virginia Company of London: The Court Book* (Washington DC: Gov't Printing Office, 1906) 94; Williams, note 12, 214–17; I *The Records of the Virginia Company* (Washington DC: Gov't Printing Office, S M Kingsbury (ed), 1933) 71–87.

between England and France in the New World. The war left the English Crown deeply in debt. Consequently, the Crown got more involved in colonial governance to try to prevent such problems and King George III imposed his authority in America to control the main issues that led to conflicts; trade and land purchases with Indian nations.[15]

The Crown took three primary steps that were extremely unpopular in America. First, it imposed taxes on the colonists, including the 1764 Stamp Act, to pay for the debts incurred in protecting the colonies in the French and Indian War, and to finance the costs of keeping troops in America to maintain the peace and to control the colonists' actions against the Indian nations. Second, the Crown centralized the control of Indian affairs in itself and established two Indian districts in America with sole jurisdiction over Indian affairs. The King then appointed the superintendents who were to manage the districts. Finally, and most significantly, the King asserted his authority over Indian affairs and exercised his Discovery power by taking control of all the trade with Indians and all sales of tribal lands. George III did this by issuing the Royal Proclamation of 1763. The Proclamation shows clearly that his government understood its Discovery powers, including preemption and other elements. The royal actions undertaken to control the commercial and political relationships with tribal nations were very unpopular with American colonists, and were even cited in the US Declaration of Independence as part of the justifications for the American Revolution.[16]

The Proclamation of October 1763 drew a boundary line along the crest of the Appalachia and Allegheny mountains over which British citizens were not to cross. In essence, the King defined Indian country, Indian lands, as all territory west of that line to the Mississippi River, where England's claim ended. England had gained an internationally recognized Discovery claim to this area in February 1763 when France ceded all its claims in Canada and east of the Mississippi to England to settle the French and Indian War. King George now exercised his new Discovery authority over this area and stated in the Proclamation that the tribes in this territory 'live under *our protection*' and that it was essential to colonial security that the Indian nations not be 'disturbed in the possession of such parts of *our dominions and territories* as, not having been ceded to or purchased by us, are reserved to them'. In this statement, George III expressly claimed his Discovery title to tribal lands, his right of preemption over these lands, and his duty to protect and civilize Indian people. Notice that he called Indian country

---

[15] Dorothy V Jones, *License for Empire: Colonialism by Treaty in Early America* (Chicago: University of Chicago Press, 1982) 36; Sosin, note 5, 28–31, 45–6, 48–9, 51, 56, 79–83; Fred Anderson, *Crucible of War: The Seven Years' War and the Fate of Empire in British North America, 1754–1766* (New York: Alfred A Knopf, 2000) xv, xix, 85, 221, 565–7.

[16] Sosin, note 5, 80–98; Anderson, note 15, 85, 221, 565–7; 'The Declaration of Independence' in *Basic Writings of Thomas Jefferson* (New York: Willey Book Co, Philip S Foner (ed), 1944) 21, 23–4.

'our dominions' even though the lands had not yet 'been ceded to or purchased by' England.[17]

George III claimed that the Indian governments between the Allegheny and Appalachia Mountains and the Mississippi River lived under his 'protection', and that they were currently in 'possession' of his 'dominions and territories' even though the Indian nations had not yet 'ceded' the lands to the King nor had the King yet 'purchased' them. This is an express allegation of several of the elements of the international law of Discovery. The King accurately stated the rights defined by first discovery, preemption, European title, the limited Indian title to possess and use their lands, and the limited tribal sovereign and commercial rights to deal only with the discovering European country.

The King then exercised even more of his Discovery powers. He ordered that none of his colonial governors or military commanders could allow surveys or grant titles in this area, and that none of his subjects could purchase or settle on Indian lands without Royal permission. Further defining his power, the King said that these Indian lands were 'reserve[d] under our sovereignty, protection, and dominion, for the use of the said Indians…'. The King also took control of all trade with Indians by requiring traders to post bonds to ensure good conduct and to be licensed by Royal governors. The Proclamation and the King's conduct demonstrated clearly that the Crown understood its alleged Discovery powers over the Indian nations and the lands in North America. The Proclamation also foreshadowed the definition of Discovery accepted by the US Supreme Court that the discovering European countries acquired title in tribal lands subject to the later transfer to the European government of the tribal rights of use and occupancy.

The Crown's Royal Proclamation and Parliament's taxation laws led to intense dissatisfaction among the colonists, and then to rebellion and the war for independence. The attitude of the colonists towards the Proclamation was well demonstrated by George Washington, who had always been active in buying Indian lands, and by Benjamin Franklin and other American Founding Fathers. Notwithstanding the King's Proclamation, which Washington thought was just 'a temporary expedient to quiet the Minds of the Indians', he made secret arrangements to continue buying Indian lands. The colonists deeply resented being taxed by Parliament since they did not have an elected representative in Parliament. Further problems developed between the Crown and the colonies from the Crown's exercise of its Discovery authority to control the Indian trade and to stop colonists from buying Indian lands. All of these actions demonstrated clearly that the Crown understood its Discovery powers when it worked to bring Indian affairs exclusively within the control of the central Royal government.[18]

---

[17] I Henry Steele Commager, *Documents of American History* (New York: Appleton-Century-Crofts, 8th edn, 1968) 47, 48; Sosin, note 5, 21–2, 73; *Select Charters and Other Documents*, note 8, 261–2, 266.

[18] *George Washington Writings*, note 5, 125; *The Writings of Benjamin Franklin*, note 10, 488–9.

B. American State Law of Discovery

After the American Revolutionary War, the new state governments and courts continued using Discovery to control sales of Indian lands and interactions with Indian nations because they assumed that these powers now belonged to their governments. It is interesting, and more than a little ironic, to watch how the new state and federal governments consolidated the Discovery authority and total control over Indian affairs into their central governments in the identical fashion that King George III had attempted.

The new American states struggled against the federal government for preeminence in Indian affairs because they claimed that Discovery powers had devolved from England to the states after they declared their independence and had not passed to the national Congress. The solution to this issue required an important compromise that led to the adoption of the 1787 US Constitution and the formation of the present day US government. We will now track the acceptance of Discovery into the laws of the new American states long before the *Johnson* case was decided in 1823.

1. State laws

The new 13 American states began adopting constitutions and enacting laws after declaring independence from England. They continued, not surprisingly, to assert the same Discovery and sovereign powers over tribal lands and Indians as they had during colonial times. Several states immediately enshrined in their new constitutions their alleged Discovery authority and various elements of the Doctrine. In Virginia's 1776 constitution, for example, the state claimed the right of preemption over Indian lands when it mandated that 'no purchase of lands shall be made of the *Indian* natives but on behalf of the public, by authority of the General Assembly'. The state was plainly attempting to exercise the Discovery authority of preemption.[19]

In New York's 1777 constitution, the state claimed preemption power over Indian lands and even applied that authority retroactively. Section 37 provided that:

no purchases or contracts for the sale of lands, made since the fourteenth day of October...one thousand seven hundred and seventy-five, or which may hereafter be made with or of the said Indians...shall be binding on the said Indians, or deemed valid, unless made under the authority and with the consent of the legislature of this State

---

[19] *The First Laws of the State of Virginia* (Wilmington, DE: M Glazier, John D Cushing (ed), 1982) 35.

New York further enforced this provision by enacting a law in 1788 which imposed criminal sanctions on any violation of the constitutional ban on private purchases of Indian lands.[20]

In 1776, North Carolina also placed Discovery principles into its constitution. North Carolina even went far beyond the elements of Discovery by claiming that Indian nations only possessed real property rights if their rights had been recognized by the colonial legislature or were recognized by the state legislature in the future: 'this Declaration of Rights shall not prejudice any nation or nations of Indians, from enjoying such hunting-grounds as may have been, or hereafter shall be, secured to them by any former or future Legislature of this State'. In Tennessee's 1796 constitution, the state claimed the same sovereign and land rights of Discovery that had existed under the royal charters.[21]

Georgia also placed express Discovery claims in its constitution. Georgia alleged that its new status as a state and its constitution did not prevent its legislature from exercising authority to 'procure an extension of settlement and extinguishment of Indian claims in and to the vacant territory of this State [and that] no sale of territory...shall take place...unless...the Indian rights shall have been extinguished thereto'. In this provision Georgia was claiming the sovereign and real property aspects of Discovery and that it was the only government that could deal with tribes and extinguish Indian titles. Georgia also recognized the *terra nullius* or vacant country element of Discovery and tribal rights in land. These constitutional provisions demonstrate that many states assumed from their beginnings that they possessed the power of Discovery.[22]

Furthermore, the laws that the new states enacted in Indian affairs demonstrated their belief that England's Discovery authority had transferred to the states. Virginia, for example, immediately took control of Indian land sales, and as early as June 1776 insisted on its legislature's right to decide the validity of titles held by individuals from Indians. In May 1779, Virginia responded to two years of petitions from land companies and individuals who objected to Virginia's constitutional prohibition on Indian land sales. These parties tried to get the legislature to ratify the titles they had allegedly purchased directly from tribes pre-1776. The state ultimately said no and in a 1779 law declared all such purchases void because they had occurred within Virginia's territory and without the permission of the colonial or state governments. This law reaffirmed that only Virginia possessed the 'exclusive right of preemption' over Indian titles within its borders.[23]

---

[20] NY Const art 37 (1777); NY Act of March 18, 1788, Sess 11, ch 85; 2 Greenl ed Laws 194.
[21] NC Const art I, § 25 (1776); TN Const art XI, § 32 (1796).
[22] GA Const art I, § 23 (1798).
[23] Onuf, *Jefferson's Empire*, note 6, 83; *First Laws of the State of Virginia*, note 19, 103–4; *Marshall v Clark* 8 Va 268, 1791 WL 325, at *3 (VA Sup Ct 1791); II *Papers of George Mason*, note 2, 746, 752.

Numerous other states enacted similar laws which demonstrated the wide-spread acceptance of Discovery, its elements, and the assumption that the states held the preemption power over tribal lands. Connecticut took control of such sales in 1776 and banned them unless they were allowed by the state assembly. In 1783, 1789, and 1802, North Carolina statutorily declared purchases of Indian lands to be void unless they had been or were approved by the colonial or state governments, and it took steps to control other activities on tribal lands. In 1780, 1783, 1784, and 1787, Georgia passed laws that declared null and void attempts by private parties to purchase Indian lands. In 1798, Rhode Island tried to take total control of Indian affairs within its state, including the sales of Indian lands. Pennsylvania likewise exercised its Discovery right of preemption and controlled Indian land sales. All of the states also relied on the *terra nullius* element of Discovery and 'simply continued the old British practice of treating traditional native hunting grounds as *terra nullius*, free, ownerless land'.[24]

Several states vied with the federal government for authority over Indian affairs even long after the federal government was granted that power in the US Constitution and had asserted in federal laws all the Discovery and political authority that any American government could exercise over tribes. Some obstinate states even signed treaties with tribal governments and bought tribal lands after a 1790 federal law forbade such state actions. When the US Secretary of War warned New York Governors Clinton and John Jay that a 1795 treaty between New York and an Indian nation would violate federal law, the state ignored the warnings and concluded the treaty anyway. New York also continued to legislate regarding Indian affairs and to engage in treaty making with tribes well into the 1830s, leading to Discovery law suits that federal courts had to decide in the twenty-first century. From the foregoing evidence, it is obvious that state governments well understood the Doctrine of Discovery and wanted to exercise its powers over the Indian nations and their lands and citizens.[25]

---

[24] *Laws of the Colonial and State Governments*, note 3, 18, 34, 50, 65–71, 148, 171–3; *The First Laws of the State of Connecticut* (Wilmington, DE: M Glazier, John D Cushing (ed), 1982) 101–2; *Danforth v Wear* 22 US (9 Wheat) 673, 677–8 (1824); *Sacarusa & Longboard v William King's Heirs* 4 NC 336, 1816 WL 222 (NC Sup Ct 1816) (1802 law); *Patterson v The Rev. Willis Jenks et al.* 27 US (2 Pet) 216, 234 (1829); I *The First Laws of the State of Georgia* (Wilmington, DE: M Glazier, John D Cushing (ed), 1981) 288; I *The First Laws of the State of Rhode Island*, note 5, 10; *Thompson v Johnston* 6 Binn 68, 1813 WL 1243, at *2 (PA Sup Ct 1813); *Blair v McKee*, 6 Serg & Rawle 193, 1820 WL 1846 (PA Sup Ct 1820); Niall Ferguson, *Colossus: The Price of America's Empire* (New York: The Penguin Press, 2004) 35.

[25] *Tennessee v Forman* 16 Tenn 256 (1835); Tim Alan Garrison, *The Legal Ideology of Removal: The Southern Judiciary and the Sovereignty of Native American Nations* (Athens & London: University of Georgia Press, 2002) 103–24, 151, 228; *South Carolina v Catawba Indian Tribe* 476 US 498 (1986); *County of Oneida v Oneida Indian Nation* 470 US 226 (1985); *Seneca Nation of Indians v New York* 382 F 3d 245 (2nd Cir 2004); *Oneida Indian Nation v New York* 860 F 2d 1145 (2nd Cir 1988); NY Act of April 2, 1813, Sess 36; NY Act of April 12, 1822, Sess 45, ch CCIV.

2. State court cases

There are a significant number of reported state court cases that touch on Discovery issues from the early days of the American states. These cases demonstrate that state judicial branches accepted and relied on Discovery and its elements.

In 1835, long after the federal government had taken complete control over Indian affairs and Discovery, the Tennessee Supreme Court still supported state incursions in this field. In *Tennessee v Forman*, the Court upheld the authority of the state legislature to extend its criminal jurisdiction into Indian country. The Court approved of this action even though it had to expressly repudiate a US Supreme Court case which had reached the exact opposite decision just three years before. The Tennessee court instead reached back to 1823 and the Supreme Court's *Johnson v M'Intosh* decision and expressly relied on Discovery and its elements of first discovery, European title, limited tribal sovereignty, religion, and conquest to hold that the state government possessed sovereign power over Indian nations and could impose state laws in tribal territory:

[T]he principle declared in the fifteenth century as the law of Christendom, that discovery gave title to assume sovereignty over, and to govern the unconverted natives of Africa, Asia, and North and South America, has been recognized as a part of the national law, for nearly four centuries.

The Court also noted the principle of 'just war' and that Americans could fight to 'defend' themselves if Indians resisted Americans taking over tribal lands. Just as Franciscus de Victoria stated in 1532, the Court agreed that if Indians opposed American rights to occupy tribal lands Americans could 'use force to repel such resistance'.[26]

Many other state courts demonstrated their agreement with Discovery and upheld state assertions of sovereignty and jurisdiction over tribes, the imposition of state laws in Indian territory, and even the idea of royal, colonial, and state ownership of tribal lands in fee simple. In *Arnold v Mundy*, in 1821, the New Jersey Supreme Court had to decide who owned oysters planted in a river. The case was primarily about the control of fisheries by the Crown in the exercise of its sovereign powers. But in analysing that issue, the Court stated that 'when Charles II. took possession of the country, by his right of discovery, he took possession of it in his sovereign capacity'. The Court also stated that the people of New Jersey had 'both the legal title and the usufruct [use rights in land] ... exercised by them in their sovereign capacity'. According to this Court, the King and later the people of New Jersey owned tribal lands due to first discovery, possession, and as part of their sovereignty. The Court also relied on *terra nullius* because it

---

[26] *Forman* 16 Tenn 256, 258–85, 287, 332–5, 339–45 (1835); Robert J Miller, 'A New Perspective on the Indian Removal Period' (2002) 38 Tulsa LJ 181, 192–4.

claimed New Jersey was 'an uninhabited country found out by British subjects'. The Court totally ignored the fact that Indian nations were living on these lands when the English arrived.[27]

In 1807, the North Carolina Supreme Court defined the tribal real property right of 'Indian title' to be just a possessory right, just a right of occupancy and use. This is the identical definition used under Discovery. The Pennsylvania Supreme Court agreed with this idea in 1813 and noted that even though the Royal charter had conveyed to William Penn the 'immediate and absolute estate in fee in the province of Pennsylvania' he had, out of good policy and justice, 'obtained the consent of the natives' by purchasing his lands from the tribes. This Court expressly relied on the well-known elements of Discovery of the limited Indian title and preemption. The Court also stated that 'the king's right was...founded...on the right of discovery'. One judge in this case relied on the elements of first discovery, preemption, limited Indian title, religion, and civilization when he stated that Indians could not own land since 'not being Christians, but mere heathens [they were] unworthy of the earth' and that the 'right of discovery' had given the colony an interest that was 'exclusive to a certain extent [and brought]...the *Indian* to his own market, where, if he sells at all, the *Indian* must take what he could get from this his only customer'. This statement clearly demonstrates the Court's knowledge of the impact that the exclusive rights of preemption and European title had on the prices Indian tribes could receive for land when there was only one possible buyer. The judge also demonstrated the religious and cultural biases that lurk behind the Doctrine and the discounting of the human, governmental, and commercial rights of Indian nations.[28]

State courts understood Discovery well enough that they accurately foretold the application and definition of its principles in advance of US Supreme Court cases. Several state courts, for example, had already ruled on and foretold the Supreme Court's statement in *Fletcher v Peck* in 1810 that states could grant away their Discovery titles in Indian lands and give to non-Indians a future title in those lands without the consent or knowledge of the Indian nation and while Indians were still occupying and using the land. In 1808, the New York Supreme Court considered the effect of the Mohawk Nation's preexisting possession of land that the colonial government had granted to a non-Indian in 1761. The Court refused to address the issue of land ownership by the nation because it considered the issue 'of granting lands in the possession of the native *Indians*,

---

[27] *Arnold v Mundy* 6 NJL 1, 1821 WL 1269 at *10, *53, *56 (NJ Sup Ct 1821). See also *Caldwell v Alabama* 2 Stew & P 327, 396, 408, 413–16 (AL Sup Ct 1831); *Georgia v Tassels* 1 Dud 229, 231–2, 234, 237–8 (GA Sup Ct 1830); *Jackson, ex dem Smith v Goodell* 20 Johns 188 (NY Sup Ct 1822); *Jackson v Sharp*, 14 Johns 472 (NY Sup Ct 1817); *Sacarusa & Longboard v William King's Heirs* 4 NC 336, 1816 WL 222, at *3 (NC Sup Ct 1816); *Strother v Martin* 5 NC 162, 1807 WL 35, at *2–3 (NC Sup Ct 1807).

[28] *Strother v Martin* 5 NC 162, 1807 WL 35, at *4 (NC Sup Ct 1807); *Thompson v Johnston* 6 Binn 68, 1813 WL 1243 *2 and 5 (PA Sup Ct 1813).

without their previous consent…a political question…. The competency of government to grant cannot be called in question.'[29]

Also foretelling the *Fletcher* statement was the Virginia Supreme Court in 1791. In *Marshall v Clark*, the Virginia court used several elements of Discovery to decide the issue of how Indian land titles were extinguished:

> The dormant title of the Indian tribes remained to be extinguished by government, either by purchase or conquest; and when that was done, it enured to the benefit of the citizen, who had previously acquired a title from the crown, and did not authorize a new grant of the lands…

Consequently, the grant of title by the colonial government, even though at the time the land was occupied by Indians, was valid and the grantee just had to wait until the government extinguished the Indian title by purchase or conquest. The Court added that 'the Indian title did not impede either the power of the legislature to grant the land…[because] the grantee, in either case, must risque the event of the Indian claims, and yield to it, if finally established, or have the benefit of a former or future extinction thereof'. That 1791 court statement agreed exactly with how Secretary of State and later President Thomas Jefferson defined states' Discovery rights in Indian lands in 1790 and accurately foretold the *Fletcher* Court's statement in 1810.[30]

Clearly, the colonial and state governments understood and applied the Doctrine of Discovery to exercise sovereign, commercial, and real property rights over the Indian nations. From their very beginnings, these governments enshrined Discovery in their constitutions, laws, and court cases.

C. American Federal Law of Discovery

The newly created national government of the 13 states immediately adopted the Doctrine of Discovery also. This is not at all surprising in light of the widespread use of the Doctrine by the European, colonial, and state governments in North America. It is also not surprising because the exercise of Discovery powers by a national government for the 13 colonies had already been proposed by Benjamin Franklin in 1754 when he presented his Albany Plan for governing the English colonies. Franklin's plan placed all matters of 'Indian Treaties…peace or [ ] War with Indian Nations…[and] Laws as they judge necessary for the regulating all Indian Trade [and] all purchases from Indians for the Crown, of lands [or] mak[ing] new settlements on such purchases by

---

[29] *Fletcher v Peck* 10 US (6 Cranch) 87, 142–4 (1810); *Jackson, ex dem J G Klock v Hudson* 3 Johns 375, 1808 WL 477, at *5, 3 Am Dec 500 (NY Sup Ct 1808).

[30] *Marshall v Clark* 8 Va 268, 1791 WL 325 *4 (VA Sup Ct 1791); *Fletcher v Peck* 10 US 142–4; III *Writings of Thomas Jefferson*, note 7, 19–20.

granting [Indian] Lands' in the hands of the national President-General and Grand Council he proposed.[31]

In September 1774, the 13 colonies created their first national governing entity, the loosely organized Continental Congress, to manage their national affairs and the struggle for independence from England. Indian affairs were a very important aspect of political events at this time but this Congress was primarily preoccupied with the monumental task of fighting the Revolutionary War. The Continental Congress did, however, deal with Indian nations on a diplomatic and political basis, tried to control the trade with tribes, and spent significant time and money trying to gain their support in the War.[32]

The Continental Congress quickly realized its own weakness due to operating without a written constitution and well-defined powers. One of the primary powers this Congress lacked was the sole authority to deal with Indian affairs. Accordingly, the Continental Congress drafted the Articles of Confederation in 1777 which were designed to give more governing authority, taxation power, and the power of Discovery and the sole voice over Indian affairs to the central federal government. The Articles were ratified in 1781 and a new, more structured, and more authoritative federal government began operation.

1. Articles of Confederation Congress 1781–1789

The 13 American states convened a new Congress in 1781 under a written document called the Articles of Confederation. This Congress then undertook major steps to incorporate the Doctrine of Discovery into federal law and to take the Discovery authority and power over Indian affairs under the sole control of the central federal government.

Section IX of the Articles provided that Congress 'shall also have the sole and exclusive right and power of... regulating the trade and managing all affairs with the Indians...'. This language repeated the claims of sovereign control over Indian affairs that had been previously made by the Crown, the colonies, and the states. However, the states insisted on two caveats in this section that ultimately doomed the attempt of the Articles to grant Congress sole charge of Indian affairs. The caveats gave states legitimate and non-legitimate arguments to meddle in Indian affairs and to frustrate the attempts of Congress to formulate and conduct unified Indian policies. Ultimately, this impasse led to

---

[31] *Select Charters and Other Documents*, note 8, 253–6.

[32] XVIII *Early American Indian Documents*, note 2, 4, 39, 43, 59, 63, 65, 70, 84, 98, 124, 203; Miller, 18 Am Indian L Rev, note 3, 137; IV *Colonial Series: The Papers of George Washington* (Charlottesville: University of Virginia Press, W W Abbot (ed), 1988) 192–4; *Cherokee Nation v Georgia* 30 US (5 Pet) 1, 34 (1831) (Baldwin J concurring); Treaty with the Delawares, Sept 17, 1778, 7 Stat 13, II *Indian Affairs: Laws and Treaties* (Washington DC: Gov't Printing Off, Charles J Kappler (ed), 1904) 3–5.

a call for an even stronger national government and to the creation of the US Constitution of 1787.[33]

Notwithstanding the problems that developed later, the Confederation Congress exercised its Discovery powers. In 1783, a congressional committee solicited the views of General George Washington and others on how to exercise its authority to control Indian affairs. Washington wrote the committee and Congress a very influential letter in September 1783 in which he stated that the United States would not have to fight tribes for land but should instead deal with them under a policy that Washington described as 'the Savage as the Wolf'. Washington said that Indian lands would fall to the United States soon enough, without bloodshed and without wasting tax dollars on an army, as the borders of American settlement and population naturally increased and Indians naturally retreated like wild beasts and died off. Washington was also in favour of Congress controlling all Indian trade and drawing a boundary line between American settlements and Indian country. This was odd because he had abhorred these same ideas when King George III used them in the Royal Proclamation of 1763. But now that the United States was in charge of Discovery and dealing with the Indian nations, Washington thought the ideas were good policies and that the US central government should control Indian affairs.[34]

Washington also demonstrated his approval of using Discovery elements as part of US Indian policies in another letter to Congress in June 1783. He suggested that to 'combat the Savages, and check their incursions' the United States should increase its trade with Indians because that 'would be the most likely means to enable us to purchase upon equitable terms of the Aborigines *their right of pre-occupancy*; and to induce them to *relinquish our Territories*, and to remove into the illimitable regions of the West'. Washington was suggesting that Congress enforce its Discovery rights by controlling tribal commercial activities, taking advantage of the limited Indian title of occupancy, 'preoccupancy' as he called it, and exercising its preemption right to buy tribal lands. He also wanted the United States to exercise sovereign authority over tribes and move them westward. Washington was well aware that the United States had just acquired the Discovery rights from England to all the lands west of the Allegheny and Appalachia Mountains to the Mississippi River in the Treaty of Paris of 1783 that ended the Revolutionary War. Notice that Washington called tribal lands 'our Territories'. This is the exact same Discovery principle that King George III used in the Royal Proclamation of 1763 to describe Indian country as 'our dominions and territories'.[35]

[33] *Articles of Confederation* art IX (1781); Miller, 18 Am Indian L Rev, note 3, 151–2; II Phillip B Kurland and Ralph Lerner, *The Founder's Constitution* (Chicago: University of Chicago Press, 1987) 145, 529; *Cherokee Nation v Georgia* 30 US (5 Pet) 1, 64 (1831) (Thompson J dissenting); *Worcester v Georgia* 31 US (6 Pet) 515, 559 (1832).

[34] *George Washington Writings*, note 5, 536–41.

[35] Francis Paul Prucha, *Documents of United States Indian Policy* (Lincoln: University of Nebraska Press, 3rd edn, 2000) 1–2; XXVII *Writings of George Washington*, note 5, 136–7, 139; *George Washington Writings*, note 5, 529.

The Confederation Congress eagerly accepted Washington's advice and his proposals formed the basis for the first US Indian policy. Congress adopted the Doctrine of Discovery with gusto as soon as the Revolutionary War was officially ended by the Treaty of Paris in 1783. In the treaty, England ceded to the United States all its property, sovereignty, and Discovery claims to lands south of Canada and east of the Mississippi River. The moment Congress acquired these powers it adopted Washington's suggestions and the precedent of the Royal Proclamation of 1763. On 22 September 1783, Congress issued a resolution that no one could settle on or purchase Indian lands 'without the express authority and directions of the United States in Congress assembled' and 'that every such purchase or settlement, gift or cession, not having the authority aforesaid, is null and void'. This was nothing less than a statement by the Confederation Congress that it alone possessed and could exercise Discovery and preemption rights over Indian lands and peoples. Thereafter, Congress tried to enforce preemption and its exclusive sovereign power to control Indian trade, land sales, and all political and commercial interactions with Indians against American citizens, states, and Indian nations.[36]

Congress also tried to take a hard line with tribes and enforce other Discovery elements. In 1783–1784, federal officials tried to convince some tribes that they had lost their lands due to conquest because they had fought for the English in the Revolution. The defeat suffered by the English was not an actual military defeat of the tribes but the United States argued that it was a 'conquest' under Discovery. Tribal leaders scoffed at this argument and the United States gave it up. England had also tried this argument in 1751 against tribes that had fought for the French. Indian leaders argued to both England and the United States that affairs between European countries could not impact tribal lands.[37]

The Confederation Congress also tried to settle the issue with the states of which government possessed the Discovery and preemption power over the lands west of the Appalachia Mountains that England had ceded to the United States. In the treaty, England passed its property rights to the United States, its Discovery powers, but at least seven of the original 13 states still claimed to own the lands westward to the Mississippi River under their Royal charters. In fact, Massachusetts and New York sued each other over their land claims in a suit that expressly reflected their Discovery claims because they argued over 'sovereignty and jurisdiction' and 'the right of preemption of the soil'. Finally, though, all 13 states came to realize that it was in their best interests to allow Congress to

---

[36] Prucha, *Documents*, note 35, 3–4; *The World Turned Upside Down: Indian Voices from Early America* (Boston: St Martin's Press, Colin G Calloway (ed), 1994) 9; XVIII *Early American Indian Documents*, note 2, 278; III *The American Indian and the United States: A Documentary History* (New York: Random House, Wilcomb E Washburn (ed), 1973) 2140–2; *Laws of the Colonial and State Governments*, note 3, 16, 20, 23, 29.

[37] Deloria Jr and Wilkins, note 10, 11; 34 *Journals of the Continental Congress* 124–5 (May 1788); Colin G Calloway, *Crown and Calumet: British-Indian Relations, 1783–1815* (Norman: University of Oklahoma Press, 1987) 9–10.

govern the western lands. The states then began offering their western claims to Congress on the conditions that Congress assume all the states' Revolutionary War debts and that the proceeds from sales of the western lands would benefit all states. Congress accepted these conditions. The compromise well served the economic interests of the federal and state governments, but it came at the expense of the Indian nations.[38]

As a consequence of this compromise, the question of which American government would exercise Discovery powers over Indian lands in the west was settled. The Confederation Congress became the government with the undisputed power of Discovery to control the western Indian lands, the authority to buy the lands from the Indian nations, to sell land to settlers, and to organize new territories and states. The 13 original states passed whatever residual Discovery powers they possessed to Congress.[39]

The Confederation Congress began exercising that power immediately and enacted the Land Ordinance of 1784 and the Land Ordinance of 1785. These acts provided for the expansion of American settlements into the western lands, the creation of federal territories and territorial governments, new states, and the sales of Indian lands. The profits from land sales were used to pay the Revolutionary War debts. Everyone's interests were considered and accommodated, except for Indian property and commercial rights, which were mostly ignored by the Doctrine of Discovery.[40]

In 1787, the Confederation Congress enacted the sweeping Northwest Ordinance to open the western lands for settlement and incorporation into the union. This law organized the settlement of the old Northwest Territory and ultimately created the states of Ohio, Illinois, Indiana, Wisconsin, and Minnesota. The Northwest Ordinance expressly adopted several elements of Discovery: 'The utmost good faith shall always be observed towards the Indians, their lands and property shall never be taken from them without their consent; and in their property, rights and liberty, they shall never be invaded or disturbed, unless in just and lawful wars...'. This law used the elements of Indian title, the requirement of

[38] I *Documents of American Indian Diplomacy: Treaties, Agreements, and Conventions, 1775–1979* (Norman: University of Oklahoma Press, Vine Deloria, Jr and Raymond J DeMallie (eds), 1999) 14; Catherine Bowen, *Miracle at Philadelphia* (Boston: Little, Brown, 1966) 168–70; III *The Papers of Alexander Hamilton* (New York: Columbia University Press, Harold C Syrett and Jacob E Cooke (eds), 1962) 702; 33 *Journals of the Continental Congress* (Library of Congress Records, 1786) 623; *Fletcher v Peck* 10 US (6 Cranch) 87, 142 (1810); Jones, note 15, 147–8, 170; Deloria Jr and Wilkins, note 10, 81; II *Papers of George Mason*, note 2, 655–63.

[39] 2 *The Territorial Papers of the United States* (Washington DC: Gov't Printing Off, Clarence E Carter (ed), 1934) 6–9; VI *The Papers of Thomas Jefferson* (Princeton: Princeton University Press, Julian P Boyd et al (eds), 1952) 571–600; II *Papers of George Mason*, note 2, 794–5.

[40] Merrill Peterson, *Thomas Jefferson & The New Nation* (New York: Oxford University Press, 1970) 266, 281–2; Peter S Onuf, *Statehood and Union: A History of the Northwest Ordinance* (Bloomington: Indiana University Press, 1992) xiv–xix, 3, 15, 25, 46; Anthony F C Wallace, *Jefferson and the Indians* (Ann Arbor MI: University of Michigan Press, 1999) 162–3; VI *Writings of Thomas Jefferson*, note 7, 79.

tribal consent to land sales, and conquest by 'just war'. It also impliedly exercised the federal government's preemption power. It is noteworthy that this law and Discovery elements were also applied to the Pacific Northwest by Congress in 1848.[41]

Under the Articles, the Confederation Congress dealt with tribes in a diplomatic and political relationship. This Congress signed at least eight treaties with Indian tribes between 1781 and 1789. These treaties vividly demonstrated the adoption of Discovery by Congress. The elements of Discovery are well represented in the eight treaties that Congress enacted with Indian nations. The clearest example is demonstrated in a 1789 treaty when Congress agreed with six tribes that they 'shall not be at liberty to sell or dispose of [land] or any part thereof, to any sovereign power, except the United States; nor to the subjects or citizens of any other sovereign power, nor to the subjects or citizens of the United States'. This provision reflects the exact definition of preemption.[42]

In addition, Congress exercised its preemption power to buy land from tribes in treaties and to define the borders of lands that the United States would recognize as tribally owned. And the United States exercised the sovereign and commercial elements of Discovery when it took 'the sole and exclusive right of regulating the trade with the Indians, and managing all their affairs in such manner as [the United States] think proper'. The United States promised to take the tribes under its protection and the tribes acknowledged themselves 'to be under the protection of the United States and of no other sovereign whatsoever'. These treaties mirrored exactly the colonial era understanding of Discovery powers possessed by the Crown and colonies, and they defined exactly the elements of Indian title, preemption and European title, and limited tribal sovereign and commercial rights.[43]

The legal evidence demonstrates that the Confederation Congress exercised the powers of Discovery against its own citizens and state governments and over the American Indian peoples and their governments. It is also certain, however, that this Congress could have exercised even more Discovery authority if the Articles had more clearly granted Congress the sole and exclusive power to deal with all tribes and all tribal lands and had prevented the states from playing any role in these activities. But various states did meddle in Indian affairs and literally caused armed conflicts with some tribes. These problems led many people, including future President James Madison, to call for the formation of a new and stronger US government wherein the exclusive

---

[41] Prucha, *Documents*, note 35, 9; Onuf, *Statehood*, note 40, xiii; Wallace, note 40, 163; 9 Stat 323 § 14 (1848).

[42] Treaty with the Wyandot, Etc, Jan 9, 1789, Art III, 7 Stat 28; Treaty with the Six Nations, Oct 22, 1784, Art III & IV, 7 Stat 15; II Kappler's, note 32, 5–25.

[43] See eg Treaty with the Cherokee, Nov. 28, 1785, Art III & IX, 7 Stat 18; Treaty with the Choctaw, Jan 3, 1786, Art II & VIII, 7 Stat 21; Treaty with the Wyandot, Etc, Jan 9, 1789, Art I, VII, XIII, 7 Stat 28; Treaty with the Shawnee, Jan 31, 1786, Art II & V; Treaty with the Six Nations, Oct 22, 1784, Art III & IV, 7 Stat 15; II Kappler's, note 32, 5, 7, 9–10, 12–21, 24.

power over Indian affairs and land purchases would rest only in the national government.[44]

2. United States constitutional era

The call for a stronger federal government due to the weaknesses of the Articles of Confederation led to a constitutional convention and the drafting of a new Constitution by September 1787. It was ratified by a sufficient number of states by June 1788 to become effective as the national governing document. George Washington and John Adams were then sworn in as the first President and Vice-President in April 1789, and the first Congress under the new Constitution met in March 1789. This new and stronger national government wasted no time in appropriating to itself the full Discovery power over the Indian nations and completely excluding the states from Indian affairs.

a. Constitution

The drafters of the Constitution solved the problem of states meddling in Indian affairs and interfering with federal Discovery powers by placing the sole authority to deal with Indian nations in the hands of Congress. In Article I, the Constitution expressly excludes states and individuals from Indian commercial affairs by stating that only Congress has the power '[t]o regulate Commerce with foreign Nations, and among the several States, and with the Indian Tribes...'. The US Supreme Court has interpreted this language to mean that Congress has the exclusive power to regulate trade and intercourse with Indian nations, and that it has absolute power in Indian affairs.[45]

The constitutional authority to be the only entity to control commercial affairs with Indian nations, which obviously included the sole power of buying Indian lands and trading with tribes, unambiguously granted the Doctrine of Discovery powers to Congress. The President and the Senate were also granted the sole constitutional authority to control treaty making in Article VI, which includes the power to make treaties with the Indian nations. The Constitution, then, granted the Discovery power solely to the national government.

---

[44] Miller, 18 Am Indian L Rev, note 3, 151–2; I *The Records of the Federal Convention of 1787* (New Haven: Yale University Press, Max Farrand (ed), 1937) 316; Max Farrand, *The Framing of the Constitution* (New Haven: Yale University Press, 1913) 47–8; US Constitutional Convention, *Journal of the Federal Convention* (Chicago: Albert Scott, E H Scott (ed), 1893) 47; *The Federalist Papers*, No 3 and 42 (New York: New American Library, Clinton Rossiter (ed), 1961) 44 (John Jay), 268–9; 33 *Journals of the Continental Congress* (1787) 455–63; Peterson, note 40, 119; Curtis G. Berkey, 'United States-Indian Relations: The Constitutional Basis' in *Exiled in the Land of the Free: Democracy, Indian Nations, and the U.S. Constitution* (Santa Fe, NM: Clear Light Publishers, Oren Lyons and John Mohawk (eds), 1992) 208–9, 213, 218.

[45] US Const art I, § 8; *Worcester v Georgia* 31 US (6 Pet) 515, 559 (1832); *Cotton Petroleum Corp v New Mexico* 490 US 163, 192 (1989).

b. Legislative branch

The very first Congress under the new Constitution immediately began exercising the Discovery powers it had received. In the first five weeks of its existence it enacted four laws concerning Indian affairs out of just 13 laws that it
enacted during that time. The new Congress established a War Department with
responsibility over Indian affairs, and appropriated money and named federal
commissioners to negotiate treaties with tribes. Most significantly, in July 1790,
the first Congress enacted a statute that is a perfect example of preemption and
its Discovery powers. Congress passed the first of a series of Indian Trade and
Intercourse Acts which forbade states and individuals from dealing politically or
commercially with Indians nations and from buying Indian lands.

[N]o sale of lands made by an Indian, or any nation or tribe of Indians within the United
States, shall be valid to any person or persons, or to any state, *whether having the right of
pre-emption to such lands or not*, unless the same shall be made and duly executed at some
public treaty, held under the authority of the United States. (italics added)

This Act was an exercise of Congress' preemption authority and prevented states
and individuals from dealing with tribes and buying Indian lands without federal approval even if the state claimed it held 'the right of pre-emption'. Congress
could not have more clearly taken the Discovery right of purchasing Indian lands
to itself. There was no confusion in 1790 about what this Act meant. President
George Washington told Seneca Chief Corn Planter that under the 1790 Act '[t]he
General Government only has the Power to treat with the Indian Nations... No
State, nor Person, can purchase your Lands.' This Act erased any doubts about
whether states had a right of preemption even for tribes within a state's borders.
This Act used the Discovery power the Constitution granted Congress and placed
sole possession of preemption in the federal government.[46]

The 1790 Act was amended slightly several times and reenacted in 1793, 1796,
and 1799. In 1802 it was enacted as a permanent law, and it is still federal law.
Thus, Discovery and preemption are still enshrined in federal law today.[47]

The 1790 Trade and Intercourse Act also exercised Congress' constitutional
Discovery authority to regulate all commerce by American citizens and states
with Indians. The Act and its later versions required Americans desiring to trade
with Indians and tribes to secure a licence and to provide a bond. In addition, in
1796, 1799, and 1802, Congress began requiring non-Indians to obtain a federal
passport before entering Indian territory. The central government was now firmly
in charge of Indian affairs, the sovereign and commercial Discovery powers,
interactions between Americans and Indians, and the power of preemption, just

---

[46] Act of July 22, 1790, ch 23, 1 Stat 137, 138, § 4, Prucha, *Documents*, note 35, 15; *Oneida
Indian Nation v New York* 860 F 2d 1145, 1159 (2nd Cir 1988).

[47] 25 USC § 177 (2000); Act of March 1, 1793, ch 19, 1 Stat 329; Act of May 19, 1796, ch 30,
1 Stat 469; Act of March 3, 1799, 1 Stat 743; Act of March 30, 1802, ch 13, 2 Stat 139.

as George III had tried to do in the Royal Proclamation of 1763, and just as the Confederation Congress had tried to do with its Proclamation of 1783.

In 1795, Congress continued exercising its power over the sovereignty of the tribal nations by completely monopolizing all trade and commercial interactions with tribes. At President Washington's urging, Congress established federal trading posts across the Indian frontier to conduct all the trade with tribes. Congress repeatedly renewed this bill at the suggestion of Washington and other presidents. Ultimately, the federal government operated 28 trading posts across the frontier from 1795 to 1822.[48]

c. *Executive branch*

The first US President George Washington and his cabinet were well acquainted with their Discovery powers and they did not hesitate to use them. As already discussed, Washington was well aware of preemption, was the creator of the 'Savage as the Wolf' federal policy which assumed that Indian tribes would slowly disappear as American settlements expanded, and was involved in the Articles of Confederation government and the drafting of the Constitution. Washington was a key figure during the decades that the American colonies became organized, won their independence, created a national governing body, and worked to place the Discovery powers solely in the hands of the national government.

Washington and the federal government were heavily involved in Indian affairs in the early decades of the American republic. Dealing with tribes was the major foreign policy issue at that time, and the legislative and executive branches spent a considerable amount of time and effort on these issues. The principles of Discovery played a large role in the daily conduct of the federal government.

President Washington and his administration readily exercised the preemption power and used Discovery to develop Indian policies and sign treaties to buy Indian lands whenever possible and to limit foreign nations, American states, and individuals from dealing with American Indian tribes. John Adams, the first Vice-President and second President of the United States, was also well aware of Discovery and federal dominion over Indians, and the right to purchase Indian lands. He was cognizant of the rights Discovery recognized in the tribal nations, including Indian titles, and a right of possession and limited ownership of their lands. These are clear examples of the sovereign and real property aspects of the Doctrine of Discovery at work in the legal operations of the US government.[49]

---

[48] Robert J Miller, 'Economic Development in Indian Country: Will Capitalism or Socialism Succeed?' (2001) 80 Ore L Rev 757, 808–9; Prucha, *The Great Father*, note 7, 116, 120.
[49] XXXV *Writings of George Washington*, note 5, 299–302; X *The Works of John Adams, Second President of the United States* (Boston: Little, Brown & Co, Charles Francis Adams (ed), 1856) 359–60; Charles Royce, *Indian Land Cessions in the US*, Bureau of American Ethnology, Eighteenth Annual Report, 1896–97, part 2 (1899) 536–7.

Washington's Secretary of War, Henry Knox, demonstrated his clear under-standing of Discovery in congressional reports and various statements. In June of 1789, for example, Knox stated:

The Indians being the prior occupants, possess the right to the soil. It cannot be taken from them unless by their free consent, or by the right of conquest in case of a just war. To dispossess them on any other principle, would be a gross violation of the fundamental laws of nature . . .

This is an accurate definition of the Discovery elements of possession, preemp-tion and European title, Indian title, conquest, and just war.[50]

The first Secretary of the Treasury, Alexander Hamilton, also showed a work-ing knowledge of Discovery. In discussions on the role of federal treaty commis-sioners, Hamilton wrote that they should:

do nothing which should in the least impair the right of pre-emption or general sover-eignty of the United States over the Country [and should] impress upon the Indians that the right of pre-emption in no degree affects their right to the soil . . . excepting that when sold it must be to the United States.

Earlier in his legal career, Hamilton litigated Discovery issues. In 1785–1786, he represented the state of New York in its land claim case versus Massachusetts. The case depended entirely on which state held the preemption power to buy Indian lands during colonial times. In preparing his case, Hamilton created an extensive chart documenting the first discoveries and settlements in America of the English, Spanish, and Dutch, and he analysed the English colonial charters and the 1493 papal bull of Alexander VI. Hamilton obviously understood the ele-ments of first discovery, preemption and European title, Indian title, and tribal limited sovereign and commercial rights.[51]

In 1790–1793, the first Secretary of State Thomas Jefferson clearly operated under the principles of Discovery and the limitations they created on tribal sov-ereignty and property rights. Jefferson continued these efforts during his eight years as US president.

The Executive Branch was very busy in its early years in negotiating, and the Senate in ratifying, at least 100 treaties with the Indian nations between 1789 and 1823. These treaties reflect the contours of Discovery and preemption, just as did the Indian treaties with the Continental and Articles of Confederation Congresses in 1778–1779 already discussed. The most obvious examples of the exercise of Discovery by the Executive Branch in its first decades are demonstrated in five treaties from 1791 to 1808.

In 1791, the United States limited the sovereignty of the Cherokee Nation by extracting a promise that it would not engage in diplomatic relations with any countries, states, or individuals except the United States. Further, in 1794, the

---

[50] Prucha, *Documents*, note 35, 12.
[51] XIV *Papers of Alexander Hamilton*, note 38, 89–91; ibid III, 702–15.

United States promised the Seneca Nation 'the free use and enjoyment' of its reservation and that 'it shall remain theirs, until they choose to sell the same to the people of the United States, who have the right to purchase'. Then in 1795, the United States secured a promise from the Wyandot and 11 other tribes that when any of them desired to sell their lands they would do so 'only to the United States'. In 1804, the United States promised the Sauk and Fox Nations that it would 'never interrupt' the tribes' 'possession of the lands' and would protect the 'quiet enjoyment' of their lands against any intruders, and in return, secured a promise from the tribes that they would 'never sell their lands or any part thereof to any sovereign power but the United States, nor to the citizens or subjects of any other sovereign power, nor to the citizens of the United States'. In 1808, the United States also secured a promise from the Osage Nation 'disclaiming all right to cede, sell or in any manner transfer their lands to any foreign power, or to citizens of the United States...'. In addition, the United States repeatedly exercised its preemption power to buy lands from tribes. Clearly, these federal actions mirrored the specific Discovery elements of Indian title and occupancy of land, and the sovereign and preemption rights the United States acquired under the Doctrine.[52]

The Indian treaties from 1789 to 1823 also demonstrate other aspects of Discovery. The United States exercised a limited sovereignty over tribal governments by controlling their trade and commerce. The United States included a provision in almost every one of these treaties in which the tribe agreed that 'the United States shall have the sole and exclusive right of regulating their trade'. And the United States promised to protect tribes and tribes acknowledged themselves 'to be under the protection of the United States of America, and of no other sovereign whosoever...'. All of these actions were implicit and explicit acknowledgments and exercises of the sovereign, diplomatic, and commercial Discovery powers.[53]

Moreover, the Executive Branch explicitly used the Doctrine of Discovery for decades to argue its territorial claims against England, Spain, and Russia to first discovery and ownership of the Pacific Northwest. All of these countries relied on the elements of Discovery in these diplomatic disputes. Spain and Russia relinquished their claims to the United States through treaties in the 1820s and only England and the United States continued to contest their rights. The

---

[52] Treaty with the Cherokee, July 2, 1791, Art II, 7 Stat 39; Treaty with the Six Nations, Nov 11, 1794, Art III, 7 Stat 44; Treaty with the Wyandot, Etc, Aug 3, 1795, Art V, 7 Stat 49; Treaty with the Sauk and Foxes, Nov 3, 1804, Art 4, 7 Stat 84; Treaty with the Osage, Nov 10, 1808, Art 10, 7 Stat 107; II Kappler's, note 32, 29, 35, 42, 75, 97.

[53] Treaty with the Cherokee, July 2, 1791, Art II, 7 Stat 39; Treaty with the Wyandot, Etc., Aug 3, 1795, Art V & VIII, 7 Stat 49; Treaty with the Creeks, June 29, 1796, Art III & IV, 7 Stat 56; Treaty with the Creeks, Aug 7, 1790, Art II, 7 Stat 35; Treaty with the Sauk and Foxes, Nov 3, 1804, Art 1, 7 Stat 84; Treaty with the Piankashaw, Dec 30, 1805, Art II, 7 Stat 100; Treaty with the Osage, Nov 10, 1808, Art 10, 7 Stat 107; Treaty with the Wyandot, Etc, July 22, 1814, Art III, 7 Stat 118; Treaty with the Winnebago, June 3, 1815, Art 3, 7 Stat 144; II Kappler's, note 32, 25, 29, 30, 42–3, 47, 74, 89, 97, 105, 130.

United States and England never really settled the legal question of who held the superior Discovery claim to the Pacific Northwest. The two countries argued the subject for decades, signed two treaties to jointly occupy the territory in 1818 and 1827, and finally in 1846 drew the dividing line between the United States and Canada where it is today.

The foregoing illustrates clearly that the US Constitution, the Congress, and the Executive Branch utilized the Doctrine of Discovery and its elements long before the US Supreme Court adopted it as federal case law in 1823 in *Johnson v M'Intosh*. These federal entities understood the elements of Discovery and the legal property and governmental rights that Discovery granted the United States over the Indian nations and their lands.

d. US Supreme Court

In the early 1800s, issues regarding tribal lands, and thus Discovery and preemption, began to make their way onto the Supreme Court's docket. The Court's Indian law jurisprudence assumed from the start that the Doctrine of Discovery was the controlling legal principle and in 1823 the Court expressly adopted the Doctrine. In the nearly 200 years since *Johnson*, the federal courts have consistently applied Discovery to the Indian nations.

In 1810, the Supreme Court relied on the Doctrine the very first time it addressed Indian property rights. In *Fletcher v Peck*, the Court was only tangentially faced with the question whether Georgia was 'legally seised [in possession] in fee of the soil thereof subject only to the extinguishment of part of the Indian title thereon'. That was a complicated way of asking whether Georgia owned a legal interest, or a fee title, in the tribal lands within Georgia that it could transfer to others even while the Indian nation was still occupying and using the land. As state courts had already held, Georgia was allowed to do that under the Doctrine because the right of preemption and the other elements of Discovery had been passed by the English Crown to Georgia.[54]

In answering that question, the Supreme Court decided that the land lay 'within the state of Georgia, and that the state of Georgia had power to grant it'. The Court implicitly and explicitly relied on the elements of Discovery such as the rights the Crown had gained by first discovery and that Indian lands were 'vacant lands' or *terra nullius*. In addition, even the dissenting judge and the arguments of the attorneys in the case, including future president John Quincy Adams and future Supreme Court Justice Joseph Story, all expressly relied on Discovery.[55]

Chief Justice John Marshall recognized that there were doubts whether Georgia could be seised in fee simple (considered to own and possess a title) of lands still subject to the Indian title of occupancy and use, and whether Georgia

---

[54] 10 US (6 Cranch) 87, 139, 142 (1810).   [55] Ibid 121–4, 140–2, 146–7.

could transfer this title while the Indian nation was still in possession and Indian title was not yet extinguished. But the Court stated that:

the particular land…lie within the state of Georgia, and [ ] the state of Georgia had the power to grant it.… The majority of the court is of opinion that the nature of the Indian title, which is certainly to be respected by all courts, until it be legitimately extinguished, is not such as to be absolutely repugnant to seisin in fee on the part of the state.

Thus, the Court held that Georgia both possessed a limited kind of fee simple title to the Indian lands, even while the lands were still in the possession and use of the tribe, and that Georgia could transfer its title to others, and that the people to whom Georgia transferred its title took the title subject only to the future extinguishment of the Indian title of occupancy.[56]

Five years later, in *Meigs v M'Clung's Lessee*, the Supreme Court reaffirmed *Fletcher*: states possessed a limited fee simple title to Indian lands even while tribes occupied and used their lands, and that states could grant their interest in Indian lands to individuals who then had to await the future extinguishment of the Indian right of occupancy and use. Such a grant of Indian land would only become effective, of course, after the Indian title was extinguished.[57]

Fletcher and *Meigs* demonstrate the Court's implied acceptance of Discovery and preemption to decide ownership rights in Indian lands. But it took until 1823 and the *Johnson v M'Intosh* case for the Court to expressly adopt Discovery as the binding legal doctrine of American Indian law and to define its elements.

i. *Johnson v M'Intosh* (1823)

In 1823, the Court was presented with long anticipated questions regarding the nature of Indian land titles; how Indian titles were extinguished; and whether individuals could buy Indian lands. *Johnson v M'Intosh* is an extremely important case because it sets out very important principles that still govern modern day American Indian law and the rights of America's Indigenous peoples. As we will see, the decision of the Court was no surprise after the long history of the use of the Doctrine of Discovery by the English Crown and the colonial, state, and federal governments.

In June 1773, William Murray, a partner in a land speculation company, purchased land from Indians in what is now the state of Illinois. Despite being warned by British officials that he was violating the Royal Proclamation of 1763, Murray purchased two large tracts of land from the Kaskaskia, Peoria, and Cahokia Nations. In October 1775, Murray, working for another company, bought two more large tracts of land from the Piankeshaw Nation which straddle what is now the Illinois and Indiana border. The private company tried to get these land purchases ratified by the Crown and then by the colonial,

---

[56] Ibid 142–3.   [57] 13 US (9 Cranch) 11, 16 (1815).

state, and federal governments and finally turned to the federal courts in the 1820s.[58]

In the meantime, the United States was carrying out its own strategy of expansion and was creating new states out of the old Northwest Territory pursuant to the Northwest Ordinance of 1787. Pursuant to that policy, in 1803 and 1809, the federal government negotiated treaties with the same Indian nations that William Murray had dealt with in 1773 and 1775. The United States purchased enormous tracts of land from these tribes. These purchases included the lands Murray had allegedly purchased for his companies three decades before. The United States immediately began surveying the area, opening land offices, and making land sales to prospective settlers. The defendant William McIntosh purchased his land from the United States in 1815 and received title in 1818.

The plaintiffs in *Johnson* were Joshua Johnson and Thomas Graham who had inherited the disputed property in 1819. They then brought a law suit in federal court to remove William McIntosh from the property they claimed but McIntosh won the case in the trial court. On appeal to the Supreme Court, Johnson's attorneys argued in favour of the Indians' natural law rights to sell the lands they had owned and occupied since time immemorial. Even these attorneys, however, did not think that the 'savage tribes' possessed full title to their lands. Instead, they called it a 'title by occupancy' and one that was held in common by all the tribal citizens. The attorneys argued that because England and various treaties recognized a tribal right in the soil, and because Indians were not English subjects, the Royal Proclamation of 1763 could not limit the tribes' natural rights to sell their lands. In contrast, McIntosh's attorneys argued that Indians had been uniformly treated 'as an inferior race' and were not recognized as having a permanent property interest in land or the right to sell land to private individuals: 'Discovery is the foundation of title, in European nations, and this overlooks all proprietary rights in the natives.'[59]

Chief Justice John Marshall stated the issue: 'the power of Indians to give, and of private individuals to receive, a title which can be sustained in the courts of this country'. Marshall then determined the legal rule to apply. He stated that a nation or society where land is located has to make the rules of how property can be acquired and a court cannot just look to 'principles of abstract justice' or natural law. Instead, a court must look to the principles of its own government. Marshall then methodically investigated the rules of property that had been adopted in North America to see what rule applied in *Johnson*. The Court briefly examined much of the history we have already discussed and the law that developed to control the European exploration and settlement of North America. The Court noted that the legal rule for real property acquisitions and transfers applied by Holland, Spain, Portugal, France, and England in North America was the Doctrine of Discovery. The Court stated that all these countries 'relied

---

[58] *Johnson* 21 US (8 Wheat) 543, 550–1, 555, 557 (1823).   [59] Ibid 567–9.

on the title given by discovery to lands remaining in the possession of Indians'. The Court repeated that 'all the nations of Europe, who have acquired territory on this continent, have asserted in themselves, and have recognised in others, the exclusive right of the discoverer to appropriate the lands occupied by the Indians'. Marshall then traced the English Crown's title in American lands from first discovery, through grants in royal charters to the colonies, and finally to the American states and then the United States.[60]

From the foregoing evidence, Marshall reasoned that the Crown had 'absolute title' in Indian lands 'subject only to Indian right of occupancy' and that this situation was 'incompatible with an absolute and complete title in the Indians'. Since the American states and then the United States had inherited this title:

[i]t has never been doubted, that either the United States, or the several States, had a clear title to all the lands...subject only to the Indian right of occupancy, and that the exclusive power to extinguish that right, was vested in that government which might constitutionally exercise it.[61]

Marshall then arrived at a succinct statement of the Doctrine of Discovery which he alleged that all European and American governments had accepted for acquiring land in North America: the 'principle [ ] that *discovery gave title* to the government by whose subjects, or by whose authority, it was made, against all other European governments, which title might be consummated by possession'. He also stated that 'the original fundamental principle' governing American land titles and transfers of title was 'that discovery gave *exclusive title* to those who made it'.[62]

The case would appear to have been easy to decide once the Court agreed on this legal rule because it follows naturally that if the discovering European government owned the exclusive title to Indian real property, how then could tribal chiefs transfer land titles to private individuals? In fact, Marshall stated that the case was easy. In light of the Discovery rule, the Court's answer to the issue was that the purchase of land directly from Indian nations by private individuals did not transfer a title 'which can be sustained in the Courts of the United States'. Consequently, the private land speculators lost out in their long battle to buy Indian lands directly from tribes. The Doctrine of Discovery had triumphed over any claim of exclusive real property rights or natural rights for American Indians and their tribal governments.[63]

The Court clearly recognized that under the Doctrine Indians had lost two very important rights, without their knowledge or consent, upon first discovery of their territory by Europeans. First, tribes lost the valuable governmental and property right of free alienability; that is the right to sell their real estate to whomever they wished for whatever amount they could negotiate. In addition, Indian

---

[60] Ibid 572, 582, 584.   [61] Ibid 584–5, 588.   [62] Ibid 573–4 (italics added).
[63] Ibid 604–5.

nations lost significant sovereign and commercial powers because of Discovery. They lost the political right to deal commercially and diplomatically in the international arena with any country other than their discoverer. The Court admitted that these 'legal principles' would not have been enforceable against tribes unless the Europeans and Americans were militarily strong enough to force these provisions upon tribal governments. In fact, the Court recognized that the US Discovery powers had been 'maintained and established as far west as the river Mississippi, by the sword'.[64]

It is unnecessary to quote line after line from the opinion as the Court re-emphasized and reiterated its definition of Discovery and the rights Europeans and Americans had gained by first discovery, and the rights that tribal nations had lost. The following statement though is worth quoting:

> The United States, then, have unequivocally acceded to that great and broad rule [Discovery] by which its civilized inhabitants now hold this country. They hold, and assert in themselves, the title by which it was acquired. They maintain, as all others have maintained, that discovery gave an exclusive right to extinguish the Indian title of occupancy, either by purchase or by conquest; and gave also a right to such a degree of sovereignty, as the circumstances of the people would allow them to exercise.

The Court clearly explicated and relied on the elements of Discovery: first discovery, occupancy and possession, preemption and European title, Indian title, tribal limited sovereign rights, uncivilized Indians, and conquest/just war. The European countries and later the United States claimed that by Discovery they had gained 'the ultimate dominion' over tribal lands and the 'power to grant the soil, while yet in possession of the natives' and to have a power to convey 'a title to the grantees, subject only to the Indian right of occupancy'. William Murray's private land purchases from tribes were null and void and thus Johnson's claim to own the land was rejected. Instead, McIntosh was the legal owner of the property because he received his title from the United States which had acquired the land through the exercise of its right of preemption.[65]

It bears repeating that this 1823 decision determined the validity of purchases of Indian lands made by private British citizens in 1773 and 1775. This was when the 13 colonies were still English possessions. Thus, when the Supreme Court invalidated those private purchases it did so because the Doctrine of Discovery was the controlling law in the colonial era for buying Indian lands under international law, the colonial common law and statutory laws, and under the Royal Proclamation of 1763. The Supreme Court did not just make up a new legal rule in *Johnson v M'Intosh* that only applied from 1823 forward. Instead, the Court adopted and further defined Discovery and ratified all the prior actions of the American colonial, state, and federal governments in using Discovery and its

---

[64] Ibid 587–90.

[65] Ibid 574, 587. See generally Lindsay G Robertson, *Conquest by Law: How the Discovery of American Dispossessed Indigenous Peoples of Their Land* (Oxford: Oxford University Press, 2007).

elements to control sales of tribal lands and the political and commercial interactions with Indian nations and their citizens.

ii. Cases subsequent to *Johnson*

The federal courts have continued to follow the precedent of *Johnson v M'Intosh* and have enforced the Doctrine of Discovery against the Indian nations and the states, and have continued to recognize the federal Discovery power in dozens of cases since 1823. In many cases, the courts followed the *Johnson* holding that Discovery gave the United States sovereign and real property rights over tribes and tribal lands. In other cases, the courts invalidated state actions that interfered with the federal government's exclusive sovereign and preemption powers to be the only government allowed to buy Indian lands and to deal politically with tribes.

In two very important Indian law cases in 1831 and 1832, the Supreme Court touched on issues of Discovery and demonstrated its continued adherence to the Doctrine. In *Cherokee Nation v Georgia*, the Court had to decide whether the Cherokee Nation was a 'foreign state' for constitutional purposes when the nation sued Georgia in the Supreme Court to prevent Georgia from imposing its laws in Cherokee territory. In a fractured decision, in which the six justices wrote three opinions, all three opinions relied on the Doctrine in their analysis. Chief Justice Marshall clearly pointed out that Discovery had limited tribal sovereignty and real property rights and that this played a significant part in his determination that Indian nations were not 'foreign' states and thus the Cherokee Nation could not sue Georgia directly in the Supreme Court:

[I]n any attempt at intercourse between Indians and foreign nations, they are considered as within the jurisdictional limits of the United States.... They occupy a territory to which we assert a title independent of their will, which must take effect in point of possession when their right of possession ceases. Meanwhile they are in a state of pupilage. Their relation to the United States resembles that of a ward to his guardian.

Marshall also demonstrated that tribal nations had lost some of their international sovereign and commercial rights due to Discovery because the United States and foreign nations considered tribes to be 'so completely under the sovereignty and dominion of the United States that any attempt to acquire their lands, or to form a political connection with them would be considered by all as an invasion of our territory, and an act of hostility'. Marshall directly relied on several of the elements of Discovery in making these statements.[66]

In other opinions, Justice Johnson relied on 'the right of discovery' and the sovereignty, dominion, and exclusive right of preemption granted by international law to the first European discoverers and then the United States as evidence that tribes were never even considered political states. And Justice Baldwin agreed

---

[66] *Cherokee Nation v Georgia* 30 US (5 Pet) 1, 17–18 (1831).

that the case should be dismissed because tribes had signed treaties placing themselves under the protection and commercial control of the United States and had never been treated, Baldwin claimed, as foreign states by any Congress of the United States. The reason he said that tribes had never been considered to be foreign states was because the 'ultimate absolute fee, jurisdiction and sovereignty' in their lands had always been held, under the Doctrine of Discovery, by the Crown, colonies, states, and then the United States. The principles of Discovery played a significant part in these three opinions.[67]

In 1832, the Court decided in *Worcester v Georgia* whether Georgia's laws could apply in Indian country to criminalize activity by a New England missionary who was living in Cherokee territory with the permission of the nation. The Court held that the laws of Georgia could have no effect in Indian country and were void because they conflicted with the federal Constitution, treaties, and federal laws which established that all relations between Americans and Indians were the exclusive business of the federal government. In reaching this decision, Chief Justice Marshall discussed some of the history of Discovery in the New World and utilized its elements.

In looking back, Marshall seemed to disparage the Doctrine because he said it was 'difficult to comprehend' how inhabitants of one part of the globe could claim property rights and dominion over the inhabitants of other places or how 'the discovery of either [could give] the discoverer rights...which annulled the pre-existing rights of ancient possessors'. Marshall also stated that it was 'extravagant and absurd' for England to claim that its 'feeble settlements made on the sea coast...acquired legitimate power by them to govern the people, or occupy the lands from sea to sea...'. He even asked a rhetorical question as to why explorers sailing along a coast could acquire for European governments property rights and dominion over the native people. Notwithstanding these concerns, Marshall and the Court clearly relied on the elements of Discovery and preemption in deciding this case. In fact, Marshall stated five times that the Court had to face 'the actual state of things', and that the reality was that 'power, war, conquest, give rights, which, after possession, are conceded by the world...'. The rights he was talking about were the preemptive rights that Europeans and then the United States held over tribes and the Discovery rights the United States held to be the only power allowed to deal politically and commercially with the 'discovered tribal nations'. The Court even quoted approvingly the 1823 *Johnson* opinion that 'discovery gave title to the government by whose subjects or by whose authority it was made, against all other European governments, which title might be consummated by possession'. The *Worcester* Court in 1832 plainly relied on *Johnson* and perpetuated the Doctrine of Discovery.[68]

---

[67] Ibid 22–3, 26–7, 33–5, 37–40, 45, 48–9.
[68] 31 US (6 Pet) 515, 537–8, 542–9, 551–2, 559–62 (1832).

We must also note the Supreme Court's use of the Discovery elements of *terra nullius* and contiguity. In 1842, the Court stated that:

[the] English possessions in America were not claimed by right of conquest, but by right of discovery. For, according to the principles of international law... the absolute rights of property and dominion were held to belong to the European nation by which any particular portion of the country was first discovered.... the territory occupied was disposed of by the governments of Europe, at their pleasure, as if it had been found without inhabitants.

In 1846, the Court again noted *terra nullius* when it stated that 'the whole continent was divided and parceled out, and granted by the governments of Europe as if it had been *vacant and unoccupied land*'.[69]

The most striking example of the Court applying Discovery is the 1955 case of *Tee-Hit-Ton Indians v United States*. In *Tee-Hit-Ton*, a clan of Tlingit Indians sued the United States for timber the United States had cut and sold from lands the Tee-Hit-Tons claimed. The Federal Court of Claims held that the clan possessed original Indian title or the Indian right of occupancy to the lands but because Congress had never specifically recognized the clan's title they did not possess legally recognizable rights in the land or timber.

Before the Supreme Court, the tribe argued that it had full ownership of the land, had continuously occupied and used it since time immemorial with no interference from Russia or the United States, and that Congress had enacted laws that recognized and confirmed its right to occupy the land. The United States claimed that if the tribe possessed any property interest at all it was only 'the right to the use of the land at the Government's will'. The Court stated that there was no evidence that Congress had ever recognized or granted the tribe ownership or permanent rights in the land. Thus, the Court had to address the meaning of 'Indian title' under the principles of Discovery.[70]

The Court then turned the Doctrine of Discovery and *Johnson* inside out. The Court stated that questions regarding Indian title were 'far from novel' and it was well settled that 'after the coming of the white man' tribes held their lands 'under what is sometimes termed original Indian title or permission from the whites to occupy. That description means mere possession not specifically recognized as ownership by Congress.' That statement is false. In contrast, *Johnson* and numerous other Supreme Court cases called the Indian real property right a legal right of use, occupancy, and possession and that it was a protectable property right, a title which was 'as sacred as the fee [title] of the whites'. Furthermore, Congress had expressly and continuously recognized since the Northwest Ordinance of 1787, the 1790 Trade and Intercourse Act, and in numerous treaties that Indian lands could only be purchased by the United States when tribes consented. The

---

[69] *Martin v Waddell's Lessee* 41 US 367, 409 (1842); *United States v Rogers* 45 US 567, 572 (1846).
[70] 348 US 272, 277 (1955).

Indian nations possessed original property rights in their lands that did not rely on 'permission from the whites' as the *Tee-Hit-Ton* Court incorrectly stated.[71]

The Court went even further:

> After conquest they were permitted to occupy portions of territory... This is not a property right but amounts to a right of occupancy which the sovereign grants and protects against intrusion by third parties but which right of occupancy may be terminated and such lands fully disposed of by the sovereign itself without any legally enforceable obligation to compensate the Indians.

This statement is also false. First, the United States obtained virtually all Indian lands in America by treaty purchases with tribal consent and not by military conquest (it is a different question whether the treaties were fair and legitimate transactions), and the Supreme Court had always recognized tribal rights to land because it was a title 'as sacred as the fee of the whites', and authorized tribal legal actions to protect their rights in land.[72]

Six justices of the *Tee-Hit-Ton* Court, however, accepted the idea that Indian lands had been acquired by physical military conquests which had terminated the Indian title. The Court said '[e]very American schoolboy knows that the savage tribes of this continent were deprived of their ancestral ranges by force' and that even the land sales that took place were 'not a sale but the conquerors' will that deprived [Indians] of their land'. This statement is also false and flies in the face of the proven fact that the vast majority of Indian lands in America were purchased with tribal consent at treaty sessions and were not taken outright by military conquests.[73]

The Court ended its opinion with yet another false statement. The Court did not choose, it said, 'harshness' over 'tenderness' towards Indians but left to Congress 'the policy of Indian gratuities for the termination of Indian occupancy of Government-owned land rather than making compensation for its value a rigid constitutional principle'. This Court ignored that it was already the law and policy of the United States established in the Northwest Ordinance of 1787 and the 1790 Trade and Intercourse Act and in the United States' entire treaty-based land-purchasing policy with the Indian nations to always buy Indian lands and only with tribal consent. Consequently, the *Tee-Hit-Ton* Court went far beyond the meaning of Discovery and the holding of *Johnson v M'Intosh* when it allowed the federal government to take the Tee-Hit-Ton's property without consent and without paying compensation.[74]

In 2005, the Supreme Court was faced with yet another case that raised issues of Discovery and its impact on tribal legal rights in the twenty-first century.

---

[71] Ibid 279. See eg *County of Oneida v Oneida Indian Nation* 470 US 226, 234–5 (1985); *Mitchel v United States* 34 US (9 Pet) 711, 746 (1835).   [72] 348 US 279.

[73] 348 US at 289–90. See eg Stuart Banner, *How the Indians Lost Their Lands: Law and Power on the Frontier* (Cambridge: Harvard University Press, 2007).   [74] 348 US 291.

Although the Court decided the case without relying on Discovery it did say in a footnote:

Under the 'doctrine of discovery,' *Oneida II,* 470 U.S. 226, 234 (1985), 'fee title to the lands occupied by Indians when the colonists arrived became vested in the sovereign-first the discovering European nation and later the original States and the United States,' *Oneida I,* 414 U.S. 661, 667 (1974). In the original 13 States, 'fee title to Indian lands,' or 'the pre-emptive right to purchase from the Indians, was in the State.' *Id.,* at 670; see *Oneida Indian Nation of N.Y. v. New York,* 860 F.2d 1145, 1159–1167 (C.A.2 1988).[75]

In that case, the Oneida Indian Nation of New York alleged that for nearly 200 years the state of New York and a county and various cities had interfered with federal Discovery powers in Indian law. The federal trial court agreed with the nation after reviewing the history of federal Indian policy and the federal power of preemption under the 1790 Trade and Intercourse Act. The Second Circuit US Court of Appeals also reviewed the history of land purchases from the Oneida Nation under state and federal treaties.[76]

D. Fundamental Principles of Federal Indian Law

There are three fundamental Indian law principles that have been developed by the Supreme Court. These principles still control federal Indian law in the United States to this day. They developed from the Doctrine of Discovery.

1. Plenary power

The plenary power doctrine holds that Congress has broad authority in Indian affairs. It has the authority, for example, to enact laws that can benefit or injure Indian nations and their citizens. Only in recent times did the Supreme Court decide that congressional actions pursuant to its plenary power in Indian law can even be reviewed by federal courts. Even then, the courts use the lowest level of judicial constitutional review. In the long history of congressional acts regarding Indian nations and peoples, no federal law has ever been overturned because Congress exceeded its plenary power in Indian law.[77]

---

[75] *City of Sherrill New York v Oneida Indian Nation of New York* 544 US 197, 203 n 1 (2005).

[76] *Oneida Indian Nation of New York v The City of Sherrill, New York, et al.* 145 F Supp 2nd 226, 233–6 (ND NY 2001), *aff'd in part, vacated and remanded in part, Oneida Indian Nation of New York v City of Sherrill, New York* 337 F 3d 139 (2nd Cir 2003), *rev'd,* 125 S Ct 1478 (2005); *Oneida Indian Nation of New York v City of Sherrill, New York* 337 F 3d 139, 146–50, 158–65 (2nd Cir 2003), *rev'd,* 544 US 197 (2005).

[77] *Felix S Cohen's Handbook of Federal Indian Law* (Charlottesville: Michie Company, Rennard Strickland et al (eds), 1982 edn) 207–57; Charles F Wilkinson, *American Indians, Time, and the Law* (New Haven: Yale University Press, 1987) 78–9; *Morton v Mancari* 417 US 535, 551–2 (1974).

The Supreme Court has stated that the Interstate/Indian Commerce Clause of the US Constitution, which we reviewed above in which Congress has the authority to regulate commerce with the Indian tribes, 'provides Congress with plenary power to legislate in the field of Indian affairs...'. The Court has also pointed out that plenary power comes from other constitutional provisions such as the treaty-making power, the Property Clause, the Supremacy Clause, and the Necessary and Proper clause which gives the federal government the authority to carry out its enumerated powers.[78]

While the Supreme Court has named several sources for the plenary power principle, it has apparently never recognized the one source that appears obvious, the Doctrine of Discovery. In fact, it seems beyond question that Discovery and the justifications behind the Doctrine spawned the idea that the national government held dominion and domination over the Indian nations because they lost sovereign, diplomatic, property, and commercial rights immediately upon first discovery. The other elements of Discovery, that Christian and European civilizations were superior and would triumph over the Indian nations, were also brought to this continent by England, France, and Spain and have remained part of the legal regime of the American colonial, state, and federal governments. As discussed above, Discovery also created the idea that Euro-American governments held a limited fee title in the lands that Indians had lived on and owned for centuries. It appears obvious that the plenary power doctrine springs from Discovery.

The Court also developed the idea of a heightened congressional power over Indian nations based on their alleged helpless and destitute conditions. The Court has always assumed the impoverished condition of Indians and their tribal governments as part of the justification for a duty to care for Indian tribes, even when that 'fact' was false. In an 1886 case, the Court analysed that the duty of the United States to protect Indians requires that Congress have sufficient power over Indians and tribes to carry out its duty. This overarching power is part of the plenary power doctrine. Do not forget that the idea of some kind of duty or guardianship over Indians also came from Discovery principles and the Royal charters of the early 1600s. However one examines the subject, it appears that Discovery played a major role in the development of the plenary power principle.[79]

2. Trust doctrine

The federal government is also considered to have a guardian, trustee, and fiduciary responsibility towards tribes based on its nearly unchecked plenary power over Indians and tribal governments. Principles of general trust law, and the alleged helplessness of tribes, led to the rise of the trust doctrine as a corollary

---

[78] *Cotton Petroleum Corp v New Mexico* 490 US 163, 192 (1989).
[79] *United States v Kagama* 118 US 375, 381 (1886).

to plenary power. In exercising their extremely broad authority in Indian affairs, Congress and the Executive Branch are charged with the responsibilities of a guardian to act on behalf of the dependent Indian people and their governments. The United States has accepted this responsibility and has 'charged itself with moral obligations of the highest responsibility and trust' and it judges its own conduct towards tribes 'by the most exacting fiduciary standards'.[80]

Many of the same justifications and Supreme Court cases that created plenary power also led to the development of the trust doctrine. The idea of a trust relationship began developing in Supreme Court case law in 1831 when the Court considered the status of the Cherokee Nation. In that case, the Court erroneously stated that the nation was dependent on the United States for its 'protection' and 'wants' and was in a 'state of pupilage' with the federal government. The *Cherokee Nation* Court then went on to state that the Nation's 'relation to the United States resembles that of a ward to his guardian'.[81]

The next major pronouncement on the subject of the trust doctrine came in 1886 in *United States v Kagama*. There, the Supreme Court considered whether Congress could extend federal criminal jurisdiction into Indian country and what power Congress might possess to have this authority. The Court expressly refused to rely on the Interstate/Indian Commerce Clause and instead started its analysis by looking at the heavy responsibility the United States has to care for Indians and their governments. Since the 'Indian tribes *are* the wards of the nation... [and] communities dependent on the United States', the Court held that '[f]rom their very weakness and helplessness' a duty arose to protect tribes under a trust responsibility and that this duty must include whatever powers are necessary to carry out the protective duty.[82]

The trust doctrine plainly had its genesis in the Discovery Doctrine. The papal bulls in the fifteenth century placed Christian guardianship duties on Spain and Portugal to convert and protect Indigenous peoples. English Royal charters ordered the colonists to convert and save American Indians. In colonial times and in the early American states, many colonies and states enacted laws that appointed citizens to be trustees and guardians to manage and allegedly protect tribal rights and to civilize and convert Indians. The federal treaties with Indian nations also contained promises by the United States to protect tribes, to control and support their commercial activities, and to provide educational and medical care. There is a long history behind the idea that Euro-Americans had a duty to care for the best interests of Indians. This thinking came largely from the Eurocentric ideas of Discovery that uncivilized, infidel savages needed to be saved by Euro-Americans. Interestingly, Chief Justice John Marshall relied on several Discovery elements when he stated in *Cherokee Nation* that Indian nations were the wards of

---

[80] *Seminole Nation v United States* 316 US 286, 297 (1942); *United States v Mitchell* 463 US 206, 224–6 (1983); *Cherokee Nation v Georgia* 30 US (5 Pet) 1, 17 (1831).
[81] *Cherokee Nation* 30 US 17.   [82] 118 US 375, 383–4 (1886).

the United States. He pointed to the limited Indian title, the right of preemption and European title that was gained by first discovery, and issues of possession as part of the proof that tribes were in a dependent relationship. 'They occupy a territory to which we assert a title independent of their will, which must take effect in point of possession when their right of possession ceases.' Consequently, since Marshall relied on the Doctrine of Discovery when he initially defined the trust responsibility, there is no question but that Discovery played a significant role in the development of this basic Indian law principle.[83]

3. Diminished tribal sovereignty

The third fundamental principle of federal Indian law explicated by the Supreme Court is the diminished tribal sovereignty principle. It is closely related to the other two basic principles and also flows directly from Discovery. In fact, the Discovery Doctrine is the origination of the idea of diminished tribal powers because tribal sovereignty, commercial, diplomatic, and real property rights were assumed to have been limited automatically upon first discovery by Euro-Americans. This Eurocentric, ethnocentric thinking assumed that Indigenous people were savages and inferior to 'civilized' Christian Europeans.

In pre-contact times, the hundreds of Indian nations in what is now the United States had a wide array of governments ranging from loosely organized political structures in small tribal bands to complex and sometimes even autocratic ruling bodies that controlled large populations. These tribes exercised nearly unlimited sovereignty over their territories, varying amounts of political control and sovereign power over their citizens, and a sovereign status that existed completely independent from the European and American governments. Yet the third fundamental principle of federal Indian law holds, right out of Discovery, that tribal sovereignty was automatically and immediately diminished upon contact with Euro-Americans.[84]

The discussion above demonstrates graphically that the Doctrine of Discovery is not just an interesting relic of American legal history but that it is still the law in the United States and impacts American Indians and their governments on a daily basis. The Doctrine is actively applied by the United States to Indians and tribal governments today and is a major component of modern day federal Indian law. Commentators have noted, in fact, that Discovery and the Supreme Court's opinion in *Johnson v M'Intosh* 'influence[d] all subsequent thinking' in federal Indian law. Consequently, the Doctrine still legally limits tribal sovereign, commercial, and real property rights today in the United States. We will see that

[83]   Robert A Williams, Jr, *The American Indian in Western Legal Thought: The Discourses of Conquest* (New York: Oxford University Press, 1990) 103; *Laws of the Colonial and State Governments*, note 3, 12, 16–17, 22, 37, 45, 59, 136, 142, 146, 150, 154; *Cherokee Nation* 30 US 17.
[84]   Miller, 80 *Ore L Rev*, note 48, 767–9, 781–5; *Cohen's Handbook*, note 77, 229–32; *Talton v Mayes* 163 US 376 (1896).

the vestiges of Discovery are reflected in far more than just the definition of the limited Indian title, the occupancy and use rights in tribal lands, but that they are also evident in more than 200 years of American Indian policies and history.[85]

The Doctrine of Discovery obviously played a major role in the legal history of the American colonies, states, and federal governments. Discovery and its elements were adopted and applied by European and American governments to claim rights in North America and to define and limit tribal natural law rights to their lands and to their legal, political, and commercial rights. There is no question that England and other European countries applied the international law Doctrine of Discovery in North America. There is also no question that Discovery was then incorporated into American law and that it became a predominant feature in the law of the colonial era and in American state and federal law and has been a crucial factor in the territorial expansion of the United States and the confiscation of the rights of America's Indigenous peoples.

---

[85] Russell Lawrence Barsh and James Youngblood Henderson, *The Road: Indian Tribes and Political Liberty* (Berkeley, CA: University of California Press, 1980) 49; Robert A Williams, Jr, 'The Algebra of Federal Indian Law: The Hard Trail of Decolonizing and Americanizing the White Man's Indian Jurisprudence' (1986) Wisc L Rev 219, 257; Note, 'International Law as an Interpretive Force in Federal Indian Law' (2003) 116 Harv L Rev 1751, 1753.

3

The Doctrine of Discovery in United States History

In the previous chapter, we looked primarily at the legal examples of how the United States adopted Discovery and used it against tribal nations and Indigenous peoples. In this chapter, we focus on the historical events that demonstrate the United States' use of the Doctrine after the adoption of the US Constitution in 1789.

In this examination, we must remember the foundational US Indian policy as stated in 1783 by General (and later President) George Washington—the 'Savage as the Wolf'. As he explained to Congress, the expectation of the United States was that Indian lands and resources would naturally be acquired by Americans. Washington compared Indians to animals that would naturally retreat and lose their lands to the advance of the United States. The US government operated under this policy until the 1960s.

We will examine the Doctrine throughout American history by looking at specific time frames that parallel some distinct historic eras of federal Indian policies. This will help us focus on American expansion and the treatment of Indigenous peoples as Discovery was applied in these eras when the United States came to control Indian peoples and tribal governments and to acquire the vast majority of their lands and assets.

A. 1789–1830

Thomas Jefferson was the first US Secretary of State from 1790 to 1793 and the third US President from 1801 to 1809. He personifies the use of Discovery against American Indians because he understood the Doctrine and used it regularly in his work as a private lawyer, state official, Secretary of State, Vice-President, and President. Jefferson had studied and applied the colonial and state laws of Virginia and he knew that to 'acquir[e] lands' the colonial government must have 'cleared [ ] the Indian title ... from the Indian proprietors'. Jefferson understood that under Discovery the state had the 'sole and exclusive power of taking convey-ances of the Indian right of soil' and that 'an Indian conveyance alone could give

no right to an individual...'. In these statements, Jefferson accurately foretold
the Supreme Court's definition of Discovery in *Johnson v M'Intosh* in 1823.[1]

As President, Jefferson began instituting the 'Savage as the Wolf' policy and
made the acquisition of Indian lands the primary goal of his eight-year administration. During this time, the United States enacted 28 treaties with tribal governments and purchased millions of acres of land east of the Mississippi River
under the Discovery element of preemption. Jefferson also began implementing
what is known as the Removal policy to move Indians west of the Mississippi
River. Jefferson plainly saw that his policies meant the destruction of Indian cultures, societies, and governments because he had: 'little doubt... [of] the various
ways in which their history [Indians] may terminate, and... that it is for their
interest to cede lands at times to the United States'.[2]

1. Secretary of State Jefferson

During his tenure as Secretary of State, Jefferson applied the Doctrine in his
everyday work involving foreign countries and tribal nations. In June 1792, for
example, Jefferson had an illuminating exchange about Discovery and Indian
rights with the English diplomat Sir George Hammond. In fact, Hammond
asked Jefferson what the US rights were 'in the Indian soil' in the lands west of
the Appalachia and Allegheny Mountains. Jefferson's explanation invoked many
elements of Discovery including preemption, Indian title, US sovereignty over
the Indian nations, the exclusion of other governments from dealings with tribes,
and international law aspects. Jefferson explained that the United States had:

1st. A right to preemption of their [Indian] lands; that is to say, the sole and exclusive
right of purchasing from them whenever they should be willing to sell. 2d. A right of
regulating the commerce between them and the whites. Did I suppose that the right of
preemption prohibited any individual of another nation from purchasing lands which
the Indians should be willing to sell? Certainly. We consider it as established by the usage
of different nations into a kind of *Jus gentium* [international law] for America, that a white
nation settling down and declaring that such and such are their limits, makes an invasion
of those limits by any other white nation an act of war, but gives no right of soil against
the native possessors. [Hammond asked do English traders have to stay out? 'Yes']

---

[1] Robert J Miller, *Native America, Discovered and Conquered: Thomas Jefferson, Lewis and Clark, and Manifest Destiny* (Westport, CT & London: Praeger Publishers, 2006) 59–97; Frank L Dewey, *Thomas Jefferson Lawyer* (Charlottesville, VA: University Press of Virginia, 1986) xi, 14–15, 22, 25, 30–1, 33, 35–6; Merrill Peterson, *Thomas Jefferson & The New Nation* (New York: Oxford University Press, 1970) 22, 118, 121; II *The Writings of Thomas Jefferson* (Washington DC: US Gov't Printing Off, Andrew A Lipscomb and Albert Ellery Bergh (eds), 1903) 131–3, 187–9; James P Ronda, 'Introduction' in *Thomas Jefferson and the Changing West* (St Louis, MO: Missouri Historical Society Press, James P Ronda (ed), 1997) xiv.

[2] Miller, note 1, 68–75, 86–91; Ronda, 'Introduction,' note 1, xiv; Roger G Kennedy, *Mr. Jefferson's Lost Cause: Land, Farmers, Slavery, and the Louisiana Purchase* (Oxford: Oxford University Press, 2003) 68, 251–2; X *Writings of Thomas Jefferson*, note 1, 357–9.

Jefferson also demonstrated his understanding that Discovery limited tribal sovereign rights: 'an established principle of public law among the white nations of America, that while the Indians included within their limits retain all other national rights, no other white nations can become their patrons, protectors, or mediators, nor in any shape intermeddle between them and those within whose limits they are'.[3]

Jefferson was also called upon to render legal opinions about Discovery. He repeatedly utilized its elements including first discovery, preemption, Indian title and rights of occupancy and use, the limits on tribal property, sovereignty, and commercial rights, contiguity, *terra nullius*, and the need to 'civilize' Indian people to define European and Indian property rights and diplomatic and commercial rights in North America.[4]

In 1790, he was asked by the US House of Representatives to examine North Carolina's claims over the Cherokee Nation. Jefferson stated that the Indians 'were entitled to the sole occupation of the lands within the limits guaranteed to them' and that 'North Carolina, according to the *jus gentium* [international law] established for America by universal usage, had only a right of pre-emption of these lands against all other nations:...and the right of occupation could not be united to it till obtained by the United States from the Cherokees'. The Cherokee Nation, Jefferson wrote, 'possess the right of occupation, and [North Carolina has] the right of preemption'. Thus, North Carolina held the incomplete 'European title' and it could not become a complete fee simple title until the United States extinguished the 'Indian title' of use and occupancy.[5]

In 1791, he issued an opinion on the rights Spain had gained by the element of conquest in Indian lands in Georgia. He doubted that 'the possession of half a dozen posts [over] seven or eight hundred miles extent, could be considered as the possession and conquest of that country'. He also wrote in 1791 to the Secretary of War and in 1793 to the US House that Indians held the right to occupy their lands independent of the states' rights of preemption. Virginia, he said by way of an example, could only grant actual possession of land after 'a purchase of the Indian right' because the tribal 'right of occupation' was still valid since it had 'never been obtained by the United States'.[6]

The potential of expanding the US borders to the Pacific Ocean also arose during Jefferson's time as Secretary. In May 1792, the American Robert Gray sailed his ship *Columbia Redidiva* into the mouth of an unknown river in the Pacific Northwest of the North American continent. He named the river Columbia, after his ship. Jefferson was well aware that Gray's discovery 'gave the United States a claim recognized by the polity of nations...over the valley and watershed of the river and over the adjacent coast'. Jefferson also knew exactly what this

---

3 XVII *Writings of Thomas Jefferson*, note 1, 328–9, 333; ibid IX, 100–3; ibid III, 426.
4 III *Writings of Thomas Jefferson*, note 1, 19.
5 VIII *Writings of Thomas Jefferson*, note 1, 99–101.
6 III *Writings of Thomas Jefferson*, note 1, 164, 168, 175, 218–20; ibid VIII, 220, 226–7.

claim meant for the native people who lived in the area. In 1792, he instructed American diplomats on the rights that Discovery recognized in Indian nations: 'You know that the frontiers of [Spain's] provinces, as well as of our States, are inhabited by Indians holding justly the right of occupation, and leaving to Spain and to us only the claim of excluding other nations from among them, and of becoming ourselves the purchasers of such portions of land, from time to time, as they may choose to sell.'[7]

2. President Jefferson

From 1801 to 1809, as the third president, Thomas Jefferson continued to expressly rely on Discovery in his interactions with Indian nations and foreign countries as he worked to expand America's borders. For example, Jefferson often accurately explained preemption to tribal leaders who visited him in Washington DC. He told these chiefs that they owned their lands and possessed the legal rights of use and occupancy, and that the United States was the only possible buyer of their lands whenever they were willing to sell. He even gave tribal leaders copies of the federal Trade & Intercourse Act and explained that American law did not allow individual Americans or states to buy tribal lands.[8]

The Doctrine is also plainly visible in Jefferson's planning for the Lewis and Clark expedition and his attempts to exercise political and commercial control of the Louisiana Territory. He also used Discovery to accomplish his vision to acquire the Pacific Northwest of the American continent from the native nations and European rivals.[9]

3. Lewis and Clark expedition

The Lewis and Clark expedition of 1803–1806 was the physical manifestation of the Doctrine of Discovery in the Louisiana Territory (that part of the United States west of the Mississippi River and east of the Rocky Mountains) and in the Pacific Northwest of the United States. Thomas Jefferson used the expedition to strengthen the American claim to the Northwest under international law and Lewis and Clark performed the well-recognized rituals of Discovery in the Louisiana Territory and the Pacific Northwest, including establishing the American outpost of Fort Clatsop at the mouth of the Columbia River. Lewis and Clark also began to bring the Indian nations within the American political and commercial orbit. Just as Jefferson planned, the expedition became part of the evidence that the United States used for decades against England, Spain, and Russia

---

[7] Bernard DeVoto, *The Course of Empire* (Boston: Houghton Mifflin, 1952) 323–8; VIII *Writings of Thomas Jefferson*, note 1, 416–17; ibid I, 337–8, 340–1.

[8] XVI *Writings of Thomas Jefferson*, note 1, 394–5, 398–9, 400–2, 467, 472.

[9] Ronda, 'Introduction,' note 1, xiv; Joseph J Ellis, *American Sphinx: The Character of Thomas Jefferson* (New York: Alfred A Knopf, 1998) 212.

to prove the American claims of first discovery, actual occupation, and ownership of the Pacific Northwest.[10]

In the instructions Jefferson personally drafted for Meriwether Lewis, the primary purposes of the expedition involved Indians, tribal governments, and various elements of the Doctrine. The expedition was clearly designed to open these new areas to American influence and to control and dominate trade and political interactions with the tribes. Lewis and Clark carried out the instructions and pursued Discovery goals in several ways. First, the explorers delivered a message to the Indian nations of the United States' new authority over them. Lewis wrote out a 2,500-word speech that was the template for the 50 or more official tribal encounters that occurred during the expedition. These speeches demonstrate how pervasively the elements of Discovery were used by Lewis and Clark to spread the news of the authority of the United States in the Louisiana Territory and Pacific Northwest.[11]

In speeches to tribal leaders, Lewis repeatedly called them 'children' and Jefferson their new 'father'. He informed them that their old fathers, the French and Spanish, were now gone forever. In essence, Lewis was telling Indians that they were now American subjects and Jefferson was their only protector. Lewis and Clark also distributed American flags, medals, and army uniforms 'as a pledge of the sincerity with which [Jefferson] now offers you the hand of friendship'. Lewis pointed out that the tribes had better accept Jefferson's advice:

[Our great chief] commanded us…to council with yourselves and his other red-children…to give you his good advice; to point out to you the road in which you must walk to obtain happiness. He has further commanded us to tell you that when you accept his flag and medal, you accept therewith his hand of friendship, which will never be withdrawn from your nation as long as you continue to follow the councils which he may command.[12]

---

[10] Miller, note 1, 99–114; DeVoto, note 7, 323–8, 411, 420, 430, 512, 527–8, 538–9, 549; Peter S Onuf and Jeffrey L Hantman, 'Introduction: Geopolitics, Science, and Culture Conflicts' in *Across The Continent: Jefferson, Lewis and Clark, and the Making of America* (Charlottesville: University of Virginia Press, Douglas Seefeldt, Jeffrey L Hantman, and Peter S Onuf (eds), 2005) 4; Ellis, note 9, 212; James P Ronda, *Astoria & Empire* (Lincoln: University of Nebraska Press, 1990) 43, 327; Peterson, note 1, 746, 904; *The Journals of Lewis and Clark* (Boston: Houghton Mifflin, Bernard DeVoto (ed), 1953) xxxiii–xxxv, l; X *The Writings of Thomas Jefferson*, note 1, 445–6; VI *American State Papers: Documents, Legislative and Executive, of the Congress of the United States*, 666–70; Ronda, 'Introduction', note 1, xiv.

[11] James P Ronda, *Lewis and Clark among the Indians* (Lincoln: University of Nebraska Press, 1984) 3, 9, 20–1, 79, 81; I *Letters of the Lewis and Clark Expedition with Related Documents 1783–1854* (Urbana, IL: University of Illinois Press, Donald Jackson (ed), 2nd edn, 1978) 10–13, 19–20, 173–5, 183–9, 203; 3 *The Definitive Journals of Lewis and Clark* (Lincoln: University of Nebraska Press, Gary E Moulton (ed), 1987) 156 (hereinafter Moulton); George Berndt, 'Comparing Lewis & Clark's speeches to the Otos and the Yankton Sioux', *We Proceeded On* 38 (August 2005) (Second Tribal Council, 30 August 1804).

[12] I *Letters*, note 11, 205–7; Second Tribal Council, note 11.

Lewis also drove home the point that the United States was now the only sovereign in the Louisiana Territory with which the Indian nations could deal in a diplomatic and commercial fashion. Tribal leaders were instructed to throw away 'all the flags and medals which you may have received from your old fathers the French and Spaniards' because it was 'not proper since you have become the children of the great chief… of America, that you should wear or keep those emblems of attachment to any other great father…'.[13]

Historians call the medals, flags, and uniforms that Lewis and Clark distributed sovereignty tokens, because by accepting these gifts Indian chiefs allegedly demonstrated their allegiance to the United States. Lewis and Clark believed that these objects carried this meaning. In fact, they repeatedly emphasized the Discovery significance of these items because they said their 'Government looked upon those things as the sacred emblems of the attachment of the Indians to their country'.[14]

Lewis and Clark also apparently thought they were naming chiefs and changing tribal governments. Lewis advised the Yankton Sioux Nation to 'obey the councils of such chiefs as your Great father may from time to time cause to be appointed among you from your Own nation; and those particularly who are this day acknowledged by us as Chiefs…'. One member of the expedition also showed his similar understanding about the August 1804 council with the Otoe and Missouri Nations: 'the Indians… appeared well pleased with the change of government, and what had been done for them. Six of them were made chiefs…'.[15]

Jefferson's goal for the Lewis and Clark expedition included acquiring American ownership of the Pacific Northwest. In fact, it was one of Jefferson's primary objectives for the expedition and he used the Discovery Doctrine in this attempt. This objective for Lewis and Clark is a well-recognized fact. A Canadian historian, Kaye Lamb, stated that '[t]he chief purpose of the Lewis and Clark expedition was to cross this new [Louisiana] territory and bolster American claims to the further areas beyond the Rocky Mountains'. Historian Bernard DeVoto also wrote that Jefferson expected Lewis and Clark 'to buttress the American claim to the Oregon country' and 'that to secure the Columbia country… was certainly the most urgent of Jefferson's purposes'. After the expedition, the United States made these exact Discovery arguments against Spain, Russia, and England for four decades that the Lewis and Clark expedition proved that the United States owned the Pacific Northwest under international law. In 1823, for example, the United States argued that it had jurisdiction and sovereignty over the Northwest based

---

[13] I *Letters*, note 11, 208; 5 Moulton, note 11, 111; Second Tribal Council, note 11.

[14] 5 Moulton, note 11, 79–80; James P Ronda, *Finding The West: Explorations with Lewis and Clark* (Albuquerque, NM: University of New Mexico Press, 2001) 71; Ronda, *Lewis and Clark*, note 11, 92, 193; Francis Paul Prucha, *Indian Peace Medals in American History* (Madison, WI: Historical Society of Wisconsin, 1971) xiv, 8, 11, 13, 20, 91; I *Letters*, note 11, 205; Second Tribal Council, note 11; 3 Moulton, note 11, 242.

[15] Second Tribal Council, note 11; 10 Moulton, note 11, 25 (Patrick Gass).

'upon their first discovery of the river Columbia, followed up by an effective settlement at its mouth...by Lewis and Clarke'. In 1826, the United States argued that its ownership was based on:

> By virtue of the first, prior discovery...subsequent settlement within a reasonable time...the right of occupancy, and ultimately of sovereignty...Captains Lewis and Clark...explored the course of the Columbia.... [and] erected the works called Fort Clatsop, and wintered in 1805 and 1806...According to the acknowledged law and usages of nations, a right to the whole country drained by that river. The United States has as strong a claim as any country ever had to vacant territory.[16]

The expedition became a crucial part of America's Discovery claim to the Northwest. But Jefferson realized that the expedition was only a temporary occupation of the Columbia region and that under international law the United States had to permanently occupy the area. Thus, he encouraged the American fur trader John Jacob Astor to build a permanent trading post at the mouth of the river because as Jefferson wrote Astor in 1808: *'All beyond the Mississippi is ours exclusively.'* And, after the trading post Astoria was established, Jefferson wrote of its importance to America's claim to the Pacific Northwest. The American government also relied heavily on these facts and argued for decades that Robert Gray's first discovery in 1792, the Lewis and Clark expedition in 1803–1806, and the building of Astoria by May 1811 proved that the United States owned the Northwest under Discovery because it found it first and followed that discovery up in a reasonable time by permanent occupation. The United States claimed that it met all the necessary elements to turn its first discovery claim into full title and ownership of the Northwest under international law.[17]

In light of the foregoing evidence, it is no surprise that the members of the expedition were also aware of the Discovery implications of their voyage. In the very last entry in his diary of the expedition, Private Whitehouse demonstrated his understanding of Discovery and that the United States now owned the Pacific Northwest: 'By unfolding Countries; hitherto unexplored, and which I presume, may be considered as a part belonging to the United States, [the expedition] will be received as a faithful tribute to the prosperity of my Country.'[18]

Lewis and Clark also used the European rituals of Discovery by marking the landscape and leaving symbols of their discovery, presence, and occupation of

---

[16] *Journals of Lewis and Clark*, note 10, xxxv, l; W Kaye Lamb, 'Introduction' in *The Journals and Letters of Sir Alexander Mackenzie* (London: Cambridge University Press, W Kaye Lamb (ed), 1970) 1, 42, 518 n 4; Ronda, *Finding The West*, note 14, 62–4; DeVoto, note 7, 420, 430, 512, 527–8, 538–9, 549; VI *American State Papers*, note 10, 666–70; ibid V, 533–8; Miller, note 1, 67–8, 74–5, 82–4, 109–10.

[17] XIII *Writings of Thomas Jefferson*, note 1, 432–4; Peterson, note 1, 904; Frederick Merk, *The Oregon Question: Essays in Anglo-American Diplomacy and Politics* (Cambridge: Belknap Press of Harvard University, 1967) 4, 14–15, 29, 399; William Plumer, *Memorandum of Proceedings in the U.S. Senate, 1803–1897* (New York: Macmillan, Everett Somerville Brown (ed), 1923) (2 December 1806) 520; Ronda, *Astoria*, note 10, xii, 44; XII *Writings of Thomas Jefferson*, note 1, 28.

[18] I *Letters*, note 11, 113, 210; 3 Moulton, note 11, 14, 152–3, 170 & n. 10; ibid vol 11, 7.

the Northwest. They often recorded that they carved and branded their names on trees and sandstone cliffs. Moreover, Lewis even took a branding iron on the voyage that contained the words 'M. Lewis Capt. U.S. Army'. This branding and marking activity had legal significance under the Doctrine of Discovery just as did the rituals that had been performed for centuries by Europeans and Americans to prove Discovery claims. In addition, they spent an enormous amount of time mapping and naming the features of the landscape. Mapping was a well-recognized European method for making Discovery claims. Explorers had to be able to prove where they had been and the new lands they had found. And Lewis and Clark gathered native people to conferences to deliver their speeches and to perform Discovery procedures. All of their rituals mimicked centuries-old English, Portuguese, Dutch, and French rituals.[19]

Lewis and Clark also chose to build forts and operate them under military protocols in the winters of 1804–1805 and 1805–1806. The Discovery significance of building a permanent monument to their occupation of the Pacific Northwest is obvious. For centuries, England, France, and Spain had built forts and trading posts to prove their occupation of locations in North America.[20]

The best evidence that Lewis and Clark operated under the elements of Discovery is a document they left in Fort Clatsop in the Pacific Northwest in March 1806. This document was 'legal' evidence of the occupation of the Northwest by the United States. Lewis and Clark first listed the names of all the members of the expedition and drew a map of their route. They then hung the document in the Fort and gave copies to Indian chiefs to give to any passing ship captain. The document proclaimed to the world that American soldiers had crossed the continent and lived on the Pacific coast:

The object of this list is, that through the medium of some civilized person who may see the same, it may be made known to the informed world, that the party consisting of the persons whose names are hereunto annexed, and who were sent out by the government of the U' States in May 1804 to explore the interior of the Continent of North America, did penetrate the same by way of the Missouri and Columbia Rivers, to the discharge of the latter into the Pacific Ocean, where they arrived on the 14th day of November 1805, and from whence they departed the [blank] day of March 1806 on their return to the United States....

Lewis and Clark wanted a 'civilized person', that is someone other than Indians, to testify to their crossing the continent and occupying the Columbia River. Europeans would not have believed the story if it were told only by Indians. Lewis

---

[19] 6 Moulton, note 11, 81, 106–7; ibid vol 4, 276; ibid vol 11, 192–3; DeVoto, note 7, 512; Patricia Seed, *Ceremonies of Possession in Europe's Conquest of the New World, 1492–1640* (Cambridge: Cambridge University Press, 1995) 1–2, 5–6, 17–19.

[20] Seed, note 19, 17–19; Edmond Atkin, 'Reasons for French Success in the Indian Trade' in *Major Problems in American Indian History* (Toronto: Heath and Company, Albert L Hurtado and Peter Iverson (eds), 1994) 143; Stephen Dow Beckham, *Lewis and Clark: From the Rockies to the Pacific* (Portland, OR: Graphic Arts Center, 2002) 11, 92.

and Clark also wanted 'the informed world', that is Europeans, to know that an American expedition had crossed the continent, built Fort Clatsop, and occupied the Pacific Northwest.[21]

4. Louisiana Purchase

In 1803, just after Meriwether Lewis departed Washington DC on his expedition, the United States purchased France's Discovery rights in the Louisiana Territory. The Louisiana Purchase and Jefferson's comments and actions surrounding the transaction are further examples of Discovery principles at work in American history.

Now that the United States had purchased France's sovereign, commercial, and preemption rights in the Louisiana Territory, the Lewis and Clark expedition took on a major new objective. Consequently, on 22 January 1804, President Jefferson wrote a new letter of instruction to Lewis and explained that he should begin exercising America's newly acquired Discovery powers over the Indian nations in Louisiana.

The President wrote Lewis that he could now more directly propose trade relations between the tribes and the United States than he could have before the Purchase. He also instructed Lewis to proclaim the United States' sovereignty.

When your instructions were penned, this new position [the Louisiana Purchase] was not so authentically known as to effect the complection of your instructions. *Being now become sovereigns of the country, without however any diminution of the Indian rights of occupancy* we are authorised to propose to them in direct terms the institution of commerce with them. It will now be proper you should inform *those through whose country you will pass*, or whom you may meet, that their late fathers the Spaniards have agreed to withdraw... that they have *surrendered to us all their subjects... that henceforward we become their fathers and friends...* (italics added)

Under Discovery elements, Jefferson knew that the United States was now the sovereign of the Louisiana Territory and in sole possession of the Indian trade.[22]

Jefferson was, of course, very interested in the exact borders of the Louisiana Territory. In 1804, he personally researched this question and drafted a 40+ page paper entitled *The Limits and Bounds of Louisiana*. This document is filled with Jefferson's reliance on the elements of Discovery to establish the borders of the Territory. He cited international law and the rights Europeans claimed in North America due to first discovery, symbolic possession, actual occupancy, contiguity, and the discovery of rivers. For example, he relied on France's Discovery claims on the Gulf Coast and up the Mississippi River which were established by explorers 'tak[ing] possession... [and] building and garrisoning forts'. Jefferson

---

[21] 6 Moulton, note 11, 429–31.
[22] I *Letters*, note 11, 165; Ronda, *Lewis and Clark*, note 11, 133.

claimed that 'from these facts... France had formal & actual possession of the coast from Mobile to the bay of St. Bernard, & from the mouth of the Misipi up into the country as far as the river Illinois'. Jefferson also argued that France had complied with 'the practice of nations, on making discoveries in America' and this included a 'principle that "when a nation takes possession of any extent of sea-coast, that possession is understood as extending into the interior country to the sources of the rivers emptying within that coast, to all their branches, & the country they cover" '. Due to these acts of occupancy and possession, Jefferson concluded that France had 'a virtual and declared possession'.[23]

Jefferson also relied on contiguity arguments in deciding where the boundary of the Territory should be marked between Spanish and French settlements. He drew the line 'midway between the adversary possessions of Mobile & Pensacola' because Discovery required a boundary to be 'midway between the actual possession of the two nations...'. In conclusion, Jefferson wrote that all the waters and country 'are held and acted on by France' and that France's 'titles derived, 1. from the actual settlements on the [Mississippi] river and it's waters, 2. from the possession of the coast, & 3. from the principle which annexes to it all the depending waters'. He even appears to have thought that the Pacific Northwest was part of Louisiana.[24]

Jefferson also well understood what the United States had purchased from France: the Discovery claim to a limited form of sovereign, political, and commercial power over the Indian nations and the right of preemption. Jefferson demonstrated his understanding of these legal principles in messages to the US Senate on 15 January 1808 and the US House on 30 January 1808 that 'the United States should obtain from the native proprietors the whole left bank of the Mississippi'. Jefferson knew that the United States owned the powers of Discovery, limited sovereignty, and the sole right of commercial dealings with the native peoples in Louisiana and the preemption right to buy the lands west of the Mississippi, on its 'left bank', from the tribal governments. Jefferson wrote Congress on other occasions of the US right 'of retaining exclusive commerce with the Indians on the western side of the Mississippi' and 'to procure the Indian right of soil, as soon as they can be prevailed on to part with it, to the whole left bank of the Mississippi'.[25]

---

[23] Thomas Jefferson, 'The Limits and Bounds of Louisiana' in *Documents Relating to the Purchase and Exploration of Louisiana* (Boston: Houghton, Mifflin & Company, 1904) 24–37.

[24] Ibid 40–5; *Annals of Congress*, 8th Congress, 1st Session (8 March 1804) 1124; Donald Jackson, *Thomas Jefferson & the Stony Mountains* (Urbana, IL: University of Illinois Press, 1981) 108–9; IV *Writings of Jefferson*, note 1, 515–17; William Earl Weeks, *John Quincy Adams and American Global Empire* (Louisville, KY: The University Press of Kentucky, 1992) 26–8.

[25] 1 *A Compilation of Messages and Papers of the Presidents* (Washington DC: Bureau of National Literature, James D Richardson (ed), 1913) 346, 360, 363–5, 421, 422, 426; I *Letters*, note 11, 61; Anthony F C Wallace, *Jefferson and the Indians: The Tragic Fate of the First Americans* (Ann Arbor, MI: University of Michigan Press, 1999) 224, 255; 10 *The Works of Thomas Jefferson* (New York: Putnam, Paul Ford (ed), 1905) 14.

These examples from Jefferson's career demonstrate conclusively that he operated under the Doctrine of Discovery and regularly used Discovery elements in dealing with the Indian nations and foreign countries.

5. Jefferson and Madison administrations

The United States undertook other Discovery-related actions under the administrations of Jefferson and his successor James Madison. In April 1805, for example, American diplomat James Monroe wrote to a Spanish diplomat and used the elements of first discovery, possession, international law, contiguity, and preemption to argue America's rights in the Louisiana Territory. In 1807, Secretary of State James Madison highlighted the United States' right to the Oregon country or Pacific Northwest in negotiations with England. Madison also argued with English officials in 1806 and 1807 about the United States' exclusive right to commercial and political interactions with the Indian nations and Indians inside American territory. These American diplomats were using Discovery to protect American claims in the Louisiana Territory and Pacific Northwest.[26]

Even more directly, in 1814, the new Secretary of State James Monroe argued that England had no claim on the Pacific coast because the United States had occupied the mouth of the Columbia River first. English and American diplomats then engaged in remarkable discussions about the Discovery rights and powers of each country vis-à-vis the Indian nations, their lands, and their sovereignty, and commercial rights. Each side emphasized their Discovery rights under the 'established maxim of public law' regarding 'Indians residing within the United States'. They discussed that under 'public law' when Europeans recognized boundaries in the New World they gave 'up to the nation in whose behalf it is made, all the Indian tribes and countries within that boundary'. These rights included 'the rights of soil and sovereignty over the territory which they inhabit' and 'the right of purchasing [land] by treaty from the Indians...'. The American diplomats pointed out that England had assumed the rights of sovereignty and preemption over Indians and their lands under the Royal Proclamation of 1763 and in Crown and colonial treaties and land purchases. The Americans stated that the 'law of nations' and 'the legitimacy of colonial settlements in America' worked to 'the exclusion of all rights of uncivilized Indian tribes'. The US diplomats expressly insisted on the US right of preemption because Indian nations did not have 'the right to sell their lands to whom they pleased' or 'to dispose of their lands to any private persons, nor to any Power other than the United States...'.[27]

---

[26] *Congressional Globe*, 25th Congress, 2nd Session (May 1838) 566; II *American State Papers*, note 10, 662–5; ibid vol III, 85–6, 126, 185–6.

[27] Ronda, *Astoria*, note 10, 309–10; III *American State Papers*, note 10, 706, 712–16, 720, 724, 731.

6. US Congress

The US Congress was well aware of the Doctrine and engaged in extensive discussions about Discovery and the Pacific Northwest. In 1820, Congressman John Floyd called on Congress to make the Oregon Country, the Pacific Northwest, part of the United States. A US House committee then proposed that the United States occupy the Columbia River and 'extinguish the Indian title'.[28]

The committee's report recounted the history of European discovery and claims in the New World. The committee concluded that the United States should extend its jurisdiction to control the Pacific Northwest based upon 'the usage of all nations, previous and subsequent to the discovery of America ... [and that] the title of the United States to a very large portion of the coast of the Pacific ocean to be well founded'. The committee also justified expanding the United States to the Oregon country to serve other Discovery goals such as converting and civilizing Northwest natives to protect them and instruct them in agriculture and mechanic arts.[29]

Floyd proposed in 1822 and 1823 that Congress require the President to occupy 'that portion of the territory of the United States on the waters of the Columbia', to extinguish the Indian title, give land to settlers, and form a federal territory named 'Origon'. He argued that Oregon was already part of America, that the United States should occupy it by building forts and 'extinguish the Indian title'. Many others joined in his call.[30]

Another congressman saw no problem with America displacing the Indigenous people of the Northwest because he claimed Indians had retreated westward the same as the animals. He was not worried if Indians were ultimately injured because civilization and Christianity were on the march. One member of Congress stated: 'To diffuse the arts of life, the light of science, and the blessings of the Gospel over a wilderness, is no violation of the laws of God; it is no violation of the rights of man to occupy a territory over which the savage roams, but which he never cultivates, and which he does not use for the purposes for which it was designed—the support of man. ... It is as much the order of nature that the savage should give place to the civilized man, as it is that the beast should give place to the savage man.'[31]

---

[28] *Annals of Congress*, 16th Congress, 2nd Session 679; 3 *Overland to the Pacific: A Narrative-Documentary History of the Great Epochs of the Far West* (Denver: Denver Public Library, Archer Butler Hulbert (ed), 1932–41) 42, 45; II *American State Papers*, note 10, 629–34.

[29] *Annals of Congress*, 16th Congress, 2nd Session 679; 3 *Overland to the Pacific*, note 28, 42, 45.

[30] 3 *Overland to the Pacific*, note 28, 52; *Annals of Congress*, 17th Congress, 2nd Session 396–409, 682–3; Edward Gaylord Bourne, 'Aspects of Oregon History Before 1840' (1906) VI Oregon Historical Quarterly 264.

[31] *Annals of Congress*, 17th Congress, 2nd Session, 396–409, 682–3; Bourne, note 30, 264.

In 1826, Congressman Baylies chaired yet another committee to study US expansion to the Pacific Northwest. This committee's report analysed so many elements of Discovery that we can only note a few instances. First, the Committee investigated 'the right of sovereignty and domain which appertains to the United States over the territory claimed by them on the Pacific Ocean'. It then set forth 'the progress of discovery, occupation, and settlement...for the purpose of illustrating the title of the United States' and examined 'all claims to discovery and title of the territory'. The committee concluded that '[t]he American title is founded on occupation, strengthened (as the committee believe) by purchase, by prior discovery of the river, and its exploration'. The Committee also relied on contiguity as having created an American claim to all the land 600 miles inland from Astoria. The Committee recounted this evidence 'of the progress of discovery and occupation on the Northwest coast...[to demonstrate] the claims of all civilized nations to any portions of this coast...'.[32]

7. Monroe administration

In the treaty that ended the War of 1812 between England and the United States, the parties agreed to return all properties captured during the war. England was in no hurry, however, to return Astoria. In 1817, the new Secretary of State John Quincy Adams and the new President James Monroe grew tired of arguing over Astoria and they ordered American representatives to retake possession of the post using Discovery rituals. As they wrote to each other, the mission was designed 'to assert the [American] claim of territorial possession at the mouth of Columbia river'. And, as Adams wrote separately the mission was 'to resume possession of that post [Astoria], and in some appropriate manner to reassert the title of the United States'.[33]

Diplomat John Prevost and Captain William Biddle were then ordered to take possession of Astoria. President Monroe and Secretary Adams ordered Biddle and Prevost to sail to the Columbia and to 'assert there the claim of sovereignty in the name of...the United States, *by some symbolical or other appropriate mode of setting up a claim of national authority and dominion*' (italics added). This directive was nothing less than the government ordering them to perform Discovery rituals.[34]

Biddle and Prevost arrived at Astoria at different times. Captain Biddle went ashore in two places and performed Discovery rituals to assert America's claim

---

[32] *House Report No 213*, 19th Congress, 1st Session (1926) 5–6, 8–12; 3 *Overland to the Pacific*, note 28, 12.

[33] VI *The Writings of John Quincy Adams 1816–1819* (New York: Macmillan Co, Worthington Chauncey Ford (ed), 1916; New York: Reprint, Greenwood Press, 1968) 204–5, 366, 372–3.

[34] Merk, *The Oregon Question*, note 17, 17–18, 22–3; III *American State Papers*, note 10, 731; ibid vol IV, 377, 852; William Earl Weeks, *Building the Continental Empire: American Expansion from the Revolution to the Civil War* (Chicago: Ivan R Dee, 1996) 50; Weeks, *John Quincy Adams*, note 24, 50; Ronda, *Astoria*, note 10, 310–15, 308–10.

to the Pacific Northwest. On the north side of the mouth of the Columbia River, and in the presence of Chinook Indians, Biddle raised the US flag, turned up soil with a shovel (just like the livery of seisin ritual from feudal times), and nailed up a lead plate which read: 'Taken possession of, in the name and on the behalf of the United States by Captain James Biddle, commanding the United States ship Ontario, Columbia River, August, 1818.' He then repeated this Discovery ritual on the south side of the Columbia.[35]

Prevost arrived at Astoria a month later on a British ship. The Captain had been instructed to cooperate in restoring America's claim to Astoria. The English flag was lowered and the US flag raised in its place and the English troops fired a salute and papers of transfer were signed. The American claim of Discovery to the trading post was again legally in place.[36]

a. *Treaties with England 1818 and 1827*

England and the United States continued to dispute their Discovery claims to the Pacific Northwest even after England relinquished symbolic occupation of Astoria. They negotiated for three decades regarding the region. In diplomatic exchanges, they argued about which country held the right of first discovery and first occupied the area so as to gain the title recognized under international law. The United States repeatedly argued its first discovery rights due to Robert Gray's 1792 discovery of the Columbia River; Lewis and Clark's exploration of that river from east to west and their occupation of Fort Clatsop and the region in 1805–1806; and John Jacob Astor's construction in 1811 of the trading post Astoria, the first permanent settlement.[37]

English officials disputed the American arguments and whether accidental discovery unattended by exploration or taking possession and 'the exploration of [the Columbia], by Lewis and Clark, in 1805–6' constituted ownership. England instead argued its claim to the Northwest and expressly relied on the elements of Discovery. England claimed first discovery by Francis Drake in the mid-1500s; the trade and exploration that England commenced in the region in the late 1700s; the cession by Spain to England of trading and settlement rights in the region in 1790; and the fur trading activities of the North West Company down the Columbia.[38]

---

[35] Merk, *The Oregon Question*, note 17, 22–3; III Oregon Historical Quarterly (Sept 1902) 310–11; XIX Oregon Historical Quarterly (Sept 1918) 180–7; XX Oregon Historical Quarterly (Dec 1919) 322–5; Michael Golay, *The Tide of Empire: America's March to the Pacific* (New York: John Wiley & Sons, Inc, 2003) 15, 63; DeVoto, note 7, 512.

[36] Ronda, *Astoria*, note 10, 314–15; Merk, *The Oregon Question*, note 17, 23–4; *House Document No 112*, 17th Congress, 1st Session, 13–19; Golay, note 35, 65.

[37] III *American State Papers*, note 10, 185, 731; ibid vol IV, 377, 381, 452–7, 468–72; Merk, *The Oregon Question*, note 17, 4, 14–23, 42, 47, 51, 110, 156, 165–6, 399; VI *Writings of John Quincy Adams*, note 33, 400.

[38] V *American State Papers*, note 10, 555–7; ibid vol VI, 663–6; Merk, *The Oregon Question*, note 17, 403.

These legal and diplomatic arguments demonstrate the importance the United States and England placed on the Doctrine of Discovery. These diametrically opposed positions, however, were never settled by a court although England did propose several times that a European monarch mediate the issue. Instead, both countries decided to jointly occupy and use the region. They signed a treaty in 1818 that provided both parties free use and access to the Pacific Northwest for 10 years.

The 1818 treaty expressly left each party's rights intact yet unresolved. However, John Quincy Adams and American diplomats continued to negotiate with English officials about their Discovery claims. In these discussions, each party expressly relied on the elements of first discovery, symbolic occupation, permanent and actual occupation, *terra nullius* (vacant lands), and claims to areas contiguous to discovered lands and river drainage systems. American diplomats argued that England's claim on the Pacific coast lay between the 51st and 54th parallels. According to Secretary Adams, the territory south of the 51st parallel 'was American by prior right of discovery'. American diplomats claimed that the United States held the 'absolute and exclusive sovereignty and dominion' of the Northwest based 'upon their first, prior discovery' of 'the mouth of Columbia river by Captain Gray [and] ... the whole territory drained by that river'. First discovery gave the United States 'a right to occupy, provided that occupancy took place within a reasonable time, and was ultimately followed by permanent settlements and by the cultivation of the soil ...'. These diplomats claimed the United States possessed and permanently occupied this 'vacant territory' and owned it 'on the ground of contiguity to territory already occupied'. The United States claimed it held the title to this area under international law, 'the established usage amongst nations'. In rebuttal, the English Foreign Secretary denied the US claims and told Adams that England would continue to follow international law and consider all lands west of the Rocky Mountains to be 'a vacant territory' and open to all until 'acquired, by actual occupancy and settlement'.[39]

In 1823, Secretary Adams argued that the American claim was strengthened due to the United States acquiring Spanish Discovery rights under the Adams-Onis Treaty of 1821. Adams asserted that Spain was 'the only European power who, prior to the discovery of the [Columbia] river, had *any* pretensions to territorial rights on the NW Coast of America'. Adams also relied on contiguity under international law when he stated that '[t]he waters of the Columbia river extend ... [t]o the [Louisiana] territory ... immediately contiguous to the original possessions of the United States, as first bounded by the Mississippi, they consider their right to be now established by *all the principles which have ever been applied to European settlements* upon the American hemisphere.'[40]

[39] IV *American State Papers*, note 10, 331, 377, 452–7, 468–72; ibid vol V, 436–7, 446–7, 449, 554–8, 791; ibid vol VI, 644, 652–3, 657, 661–70; Merk, *The Oregon Question*, note 17, 4, 14–35, 42, 47, 51, 68–9, 110, 156, 164–6, 185–8, 395–412.
[40] V *American State Papers*, note 10, 446–7; Albert K Weinberg, *Manifest Destiny: A Study of Nationalist Expansionism in American History* (Gloucester, MA: Peter Smith, 1958) 136.

England and the United States never settled their conflicting Discovery arguments. Instead, in 1827, they concluded another treaty of joint occupancy, free travel, and free use of the Northwest for English and American citizens.

b. Treaty with Spain

In 1817, Secretary of State Adams began negotiating with the Spanish Ambassador Don Luis de Onis regarding Florida, the boundaries of the Louisiana Territory, and a border on the Pacific. Both parties vigorously disputed their Discovery claims. In 1818, Onis argued Spain's 'rights of discovery, conquest, and possession [under] . . . the law of nations'. Adams countered by invoking 'the general practice of the European nations' and first discovery, possession, contiguity, ownership of river drainage systems, and preemption to prove the boundaries of Louisiana. After many proposals, an agreement was signed in 1819 granting to the United States Spain's claim to lands across the continent and on the Pacific between the 42nd and 54th parallels, which was allegedly the southern edge of Russia's Discovery claim.[41]

c. Treaty with Russia

By 1809, Russia was actively trying to control trade along the Pacific Northwest coast due to Discovery. John Quincy Adams and President Monroe used the elements of Discovery to dispute the Russian claim. In 1822, Adams asked Russia for an explanation under international law justifying its position. Russian diplomats relied on 'discovery, occupancy, and uninterrupted *possession*'. Adams rejected most of these claims and especially any claim based on the element of contiguity.[42]

Adams did not dispute, however, that Russia could make legitimate arguments under Discovery to present day Alaska and the coast of British Columbia. Therefore, he negotiated a treaty in which Russia agreed to restrict its claim to north of the 54th parallel. (That demarcation line is familiar to Americans because it was a slogan in the presidential election of 1844 for the United States to take the entire Pacific Northwest: 'fifty-four forty or fight'.) The primary significance of the Russian and Spanish treaties to the United States was that now two of America's European rivals for ownership of the Pacific Northwest were removed.

B. 1830–1850

President Jefferson had expressly raised the idea of removing eastern Indians west of the Mississippi River as early as 1803. He wrote a Territorial Governor that the American settlements 'will gradually circumscribe and approach the Indians,

---

[41] IV *American State Papers*, note 10, 455, 470; *The Diary of John Quincy Adams 1794–1845* (New York: Charles Scribner's Sons, Allan Nevins (ed), 1951) 211; Weeks, *John Quincy Adams*, note 24, 73, 119–20.
[42] Jackson, note 24, 53; V *American State Papers*, note 10, 436–7, 446, 449, 791; VII *Writings of John Quincy Adams*, note 33, 212–15; Weeks, *John Quincy Adams*, note 24, 79–81.

and they will in time either incorporate with us as citizens of the United States, or remove beyond the Mississippi...'. He also wrote other officials that the United States could tempt Indians to move west of the Mississippi by using the Louisiana Territory as 'the means of tempting all our Indians on the east side of the Mississippi to remove to the west...'.[43]

Jefferson explained his thinking on Removal and Indians to ex-President John Adams in 1812. Jefferson said that to deal with 'backward' tribes the United States 'shall be obliged to drive them, with the beasts of the forest into the Stony mountains'. Jefferson obviously had the same vision for Indians as Washington's 'Savage as the Wolf' policy.[44]

The federal policy of Indian removal that ran from 1830 to 1850 is most often blamed on President Andrew Jackson because Congress enacted the Removal Act in 1830. This Act required tribal consent for the sale of lands (as required by Discovery) but the United States forced this policy on the eastern tribal governments by coercive actions. It led to enormous losses of tribal lands and assets, and lives too, on the infamous 'Trail of Tears' that followed the removals.[45]

1. Manifest Destiny

Following the Lewis and Clark expedition, Americans gradually began to develop the idea that the United States would soon cross the continent and own all the lands of the native peoples. By the mid-1840s, this idea coalesced under the phrase 'Manifest Destiny'. This phrase represents the principle that the United States would expand to the Pacific Ocean under divine direction. The Doctrine of Discovery was the primary force behind this idea.

In July 1845, 'Manifest Destiny' was first expressed in an editorial written by John O'Sullivan about America annexing Texas. O'Sullivan denounced foreign nations who were allegedly 'checking the fulfillment of our manifest destiny to overspread the continent allotted by Providence for the free development of our yearly multiplying millions'. In December 1845, he wrote a very influential editorial about the Pacific Northwest entitled 'The True Title' in which he created a new slogan that justified American expansion and became part of the national vocabulary.[46]

---

[43] X *Writings of Thomas Jefferson*, note 1, 371, 391, 393–4, 401–2; ibid vol XVI, 285; Jackson, note 24, 112; 4 *The Works of Thomas Jefferson*, note 25, viii, 244, 500; Ronda, *Finding The West*, note 14, 62.

[44] II *The Adams-Jefferson Letters* (Chapel Hill, NC: University of North Carolina Press, Lester J Cappon (ed), 1959) 308.

[45] Francis Paul Prucha, *The Great Father: The United States Government and the American Indians* (Lincoln: University of Nebraska Press, 1995) 183–269.

[46] 'Annexation' (July 1845) 17 United States Magazine and Democratic Review 5 (quoted in Julius W Pratt, 'The Origin of "Manifest Destiny"' (No 4 July 1927) 32 The American Historical Rev 795, 798; *New York Morning News*, 27 December 1845 (quoted in Pratt, ibid, 795–6).

O'Sullivan used the Doctrine of Discovery in his argument that the United States already held legal title to the Pacific Northwest:

Our *legal title* to Oregon, so far as law exists for such rights, is perfect. Mr. Calhoun and Mr. Buchanan [Secretaries of State] have settled that question, once and for all.... Not a foot of ground is left for England to stand upon, in any fair argument ... [U]nanswerable as is the demonstration of our legal title to Oregon ... we have a still better title than any that can ever be constructed out of all these antiquated materials of *old black-letter international law*. Away, away with all these cobweb tissues of *right of discovery, exploration, settlement, continuity*, &c.... our claim to Oregon would still be best and strongest. And that claim is by the right of our *manifest destiny to overspread and to possess the whole of the continent* which Providence has given us for the development of the great experiment of liberty and federated self-government ... for any purpose of human *civilization*.... The God of nature and of nations has marked it for our own ... (italics added)

'Black-letter international law', 'civilization', the 'right of discovery, exploration, settlement, continuity'—there is no question that O'Sullivan invoked the elements of Discovery to justify America's legal title to Oregon.[47]

Manifest Destiny plainly had a racial component just as did Discovery. Americans felt they had the leading role in educating, civilizing, and conquering the continent and dominating American Indians and Mexicans. Many white Americans applied the same language they had used for centuries about Indians—inferior, savage, uncivilized, and a hopeless future—to Mexicans. In 1847, for example, one writer stated that the Mexican destiny was the same as Indians, to amalgamate into the 'superior vigor of the Anglo-Saxon race, or they must utterly perish'.[48]

2. President James K Polk

In the 1844 presidential election, the Democratic Party brought Manifest Destiny and Discovery issues to a head because the party platform demanded the annexation and occupation of Texas and Oregon. The party stated that 'our title to the whole of the Territory of Oregon is clear and unquestionable; that no portion of the same ought to be ceded to England or any other power; and that the

[47] *New York Morning News*, 27 December 1845, note 46; *Reprint of Documents: Manifest Destiny and the Imperialism Question* (New York: John Wiley & Sons Inc, Charles Sanford (ed), 1974) 10; Sam W Haynes, *James K Polk and the Expansionist Impulse* (New York: Longman, 1997) 87–90, 99; Reginald Horsman, *Race and Manifest Destiny: The Origins of American Racial Anglo-Saxonism* (Cambridge: Harvard University Press, 1981) 86; Anders Stephanson, *Manifest Destiny: American Expansion and the Empire of Right* (New York: Hill and Want, 1995) 21–7, 46–7, 55–60.

[48] Thomas R Hietala, 'This Splendid Juggernaut: Westward a Nation and its People' in *Manifest Destiny and Empire: American Antebellum Expansionism* (College Station, TX: University of Texas Press, Sam W Haynes and Christopher Morris (eds), 1997) 53; Horsman, note 47, 1, 3, 5, 82–5, 89–93, 207–8.

re-occupation of Oregon and the reannexation of Texas at the earliest practicable period are great American measures'.[49]

The Democratic candidate, James Polk, campaigned vigorously on this theme. His election slogan was the warlike statement about Oregon—'Fifty-four forty or fight'. Polk was claiming the Pacific Northwest into much of present day British Columbia, Canada. The election was considered to be about expansion and when Polk won he declared a mandate for American expansion. It is no surprise, then, that Texas was annexed, the Pacific Northwest acquired, and a war of territorial conquest commenced with Mexico within less than two years.[50]

In his inaugural address, Polk claimed Oregon under Discovery. In discussing 'our territory which lies beyond the Rocky Mountains', he stated that the United States 'title to the country of the Oregon is clear and unquestionable' and that '[t]he title of numerous Indian tribes to vast tracts of country has been extinguished' and that American settlement of Oregon was a beneficial outcome. Furthermore, in his first annual message to Congress, Polk discussed Oregon at length. He asserted that 'our title to the whole Oregon Territory...[is] maintained by irrefragable [irrefutable] facts'. Polk asked Congress to extend federal protection, laws, and civil and criminal jurisdiction to US citizens in Oregon and to control tribal commercial and political relations. He also requested the grant of land to the 'patriotic pioneers who...lead the way through savage tribes inhabiting the vast wilderness'.[51]

In September 1845, Polk's administration resumed the decades old negotiations with England on the boundary line in the Northwest and argued for the 54th parallel. The United States finally agreed, however, in an 1846 treaty with England to the 49th parallel where the border remains today. Thus, England relinquished its Discovery claim to the Oregon country and American Manifest Destiny to the Pacific Ocean was ensured. Secretary of State James Buchanan foresaw America's 'glorious mission...[of] extending the blessings of Christianity and of civil and religious liberty over the whole of the North American continent'.[52]

The United States quickly absorbed Oregon into the Union. In August 1848, Congress created the Oregon Territory and applied the Northwest Ordinance of 1787 and its use of Discovery principles in the Territory. In September 1850, Congress began giving land to settlers even though the Indian titles had not yet been extinguished. This assumption that Indian lands were already federal property to some extent reflected Discovery and the understanding that the United States could grant its title even before the Indian title was extinguished and while Indians still occupied the lands.

[49] Weeks, *Building the Continental Empire*, note 34, 105; VI Oregon Historical Quarterly, note 30, 271.
[50] 4 *Compilation*, note 25, 381; Ray Allen Billington, *The Far Western Frontier, 1830–1860* (Evanston, IL: Harper & Row, 1956) 155.
[51] 4 *Compilation*, note 25, 380–1, 392–7; Haynes, note 47, 70; Billington, note 50, 156–7.
[52] Haynes, note 47, 98–9.

3. Mexican-American War 1846–1848

In keeping with his perceived election mandate to expand America, President Polk commenced the Mexican-American War in 1846. The war led to the cession to the United States in 1848 of an enormous amount of territory including California and the present day United States Southwest. The discovery of gold in California in 1849 and the increasing use of the Oregon Trail led to a massive migration of Americans to these new American territories.

4. American settlers

In 1828, one prominent advocate of settling Oregon submitted a memorial to Congress for the government to form a colony on the Pacific Northwest coast. He relied on the elements of Discovery and argued that Congress should give Americans land in the Northwest so they could aid in 'colonizing a part of the American territory bordering on the Pacific Ocean'. These advocates also claimed they wanted to protect American 'rights and property on the North-West Coast, and [work] for the peace and subordination of the Indians'. They hoped to spread 'the refined principles of a republican government, and Christianity' and to 'open this wilderness to the skilful and persevering industry of civilized man'. All they asked was that Congress grant them jurisdiction, fee simple titles, and to extinguish the Indian title. Other groups were also interested in Oregon so they could plant a 'Christian settlement... [and] spread civilization and Christianity among the Indians... [to settle the] savage wilderness'.[53]

American missionaries also played an important role in opening the Oregon Trail and working to extend the elements of Discovery and Manifest Destiny to Oregon from 1833 onward. After the Astorians from 1811 to 1814, missionaries were the first Americans to permanently occupy the region. In 1834, for example, the Methodist Jason Lee travelled to Oregon and settled south of the Columbia River. In just two short years, the Americans who settled around Lee's settlement outnumbered the English in the Northwest. By 1839, Lee was asking Congress to establish American jurisdiction over the region. By the end of 1840 there were 500 Americans in the Willamette Valley of Oregon, and in 1843 alone, 900 more Americans arrived. Three thousand more Americans arrived in 1845 and immediately petitioned Congress for federal services.[54]

[53] *House Document No 139*, 20th Congress, 1st Session (11 February 1828) 3–5, 25–7; *House Report No 25–101*, (1839) 4, 24–6; VI Oregon Historical Quarterly, note 30, 271.
[54] Frank McLynn, *Wagons West: The Epic Story of America's Overland Trails* (New York: Grove Press, 2002) 9; William H Goetzmann, *Exploration and Empire: The Explorer and the Scientist in the Winning of the American West* (New York: Alfred A Knopf, 1966) 159; Billington, note 50, 70–1, 79–81.

C. 1850–1887

The rapid growth of the United States from 1846 to 1848 as a result of the Mexican-American War produced a modification of the Indian Removal policy. The enormous migration of Americans to the California gold fields and Oregon Territory caused the United States to enact a new Indian policy and a new way of applying Discovery against Indian nations. The United States now created the idea of confining tribes and Indians on small and isolated areas called reservations. The new policy began in California and Texas and lasted throughout this time period. In the Oregon Territory and elsewhere, the United States negotiated treaties with tribes to extinguish the Indian title and to move Indians away from the valuable farming, mining, grazing, and timber lands that Americans desired. The United States continued to exercise its Discovery powers by completely controlling Indian affairs and using its constitutional Discovery authority through treaty making and otherwise to totally dominate Indian nations. In addition, the United States continued to exercise its preemption power to buy land from tribes through the treaty process.[55]

D. 1887–1934

The increasing domination of the United States over Indian nations, the 'Savage as the Wolf' policy, and the Doctrine of Discovery became even more evident in what is called the Allotment and Assimilation era of federal Indian policy. The United States now more strongly than ever exercised its Discovery power over Indians without tribal input or consent. Congress radically altered the policies of the treaties and the Reservation era of federal policy and breached the limits of its alleged Discovery powers. Congress now unilaterally altered the nature of tribal property rights when it enacted the General Allotment Act of 1887. The goal of this legislation was to break up tribal ownership of reservations, open reservations for non-Indian settlement, and to end tribal existence. Congress accomplished this task by dividing, or allotting, many reservations into 160, 80, and 40 acre plots that were then granted in individual ownership to individual Indians. Reservation land in excess of what was needed to allot a share to each tribal citizen was called 'surplus' and was sold to non-Indian settlers who then moved onto reservations. A significant amount of the land allotted to tribal citizens was ultimately lost by voluntary sales and state tax foreclosures. The Allotment era resulted in a loss of two-thirds of all tribally owned lands from 1887 to 1934. In

---

[55] Prucha, *The Great Father*, note 45, 315–18, 340–50, 354–92; Stephen Dow Beckham, *Ethnohistorical Context of Reserved Indian Fishing Rights: Pacific Northwest Treaties* (Portland, OR: Lewis & Clark College, 1984) 8–11.

1887, tribal governments owned 138 million acres but by 1934 that number had shrunk to 48 million acres, of which 20 million acres were arid or semi-arid.[56]

In the Allotment era, the federal government unilaterally expanded its Discovery powers of preemption and sovereignty over tribal governments. The forced allotments of communally owned tribal lands into individual ownership and the confiscation of 'surplus lands' and their sales to non-Indians were conducted almost completely without tribal consent and in fact against the active opposition of most tribal governments. Forced transfers of tribal lands without consent was a direct violation of the preemption element of Discovery. As President Jefferson and others had explained, and as federal law provided, tribes and Indians could occupy, use, and live on their lands forever if they wished and they had to consent to any sales. The Allotment Act, however, was a dramatic example of the United States expanding Discovery power far beyond its legal definition.

Also during this era of Indian policy, the United States exercised its alleged authority to force assimilation on Indians. Straight out of the fifteenth century papal bulls and the sixteenth and seventeenth century English colonial charters, civilization, citizenship, education, and religious conversion of Indians became federal objectives. As early as 1870, President U S Grant handed control of many reservations to various Christian religions and the federal government even deeded tribal lands to religions to operate missions and schools. In the 1880s, the federal government began operating boarding schools to civilize Indians. The goal of these schools was aptly stated by the creator of the first one: Captain Henry Pratt said 'kill the Indian, save the man'. During this same time period, the Bureau of Indian Affairs attempted to take absolute control of Indian life and to squeeze out Indian governments, religions, and cultures.[57]

The US Indian policy since the early 1960s is called the Self-Determination Era. It is a far more respectful and humane policy in which the United States supports tribal governments and Indians in self-governance, economic development, and self-determination efforts. But Discovery and *Johnson v M'Intosh* are still fundamental principles of federal Indian law. The United States continues to hold the dominant position in Indian affairs and exercises enormous control over tribal political, commercial, and land issues. The Doctrine of Discovery continues to be the controlling legal precedent for federal interactions with Indian nations.

---

[56] General Allotment Act, 24 Stat 388 (1887); Prucha, *The Great Father*, note 45, 659–73; John Collier, *The Purposes and Operation of the Wheeler-Howard Indian Rights Bill, Hearings on H.R. 7902 Before the Senate and House Committees on Indian Affairs*, 73rd Congress, 2nd Session (1934) 15–18.

[57] Prucha, *The Great Father*, note 45, 512–19, 609–10; Vine Deloria Jr, *God is Red: A Native View of Religion* (Golden, CO: Fulcrum Publishing, 2nd edn, 1994) 238–41; Robert J Miller, 'Exercising Cultural Self-Determination: The Makah Indian Tribe Goes Whaling' (2001) 25 Am Indian L Rev 165, 199–206.

E. Conclusion

From the earliest days of European explorations and claims in North America, and from the establishment of the English colonies and the American states and United States, the Doctrine of Discovery has been the primary legal principle that controlled Euro-American claims and rights, and the rights and lives of Indian peoples and their nations. This legal principle does not respect Indigenous rights or native peoples and governments. Discovery and its racial, religious, and ethnocentric view of the superiority of Euro-American civilizations does not even consider Indigenous human, sovereign, or commercial rights.

Furthermore, the Doctrine of Discovery and Manifest Destiny foretold a very grim future for America's native peoples. In 1825, for example, US Secretary of State Henry Clay stated that it was 'impossible to civilize Indians.... They were destined to extinction...'. One US Senator asked the Senate rhetorically in 1825 whether the West was 'to be kept a jungle for wild beasts? No. It is not in the order of Providence. The earth was designed for man.... Their march onward, therefore, to the country of the setting sun, is irresistible.... our destinies, what-ever they may be, were placed, in this particular context, beyond our control.' One author stated that 'since the days of earliest settlement, many whites had believed that the American continent was reserved for them by Providence and that Indians should accordingly surrender it and disappear'. When US Senator Thomas Hart Benton was asked in the 1830s whether American expansion would cause the extinction of Indians he replied, 'I cannot murmur at what seems to be the effect of divine law... The moral and intellectual superiority of the White race will do the rest...'. And, as Americans clashed with Indians in Wyoming in 1870, a newspaper noted: 'The rich and beautiful valleys of Wyoming are des-tined for the occupancy and sustenance of the Anglo-Saxon race.... The Indians must stand aside or be overwhelmed.... The destiny of the aborigines is written in characters not to be mistaken... the doom of extinction is upon the red men of America.' Finally, an international law scholar stated in the mid-1800s what Discovery did to Indigenous peoples: 'the heathen nations of the other quarters of the globe were the lawful spoil and prey of their civilized conquerors'.[58]

These opinions were not new or startling ideas to Americans at the times they were stated. In fact, under the Doctrine of Discovery, these objectives were the intended results of policies that treated American Indians as the 'Savage as the Wolf'.

---

[58] Harry L Watson, *Liberty and Power: The Politics of Jacksonian America* (New York: Farrar, Straus & Giroux, 1990) 53, 105; *1 Congressional Debates (1825) 689; Reprint of Documents*, note 47, 46, 70; Horsman, note 47, 1, 3, 5, 110, 195, 300–3; Stephanson, note 47, 54–7; Hietla, *Manifest Destiny and Empire*, note 48, 53; Henry Wheaton, *Elements of International Law* (Philadelphia: Lea & Blanchard, 3rd edn, 1846) 210.

4

The Doctrine of Discovery in Canada

A. The Earth is Our Mother: Meta-Indigenous Conceptualizations of Our Relationship with Our Land

It is one of those generalizations or stereotypes that have its inception in a truism: 'The Earth is Our Mother'. Many of us are loathe speaking it[1] as saying it risks perpetuating the generalization and entrenching a misunderstood notion of what 'mothering' means. In order to understand Indigenous relationships with our land, western conceptualizations of animus need to be left behind. In many Indigenous cultures the earth has animus, is living, and is perceived as a provider and giver of life. As such, the earth itself gives birth to all creatures. The grain of truth in what has become a stereotype is this: it is one of those facts, an actual understood fact, and based upon our reason that we can say 'The earth is our mother'. No one can own your mother. No one can take your mother away. No one would give their mother away. No one could acknowledge that their mother could be owned. No one would view transference, by force or by will, as even possible.

How, therefore, is it possible to change the relationship between ourselves as Indigenous (in my case Cree—*Neheyiwak*) peoples and our mother? To start, you have to shift your mindset from 'might makes right'. As nations, we certainly negotiated treaties with other Indigenous nations and made peace with shared relations with the land. In no way did this change the nature of our relationship with the land—it merely added to the complex relationships that existed between the land and a larger family. As peoples responsible for that land (relatives with an obligation to family) your obligation became greater when more people entered into a relationship with the land.

To be able to understand the complex nature of these relationships, 'inherency' needs to be understood and contextualized. In my understanding, an inherent right[2] to the land exists because we, as original peoples, inherited that

---

[1] In drafting these chapters, I found myself unable to write about any sort of non-Indigenous doctrine related to our traditional territories. Once I decided to address our relationship with our lands and the effects that non-Indigenous doctrine have had on our relationships (as Indigenous peoples) with our lands, I found myself able to write about newcomer doctrine and indoctrination.

[2] The notion of 'rights' does not quite encompass the nature of this discussion. While Canadian courtrooms deal principally with the notion of Aboriginal rights, the word 'rights' speaks to the

relationship from our ancestors. In this regard, language is (as Bishop Avila conveyed) 'the perfect instrument of empire'.[3] To some degree, this was precisely true: our meanings, philosophies, world views and laws cannot be detailed fully in a manner which approximates their meaning in English. As words are squashed into English word boxes, concepts run over the top like spring water in a barrel.

So, it is important to acknowledge and define our relationships and the laws related to our relationships in a way that is meaningful to us as Indigenous peoples. It is one of the truisms in our culture that we understand the earth to be our mother—but mother has many more meanings attached to it than the English word would denote. Within that word are bundles, bundles of meaning. Included within that familial relationship is the understanding that we have a relationship with the land that is reciprocal. It has cared for us. We must care for it. The bones of our ancestors turned into dust and are now a part of the earth. Integral to that understanding is this one: there is no possibility that someone whose bones, histories, and laws were not birthed or placed in that land over thousands of years could come and 'take it'.

This is our law. If we were to be frank about it, and examine this from an Indigenist perspective, it would be accurate to say that in occupying our traditional territories, colonizers broke and continue to break Indigenous laws. It has been repeated so many times as to become almost without meaning in popular culture, but the statement has its origin in something that is most true: our mother cared for us, we must care for our mother, and we are linked to all the generations before and all that come after because of our mother. It may be elementally stated but make no mistake, this is a complex legal regime comprised of responsibility, obligations, reciprocity, and interrelationships.

B. Indigenous Ideologies and Understandings

Harold Cardinal and Walter Hildebrandt, after working with Elders from the Treaty 6 area[4] of Canada, addressed the notions of relations and reciprocity thus:

Powerful laws were established to protect and to nurture the foundations of strong, vibrant nations. Foremost amongst these laws are those related to human bonds and relationships known as the laws relating to *miyo-wicehtowin* [author's note: 'having or

---

primacy of humans and the hierarchy of humanities. In an Indigenous conceptualization of the relationship that original peoples have with our lands 'obligations' and 'reciprocity' speak better to this than the term 'rights' does. Patricia Monture wrote of this in 'The Roles and Responsibilities of Aboriginal Women' (1992) 56 Sask Law Rev 237. Also discussed in an interview with Métis Maria Campbell, Elder in Virtual Residence, Athabasca University (Edmonton, 28 September 2009).

   [3] Lewis Hanke, *Aristotle and the American Indians: A Study in Race Prejudice in the Modern World* (London: Hollis and Carter, 1959) 8.

   [4] Harold Cardinal and Walter Hildebrandt, *Our Dream is That Our Peoples Will One Day Be Clearly Recognized as Nations* (Calgary: University of Calgary Press, 2006).

possessing good relations']. The laws of *miyo-wicehtowin* include those laws encircling the bonds of human relationships in the ways in which they are created, nourished, reaffirmed, and recreated as a means of strengthening the unity among First Nations people and of the nation itself.[5]

In terms of a meta-Indigenous understanding that can be arrived at based upon *Neheyiwak* 'law', it might be useful to state that those laws which determined how humans would interact with themselves and their environments provided a template for how Indigenous peoples understood lawful behaviour. Those laws were and often still are the requirement, and the requirement found support in codes which govern(ed) conduct. That reciprocal relationship between original peoples, lands, and their Creator provides the basis for our ongoing relationship and is the source of our sovereignty as peoples Indigenous to our lands. Cardinal and Hildebrandt wrote of this:

The Elders emphasize the sacredness of the Earth, and in particular the sacredness of the Peoples' Island—North America—that was given to their peoples to live on. The Elders say that the Creator gave the First Nations peoples the lands in North America. The Elders maintain that the land belongs to their peoples as their peoples belong to the land. The land, waters, and all life-giving forces in North America were, and are, an integral part of a sacred relationship with the Creator. The land and water could never be sold or given away by their Nations. For that reason, the Elders say that the sacred Earth given to the First Nations will always be theirs. But more than land was given by the Creator.

'*Iyiniw miyikowisowina*' (that which has been given to the peoples) and '*iyiniw saweyi-htakosiwin*' (the peoples' sacred gifts)... The Elders are emphatic in their belief that it is this very special and complete relationship with the Creator that is the source of the sovereignty that their peoples possess.[6]

In short, the connection, relationship, and 'right' to the land were and are inviolable. An understanding that can be taken from this is that the relationship of Indigenous peoples with their traditional territories could not be altered by the arrival of non-Indigenous peoples, regardless of the theory or doctrine that they brought with them. The ideology that the Treaty 6 Elders refer to is one which supports a vision in which lawful adherence (that is, following Indigenous laws of the land) would be expected and maintained. The same Elders note that there was some understanding that some portions of Indigenous land would be shared.[7] The shared understanding of settler peoples was addressed repeatedly in ceremonies and gatherings governed by Indigenous law.[8]

Settlers initially adhered to the Indigenous laws governing settlement and those governing settler and original peoples' relationships. The myth of discovery and of adherence to Doctrinal tenets has been perpetuated over time, but the

---

[5] Ibid 15.   [6] Ibid 10–11.   [7] Ibid 15.

[8] Ibid 7. 'In the view of the Elders, the treaty nations—First Nations and the Crown—solemnly promised the Creator that they would conduct their relationships with each other in accordance with the laws, values, and principles given to each of them by the Creator.'

likelihood is that settlers adhered to Indigenous laws until they had the economic, numeric, or military power to enforce their own boundaries. This most certainly could be done and be understood to be done in the furtherance of 'happy and noncoercive relations'. In that regard, there could have existed an understanding of mutuality—a space where Indigenous ideology and laws naturally occupied the same space as settler principles with no seeming conflict.

The perception that any sort of 'discovery' occurred likely was perpetuated by stereotypical imagery of savage peoples with no governance, laws, or economies 'rescued' by the coming of settlers. To that degree, the notion of discovery likely occupied the space that natural Indigenous rule, law, and societies could not occupy in colonizing minds.

C. Indigenous Identification of Problems with Colonial Research, History, and Narrative

The word 'law' has its origin in non-Indigenous etymology. While we have some comparable and translatable terminology and concepts, it is many Indigenous peoples' shared experience that 'law' does not translate. Law is just one word which describes the ways in which we can live most kindly together. Philosophy and doctrine, in terms of most Indigenous citizens, were predicated on notions of kindness, respect, and peace. Doctrinal knowledge, if such a thing can be said to exist in our nations (for if English words cannot capture Indigenous essence, who knows to what degree English theories preclude Indigenous understanding), surely must include the knowledge that new inhabitants must negotiate their use of land with the original inhabitants. Certainly, it can be stated without much argument that those negotiations must be such that the original inhabitants must benefit from them or they would not enter into them. Additionally, it can likely be concluded that no original inhabitant could or would possess the autonomy to alter their family's (nation's) relationship with the land without consensus. Our legal histories[9] show this to be true—in our languages and in English.

For in both Indigenous and non-Indigenous cultures language is inseparable from its history. Legal traditions and/or statutes are inseparable from language. Interpretation is reliant upon a commonly held understanding of the meaning entrenched in language. Weighted and biased language hides the sizeable footprint that imperialism leaves in Canadian legal discourse. For these reasons, separating notions of 'Aboriginal rights' and 'Aboriginal title' from the notions of *terra nullius* (erasure) and the Doctrine of Discovery (savages requiring civilization)

---

[9] As legal orders are inseparable from relationships, relationships inseparable from life forms, and life forms from governance, law is inextricable from its history (and its history from its contemporary existence). Cardinal and Hildebrandt, ibid 14, detail the Cree peoples' relationships/ *wahkotowin* as 'the laws governing all relations'.

is impossible. Each word is a bundle,[10] housing within it the legal histories and Western etymology of the word. Those legal histories and the rationale for colonization of Indigenous lands are entrenched within the legal histories of settler nations and it is the height of absurdity to think that the histories and the settler lawful racialization of Indigenous peoples and the usurpation of Indigenous lands are not housed within the scheme.

In and over time, the use of the phrase 'Doctrine of Discovery' becomes unacceptable and commonly understood to house meaning which includes the notion of Indigenous submission, inferiority, and capitulation. In most circles, it is not acceptable to validate or address the Doctrine as an actuality. Not speaking its name has not served to invalidate its existence, however. As a tool of empire with historic roots to imperialist and colonial thinking, law making, and enforcement, it would be folly to think that de-racializing the surface de-systematizes the system which perpetuates itself based upon Indigenous (rights, claims, laws, peoples) inferiority. The notion of the 'universalized truth' is as relevant today to Indigenous peoples' existences as it was to the popes who issued the papal bulls (notably, Pope Innocent IV was a lawyer). In contemporary Canada, papal imperialism has found itself replaced with judicial and legislative imperialism[11] and it would not be too harsh to state that the inability of the Canadian judiciary and legislators to even entertain the notion of Indigenous legal orders as determinants of Indigenous land is not just a matter of reliance on precedent, but is equally a matter of reliance upon historico-legal absolutism. The ensuing cases are 'cleaned up' and on their face possess none of the early commonly held racialized understandings about Indigenous peoples and their incapacity regarding land, but the understanding, interpretation, and belief is entrenched within the legal order, legislative presumptions, and interpretative tools: Canadian law is a tool of empire.

D. The Doctrine of Discovery

1. Defined

The word 'doctrine' has roots firmly embedded in dogma. Organized religion, military organizations, and law are all inheritors of a number of doctrines/shared understandings. Embedded within the notion of doctrine is some sort of rightfulness (righteousness) that both defines and reifies the doctrine.

---

[10] Interview with Maria Campbell (Métis Nation), Elder in Virtual Residence, Athabasca University (Edmonton, 28 September 2009).

[11] I would define the categorization of both as 'legal imperialism'. A workable definition of this would be: the systematized enforcement of colonizer legal standards within the systems of law making and legal enforcement. Adherence to and perpetuation of the same through the application to original peoples results in the manifestation of legalized racial/cultural superiority which privileges colonial laws and beliefs and contributes to the erasure of Indigenous legal orders, values, and beliefs.

The notion of 'Discovery' is one that is based in first time: first time encounter, first time in your knowledge, first observation. That the Doctrine of Discovery has lost that meaning—of a first encounter—and that it has become subsumed in an understanding of 'finding' land, a nation, a people is difficult to understand unless you consider the intent and role of the Doctrine.

For the purposes of this chapter and the next, the Doctrine of Discovery will be defined as a dogmatic body of shared theories (informing theory, law, and understanding) pertaining to the rightfulness and righteousness of settler belief systems and the supremacy of the institutions (legal, economic, governmental) that are based upon those belief systems. The shared theories have been predicated on a notion of 'first' or 'discovery' as original peoples/Indigenous peoples in their own territories did not share settler theory or understandings or settler legal, economic, or governmental institutions and were deconstructed as non-existing in order to allow for 'rightful' and righteous settlement of Indigenous peoples' lands. The Doctrine has been utilized as a rationale to take Indigenous lands on the basis of Indigenous peoples' constructed and Doctrinally defined deficiencies and inhumanity.

2. Sources

The Doctrine of Discovery has its origins in the notion of superiority. The Doctrine is built upon this largely racialized philosophy: those who were superior had superior rights to those who were inferior. 'Infidel' inferiority was predicated upon notions of correspondence with the imperialist defined notions of humanity. Finding the basis in religious theology, the Old World was understood to exist by virtue of the theology which defined colonizing nation inhabitants as possessing direct relationships to the Supreme Power through His representatives on earth. Those who were unrelated to the representatives were understood to be opposed to and conflicting with the authority. They were also understood to possess lesser humanity. This understanding led, further, to the supremacist understanding that those who did not share imperialist religious beliefs and who did not act in accordance with those beliefs, were lesser humans. Lesser humans had, as well, lesser rights: to liberty, to property, to life. This list of infidels included Indigenous peoples within the 'New World'.

Entrenched within the imperialistic understanding of the lack of humanity of Indigenous peoples was the notion of Indigenous peoples' inferior relationship with/rights to their land. Conceptions of the 'New World' and Indigenous peoples were based upon imaginary, misconstrued, or fear-based constructions of peoples whose individual traits, philosophies and values, and systems (government, land holding, laws, etc) differed from their own. Casting imperial law as normative and Indigenous law as non-existent or abnormal played a distinct role in the implantation of beliefs about the rightfulness of European property laws.[12] Additionally, situating Indigenous nations as 'savage' and lawless inverted reflections of imperial nations meant that rightful and righteous force and/or authority could be applied and used to justify settler invasion.[13]

One of the most potent tools available to settler governments and their appointed 'explorers' in the invasion of Indigenous lands was imperial law. Possessing origins in imperial religion,[14] imperial law itself was most useful in shaping the imperial agenda and in controlling the exploitation of Indigenous peoples, lands and resources. Robert Williams wrote of this: 'The manipulability of legal discourse one of the indispensable instruments of power deployed by the West's will to empire.'[15] The notion of papal supremacy housed within it the rights of dominium which, in imperial understanding, were the greatest rights to be held in relationship to land on earth. This, Williams writes, was the source of the right of 'discoverer's authority' and the 'divine discovery and the authority of God over godless'.[16]

Indigenous peoples who lived in accordance with their own and different set of philosophies, laws, values, and principles were easily dismissed as land owners and as humans. Nationhood was presumed to exist only within those peoples who chose to live in accordance with the religion-derived laws and principles of imperial peoples. Laws were presumed to exist only for and by the peoples who subscribed to imperial belief systems. Property was presumed to follow only those who could understand, worship, and hold dominium. Infidels were defined by what we were perceived not to possess:

By their (infidel nations) rejection of the true God and his chosen vicar the pope, all pagans were presumed to lack rights to property and lordship. The pope held unquestioned universal jurisdictional authority on earth over all the Church's subjects, real or potential. Resistance to that authority constituted resistance to God's law. The papacy possessed the power not only to punish the deluded pagans but also to assume the rule over their territories, which rightly belonged to Rome in the first place.[17]

Religion, language, and law proved to be profoundly powerful tools in advancing the imperial agenda.[18] Church doctrine legitimated legal discourse and laws pertaining to conquest and discovery.[19] The Constance Debates on the Rights of

---

[12] Robert A Williams, *The American Indian in Western Legal Thought: The Discourses of Conquest* (Oxford: Oxford University Press, 1990) 25.

[13] Williams notes that notions of 'authority' and 'administration' are borrowed from Roman jurisprudence. Ibid 27.

[14] Williams notes that Pope Innocent IV 1243–54 was a lawyer and that he 'fully elaborated the legal discourse for determining the rights and status of pagan peoples'. Ibid 27. Williams also writes that '[t]he hierocratic canonists and their Romanized legal methodology complemented perfectly the Crusade-era papacy's own absorbtive, imperial goals'. Ibid 40. The understanding, Williams writes, was the no person had authority that was greater than Christ's but that papal authority was derived from this. [15] Ibid 37.

[16] Ibid 40. [17] Ibid 41.

[18] At ibid 46, Williams says that Innocent provided a divinely oriented, totalizing epistemology in support of the Church's medieval views.

[19] At ibid 60, Williams said: 'Formal acceptance of the medieval cannon lawyer-pope's positions on infidel rights as the official doctrine of the Roman Church provided the discursive legitimating

Infidels,[20] the issuance of papal bulls,[21] the Spanish encomienda,[22] the Laws of Burgos,[23] and the debates at Valladolid[24] were all central to the construction of notions of Indigenous inferiority and to the legitimating of imperialist assumptions of power. Religion and law legitimate and language rationalizes the 'hierocratic assertions of jurisdictions over infidel peoples'.[25] All served to authorize and validate conquest and discovery.

Territoriality and discovery predicated upon the duality of imperial and Indigenous peoples (good versus evil, lawful versus lawless, rightful versus wrongful, righteous versus immoral, land owner versus occupant) justified and facilitated imperial land grabs in North America. King Henry VII granted a 1497 Charter of Conquest to John Cabot to 'occupy and possess all such towns, cities, castles, and lands' belonging to heathen and infidel persons.[26] It is thought that he made the voyage to Bona Vista (Newfoundland) in 1497.[27] Only the 1497 voyage is recalled 'in the letters patent of 1498'.[28]

Exploration and the new imperial imperative behind colonial expansion was due to a number of factors, but chief among them is the fact that Elizabeth ascended to the throne at a time when the Crown was relatively impoverished.[29]

---

foundations for the first legal discourses of conquest that emerged from the early colonizing experiences of Portugal and Spain.'

[20] The Constance Debates on the Rights of Infidels (ibid 62) in which the Constance Council of 1414 had to resolve claims to St Peter's chair by three rival popes. At ibid 64, Williams writes: '[P]agans, who were presumptively not in a state of grace, similarly lacked dominium and thus could be deposed of their property and leadership by righteous Christians.' Williams writes that these findings legitimated attacks on pagan nonbelievers.

[21] Pope Eugenius issued a bull authorizing conversion (ibid 72) of Indigenous peoples in the Canary Islands. Williams, ibid 79, considers Pope Alexander's three papal bulls which addressed the rights of Spain with regard to 'barbarous' peoples. Under one papal bull (ibid 80), the Pope could place non-Christian people under the tutelage and guardianship of the first Christian nation discovering the lands as long as peoples reported by the 'discovering' nation to be 'well disposed to embrace the Christian faith'.

[22] At ibid 84, Williams notes that Encomienda were used in the Spanish 'New World' and were groups of Indian villages 'commended' to an individual. People who were in control of them had legal and military obligations to the Crown.

[23] Williams writes, at ibid 87, that the genocidal fury of the Spanish colonies forced King Ferdinand to convene a council of royal theologians and canon law scholars in 1512 to discuss Indian capacity and character and the role of conversion, subjugation, remediation, and forceful removal in its 'conquering'.   [24] Williams discusses the same at ibid 95 and 96.

[25] Ibid 79. Williams wrote, with respect to the Spanish bulls, as regards Antonio de Nebrija's Spanish *Grammatica* that when Queen Isabella asked Bishop Avila what it was for, his answer was reportedly 'Language is the perfect instrument of empire.' Ibid 74.   [26] Ibid 121.

[27] Henry Harrisse, *John Cabot, The Discoverer Of North America And Sebastian, His Son: A Chapter Of The Maritime History Of England Under The Tudors, 1496–1557* (London: Stevens, 1896). There is debate about whether the landing occurred in 1497 or in 1493. Sebastian Cabot wrote that it occurred in M.CCCC.XCIIII on 24 June in the morning. Ibid 56.

[28] Ibid 61. Schoolcraft concludes that John Cabot sailed under the British flag and that 'the continent of North American was discovered ... in the year 1497'. Henry R Schoolcraft, *The American Indians Their History, Condition And Prospects, From Original Notes And Manuscripts* (Buffalo: G H Derby, 1851) 62.   [29] Williams, note 12, 134.

3. Theory

In an American context, Robert Miller has outlined 10 distinct elements of the Doctrine of Discovery as employed in, at least, Oregon. Those distinct elements are: first discovery, actual occupancy and current possession, preemption/ European title, Indian title, tribal limited sovereign and commercial rights, contiguity, *terra nullius*, Christianity, civilization, and conquest.[30]

Perhaps the Doctrine of Discovery in what became known in Canada is better known in terms which include and expand upon Professor Miller's model. Examining that in a critical Indigenous theoretical manner and addressing it in a Canadian context, distinct elements in Canada might include:

A. The 'Savage' Period
   1. The assertion of first discovery by Europeans;
   2. Nation to nation dealings by the settlers;
   3. Actual occupancy and possession;
B. Ownership/Owned
   4. The assertion of European title;
   5. Creation of the notion of Indian title;
C. Obliged/awareness of obligations
   6. The attempted limitation of Indigenous sovereignty;
   7. Attempted domesticization (Christianization, assimilation, and usurpation);
D. Narrowing the Obligations
   8. The evolving conceptualization of limited (by discovery) sovereignty, rights, and title.

4. Practice

Canadian law has never used either "discovery" or "terra nullius". Our legal tradition has been so self-confident, so arrogant, that it felt no need to have any legal theory justifying British colonialism.[31]

In practice, Indigenous nations in the territory north of the United States were faced with a different set of circumstances. French and English warring and tensions necessitated cooperation by and union with the Indigenous peoples in what was to become known as Canada. 'Discoverers' who landed on Indigenous nations were similarly armed with notions of rightful and righteous land acquisition in the name of the Crown (who acquired the same in the name of a Supreme Being). However, 'discovering' Indigenous lands when competing with other imperial nations necessitated reciprocal relations with Indigenous peoples. Indigenous

---

[30] Robert J Miller, *Native America, Discovered and Conquered: Thomas Jefferson, Lewis and Clark, and Manifest Destiny* (Westport, CT and London: Praeger Publishers, 2006) 3–5.
[31] Douglas Sanders, 'The Supreme Court Of Canada and the "Legal And Political Struggle" Over Indigenous Rights' (1990) 22 Canadian Ethnic Studies 122, 122.

peoples would be asked to provide loyalty and protection for mutually beneficial trades and trading. As well, there was substantial violence, fear, and conflict
which made Indigenous peoples' cooperation essential to settler survival.

In this regard, there is much support for the notion that, while perhaps
regarded as pitiable ones, settler peoples did engage with the Indigenous nations
as nations.[32] The practice was not to regard the First Peoples as non-entities,
but to engage them to the degree their territory was required and their cooperation was warranted. In some cases, this meant dealing with the nations in treaty
agreements. In others, it meant dealing with First Nations as problems to be dealt
with. There was no language and no law that dealt with the nations as other than
sovereigns[33] and the nature of treaties and agreements that followed colonizer
landing on Indigenous lands were predicated on notions of nationhood, authority, and autonomy.[34]

Modern case law addressing early treaties with Indigenous peoples in the territory that became known as Canada addresses the notion of reciprocal relations
and the requirement of Indigenous alliances in order to address threats from
other colonial nations.[35]

E. The Doctrine of Discovery in Canada: Early Era

John Cabot was followed by Jacques Cartier who left St Malo, France on 20 April
1534, arriving on the coast of Newfoundland 20 days later.[36] Schoolcraft notes
that on the 10th of June of the same year includes the first description of the original occupants of the territories.[37] Cartier later went on to observe the gulf of the
St Lawrence[38] and returned on a second journey.[39]

It should be noted that the exploration of Indigenous territories and lands was
not acceptable to the original inhabitants. Chief Donnacona (Haudenosaunee)
and 10–12 other chiefs with more than 500 Indigenous citizens, boarded Cartier's

---

[32] The nation to nation relationship is addressed later in the chapter.

[33] It has often been argued that the First Nations were regarded as either sovereigns or 'savages',
but there was a demonstrated cognizance that the original occupants of their territories could be
either or both, depending on the circumstance (the application of foreign laws or the recognition
of land rights).

[34] Treaties and agreements are discussed in Chapter 4. Judicial interpretations of the same are
discussed in Chapter 5.

[35] See eg *R v Marshall* [1999] SCJ 55 (Supreme Court of Canada) and *R v Marshall* [1999] SCJ
66 (a Supreme Court of Canada case) <http://www.quicklaw.com>.

[36] Schoolcraft, note 28, 331.

[37] Ibid 332–3. The description includes the phrase 'wild and unruly' to describe the male original inhabitants.

[38] At ibid 335 it is noted that they met with some of the original occupants ('wild men') and
were provided with cooked seal and gave hatchets, knives, and beads in return.

[39] Leaving St Malo on 19 May 1535, Cartier brought three ships and arrived on the coast of
Newfoundland on 7 July. Ibid 338.

vessels 'to protest against the intended voyage of exploration'.[40] 'Protest' is a mild description. From a reading of the work, it is easy to see that the leadership and citizenship of the First Nations attempted to dissuade the imperial journey verbally, physically, and spiritually.[41] If settler peoples in Indigenous peoples' territories were in any way considering themselves than fully connected to their lands and the peoples primarily responsible for it, it would seem unlikely that they would have to continue to entertain, soothe, and meet with the Indigenous leadership demonstrated at least that Cartier entertained the notion of an Indigenous continuing relationship with the land.

Canadian and world history has, to some degree, mythologized the nature of the relationships between First Peoples and settler peoples. Sanders writes of this:

There are many myths about this early period. The reality was not peaceful negotiations leading to treaties. The history was much more brutal, with extensive warfare and the extermination of whole tribes. Treaties were often signed after warfare, when terms could be dictated. Modern historians see even the famous treaties with the Iroquois confederacy not simply in terms of rights, but as part of British political strategies designed to deal with the French and with the other tribes further inland.

The history involves warfare, brutality and manipulation. But it also clearly involves European colonial powers seeking to gain rights from the tribes, whether by warfare, alliances or negotiation. The tribes were outside the political power of the European colonizers and needed to be brought into the new colonial order in some way.

This early recognition of the independence of the tribes was gradually undermined as European colonial powers gained greater and greater control in North America. When the British defeated the French, Indians could no longer play one colonial power off against another.[42]

That those rights were inherent in the Indigenous nations as First Peoples and that it was commonly held that some sort of divesting of Indigenous sovereignty must occur (with or without Indigenous peoples' knowledge) was evinced by settler consent and compliance to initiating relationships with the original peoples.

Additionally:

Written treaties between tribes and European powers go back to the early 17th century. International practice on treaties was flexible in that period. International law accepted

---

[40] Ibid 341.

[41] Ibid 341 and 342. The attendance on the ship was accompanied by entreaties, provision of presents, requiring Cartier to participate in ceremony and sending men 'wrapped in skins, besmeared and provided with horns' to the side of Cartier's vessels 'importing ill tidings to the French ... to inform them that, there was so much ice and snow in the country, that whoever entered it, must die'. Cartier was not to be stopped; he made a third voyage on behalf of King Francis I, leaving on 23 May 1540. Ibid 350. Harrisse, note 27, 105 (and many other sources) notes that the third voyage arrived on the northeast coast of Newfoundland on 23 May 1541. It is commonly thought that Cartier kidnapped two male Iroquois citizens and returned to France with them.

[42] Sanders, note 31, 123.

that there were a range of political entities, not simply the single modern model of the sovereign state. In the law of the period it was not remarkable for tribes to be recognized as natural political communities, with whom international relations could be established.[43]

Those treaties, over time, came to have meaning affixed to them that not only mirrored imperialist policy and understandings, but which were used to perpetuate the imperial notion of the rightfulness of the myth of discovery.

1. Colonizer philosophies and law

As colonizer philosophies were built upon imperialist and racialized understandings about Indigenous peoples' inhumanity, so too was the law. By perpetuating the notion of Indigenous peoples as inhuman, it became easier to deny Indigenous peoples the qualities of humans: the ability to identify and name citizens, the capacity to own property, and the ability to hold governmental authority. Entrenched in the notion of Indigenous inhumanity was the understanding that if Indigenous peoples, communities, and nations were antithetical to 'civilized peoples', then the rights that accompany them could not be understood in the same way as settler rights. The Doctrine of Discovery, therefore, came to be understood as a means by which to contrast and compare Indigenous and non-Indigenous humanity in order to arrive at a privileging approach to rights determination. Settler rights and settler governments, in order to rationalize the unjust 'taking' of Indigenous lands (in other comparable situations, and perhaps in this one, this would be labelled 'invasion') had to legitimize settler authority by ostensibly delegitimizing Indigenous authority. In this way, imperial philosophy created the imperial law related to settlement ('discovery') which explicitly (then) and implicitly (now) subordinated Indigenous interests, rights, and authorities to settler interests, rights and, authorities. Settler standards were understood by settlers and recorded in written text as *the* law— the normative standard—which became prescriptive and which mandated Indigenous inferiority (in rights, in land claim, and in law). All of these reasons, entrenched and normatively established, became the basis for the matter of fact denial of Indigenous sovereignty. That the fact was most assuredly a European fact seemed to be of little import:

There are legal reasons why international law permitted the assertion of British and French sovereignty over Aboriginal people, and apparently authorized the denial of Aboriginal governmental authority. However, those legal reasons can and ought to be subjected to normative scrutiny. International law at the time of European contact, according to the doctrine of discovery, viewed Aboriginal nations as inferior to European nations and therefore did not recognize the fact of Aboriginal sovereignty in North America. As a result, mere settlement, as opposed to conquest or treaty, was sufficient to assert

---

[43] Ibid 122–3.

sovereignty over Aboriginal peoples on the continent. The justification offered by inter-national law in support of this conclusion rests on racist premises; as a result it is norma-tively unacceptable by Aboriginal and non-Aboriginal standards alike as a reason to deny Aboriginal people a right of self-government.[44]

'Mere settlement' as a standard was used to justify and legitimate settler sover-eignty at the moment it was asserted, regardless of the fact that other humans lawfully and rightfully inhabited the territories that were subject to some sort of blanket notional prerogative which manifested by virtue of the superiority of the people asserting sovereignty.[45]

2. Colonizing belief and peoples

The 1670 Royal Charter of the Hudson's Bay Company (HBC),[46] signed by King Charles II, was essentially a gift to his cousin Prince Rupert (whom the King pronounced first governor of the company). The Charter provided Prince Rupert and his company of explorers with the resources and administrative capacity to explore and 'discover' the north-west of what was to become Canada in order to find 'some Trade for Furs, Minerals, and other considerable Commodities, and by such their Undertaking, have already made such Discoveries as do encourage them to proceed further in Pursuance of their said Design, by means whereof there may probably arise very great Advantage to Us and Our Kingdom'.[47]

Commerce did indeed follow settlement, with Charles II's pronouncement of the creation of the body corporate and politique, 'The Governor and Company of Adventurers of England, trading into Hudson's Bay, and them by the Name of the Governor and Company of Adventurers of England, trading into Hudson's Bay, one Body Corporate and Politique, in Deed and in Name, really and fully for ever, for Us, Our Heirs and Successors . . .'.[48]

---

[44] Patrick Macklem, 'Normative Dimensions of an Aboriginal Right of Self-Government' (1995) 21 Queen's LJ 173, 186–7.

[45] 'Mere settlement' has become entrenched in Canadian law and continues as a Canadian legal justification for the denial of Indigenous sovereignty.

[46] Royal Charter of the Hudson's Bay Company (as transcribed and produced for Project Gutenberg by Sean Barrett, Charles Franks, and the Online Distributed Proofreading Team from images generously made available by the Canadian Institute for Historical Microreproductions) <http://www.hbc.com/hbcheritage/collections/archival/charter/charter.asp>.

[47] Ibid. A monarchy monopoly on the rights to trade and commerce all of the land, other than that 'actually possessed by any of our Subjects, or by the Subjects of any other Christian Prince or State' was included in the Charter.

[48] Ibid. There was no separation of monarchy, state, economy, or law:

Times hereafter shall be, personable and capable in Law to have, purchase, receive, possess, enjoy and retain, Lands, Rents, Privileges, Liberties, Jurisdictions, Franchises, and Hereditaments, of what Kind, Nature or Quality soever they be, to them and their Successors; and also to give, grant, demise, alien, assign and dispose Lands, Tenements and Hereditaments, and to do and execute all and singular other Things by the same Name that to them shall or may appertain to do. And that they, and their Successors, by the Name of The Governor and Company of Adventurers of England, trading into Hudson's Bay, may plead, and be impleaded, answer, and be answered, defend, and

If commerce followed settlement, then it also preceded law. Law making and law enforcement process were entrenched in the HBC Charter, in a document that looked very much like a hybrid between minutes of incorporation and a Constitutional document.[49] The Charter provided:

AND FURTHERMORE, of our ample and abundant Grace, certain Knowledge, and mere Motion, WE HAVE granted, and by these Presents for Us, Our Heirs and Successors, DO grant unto the said Governor and Company, and their Successors, that they, and their Successors, and their Factors, Servants and Agents, for them, and on their Behalf and not otherwise, shall for ever hereafter have, use and enjoy, not only the whole, entire, and only Trade and Traffick, and the whole, entire, and only Liberty, Use and Privilege, of Trading and Trafficking to and from the Territory, Limits and Places aforesaid; but also the whole and entire Trade and Traffick to and from all Havens, Bays, Creeks, Rivers, Lakes and Seas, into which they shall find Entrance or Passage by Water or Land out of the Territories, Limits or Places, aforesaid; and to and with all the Natives and People, inhabiting, or which shall inhabit within the Territories, Limits and Places aforesaid; and to and with all other Nations inhabiting any of the Coasts adjacent to the said Territories, Limits and Places which are not already possessed as aforesaid, or whereof the sole Liberty or Privilege of Trade and Traffick is not granted to any other of Our Subjects. AND WE of our further Royal Favour, and of Our more especial Grace, certain Knowledge, and mere Motion,

And, in Case any Crime or Misdemeanor shall be committed in any of the said Company's Plantations, Forts, Factories, or Places of Trade within the Limits aforesaid, where Judicature cannot be executed for want of a Governor and Council there, then in such Case it shall and may be lawful for the chief Factor of that Place and his Council, to transmit the Party, together with the Offence, to such other Plantation, Factory, or Fort, where there shall be a Governor and Council, where Justice may be executed, or into this Kingdom of England, as shall be thought most convenient, there to receive such punishment as the Nature of his Offence shall deserve.

From this, it can be seen that for many years the traders were the law and the law was informed by the economy. With specific instructions from the King

be defended, in whatsoever Courts and Places, before whatsoever Judges and Justices, and other Persons and Officers, in all and singular Actions, Pleas, Suits, Quarrels, Causes and Demands, whatsoever, of whatsoever Kind, Nature or Sort, in such Manner and Form as any other. Our Liege People of this Our Realm of England, being Persons able and capable in Law, may, or can have, purchase, receive, possess, enjoy, retain, give, grant, demise, alien, assign, dispose, plead, defend, and be defended, do, permit, and execute. And that the said Governor and Company of Adventurers of England, trading into Hudson's Bay, and their Successors, may have a Common Seal to serve for all the Causes and Businesses of them and their Successors, and that it shall and may be lawful to the said Governor and Company, and their Successors, the same Seal, from time to time, at their Will and Pleasure, to break, change, and to make anew, or alter, as to them shall seem expedient.

[49] The document provides: 'WE WILL to be duly observed and kept under the Pains and Penalties therein to be contained; so always as the said Laws, Constitutions, Orders and Ordinances, Pines and Amerciaments, be reasonable, and not contrary or repugnant, but as near as may be agreeable to the Laws, Statutes or Customs of this our Realm.'

to 'Trade and Traffick with *Natives and People*' living in the Indigenous peoples' territories and the understanding that there may be a need to transit those who committed crimes to a plantation, factory, or fort where justice could be executed, it can be argued that those who made money also made judicial decisions.[50]

The government of Canada's position on this is quite clear:

But the charter granted the Hudson's Bay Company a trading monopoly in this region and bestowed upon them sovereignty rights to the region. The company had the authority to establish and enforce laws, to erect forts and to enter into agreements with the aboriginal people they met. The company was, in effect, a commercial fiefdom, protected by the British Crown but in all other respects an autonomous power.[51]

The notion that a Charter granted by a King never seen, to a land filled with its original occupants, over which the laws of the original nations were still in operation, could usurp and replace all authorities just by virtue of sending his delegates to the original occupants' territory seems ludicrous to many. There is strong argument to support that this Canadian governmental characterization of the easy colonial relationship with unjustified assertions of power and authority was and is a colonial reality. In any reading of the HBC Charter, it is easy to see that the roots of economic domination and imperial dominion were so intertwined as to prove a formidable occupant of the territory.

The occupant company had a trade monopoly that continued until 1820. In that year, the Hudson's Bay Company merged with the North West Company. Until 1870[52] the merged companies acted as the economic driver and as the de facto non-Indigenous form of governance in the territory listed in the Charter. In this year, the HBC transferred control of the territories stipulated in the Charter to the Crown. The government of Canada writes of this:

The land holdings of the company at one time were so vast that it controlled most of what is now Western Canada. This continued until 1870, when the company signed an agreement, the Deed of Surrender, transferring control of almost all its land to the British Crown. The British Crown in turn transferred control of these lands to the newly formed Dominion of Canada. The provinces of Manitoba, Saskatchewan and Alberta would eventually be carved out of Hudson's Bay Company lands.[53]

The 200-year de facto commercially-motivated and informed governance structure had profound impact upon Indigenous nations, communities, and families. It did not replace Indigenous governments or laws, but it most likely (as was the case with regard to Indigenous territories and nations) encroached on the border of those.

[50] Government of Canada, 'Key Economic Events' <http://www.canadianeconomy.gc.ca/english/economy/1670Hudsons_Bay_Company.html>.   [51] Ibid.
[52] Ibid.   [53] Ibid.

F. Early Documentation

1. Constitutional documents

The Royal Proclamation was proclaimed in force following the Seven Years War, in 1763. There was no way King George III could have known that the Proclamation would live and take its place in modern Canadian law and governance.[54] The Royal Proclamation[55] addressed the Crown wish to administer and regularize boundary and jurisdictional interests in the territories they had so recently settled upon. Interaction between the Indigenous peoples and settlers on the Indigenous territories possessed the potentiality to result in conflict. In declaring the Proclamation, the Crown was attempting to address, administratively, the unlawful settlement of and incursion into Indigenous territories. That the Proclamation itself broke several Indigenous laws, it can be presumed, went largely unnoticed. The notion of Indigenous consent (in line with the notion of Indigenous jurisdiction and legal acknowledgement of Indigenous land holdings) was built into the Proclamation. However, the Crown placed Crown consent ahead of Indigenous consent in the chain of potential land acquisition. This, in addition to the inclusion of political and legal understandings which were legally unintelligible[56] to Indigenous peoples (ie Crown sovereignty), resulted in a document which asserted protectionism but was in itself grounded in the same notions of superiority which it sought to protect Indigenous peoples from. Borrows writes of this:

To alleviate conflict, the Royal Proclamation was declared to delineate boundaries and define jurisdictions between First Nations and the Crown. The Proclamation attempted to convince First Nations that the British would respect existing political and territorial

---

[54] Canadian Charter of Rights and Freedoms being Part I of the Constitution Act 1982 s 25 reads in its entirety:

The guarantee in this Charter of certain rights and freedoms shall not be construed as to abrogate or derogate from any aboriginal, treaty or other rights or freedoms that pertain to the aboriginal peoples of Canada including
  (a) any rights or freedoms that have been recognized by the Royal Proclamation of October 7, 1763; and
  (b) any rights or freedoms that now exist by way of land claims agreements or may be so acquired.

[55] One author has called the Proclamation a 'treaty between First Nations and the Crown which has never been abridged or repealed, and which stands as a positive guarantee of First Nations self-government'. John Borrows, 'Constitutional Law from a First Nation Perspective: Self-Government and the Royal Proclamation' (1994) 28 Univ of British Columbia L Rev 1–47, para 4 <http://www.quicklaw.ca>.

[56] It should be noted that legal unintelligibility is linguistically, culturally, philosophically, and ethically informed. It is not merely a matter of written or spoken recording systems coming into conflict. Unintelligibility does not mean 'unknown', it may certainly mean not only a lack of shared systemic or linguistic meanings, but it can also mean that certain concepts and understandings are untranslatable.

jurisdiction by incorporating First Nations' understandings of this relationship in the document. The Proclamation does this by implying that no lands would be taken from First Nation peoples without their consent. However, in order to consolidate the Crown's position in North America, words were also placed in the Proclamation which did not accord with First Nations' viewpoints of the parties' relationship to one another and to the land. For example, the British inserted statements in the Proclamation that claimed 'dominion' and 'sovereignty' over the territories First Nations occupied. In placing these divergent notions within the Proclamation the British were trying to convince Native people that there was nothing to fear from the colonists, while at the same time trying to increase political and economic power relative to First Nations and other European powers.[57]

What appears from this is that the inherency and autonomy of Indigenous nations is, if tacitly, acknowledged. Certainly, English inherency of authority and autonomy is recognized. The notion that Indigenous rights are different than mere property rights (thus necessitating non-Indigenous governmental assurances of non-intrusion) is affirmed in the document.

The inclusion of consent as a precursor to the 'taking' of Indigenous lands is not a nicety. Entrenched in that understanding is the knowledge that not doing so would result in consequences that would impact the colonial settler peoples and government. Intrinsic to that consent is the (wrongful) notion of delegated inherency, and also some (wrongful) notion of a degree of delegated authority. That is, it can be stated with some assurance of accuracy that the colonial government assigned itself responsibility to make determinations about the rightfulness of transfer of Indigenous lands. Assigning itself legal capacity does indeed speak to the notion that colonial settlers incorrectly understood Indigenous peoples to have no laws, no standards, or understandings related to land and land transfer. However, by assigning itself legal capacity (and in the long term a duty) it also held itself out as expert in relation to lands and laws related to lands. The intellectual issue and ethical issue are not reflected in the legal issues that have arisen. The issue as this author understands it is this: Indigenous peoples had an expectation of continued relationships with our land, and that there would be protection of those relationships from intrusion by Her Majesty. No understanding of diminished sovereignty or the usurpation of authority (legal and otherwise) could or would have been understood. That the written text of the document continues to perpetuate the understanding that Indigenous peoples have a special relationship with our land is an important understanding. That it was understood to mean that Indigenous peoples were not capable of protecting their land was not necessarily so. That, legally, it has become an entrenched standard used to support some notion of Canadian 'legal carbon dating' the assertion or existence of non-Indigenous sovereignty is undoubtedly an issue entrenched within western legal traditions and mythology.

---

[57] Borrows, note 55, para 27.

Upon the formation of Canada,[58] Canada constitutionalized its obligation to and relationship with Indigenous peoples in section 91(24) of the (formerly) British North American Act 1867.[59] In a section dealing with the distribution of legislative powers, the powers of federal parliament (the legislative authority of the Parliament of Canada) were extended to Indian peoples and lands.[60]

Constitutionalizing the authority to make laws related to 'Indians, and Lands reserved for the Indians' accomplished at least three things: (1) Canada purported to (ostensibly) give itself Canadian legal authority for the lands (traditional territories, reserves, and other terrain) that Indigenous peoples had been occupants of and have had a relationship with since time immemorial. (2) It constitutionalized the relationship between 'Indians' and the government of Canada. (3) It linguistically 'captured' Indigenous peoples as 'Indians' and created a legal category of peoples who were to have a special relationship with the government of Canada.[61] Within the legislative authority Canada granted itself pursuant to section 91 were other such subjects (objects) as trade and commerce (2), census (6), navigation and shipping (10), currency and coinage (14), divorce and marriage (26), and criminal law (27).[62]

The objectification of 'Indians'—owning by naming and administering—is directly linked to and reminiscent of the Hudson's Bay Charter and the Royal Proclamation in that the government of the day presumed legislative and administrative authority for Indigenous peoples (in this case, Canadian legally defined and undifferentiated Indigenous peoples). It is no exaggeration to state that presumed legislative and administrative authority was tantamount to ownership. Housing the legal Indian not only constructed some notion of responsibility but also postponed for almost a century the necessity of discussion with Indigenous peoples as original peoples. As a result, there was no justification required for the infringement of Aboriginal or treaty rights until 1982.[63]

---

[58] Prior to Canadian Confederation, The Union Act 1840 initially joined Lower Canada and Upper Canada and established the Province of Canada (replacing the legislatures of both Upper and Lower Canada).   [59] The Constitution Act 1867.

[60] The provision provides, in its entirety:

91. It shall be lawful for the Queen, by and with the Advice and Consent of the Senate and House of Commons, to make Laws for the Peace, Order, and good Government of Canada, in relation to all Matters not coming within the Classes of Subjects by this Act assigned exclusively to the Legislatures of the Provinces; and for greater Certainty, but not so as to restrict the Generality of the foregoing Terms of this Section, it is hereby declared that (notwithstanding anything in this Act) the exclusive Legislative Authority of the Parliament of Canada extends to all Matters coming within the Classes of Subjects next hereinafter enumerated; that is to say,

24. Indians, and Lands reserved for the Indians.

[61] It should be noted that fiduciary obligations arose in each of these areas (with the degree being subject to litigation).   [62] The Constitution Act 1867 ss 2, 6, 10, 14, 26, and 27.

[63] Section 35(1) of the Constitution Act was enacted in this year. Constitution Act 1982, note 54. The meaning of the justification scheme was not fully enumerated until the *Sparrow* decision. *R v Sparrow* [1990] SCJ 49 (Supreme Court of Canada) <http://www.quicklaw.com>. Kent McNeil addresses this point, specifically, in his paper 'Section 91(24) Powers, the Inherent Right of Self-Government, and Canada's Fiduciary Obligations' (A research paper prepared for the Office of the

There is some notion of responsibility for the object Indian. The responsibility that is grounded in the attempt to usurp Indigenous lands and autonomies is one from which fiduciary duty obligations stem. However, there is also an imperial notion of ownership of the Indian that follows the Doctrine of Discovery. If the Doctrine takes its power from the notion of non-Christians requiring civilization, governments exercised that power in the next era of the Doctrine. The exercise of that power came in the form of the exercise of authority over the 'owned' Indian. Reflecting the proposition that stems from Roman law—that law serves to control, manage, and administer—the constitutional documents mentioned in this section were formulated to manage the obligation that the civilized peoples had to the uncivilized and owned peoples.

2. Treaties

The doctrines of discovery and *terra nullius* are two principles of international customary law that guided European colonization of foreign land. The doctrines stipulated that the first state to discover a new and 'empty' territory could assert their sovereignty by a symbolic act such as raising its flag or by effecting actual occupation of the territory. In the case of lands inhabited by Indigenous peoples, European settlers applied the doctrine of *terra nullius* with a unique twist, concluding that such lands were legally vacant despite the presence of bands of people organized according to their own societal customs. The Australian Court is careful to point out in *Mabo* that even this questionable assertion of sovereignty through discovery does not automatically give the incoming state full title to the land within the new territory, with the acquisition of title being guided by principles of the common law. The relevant common law provides that ownership of land cannot be asserted, even as an act of state, where land is already occupied.[64]

The (perhaps ironically) named Peace and Friendship Treaties were signed in the mid-1700s between the King's representative and Indigenous peoples on the eastern coast of Canada. The 1752 Peace and Friendship Treaty Between His Majesty the King and the Jean Baptiste Cope[65] had eight provisions in all. The Treaty was signed by 'Major Jean Baptiste Cope, chief Sachem of the Tribe of Mick Mack Indians Inhabiting the Eastern Coast of the said Province, and Andrew Hadley Martin, Gabriel Martin & Francis Jeremiah, Members and Delegates of the said Tribe, for themselves and their said Tribe their Heirs, and the Heirs of their Heirs forever...'.[66] Submisions and promises of peace,

BC Regional Vice-Chief of the Assembly of First Nations 2002) 6, <http://www.fngovernance.org/pdf/KentMcNeilFiduciary.pdf>.

[64] Kelley C Yukich, 'Aboriginal Rights in the Constitution and International Law' (1996) 30 Univ of British Columbia L Rev, para 70 <http://www.quicklaw.ca>.

[65] Peace and Friendship Treaty Between His Majesty the King and the Jean Baptiste Cope 1752, <http://www.ainc-inac.gc.ca/al/hts/tgu/pubs/pft1752/pft1752-eng.asp>.

[66] Ibid (Preamble).

the promise to bring other Indigenous peoples into peaceful alliance with the King and his subjects, the continuation of hunting and fishing, and the provision of truck houses so that the Indigenous parties might engage in commerce and trade were included in the Treaty.[67] Provisioning to the Indigenous parties for their families and the yearly presentation of presents (blankets, tobacco, powder and shot) were provided for in sections 5 and 6 of the Treaty.[68] Finally, the Treaty provided that all disputes between His Majesty's subjects and the Indigenous parties would be resolved in courts of civil judicature 'where the Indians shall have the same benefit, Advantages and Priviledges, as any others of His Majesty's Subjects'.[69] What is clear from the Treaty is that the colonizers needed Indigenous peoples' cooperation and support. What is also clear is that the economic viability of the Indigenous nations was important to His Majesty and that the nature of the relationship anticipated by the Treaty was reciprocal and mutually beneficial.

A second early treaty between Governor and Commander in Chief of the Province of Nova Scotia (on behalf of the King) and Chief Paul Laurent (on behalf of the LaHave tribe of Indians) addressed the jurisdiction and dominion of the King and the notion of peaceful coexistence between the Indigenous nation and His Majesty's subjects quite directly:

I, Paul Laurent do for myself and the tribe of LaHave Indians of which I am Chief do acknowledge the jurisdiction and Dominion of His Majesty George the Second over the Territories of Nova Scotia or Acadia and we do make submission to His Majesty in the most perfect, ample and solemn manner.

And I do promise for myself and my tribe that I nor they shall not molest any of His Majesty's subjects or their dependents, in their settlements already made or to be hereafter made or in carrying on their Commerce or in any thing whatever within the Province of His said Majesty or elsewhere and if any insult, robbery or outrage shall happen to be committed by any of my tribe satisfaction and restitution shall be made to the person or persons injured.[70]

The Treaty includes promises that the Indigenous nation's citizens will not harm the English, that they will release any English prisoners they hold, and that the nation will not ally with any of the King's enemies. Again, a truck house provision detailing the mutuality of trade was included in the 1760–1761 Treaty.[71] To what degree an acknowledgement of an Indigenous person of the King's jurisdiction and dominion can be held to be an agreement (and that it was clearly

---

[67] Ibid clauses 1, 3, and 4 respectively.

[68] Ibid clause 7 provided that 'the Indians shall use their best Endeavours to save the lives and goods of any People Shipwrecked on this Coast, where they resort, and shall Conduct the People saved to Halifax with their Goods, & a Reward adequate to the Salvadge shall be given them'. Ample evidence of reciprocal relationships and the necessity of good relations are evident in this Treaty.   [69] Ibid clause 8.

[70] Peace and Friendship Treaties Between His Majesty the King and the LaHave Tribe of Indians 1760–1 <http://www.ainc-inac.gc.ca/al/hts/tgu/pubs/pft176061/pft176061-eng.asp>.

[71] Ibid.

understood by the signatory) is of course questionable. The notions of foreign authority over Indigenous lands and the eradication of Indigenous governance, autonomy, and relationship with and responsibility for land need to be examined. While there is no discussion of conveyance or surrender, the understanding that jurisdiction for the province is housed in the King is not supported by the understanding that there is a distinction to be made between the tribe and His Majesty's subjects or dependents. Shared nationhood was not anticipated by this treaty. If the Doctrine of Discovery presumes Indigenous inferiority, then these treaties may be predicated on an associated axiom of the rightfulness of His Majesty's blanket authority to assume jurisdiction over territory.

The 1850 Robinson Treaty, which addressed the rights related to Indigenous territory on Lake Superior, was signed by 'Ojibewa' chiefs on behalf of the Indigenous nations and William Benjamin Robinson on behalf of the Queen. The Treaty included the following provision:

… the said chiefs and principal men do freely, fully and voluntarily surrender, cede, grant and convey unto Her Majesty, Her heirs and successors forever, all their right, title and interest in the whole of the territory above described, save and except the reservations set forth in the schedule hereunto annexed, which reservations shall be held and occupied by the said Chiefs and their Tribes in common, for the purpose of residence and cultivation, and should the said Chiefs and their respective Tribes at any time desire to dispose of any mineral or other valuable productions upon the said reservations, the same will be at their request sold by order of the Superintendent General of the Indian Department for the time being, for their sole use and benefit, and to the best advantage.[72]

The inclusion of the cede, release, and surrender provision addressed the 'rights, title and interest' of the Indigenous nations. There was an exchange anticipated by the Treaty. The Indigenous nations were to receive 2,000 pounds and a perpetual annuity of 500 pounds as a result of the Treaty.[73] Continuing mineral rights on lands reserved for the Indigenous peoples were anticipated by the Treaty. While included in the Treaty, the ability to sell the rights or reserve land was subject to Crown approval. The notion of protectionism educes the premise of the Royal Proclamation (and which is referent to the false notion of the childlike or exploited nature of Indigenous peoples integral to the Doctrine of Discovery): Indigenous people require protection from the Crown's subjects. The rights to hunt and fish over the territory, treaty annuities, and a promise not to hinder Her Majesty's subjects who are exploring for minerals or 'other valuable productions' were included in the document.

Similarly, the Robinson Treaty of 1850 signed by the 'Ojibewa' Indians of Lake Huron and William Benjamin Robinson on behalf of the Queen addressed

[72] Copy of the Robinson Treaty Made in the Year 1850 with the Ojibewa Indians of Lake Superior Conveying Certain Lands to the Crown, seventh day of September, in the year of Our Lord one thousand eight hundred and fifty <http://www.ainc-inac.gc.ca/al/hts/tgu/pubs/trob/rbt2/rbt2-eng.asp>.   [73] Ibid.

the conveyance of Indigenous traditional territories to the Crown.[74] The terms included a payment of 2,000 pounds and a 'further perpetual annuity of six hundred pounds of like money, the same to be paid and delivered to the said Chiefs and their Tribes at a convenient season of each year...'.[75] In addition, similar provisions as were made in the treaty with the Indigenous peoples inhabiting the territory around Lake Superior were provided.[76]

The exacting of promises not to interfere with exploration provides some contextualization of the rationale for the Treaty. It also addresses the fallacy of Indigenous citizenship transmuting to Canadian citizenship upon 'discovery', treaty making, or some other constructed event.

There are a number of other treaties with First Nations that were signed after the Robinson-Huron Treaties and before the numbered Treaties which Her Majesty held out as conveyances and a surrender of title. The Douglas Treaties (1850–1875) signed between coastal Indigenous nations and the Hudson's Bay Company were quite uniform in their construction. One term provided:

The conditions of our understanding of this sale is this, that our village sites and enclosed fields are to be kept for our own use, for the use of our children, and for those who may follow after us and the land shall be properly surveyed hereafter. It is understood, however, that the land itself, with these small exceptions, becomes the entire property of the white people for ever; it is also understood that we are at liberty to hunt over the unoccupied lands, and to carry on our fisheries as formerly.

We have received, as payment, Forty-eight pounds six shillings and eight pence.[77]

Treating the Treaty like a sale and as a transfer of the entirety of the property to 'white people for ever' is, like many of the treaties, predicated on the notion that the relationship to their land could be severed by Indigenous peoples. In actuality, it would be an exceptionally rare circumstance within which any individual would be given authority by the citizenship to do this. The concept would be a foreign one and likely to be quite incapable of translation.

The numbered treaties include 11 treaties numbered 1–11 and were signed from 1871 to 1921. There is a significant divergence between Indigenous advocates' understanding related to the Treaties and Canadian authorities' interpretation of the numbered treaties. Much has been written about the literal interpretation applied by the government of Canada in its interpretation and

[74] Copy of the Robinson Treaty Made in the Year 1850 with the Ojibewa Indians of Lake Huron Conveying Certain Lands to the Crown <http://www.ainc-inac.gc.ca/al/hts/tgu/pubs/trob/rbt/rbt-eng.asp>.   [75] Ibid.

[76] Ibid. An additional provision was provided, in the event that additional Indigenous nations should desire to become included in the Treaty: 'The said William Benjamin Robinson of the first part further agrees, on the part of Her Majesty and the Government of this Province, that in consequence of the Indians inhabiting French River and Lake Nipissing having become parties to this treaty, the further sum of one hundred and sixty pounds Provincial Currency shall be paid in addition to the two thousand pounds above mentioned.'

[77] Douglas Treaties—Conveyance of Land to Hudson's Bay Company by Indian Tribes (1 May 1850) <http://www.ainc-inac.gc.ca/al/hts/tgu/pubs/trtydg/trtydg-eng.asp>.

legal position related to the written treaties. Less well known but equally important is the understanding that there is also an oral version of the Treaties and that
the Treaties need to be understood with reference to and in the context of the
spirit and intent of the agreements. A few authors address the spirit and intent
of the Treaties and the notion that treaty making occurred between equal parties—both of which had mandates that they could not overreach.[78] Given the
limited authority of treaty signatories (Indigenous parties to the Treaty almost
universally maintain that their laws and legal orders would not allow for the
transfer, sale or ceding, releasing or surrendering of land) it is exceptionally difficult to support the interpretation of the documents as ones which could usurp
Indigenous authority for Indigenous lands.[79] Treaty 1+, between Her Majesty
and the Chippewa, Swampy Cree, and other Indigenous peoples included this
provision:

The Chippewa and Swampy Cree Tribes of Indians and all other the Indians inhabiting
the district hereinafter described and defined do hereby cede, release, surrender and yield

---

[78] The issues related to the limitations on the authority of the Indigenous signatories by the
Indigenous citizenship (and in accordance with Indigenous legal orders) are detailed in works
about the oral tradition and understood laws told by Elders with respect to Treaties 6, 7, and
8. Respectively, these legal histories, legal orders, and governmental autonomies are detailed in
the following works: Harold Cardinal and Walter Hildebrandt, *Treaty Elders*, note 4; Walter
Hildebrandt, Dorothy First Rider, Sarah Carter, Treaty 7 Elders, and Tribal Council, *The True
Spirit and Original Intent of Treaty 7* (Montreal: McGill-Queen's University Press, 1996); Sharon
Venne, 'Understanding Treaty 6: An Indigenous Perspective' in Michael Asch, *Aboriginal and
Treaty Rights in Canada: Essays on Law, Equality, and Respect* (Vancouver: UBC Press, 1997)
173–207.

[79] The numbered treaties are generally known for their inclusion of 'cede, release and surrender' provisions. For additional reading related to the provisions, see the Royal Commission on
Aboriginal Peoples, *Report of the Commission on Aboriginal Peoples* <http://www.collectionscanada.
gc.ca/webarchives/20071124130154/ and http://www.ainc-inac.gc.ca/ch/rcap/sg/ska5a1_e.
html#Appendix%20A:%20Summary%20of%20Recommendations,%20Volumes%201-5>,
recommendations providing:

2.2.4
The spirit and intent of the historical treaties be implemented in accordance with the following
fundamental principles: . . .

d) There is a presumption in respect of the historical treaties that
  • treaty nations did not intend to consent to the blanket extinguishment of their Aboriginal
    rights and title by entering into the treaty relationship;
  • treaty nations intended to share the territory and jurisdiction and management over it, as
    opposed to ceding the territory, even where the text of an historical treaty makes reference to a
    blanket extinguishment of land rights; and
  • treaty nations did not intend to give up their inherent right of governance by entering into
    a treaty relationship, and the act of treaty making is regarded as an affirmation rather than
    a denial of that right.

With regard to new treaties and agreements, the Commission recommends that

2.2.6
The federal government establish a process for making new treaties to replace the existing
comprehensive claims policy, based on the following principles:

  (a) The blanket extinguishment of Aboriginal land rights is not an option . . .

up to Her Majesty the Queen and successors forever all the lands included within the following limits...[80]

That this was an Indigenous legal impossibility and that it appeared in a language that few Chippewa and Swampy Cree could speak, let alone write, did not receive much analysis until the latter part of the twentieth century. Indeed, the notion that the 'discovery' of the territory led to the right to confine Indigenous peoples to portions of it in order to facilitate settlement of the discoverers or discovery of other types (minerals, resources, oil and gas) has not been fully examined to date.[81]

Treaty No 11:

AND WHEREAS the said Commissioner has proceeded to negotiate a treaty with the Slave, Dogrib, Loucheux, Hare and other Indians inhabiting the district hereinafter defined and described, which has been agreed upon and concluded by the respective bands at the dates mentioned hereunder, the said Indians do hereby cede, release, surrender and yield up to the Government of the Dominion of Canada, for His Majesty the King and His Successors forever, all their rights, titles, and privileges whatsoever to the lands included within the following limits, that is to say...[82]

Having expanded on that which the Canadian government understood could be ceded, released, and surrendered between 1871 and 1921 the notion it had of Indigenous landholdings narrowed as well. While this is considered by Canada to be cessation by agreement, McNeil has written of the Indigenous understanding (quoting Leroy Littlebear):

Although Canadian law allows for the surrender of Aboriginal title to the Crown, this does not mean that it is surrenderable under Aboriginal law. Leroy Little Bear has explained that Aboriginal peoples generally did not have a concept of land ownership that would have included authority to transfer absolute title to the Crown. They received their land from the Creator, subject to certain conditions, including an obligation to share it with plants and animals. Moreover, the land belongs not just to living Aboriginal persons, but to past and future generations as well. He concluded:

In summary, the standard or norm of the aboriginal peoples' law is that land is not transferable and therefore is inalienable. Land and benefits therefrom may be shared with others, and when Indian nations entered into treaties with European nations, the subject of the treaty, from the Indians' viewpoint, was not the alienation of the land but the sharing of the land.[83]

---

[80] Alexander Morris, *The Treaties of Canada with the Indians of Manitoba and the North-West Territories, Including the Negotiations on Which They Were Based, and Other Information Relating Thereto* (Toronto: Belfords, Clarke & Co, 1880) (Fifth House Publishers, Saskatoon 1991) 314.

[81] While we are often surprised by the notion of 'discovering' Indigenous territories and the dehumanization of Indigenous peoples through such ancillary legal understandings and theories as *terra nullius,* Indigenous territories are still overrun by government and corporate entities professing to 'discover' minerals and resources.

[82] Treaty No 11 (27 June 1921) and Adhesion (17 July 1922) with Reports, etc <http://www.ainc-inac.gc.ca/al/hts/tgu/pubs/t11/trty11-eng.asp>.

[83] Kent McNeil, 'Extinguishment of Aboriginal Title in Canada: Treaties, Legislation, and Judicial Discretion' (2001–02) 33 Ottawa L Rev 301–46, para 4 <http://www.quicklaw.ca>, quoting Leroy Little Bear, 'Aboriginal Rights and the Canadian "Grundnorm"' in *Arduous*

The same understanding of Indigenous illegality and extinguishment impossibility is shared by the Elders in Treaty 6, Treaty 7, and Treaty 8. The Indigenous signatories to the treaties understood themselves to be entering into agreements to share the land.[84] To the degree that there is any agreement, it was certainly not to cede, release, and surrender territoriality or responsibility for the land as such was an impossibility.

If colonial powers utilized the Doctrine of Discovery to rationalize 'taking' Indigenous lands, then the treaty policy which confined Indigenous people to reserves and allowed settlers to settle in Indigenous traditional territories and 'discover' natural resources that Indigenous citizens were not able to access was a policy which housed itself upon the doctrine. The ideology of Indigenous peoples as owned and moveable objects and controllable absolutely is a derivative of the false authority and beliefs housed in the Doctrine of Discovery.

3. Legislation

The theory of sovereignty acquired by discovery becomes entrenched in constitutional documents and treaties. It also becomes entrenched in legislation and habituated by its incorporation into legislative regimes through assumptive applicability and the assumed inferiority of Indigenous peoples. In Canada, the legislative history is rich with the notion of legislative 'othering'. Indigenous peoples are understood not to exist for the purposes of determinations related to sovereignty, to exist for the purposes of land acquisition, and to exist as non-Canadians insofar as determinations are made with respect to governance and citizenship of the nations. While Indigenous territory was assumed to be vacant for the purposes of the assertion of foreign sovereignty, there can be no doubt that Her Majesty's representatives understood that cession was quite necessary to acquire and rule Indigenous territories (whether or not there was a shared understanding in this regard is, as mentioned, a live debate). As a result, the conceptualization of the Doctrine of Discovery and the belief in the supremacy of non-Indigenous peoples which sustains and perpetuates the Doctrine becomes embedded in Canadian legislative regimes that apply to Indigenous peoples.

In this aspect, it is quite significant to follow the tendrils of imperialism from the Doctrine of Discovery as they spread to the roots of contemporary colonial ideologies. The Department of the Secretary of State for Canada was the Superintendent General of Indian Affairs, inextricably tying the colonial government to control and management of Indigenous peoples' (defined as 'Indians') lands and property in 1868.[85] Canada constructed trusts for reserved lands and mandated that they

---

Journey: Canadian Indians and Decolonization (Toronto: McClelland & Stewart, J R Ponting, (ed), 1986) 243, 247.

[84] Cardinal at Hildebrandt, note 4, 39.

[85] An Act providing for the organisation of the Department of the Secretary of State of Canada, and for the management of Indian and Ordnance Lands 1868 s 5.

could not be sold, leased, or alienated 'until they have been released or surrendered to the Crown for the purposes of this Act'.[86] Furthermore, Canada legally empowered itself to 'deal with' monies from sales of land and timber in the way it had always done (although how it had always been done was not specified in the legislation).[87] Finally, the government of Canada defined the conditions of surrender of Indian lands within the legislation. The terms under which an Indigenous nation could do so were circumscribed in accordance with western principles of good governance, which may have had nothing to do with Indigenous nations' laws, understandings, and principles related to good governance. The imperial notion of universal alienability to foreign autocrats is also embedded in the legislation. Surrender was to take place in conformance with chief(s)' assent and 'if there be more than one chief, by a majority of the chiefs of the tribe, band or body of Indians, assembled at a meeting or council of the tribe, band or body summoned for that purpose according to their rules and entitled under this Act to vote thereat' with the Secretary of State or an authorized officer present.[88]

The supposition that land is alienable and that Indigenous nations possessed no system of decision making is referential to and authenticated by the premise of the Doctrine of Discovery: Indigenous peoples were not true occupants and could not truly occupy territory. However, while the acquisition of sovereignty proceeded on that basis, occupation was presumed in the legislation for the purposes of land transfer. The territory was not presumed to be vacant and the legislation was undoubtedly enacted and applied to address the very real occupancy, possession, or the inherent territoriality of Indigenous nations.

What constituted lawful possession was without question on the minds of Canadian legislators when they enacted An Act for the gradual enfranchisement of Indians in 1869.[89] Section 1 of the legislation provided:

In Townships or other tracts of land set apart or reserved for Indians in Canada, and subdivided by survey into lots, no Indian or person claiming to be of Indian blood, or intermarried with an Indian family, shall be deemed to be lawfully in possession of any land in such Townships or tracts, unless he or she has been or shall be located for the same by the order of the Superintendent General of Indian affairs...[90]

In this way, the Doctrine of Discovery ideology related to the presumption sovereign authority (ie the power to determine the location of Indians) ran parallel to the notion of lawful possession by Indians. This territory was clearly not presumed to be vacant and there was a clear obligation that the Crown was addressing. It should be considered as well that the Crown formulated and captured in

---

86　Ibid s 6.　　87　Ibid s 7.　　88　Ibid s 8.1.

89　An Act for the Gradual Enfranchisement of Indians, the Better Management of Indian Affairs, and to Extend the Provisions of the Act 31st Victoria 1869 (Enfranchisement Act). This Act was not the first of its kind. It was preceded by the pre-Canadian (before 1867) An Act to encourage the gradual Civilization of the Indian Tribes in this Province, and to amend the Laws respecting Indians 1857. The legislation included provisions related to blood quantum and Indian identification as a result of the same.　　　　　90　Enfranchisement Act s 1.

the legislation just how much Indian was 'Indian enough' to lawfully entitle a person to share in annuities, interest or rents on lands possessed by Indians (a person of ¼ Indian blood).[91] The unification of blood quantum,[92] monies received from Indian lands, and lawful possession of those lands in one statute speaks directly to imperialism and the possibility of the same stems from the hegemonic propositions of the Doctrine of Discovery.

The statute also placed pressure on traditional Indigenous governments by attempting to enforce western standards related to governance, municipal governmental authority, and elections on Indians. Nations that had elegantly and successfully applied their authority for generations found themselves subject to foreign standards and ostensible constrictions on some of their activities.[93] Section 16 provided the terms of voluntary enfranchisement whereby an Indigenous person could elect to 'give up' Indian status. The Doctrine of Discovery is evident, to some degree, in this provision as well. Indigenous peoples legally defined as Indians were able to elect to forgo 'Indian' status (fused to some degree with citizenship and communal territoriality) in favour of national alliance with Canada. It is interesting to note that there was a choice to be made here: an election to do so is a voluntary one, a choice to select Canadian nationhood and to adopt Canadian leadership, governance, citizenship and potentially, sovereignty. If an individual chose not to enfranchise, then seemingly s/he maintained Indigenous leadership, governance, citizenship, and sovereignty. In accordance with this view, then Indigenous autonomy could be understood to continue until an Indian elected not to be subject to the laws and governments of the nations that possessed the same.

However, such a favourable interpretation of Canadian legislation would be a rarity, given the preponderance of restrictive provisions in the Canadian laws

---

[91] Enfranchisement Act s 4.

[92] More than a determination of blood quantum was made in the statute. The blood referred to was predominantly male blood. Indian women who married non-Indian men (and her children) were not considered to be Indian peoples under this Act. If an Indian woman married an Indian man from another tribe, the children of the union were considered members of his tribe, automatically (section 6). This phallo-centric ownership of Indian identity still has resonance in our contemporary nations, communities, and families.

[93] Enfranchisement Act s 10. This section provides for the removal of Chiefs from office for such things as 'dishonesty, intemperance, or immorality' and the number of Chiefs. Section 12 provides:

12. The Chief or Chiefs of any Tribe in Council may frame, subject to confirmation by the Governor in Council, rules and regulations for the following subjects, viz:
   1. The care of the public health.
   2. The observance of order and decorum at assemblies of the people in General Council, or on other occasions.
   3. The repression of intemperance and profligacy.
   4. The prevention of trespass by cattle.
   5. The maintenance of roads, bridges, ditches and fences.
   6. The construction of and maintaining in repair of school houses, council houses and other Indian public buildings.
   7. The establishment of pounds and the appointment of pound-keepers.

pertaining to Indigenous peoples. In admitting Rupert's Land and the North-Western Territory into the Dominion of Canada,[94] the issue of Indigenous territoriality and land holdings was addressed directly. In establishing the terms of the land transfer, section 30 provided:

All ungranted or waste lands in the Province shall be, from and after the date of the said transfer, vested in the Crown, and administered by the Government of Canada for the purposes of the Dominion, subject to, and except and so far as the same may be affected by, the conditions and stipulations contained in the agreement for the surrender of Rupert's Land by the Hudson's Bay Company to Her Majesty.[95]

This notion of absolute ownership upon annexation is grounded in the principles inherent in the Doctrine of Discovery. However, the Canadian government clearly demonstrated its recognition and acceptance of Aboriginal title in the statute as well.[96]

When the Canadian Department of the Interior was established in 1880, the Department ostensibly took responsibility for the 'the control and management of the lands and property of the Indians in Canada'.[97] The notion of Canadian governmental discretion, the ability to choose whether or not the provisions of this (or other) act/s applied to Indigenous peoples, has its source in authoritarian approaches to settlement in Indigenous territories. It devalues Indigenous humanity and attempts to eliminate Indigenous rights and authorities through mere disregard. Ignoring Indigenous legal orders and governmental authorities results in a constructive legislative *terra nullius*—where Indigenous sovereignty, governmental autonomy, and legal orders are supposed to be non-existent.

In 1874 the government of Canada enacted An Act to amend certain Laws respecting Indians, and to extend certain Laws relating to matters connected with Indians to the Provinces of Manitoba and British Columbia.[98] With provisions related to the prohibition of and punishment for the provision of intoxicants to

[94] An Act to Amend and Continue the Act 32 and 33 Victoria, Chapter 3; and to Establish and Provide for the Government of the Province of Manitoba 1870.   [95] Ibid s 30.
[96] Ibid s 31. Section 31 provides, with respect to the government's recognition of Aboriginal title:

31. And whereas, it is expedient, towards the extinguishment of the Indian Title to the lands in the Province, to appropriate a portion of such ungranted lands, to the extent of one million four hundred thousand acres thereof, for the benefit of the families of the half-breed residents, it is hereby enacted, that, under regulations to be from time to time made by the Governor General in Council, the Lieutenant-Governor shall select such lots or tracts in such parts of the Province as he may deem expedient, to the extent aforesaid, and divide the same among the children of the half-breed heads of families residing in the Province at the time of the said transfer to Canada, and the same shall be granted to the said children respectively, in such mode and on such conditions as to settlement and otherwise, as the Governor General in Council may from time to time determine.

[97] An Act to further amend 'The Indian Act, 1880' 1873.
[98] An Act to amend certain Laws respecting Indians, and to extend certain Laws relating to matters connected with Indians to the Provinces of Manitoba and British Columbia 1874.

Indians, the Act is noteworthy as it also extended the definition of 'Indian' to include 'and who shall participate in the annuities and interest moneys and rents of any tribe, band or body of Indians'.[99]

This was the precursor to the first incarnation of Canada's Indian Act.[100] The Indian Act 1876 consolidated previous Canadian legislation with respect to people defined as Indians. As a result, the Act enumerates specifications for a number of matters related to Indian peoples. The areas addressed include definitions for bands (any tribe, band, or body of Indians who own or are interested in a reserve or in Indian lands in common, of which the legal title is vested in the Crown, or who share alike in the distribution of any annuities or interest moneys for which the government of Canada is responsible);[101] defining the term 'Indian';[102] and defining the term 'reserve'.[103] Importantly, two other terms are defined at the outset of the legislation. At section 8, 'Indian lands' is said to mean 'any reserve or portion of a reserve which has been surrendered to the Crown'.[104] Linguistically (although many would argue not legally), this eliminates the notion of Indigenous territoriality outside of reserves. The embedded notion of non-reserve territory and lands as acquiring Canadian sovereignty exemplifies the Doctrine of Discovery axioms of deemed territorial land holding and implicitly transferred sovereign power. Additionally, the Doctrine of Discovery imperative of dehumanization as a justification for an interpretation of land as vacant and governance as absent is explicitly housed in the statute. Section 12 provides:

12. The term 'person' means an individual other than an Indian, unless the context clearly requires another construction.[105]

The relationship that Indians could Canadian legally have with land was circumscribed in the Act. Reserve lands were defined within the legislation, the capacity to hold lots,[106] the granting of location tickets,[107] the passing of estates upon death,[108] leases and other conveyances,[109] and punishments for Indians and non-Indians who unlawfully reside on, use, or trespass on Indian lands are addressed.[110]

---

[99] Ibid s 8.
[100] An Act to amend and consolidate the laws respecting Indians 1867 (ibid).
[101] Ibid s 3.1.
[102] Ibid s 3. 'The term "Indian" means *First.* Any male person of Indian blood reputed to belong to a particular band; *Secondly.* Any child of such person; *Thirdly.* Any woman who is or was lawfully married to such person ...'. The remainder of the provision deals with the circumstances arising in which peoples may or may not be determined to be Indian (ie illegitimacy, Indian women 'marry out', etc).
[103] Ibid s 6. 'The term "reserve" means any tract or tracts of land set apart by treaty or otherwise for the use or benefit of or granted to a particular band of Indians, of which the legal title is in the Crown, but which is unsurrendered, and includes all the trees, wood, timber, soil, stone, minerals, metals, or other valuables thereon or therein'.
[104] Indian Act 1876 s 8.
[105] Ibid s 12. [106] Ibid s 6. [107] Ibid s 7. [108] Ibid s 9. [109] Ibid s 11.
[110] Ibid ss 13, 16, and 17.

The terms and process for surrender of Indian lands and for the management and sale of timber are provided for in sections 25–57. The Crown required that all sales, leases, and alienation occur only after release or surrender by the Indian band to the Crown.[111] In order to have a lawful surrender, a majority vote would have to be made in favour of the same.[112] In fact, the Department assumed responsibility for all of the money matters of the Indians, going so far as to direct the nature and amount of investment monies to be directed to Indians, management of the reserve, or repairs to roads, etc, upon sale of lands, property, timber, or other sources.[113] As well, 'The proceeds arising from the sale or lease of any Indian lands, or from the timber, hay, stone, minerals or other valuables thereon, or on a reserve, shall be paid to the Receiver General to the credit of the Indian fund.'[114]

The absolute management of Indian reserve lands, land surrenders, and resource sales situated (and to some extent, still situates) authority for reserve lands in the government of Canada. The construction of this authority, this acquisition of power, is ancillary to the precepts which inform the Doctrine of Discovery. Transferring power (some would argue that only administrative power was transferred and that Indigenous peoples retain the sovereign and inherent right to make autonomous decisions) through statute reifies and rationalizes alienation and alienability. It can be read, in an Indigenist context, as an attempt to codify the usurpation of authority. For example, in the 1876 Act as well, traditional and custom Indigenous government styles and governance authorities remain unaddressed. Indeed, singular Chiefs and numerically significant councillors (with each band receiving a councillor for every 200 Indians) were legislatively entrenched as the governing body, regardless of the traditional governance system in place.[115]

The Indian Act 1876 did pull together disparate legislative enactments into one place, but it is easy to see that surrender and resource management[116] and enfranchisement[117] were key issues in the document.

---

[111] Ibid s 25.

[112] Ibid s 26(1)—only 'habitual residents' could participate in the vote. Subsection 3 provided that the Superintendent General could issue a licence to anyone (subject to band consent) 'to cut and remove trees, wood, timber and hay, or to quarry and remove stone and gravel on and from the reserve'.   [113] Indian Act 1876 s 59.

[114] Ibid s 60.

[115] Ibid s 62. It should be noted that many Indigenous nations did eventually follow the Indian Act constructed government. However, many did and still have custom and traditional governments operating instead of, in accordance with, or parallel to the statute enforced mandated band councils.

[116] The Indian Act 1876 also seems to have been a laundry list of going concerns that settler peoples had about original peoples. For example, Indians were not to be taxed on real or personal property (s 64) or land that was held in trust for them (s 65). Indians could not get mortgages (s 66) and Indians (treaty and non-treaty) could sue for debts owed them, torts, or to compel performance of an obligation (s 67).   [117] Indian Act 1876 ss 86–94.

4. Early case law

On 12 December 1888 the Judicial Committee of the Privy Council (Earl of Selborne, Lord Watson, Lord Hobhouse, Sir Barnes Peacock, Sir Montague E Smith, Sir Richard Couch) reached a decision in an appeal from the Supreme Court of Canada in *St Catherine's Milling and Lumber Company v The Queen*.[118] In what was to become the Canadian legal standard related to Indigenous land rights for almost a century, the Privy Council's Judicial Committee examined a dispute between the provincial and federal crowns in order to determine who had rights to Indian territories. It is notable that Indians were not included in the decision and were only referred to in terms of the content of the Royal Proclamation of 1763, the effect of the British North America Act 1867 on Provincial and Federal rights to Indian lands and resources, and the 'Ojibbeway' Treaty of 3 October 1873.

The lands in this case were lands identified as being within the province of Ontario border. The issue identified by the Judicial Committee of the Privy Council was whether the land in question belonged to Canada or to Ontario.[119] In order to arrive at the answer to this question, the Committee had to examine the nature of the territorial interests held in the land by virtue of the constitutional provisions, legislation, and treaty noted above. In this specific instance, the appellant logging company (St Catharine's Milling) cut timber on lands with a licence from the Dominion, but no authority from the province.[120] The Supreme Court of Canada had found in favour of the Province[121] and, as a result, the Dominion of Canada applied for intervenor status at the Judicial Committee.[122]

Lord Watson delivered the decision of the Judicial Committee.[123] Initially, he addressed the provisions of the Treaty entered into with the Ojibway leadership. Specifically, he looked to the portion of the Treaty that includes the 'cede, release and surrender' provisions.[124] Acting on the assumption that the beneficial

---

[118] *St Catherine's Milling and Lumber Company v The Queen* (1888) 14 AC 46 (also reported: 58 LJPC 54, 60 LT 197, 5 TLR 125, 4 Cart BNA 107) (a Privy Council Judicial Committee case).

[119] Ibid 542 (47).

[120] Ibid.

[121] *St Catharine's Milling and Lumber Company v The Queen* (1887), 13 SCR 577 (also reported: 4 Cart BNA 127) (a Supreme Court case). In that decision, discovery was directly addressed when (at 473–4 and 609–10) the Court held:

> That his (sic) peaceful conduct of the Indians is in a great degree to be attributed to the recognition of their rights to lands unsurrendered by them, and to the guarantee of their protection in the possession and enjoyment of such lands given by the crown in the proclamation of October, 1763, hereafter to be more fully noticed, is a well known fact of Canadian history which cannot be controverted.   [122] *St Catharine's Milling*, note 118, 542 (47).

[123] Ibid 546 (51).

[124] Ibid 546–7. Included is text to provide the reader with a notion of the thoroughness and complexity of the Treaty term:

> by which the latter, for certain considerations, released and surrendered to the Government of the Dominion, for Her Majesty and her successors, the whole right and title of the Indian inhabitants whom they represented, to a tract of country upwards of 50,000 square miles in extent. By

interest in these lands had passed to the Dominion Government, (their Crown Timber Agent)[125] the Dominion of Canada issued a permit to the milling company to cut timber from the area in dispute.

Lord Watson noted the role of timber in the dispute, but acknowledged that the real nature of the dispute was based upon '. . . determination of the larger question between that govern ment and the province of Ontario with respect to the legal consequences of the treaty of 1873'.[126] In order to be able to analyse the law and arrive at a conclusion, Lord Watson examined the historical record (available to him) and noted that the 'capture of Quebec in 1759, and the capitulation of Montreal in 1760, were followed in 1763 by the cession to Great Britain of Canada and all its dependencies, with the sovereignty, property, and possession, and all other rights which had at any previous time been held or acquired by the Crown of France'.[127] No mention was made of Indigenous sovereignty, property and possession, and all other rights. The assumption was that these moved directly from the Crown of France to the Crown of Her Majesty.

Lord Watson went on to review the Royal Proclamation of 1763,[128] noting the geographic boundaries of the same, the non-molestation and non-disturbance clause, the continuing use of 'non-ceded' lands as hunting grounds, and that no private person could purchase Indian lands.[129] Reserving under their own sovereignty lands and territories for the use of Indians,[130] the implicit assumption of colonial ownership via discovery by any European nation was evidently enough legal authority to divest Indigenous peoples of their own within the British legal traditions.

The Court held, of this authority and the divestiture of Indigenous sovereignty:

Whilst there have been changes in the administrative authority, there has been no change since the year 1763 in the character of the interest which its Indian inhabitants had in the lands surrendered by the treaty. Their possession, such as it was, can only be ascribed to the general provisions made by the royal proclamation in favour of all Indian tribes then living under the sovereignty and protection of the British Crown.[131]

---

an article of the treaty it is stipulated that, subject to such regulations as may be made by the Dominion Government, the Indians are to have right to pursue their avocations of hunting and fishing throughout the surrendered territory, with the exception of those portions of it which may, from time to time, be required or taken up for settlement, mining, lumbering, or other purposes. Of the territory thus ceded to the Crown, an area of not less than 32,000 square miles is situated within the boundaries of the Province of Ontario; and, with respect to that area, a controversy has arisen between the Dominion and Ontario, each of them maintaining that the legal effect of extinguishing the Indian title has been to transmit to itself the entire beneficial interest of the lands, as now vested in the Crown, freed from incumbrance of any kind, save the qualified privilege of hunting and fishing mentioned in the treaty.

[125] Ibid 547 (52).   [126] Ibid 548 (53).
[127] Ibid.   [128] Ibid 549 (54).   [129] Ibid.   [130] Ibid 548–9 (53)–(54).
[131] Ibid 549 (54).

Indigenous nations, presumably, would disagree that the source of their interest in their traditional territories was the beneficence and sovereign will which 'protected them'. The notion that:

[t]heir possession, such as it was, can only be ascribed to the general provisions made by the royal proclamation in favour of all Indian tribes then living under the sovereignty and protec-tion of the British Crown. That inference is, however, at variance with the terms of the instrument, which shew that the tenure of the Indians was a personal and usufructuary right, dependent upon the good will of the Sovereign[132]

was likely to be, and is, unsupportable under and in breach of Indigenous legal orders. The 'tenure of the Indians' was addressed by the Court as an ancillary issue, and they went on to find that '[t]he lands reserved are expressly stated to be "parts of Our dominions and territories;" and it is declared to be the will and pleasure of the sovereign that, "for the present," they shall be reserved for the use of the Indians, as their hunting grounds, under his protection and dominion'.[133] Deeply entrenched within this is the mythologizing of Indigenous peoples' relationships with and rights to their land. A constructed notion of dependency (dependent upon Crown rightfulness, Crown protection and dominion, Crown sovereignty and will) had to be established in order to enable a new casting of Indigenous rights and titles. Those rights, as constructed by the colonizer in accordance with the held understandings in the Doctrine of Discovery, were to be secondary, dependent, and derivative rights. In order to do so, the Committee had to address the presumed inherent supremacy of the Crown and the implicit and understood inferiority of Indigenous peoples, and therefore rights.

In order to arrive at this notion of derivative and inferior rights, Indigenous inferiority had to be constructed in the law. In this regard, Lord Watson was able to deliver: 'It appears to them to be sufficient for the purposes of this case that there has been all along vested in the Crown a substantial and paramount estate, underlying the Indian title, which became a plenum dominium whenever that title was surrendered or otherwise extinguished.'[134]

The mythical construction of an underlying and paramount estate is, at heart, grounded in the notion of the Doctrine of Discovery. Built upon the notion of inherent savagery and inability to hold land as the result of some secondary humanity, any rights that Indigenous peoples held were found to be subject to the superior and paramount title of the colonizers. While legally and lawfully impossible, the constructivist law achieved the impossible: to divest Indigenous peoples of their rights without addressing the nature of them, their lawful claim as humans, or the laws that would require settlers to resolve original Indigenous owners' rights.

The Judicial Committee went on to consider whether federal or provincial Crown rights were in place in the territory (as it was presumed that Indigenous

[132] Ibid.   [133] Ibid 550 (55).   [134] Ibid.

rights warranted no discussion) as Indigenous rights were not understood to be paramount rights:

There was no transfer to the Province of any legal estate in the Crown lands, which continued to be vested in the Sovereign; but all moneys realized by sales or in any other manner became the property of the Province. In other words, all beneficial interest in such lands within the provincial boundaries belonging to the Queen, and either producing or capable of producing revenue, passed to the Province, the title still remaining in the Crown.[135]

The Committee went on to say that that was the state of things until the British North America Act 1867:

Had the Indian inhabitants of the area in question released their interest in it to the Crown at any time between 1840 and the date of that Act, it does not seem to admit of doubt, and it was not disputed by the learned counsel for the Dominion, that all revenues derived from its being taken up for settlement, mining, lumbering, and other purposes would have been the property of the Province of Canada.[136]

The Judicial Committee also examined provincial authorities for land, mines, and minerals as included in the Act in section 109.[137] Dealt with as a straight interpretation addressing the authority of the federal Crown under section 91(24) and section 109, the Judicial Committee found that:

The enactments of sect. 109 are, in the opinion of their Lordships, sufficient to give to each Province, subject to the administration and control of its own Legislature, the entire beneficial interest of the Crown in all lands within its boundaries, which at the time of the union were vested in the Crown, with the exception of such lands as the Dominion acquired right to under[138] sect. 108, or might assume for the purposes specified in sect. 117. Its legal effect is to exclude from the 'duties and revenues' appropriated to the Dominion, all the ordinary territorial revenues of the Crown arising within the Provinces.[139]

The reasoning of the Judicial Committee was based upon the premise that Indian peoples could not be owners of their land in fee simple; had they been able to be owners it could have been held that '... the Province of Ontario could derive no benefit from the cession, in respect that the land was not vested in the Crown at the time of the union'.[140] The Judicial Committee went on to hold that

---

[135] Ibid.
[136] Ibid. The Act constructed separate provinces (Ontario and Quebec) and addressed the division of powers—in terms of what authorities were housed in the federal Crown and which were housed in the provincial Crown. Section 91(24) provided for 'Indians and lands reserved for Indians'. British North America Act 1867 s 91(24).
[137] Section 109 provides:

all lands, mines, minerals, and royalties belonging to the several Provinces of Canada, Nova Scotia, and New Brunswick, at the union, and all sums then due or payable for such lands, mines, minerals, or royalties, shall belong to the several Provinces of Ontario, Quebec, Nova Scotia, and New Brunswick, in which the same are situate or arise, subject to any trusts existing in respect thereof, and to any interest other than that of the Province in the same.

[138] *St Catharine's Milling*, note 118, 552 (57).   [139] Ibid 553 (58).   [140] Ibid.

the Indian interest was not of that nature and that as a result the 'ceded territory' was subject to the Crown's proprietary interest.[141] A result of this, the Judicial Committee continued that '[t]he ceded territory was at the time of the union, land vested in the Crown, subject to "an interest other than that of the Province in the same," within the meaning of sect. 109; and must now belong to Ontario in terms'.[142]

The rationale the Judicial Committee provided for finding that Indigenous peoples had no existing or continuing right to the resources in their traditional territories was that '[t]he treaty leaves the Indians no right whatever to the timber growing upon the lands which they gave up, which is now fully vested in the Crown, all revenues derivable from the sale of such portions of it as are situate within the boundaries of Ontario being the property of that Province'.[143] That there is a contradiction here is evident. The notion of Indigenous title is clearly tied to the treaty process (and, commensurately, Indigenous sovereignty and jurisdiction over Indigenous lands). However, the uniformity of understanding related to alienability, the lack of recognition of Indigenous continuing territoriality and capacity to give up land, and the seeming inability to cognize Indigenous nations in terms of sovereign entities are quite linked to the Doctrine of Discovery. There is a fractured understanding: Indigenous peoples are nations capable of signing treaties. Indigenous peoples have rights to the land. This understanding sits side by side with a lack of understanding, flawed reasoning: these nations have no governance or laws, so we need to intervene. These nations acknowledge our supremacy and our supremacy includes sovereignty. These nations occupy territory and we can legislatively limit the occupation; settler rights to land lie under Indigenous rights. It is hard to reconcile the knowledge of treaty making and accommodation with the idea of the superiority of colonial title, rights, laws, and governments. Perhaps this is because supremacy is not logical. Maybe the intellectual crevasse exists because racism is not easily observable and settler requirements differed from colonial dogma. Whatever the case, what is perceivable is that with the 'discovery' of Indigenous nations, imperial nations understood themselves to be vested with superior rights. Those perceived superior rights transmuted to exclusivity in negotiations with inferior rights holders and the universalized imperial assumption that Her

---

[141] 'The Crown has all along had a present proprietary estate in the land, upon which the Indian title was a mere burden.' Ibid.

[142] Ibid. Further, at 554 (59):

The fact that the power of legislating for Indians, and for lands which are reserved to their use, has been entrusted to the Parliament of the Dominion is not in the least degree inconsistent with the right of the Provinces to a beneficial interest in these lands, available to them as a source of revenue whenever the estate of the Crown is disencumbered of the Indian title.

[143] Ibid 555 (60).

Majesty's superior title, *which they received by merely showing up*, is underlying title to all territory.[144]

G. Conclusion

The Doctrine of Discovery is firmly entrenched in Canada's legal history. As such, it became firmly entrenched in Canadian notions of law, legality, and legal ownership. Canadian legal history reveals the degree to which presumptions of infidel/Indigenous inhumanity were captured and perpetuated in Canadian law. Indigenous philosophies, legal orders, and governmental orders were largely unexamined (and were certainly not well understood) by and in Canadian law. Indigenous legal orders, revealing ancient traditions and laws related to the requirement of care for your relatives (human and non-human), were disregarded. In an Indigenous legal order context, Indigenous laws were historically broken. Our relationship of protection with our mother was ignored and the legal requirement (for lack of a better term) that we reside on and take care of our mother was often unacknowledged.

[144] The discussion about the Doctrine of Discovery in the lower courts in the *St Catharine's Milling* case is telling. At the Ontario Court of Appeal, Hagarty CJO, Burton, Patterson and Osler JJA in which it was found at para 66:

The general result of the historical evidence is, I think, as correctly and as concisely stated in Story's Commentaries on the Constitution of the United States as in any other work. I quote from section 6, of the author's abridged edition of 1833: 'It may be asked, what was the effect of this principle of discovery in respect to the rights of the natives themselves. In the view of the Europeans it created a peculiar relation between themselves and the aboriginal inhabitants. The latter were admitted to possess a right of occupancy or use in the soil, which was subordinate to the ultimate dominion of the discoverers. They were admitted to be the rightful occupants of the soil, with a legal as well as a just claim to retain possession of it, and to use it according to their own discretion. In a certain sense they were permitted to exercise rights of sovereignty over it. They might sell or transfer it to the sovereign who discovered it, but they were denied authority to dispose of it to any other persons, and, until such a sale or transfer, they were generally permitted to occupy it as sovereigns de facto. But notwithstanding this occupancy, the European discoverers claimed and exercised the right to grant the soil while yet in the possession of the natives, subject, however, to their right of occupancy; and the title so granted was universally admitted to convey a sufficient title in the soil to the grantees in perfect dominion, or, as it is sometimes expressed in treatises of public law, it was a transfer of plenum et utile dominium.' This view is evidently that of the Parliament of Canada as may be gathered from the Indian Act, 1880, where 'Reserve' is defined as 'any tract or tracts of land set apart by treaty or otherwise for the use or benefit of or granted to a particular band of Indians, of which the, legal title is in the Crown, but which is unsurrendered' (para 67). I start therefore with the proposition that the title to all these Indian lands, even before what is called the surrender by the Indians, is in the Crown, without attempting by any argument of my own to prove its correctness…

R v St Catharine's Milling and Lumber Co; Regina v The St. Catharines Milling and Lumber Company [1885] OJ No 67 10 OR 196 (Ontario High Court of Justice Chancery Division) Boyd C, 10 June 1885, at paras 16, 17, and 18. This decision was appealed to the Ontario Court of Appeal in *Regina v The St Catharine's Milling and Lumber Company* [1886] OJ No 108 13 OAR 148. The case was appealed to the Supreme Court of Canada and upheld; it then went to the United Kingdom Privy Council.

The language of imperial settlement, and the legal language to support the same, were (and to some degree, are) foreign concepts to Indigenous nations. They were (and in many cases, are still) illegal or in opposition to Indigenous legal orders. If we, as First Peoples, understand ourselves not to be conquered and not to be lawfully regulated or legislated, we reach legal terrain in which understandings and legal relationships cannot be understood to be reciprocal. Empire and the laws of empire required that Indigenous inhumanity be lawfully constructed to support the empirical legal understandings of inherency. This inverted mirror image is not an historical legal understanding, but is a live issue requiring living peoples to address and deconstruct the same. Empire defined conceptualizations of 'rights', 'title', and 'discovery' cannot be considered only as historical antecedents to contemporary 'understandings'. These contemporary understandings, predicated on false notions and on the Indigenous illegal, are living understandings. As they are the loose stones upon which the landslide of Canadian law pertaining to Indigenous peoples is situated, there is an obligation to continue to question, critique, and displace them.

Inherency was the inverted mirror image of inhumanity. Section 91(24) of the Canadian Constitution Act 1867, in which we were administratively housed as a subject matter to be dealt with by Canada, cannot be readily accepted without Indigenous input, legal orders, and understanding. Similarly, the presumptive eradication of Indigenous nations' sovereignty requires constant attention; the historical record related to the same cannot be subsumed into our shared history or into Canadian legal history without protest and constant recognition of Indigenous relationships with our land, legal orders, and governmental authorities as existing legalities. Reciprocity in our relationship requires that we all evaluate laws, legality, and illegality and judicial standardization of the same every day. Canadian legal history, in this regard, is not history at all.

5

Contemporary Canadian Resonance of an Imperial Doctrine

Because of their lack of familiarity with the racist origins of the core doctrines of modern federal Indian law, most practitioners and students do not realize that every time the current Supreme Court cites to any of the core principles to uphold one of its Indian law decisions, it perpetuates and extends the racist legacy brought by Columbus to the New World of the use of law as an instrument of racial domination and discrimination against [I]ndigenous tribal peoples' rights of self-determination.[1]

The Canadian judiciary has addressed the Doctrine of Discovery in a number of its decisions. As important, judicial pronouncements in Canada have included the roots of imperial thinking and the colonial offshoots in their decisions from the earliest adjudication and assessment of the rights (in an Indigenist approach, we would label this assertion of our rights) of Indigenous peoples until the current day. Despite Douglas Sanders' statement that 'Canadian law has never used either "discovery" or "*terra nullius*"'[2] it seems that Canada has utilized colonial legal theory in its policy and statute writing. The Doctrine of Discovery in Canada may not be as evident on the face of the law as in other countries, but the assumption of authority under Discovery indisputably informs the development of policy and legislation. As a result, and as a common law country with reliance upon other common law jurisdictions, Canada also has seen the application of the legal theory of Discovery in the law applied to Indigenous peoples and in modern-day treaty writing. While entrenched in law and legal policy, the Doctrine is also rooted in Canadian history and politics.

Indigenous peoples felt the political will of the Canadian government enforced through legislative means. That the reality of the territory which came to be known as Canada was that Indigenous peoples had lived there and had

---

[1] Brenda L Gunn, 'Protecting Indigenous Peoples' Lands: Making Room for the Application of Indigenous Peoples' Laws Within the Canadian Legal System' (2007) 6 Indigenous LJ 31–69, 39 (citing Robert A Williams Jr, 'Columbus's Legacy: The Rehnquist Court's Perpetuation of European Cultural Racism Against American Indian Tribes' (1992) 39 Fed B News & J 358 (as cited in David H Getches, Charles F Wilkinson, and Robert A Williams Jr, *Cases and Materials on Federal Indian Law* (Minneapolis: West Publishing Co, 5th edn, 2005) 36–7).

[2] Douglas Sanders, 'The Supreme Court Of Canada and the "Legal and Political Struggle" Over Indigenous Rights' (1990) 22 Canadian Ethnic Studies 122, 122.

a relationship with their traditional territories since time immemorial had to be overcome. The additional reality of the earlier colonial era (see Lindberg, Chapter 4)—the requirement of peaceful trading and economic alliances—was less of a consideration which meant that the most important colonial goal was controlling Indigenous peoples and the obligations of the government of Canada to Indigenous peoples. With a developed economy in place which had devolved the role of Indigenous peoples, settlements with provisioning and colonial governments in place, Indigenous cooperation and accord was less important. For this reason, the assertion of Canadian governmental authorities from 1900 to 1969 dealt principally with Indigenous peoples as a matter to be dealt with in order to facilitate settlement in the west.

The era from 1969 to 1997 followed an era of Indigenous activism, legal challenges, and Canadian governmental response. As Indigenous peoples mobilized and began to control the dialogue about Indigenous rights and title, Canadian history and legal history began to be re-examined as well. Sovereignty, self-determination, and Indigenous governmental authority began to be discussed, debated, and reconsidered. Indigenous stories of relationships with land began to be told in the first person. The long history of attempted limitation/eradication of Indigenous sovereignty came under close scrutiny by Indigenous peoples, Canadian citizens, and the Canadian judiciary.

Canadian legislation and policy in the modern era continues to 'deal' with Indigenous issues as they arise. It can be stated with some assurance that not one non-Indigenous governmental party in power has been able to address satisfactorily issues of the historical breaches of trust with Indigenous peoples, the usurpation and denial of Indigenous authorities and lands, or the sovereignty of Indigenous peoples before the issues arise through protest, arrest, court cases, or political pressure. Policy seems to be written reactively and often has not included Indigenous people in the research or drafting. There are, of course, exceptions.[3]

More recently in Canadian legal history, case law has been centred on defining the nature of Aboriginal rights (and title) and treaty rights and how far they extend. We have begun to see Canadian courts address the evolving conceptualization of limited (by discovery) sovereignty, rights, and title. Discovery, with regard to its impact on notions of Indigenous sovereignty, is still firmly entrenched in the Canadian judicial mindset, however. Discussions of duty to consult and the potential duty to accommodate have replaced discussions of the

---

[3] The recent discussions surrounding matrimonial property on reserve have included Indigenous women's groups in the discussion and their contribution to the drafting. Minister of Indian and Northern Affairs Development and Federal Interlocutor for Métis and Non-Status Indians, 'Consultation Report on Matrimonial Real Property' (Ottawa, 7 March 2007), <http://www.ainc-inac.gc.ca. http://www.nwac-hq.org/en/documents/CR_English.pdf>. The Assembly of First Nations has been a party to the discussion about the formation of a new specific claims tribunal: Political Agreement Between the Minister of Indian Affairs and Northern Development and the National Chief of the Assembly of First Nations in Relation to Specific Claims Reform (signed 27 November 2007) (Canada–Assembly of First Nations) <http://www.afn.ca/misc/SC-PA.pdf>.

source, nature, and extent of Aboriginal and treaty rights and title. Pithy statements about the 'honour of the Crown' have replaced the prolonged and needed in-depth analysis of fiduciary duty and other duties.

A. Contemporary Documentation

1. Constitutional documentation

According to the doctrine of discovery, sovereignty could be acquired over unoccupied territory by discovery. If the territory in question was occupied, then conquest or cession was necessary to transfer sovereign power from its inhabitants to an imperial power. However, European imperial practice was to deem territory occupied by Indigenous peoples to be unoccupied, or *terra nullius*, for the purposes of acquiring sovereign power. Legally deeming Indigenous territory vacant meant that settler governments did not require conquest or cession of themselves in order to grant themselves sovereign power to rule Indigenous peoples and territories. International law deemed Indigenous territory to be *terra nullius* because European powers viewed Indigenous people to be insufficiently Christian or civilized to merit recognizing them as sovereign powers.[4]

Between 1931 and 1982, Canada was subject to the Constitution Act 1930.[5] The Act contained within it Schedules for each western territory that joined Canada as a province. In each Schedule, provision was made to address the continuing relationship between the federal government and the provincial governments. Manitoba, Saskatchewan, and Alberta[6] had the same clauses addressing the relationship each province would have with the government of Canada with regard to Indigenous ('Indian') lands. With respect to Indian Reserves,[7] Saskatchewan's Natural Resource Transfer Agreement (NRTA)[8] provides that Indian reserves within the province 'shall continue to be vested in the Crown and administered by the Government of Canada for the purposes of Canada...'.[9] Additionally, when obligations under treaty require land, the Province is mandated to set

---

[4] Patrick Macklem, 'What is International Human Rights Law? Three Applications of a Distributive Account' (2007) 52 McGill LJ 575–604, para 36 <http://www.quicklaw.ca>.

[5] Constitution Act 1930.

[6] British Columbia did not have the same provisions. This province's provision related to Indian reserves provides:

13. Nothing in this agreement shall extend to the lands included within Indian reserves in the Railway Belt and the Peace River Block, but the said reserves shall continue to be vested in Canada in trust for the Indians on the terms and conditions set out in a certain order of the Governor General of Canada in Council approved on the 3rd day of February, 1930 (P.C.208).

Memorandum of Agreement (4) British Columbia Made this twentieth day of February, 1930. Constitution Act 1930.

[7] Note that Indian territories and traditional lands are not included within the NRTA.

[8] Saskatchewan Natural Resources Transfer Agreement (Memorandum) 1930.

[9] Ibid s 10.

aside (out of unoccupied Crown lands) lands 'necessary to enable Canada to fulfil its obligations under the treaties with the Indians of the Province...'.[10] That
Indigenous territory can be taken and exchanged without negotiation with the
original peoples is a further instance of the Doctrine at work within Canada.
That there is recognition built into the NRTA of the legal requirement to settle
treaty obligations (new or existing) with Indigenous peoples is a further example
of Canadian governmental adherence to the Doctrine when it comes to sovereignty but movement away from it when it deals with Indigenous land rights.

Section 12 of the NRTA provides, in its entirety:

12. In order to secure to the Indians of the Province the continuance of the supply of
game and fish for their support and subsistence, Canada agrees that the laws respecting
game in force in the Province from time to time shall apply to the Indians within the
boundaries thereof, provided, however, that the said Indians shall have the right, which
the Province hereby assures to them, of hunting, trapping and fishing game and fish for
food at all seasons of the year on all unoccupied Crown lands and on any other lands to
which the said Indians may have a right of access.[11]

Negotiated positions and promises made during the numbered treaties with
Indigenous nations on the prairies are not reflected within this provision. Neither
Indigenous oral traditions[12] nor historical written sources[13] reflect this under-
standing. Instead, both refer to the fact that Indigenous peoples' capacity to

[10] Ibid.
[11] Ibid s 12. This section is controversial and has been the subject of litigation in Canada as it
seems to contradict the promises made in the numbered treaties with respect to the continuance
of livelihood rights (including hunting and fishing). This section is discussed at length later in the
chapter.
[12] Sharon Venne, 'Understanding Treaty 6: An Indigenous Perspective' in Michael Asch,
Aboriginal and Treaty Rights in Canada: Essays on Law, Equality, and Respect (Vancouver: UBC
Press, 1997) 173–207, 196. With respect to the Elders' understanding of the Treaty, Venne writes,
'The commissioner said that "anything that the Indian uses was to be left alone. The White Man
has nothing to do with it"'. As well, in Richard Price (ed), *The Spirit of the Alberta Indian Treaties*
(Edmonton: University of Alberta Press, 1999), interviews with a number of Elders demonstrated a
shared understanding with respect to the minerals, territoriality and land use, and the right to hunt
and fish. See Elder Lazarus Roan, 116, John Buffalo, 119, Fred Horse, 124–35.
[13] Treaty No 8 and Adhesions, Reports, Etc, 1899. Treaty No 8: Report of Commissioner for
Treaty No 8 (Department of Indian Affairs, Ottawa 1900). Report of the Commissioners for
Treaty No 8, 22 September 1899, <http://www.ainc-inac.gc.ca/al/hts/tgu/pubs/t8/trty8-eng.asp>.
In their report, the Commissioners wrote:

Our chief difficulty was the apprehension that the hunting and fishing privileges were to be cur-
tailed. The provision in the treaty under which ammunition and twine is to be furnished went far
in the direction of quieting the fears of the Indians, for they admitted that it would be unreasonable to furnish the means of hunting and fishing if laws were to be enacted which would make
hunting and fishing so restricted as to render it impossible to make a livelihood by such pursuits.
But over and above the provision, we had to solemnly assure them that only such laws as to hunting
and fishing as were in the interest of the Indians and were found necessary in order to protect the
fish and fur-bearing animals would be made, and that they would be as free to hunt and fish after
the treaty as they would be if they never entered into it.

We assured them that the treaty would not lead to any forced interference with their mode of
life...

hunt and fish was to remain unfettered and that the Indigenous peoples would '… have an equal share and equal use of your land. You cannot stop each other. You can camp and you can hunt for food where you have always hunted. This is the way you are going to live.'[14]

Under the Statute of Westminster 1931[15] the British Parliament still had power to amend Canada's constitution. This was the case until the Canada Act 1982.[16] Schedule B to that Act[17] constitutionalized (after a long period of negotiation between Indigenous national organization representatives and Canadian nation representatives) the *existing* Aboriginal and treaty rights of Aboriginal peoples in Canada. Section 35 subsection 1 provides:

35. (1) The existing aboriginal and treaty rights of the aboriginal peoples of Canada are hereby recognized and affirmed.[18]

Aboriginal peoples of Canada, according to section 35(2), 'includes the Indian, Inuit and Métis peoples of Canada'.[19] Moreover, section 35(3) clarified Canada's constitutional understanding of treaty rights and determined that they include 'rights that now exist by way of land claims agreements or may be so acquired'.[20]

While the Doctrine would certainly not support the precept upon which this section is based (that Indigenous peoples have rights, including land rights as Indigenous peoples) the limiting precept of *existing* is one which may very well be related to the philosophy entrenched in the Doctrine. Land rights certainly do exist: treaties, reserves, and Aboriginal title attest to this. However, again, the Doctrinal precept that Indigenous sovereignty was replaced or limited potentially finds life within the word *existing*.[21] Limiting rights to existing rights ignores the impact that colonization and imperialism had and continue to have on Indigenous peoples. That a history of the lack of acknowledgment of Aboriginal rights and the attempted or actual legislative removal of lands, enforcement by jail time for not adhering to enforced models of governance, and the English assumption of English sovereignty should not be addressed before arriving at an understanding of what Indigenous rights were actually able to exist reifies the Doctrinal axiom that infidel rights exist at a level below other citizens' rights.

---

[14]   Price, note 12, 132 (interview Camoose Bottle).
[15]   Statute of Westminster 1931 (UK).
[16]   The Canada Act 1982 was the United Kingdom Parliament's last Act pertaining to Canada. Canada's Constitution Act is Schedule B to the Canada Act 1982, (UK) (coming into force on 17 April 1982).   [17]   Constitution Act, ibid.
[18]   Ibid s 35(1).   [19]   Ibid s 35(2).   [20]   Ibid s 35(3).
[21]   It is this author's position and understanding that *existing* must be determined in accordance with both Indigenous and Canadian legal standards and that colonial interference and imperial dicta must be taken into account in determining the possibility of subversive, inconspicuous, transformed, or the quiet exercise of *existing* Aboriginal rights. The Supreme Court of Canada's findings with regard to the nature of 'existing' and the limitations on Aboriginal rights will be reviewed at length later in this chapter.

2. *Terra nullius*

To state that the Americas at the point of first contact with Europeans were empty unin-habited lands is, of course, factually incorrect. To the extent that concepts such as terra nullius and discovery also carry with them the baggage of racism and ethnocentrism, they are morally wrong as well.[22]

It may be difficult to find, but the notion of *terra nullius* does live within Canadian judicial decisions as they apply to Indigenous peoples. As stated in Chapter 4, the Doctrine relies on the myth of Indigenous inhumanity (and invisibility) in order that title can be found to belong to colonizers. The unquestioned importation of common law facilitates the myth, and underlying title is constructed to facilitate the Crown assertion of ownership.[23]

Patrick Macklem addresses the notion of *terra nullius*, discovery, and sov-ereignty and quite neatly ties them all together:

According to the doctrine of discovery, sovereignty could be acquired over unoccupied ter-ritory by discovery. If the territory in question was occupied, then conquest or cession was necessary to transfer sovereign power from its inhabitants to an imperial power. However, European imperial practice was to deem territory occupied by indigenous peoples to be unoccupied, or terra nullius, for the purposes of acquiring sovereign power. Because indig-enous territory was deemed vacant, neither conquest nor cession was necessary to acquire the sovereign power to rule indigenous people and territory. International law deemed indigenous territory to be terra nullius because European powers viewed indigenous people to be insufficiently Christian or civilized to merit recognizing them as sovereign powers.[24]

[22] Royal Commission on Aboriginal Peoples, *Report of the Royal Commission on Aboriginal Peoples: Looking Forward, Looking Back*, vol 1 (Ottawa: Canada Communication Group, 1996) 695.
[23] Kelley C Yukich, 'Aboriginal Rights in the Constitution and International Law' (1996) 30 Univ of British Columbia L Rev 235–78, para 76, <http://www.quicklaw.ca>. Yukich discusses three levels of the doctrine:

At this point, in order to clarify the present Aboriginal position, it is helpful to identify the three distinct levels at which the doctrine of terra nullius has been applied. *First,* the doctrine of discov-ery, giving sovereignty to the first European state to discover and occupy a new territory, depends on the fiction that a territory is uninhabited. Otherwise, the incoming state would have to conquer the territory or receive it through cession. *Second*, as a matter of municipal law, the common law of England was automatically imported into new territories. This is a step that may only occur when the mode of acquisition is settlement of an empty territory with no effective legal regime. As indige-nous peoples were perceived as too primitive to have a cognizable legal order, English law was auto-matically imported for the benefit of the settlers. If the land was viewed as having been conquered or ceded, as it should have been due to the presence of indigenous inhabitants, the law already in existence would have continued to apply until it was altered by the Crown. *Third,* once common law was accepted into the new territory, the Crown could only acquire full beneficial ownership of land that was not already occupied. This result flows from the general common law rule that own-ership cannot be acquired by occupying land that is already occupied by another. The result of the Crown's assertion of sovereignty when land is already occupied is therefore simply an acquisition of radical or underlying title sufficient to support the doctrine of tenure. It was only by conceiving of the land as vacant that the Crown was able to acquire the full beneficial ownership of all land and, in doing so, extinguish Aboriginal land ownership in one clean sweep. (Emphasis added)

[24] Patrick Macklem, note 4, para 36.

The meaning of cession must be examined and Indigenous legal orders related to the same must contribute to our understanding of the nature and (in)applicability of cession in the territory that became known as Canada. If there is no shared understanding of ceding, releasing, and surrendering, then most certainly it has to be asked, often and with an understanding of legal pluralism accompanying the dialogue: can Indigenous nations be lawfully understood to have ceded their lands if there was/is no legal or other capacity of cessation? Surely, historic Doctrine predicated on notions of racialized inferiority cannot be our only guide in this discussion.

Section 35(1), some authors have argued, does allow Canada to acknowledge full ownership of land by Aboriginal peoples. Yukich wrote, in discussing the presumption of ownership by the Crown and the role section 35(1) can play in redressing the wrong:

How then, does this generally accepted account explain how the Crown presumes to completely own land to the exclusion of Aboriginal interests that prevailed at the time of settlement? This result must also arise through the fiction that Canada, like Australia, was terra nullius when British settlers arrived. Since it is now clear that the lands were occupied on arrival, the Crown's assertion of land ownership, with its accompanying conclusion that Aboriginal ownership ceased, must be questioned, and the possibility that Aboriginal rights to full ownership of land are entrenched in s. 35(1) must be acknowledged.[25]

While the notion of *terra nullius* may no longer have the same contemporary prominence as it did in the past it has continued to reinforce the presupposed legitimacy of Crown sovereignty. Gordon Christie has written of this: 'Since the historical situation is that Aboriginal peoples were "here first," the Court must replace the old tired colonial fictions of terra nullius and "discovery" and fall back on its one remaining story, elevating this to a new level of prominence—the Crown is unquestionably recognized as the sole legitimate sovereign power.'[26]

Until Indigenous primacy and legal orders are fully honoured, that is, when Indigenous nations are able to assert the same, live the same, and have it acknowledged by colonial governments, the legitimacy of Indigenous land cession has to remain suspect and subject to constant scrutiny.

3. Treaty cases and Canadian treaty interpretation

It is essential to note that treaty making was not just for 'peace and friendship'. There were international trading alliances required and Indigenous peoples signed treaties with representatives of newcomer nations in order to facilitate trade and the development of good inter-nation (and international) relationships.

[25] Yukich, note 23, para 70.
[26] Gordon Christie, 'Aboriginal Rights, Aboriginal Culture, and Protection' (1998) 36 Osgoode Hall LJ 447–84, para 71, <http://www.quicklaw.ca>.

How settler peoples perceived those agreements at the time is indisputable. How they came to be interpreted over time is also, to some degree, a matter of economics. To the degree that economics is informed by power and authority, the Doctrine of Discovery is equally present in this discussion.

Treaties between Her Majesty and Indigenous nations were often entered into when settler economic goals came into conflict with Indigenous territoriality (it could be argued that these are the circumstances upon which most Aboriginal rights cases wind up in Canadian courts, as well). It is important to note that Indigenous representatives who served as signatories to the treaties, generally, understood the treaties to be international treaties entered into with an air of sanctity and which bound the speakers, negotiators, and participants to the promises made (in writing and orally) forever. Treaty disputes in the contemporary era are often characterized as requiring resolution as to whether a treaty right exists or does not exist. What is rarely conceded is the fact of treaty breach or infringement by the application of statute to activities and lands understood to be protected by treaty. Continuing and existing treaty rights are under constant pressure—a pressure the Indigenous parties to the treaty were assured would not ever occur.[27]

Several Canadian decisions related to treaty rights were brought forward when Canadian legislation was perceived to infringe treaty rights. The Doctrinal notion of Indigenous lawlessness and a superior non-Indigenous lawfulness can be found in the Supreme Court of Canada's decision in *R v Horseman*.[28] In this case, Mr Horseman (a treaty Indian person from the Treaty 8 territory) was charged with unlawfully trafficking in wildlife.[29] At the time that Mr Horseman killed a bear, he was hunting a moose.[30] A year later, he sold the bear hide (but got a grizzly bear licence prior to doing so)[31] and was subsequently charged. Mr Horseman's defence was that he was a Treaty 8 Indian exercising his treaty right to hunt.[32] The relevant provision of the Treaty provides:

Treaty No. 8, 1899:
And Her Majesty the Queen HEREBY AGREES with the said Indians that they shall have right to pursue their usual vocations of hunting, trapping and fishing throughout the tract surrendered as heretofore described, subject to such regulations as may from

---

[27] For a detailed discussions on the promises made to Indigenous peoples as shared in oral traditions by Elders, see Venne, note 12, Price, note 12, and Harold Cardinal and Walter Hildebrandt, *Treaty Elders of Saskatchewan: Our Dream Is That Our Peoples Will One Day Be Clearly Recognized As Nations* (Calgary: University of Calgary Press, 2000).

[28] *R v Horseman* [1990] SCJ No 39 (a Supreme Court of Canada case), <http://www.quicklaw. com>.

[29] The charge was under Province of Alberta Wildlife Act. Wildlife Act, RSA 1980, c. W-9 s 42. The section of the Act provides that 'no person shall traffic in any wildlife except as is expressly permitted by this Act or by the regulations'.   [30] *R v Horseman*, note 28, para 39.

[31] Ibid para 41.

[32] The relevant provision of the Treaty is at ibid para 15. Note 13 contains a full reference to Treaty 8 (1899).

time to time be made by the Government of the country, acting under the authority of Her Majesty, and saving and excepting such tracts as may be required or taken up from time to time for settlement, mining, lumbering, trading or other purposes.[33]

Intrinsic to the Treaty is the notion that hunting will continue. Additionally, oral evidence provided by many Elders attests to the understanding that the negotiated terms were that Indigenous peoples were forever able to hunt, fish, and pursue their livelihoods as they always had.[34] The issue in this case was characterized by the Supreme Court of Canada as whether Treaty 8 hunting rights were limited by the Alberta Natural Resources Transfer Agreement 1930 (NRTA).[35] The Court went on to find that while the Treaty did protect the right to hunt commercially, it was subject to regulation by virtue of the NRTA.[36] The Court looked to section 88 of the Indian Act[37] in determining that the right was no longer a treaty right and that therefore section 88 did not apply.

The Supreme Court of Canada had another opportunity to examine the treaty rights of Indigenous peoples as they relate to land in the 1996 *R v Badger* decision.[38] The three people charged with breaking provincial laws (and who could claim that the legislation was a breach of treaty) were all Treaty 8 Indigenous citizens defined as Indians under the Indian Act. Each was charged with an offence under the province of Alberta Wildlife Act.[39] Each was hunting. Each argued that they had a Treaty 8 right to do so. The issues as characterized by the Supreme Court of Canada were whether the Treaty 8 hunting rights were extinguished or modified by the NRTA and whether 'Indians who have status under Treaty No. 8 have the right to hunt for food on privately owned land which lies within the territory surrendered under that Treaty'.[40]

It is interesting to consider the notion of surrender and the title to 'privately owned land' which the Indigenous peoples of Treaty 8 would characterize as their traditional territories in the context of the Doctrine. Mr Badger hunted

---

[33] Treaty 8, note 13.

[34] Price, note 27. Cardinal and Hildebrandt, note 27.

[35] Alberta Natural Resources Transfer Agreement (Memorandum) 1930 s 12:

In order to secure to the Indians of the Province the continuance of the supply of game and fish for their support and subsistence, Canada agrees that the laws respecting game in force in the Province from time to time shall apply to the Indians within the boundaries thereof, provided, however, that the said Indians shall have the right, which the Province hereby assures to them, of hunting, trapping and fishing game and fish for food at all seasons of the year on all unoccupied Crown lands and on any other lands to which the said Indians may have a right of access.

[36] *R v Horseman*, note 28, paras 63 and 66. At para 66, the Court also held that the Treaty right to commercially hunt was limited but that the right to hunt for food was expanded.

[37] Discussed in the next section of this chapter at length, section 88 provides that provincial laws of general application apply to Indians unless the laws conflict with a treaty right or Act of Parliament. Indian Act 1970 s 88.

[38] *R v Badger* [1996] SCJ No 39 (a Supreme Court of Canada case) <http://www.quicklaw.com>.   [39] Wildlife Act SA 1984 ss 15(1)(c), 26(1), 27(1).

[40] Ibid note 38, para 20.

near an occupied house.[41] A second hunter, Mr Kiyawasew, hunted a moose on a snow covered field (posted and harvested the previous fall).[42] In both instances, the Court found that the lands could be understood to be occupied as they were clearly being put to a visible and incompatible (with hunting) use.[43] The irony of this finding, in terms of the finding related to occupancy, is startling. First, it is ironic that the test for occupancy requires Indigenous peoples (who were presumed not to occupy lands in order for them to be declared unoccupied Crown lands) to assume that certain signs of non-Indigenous occupancy (a house, a bare field) equate with an understanding that the property is occupied and cannot be used to hunt. The second irony is that peoples who were adjudicated to have lost their treaty right by virtue of a statute which abridged their treaty rights are held to a much higher standard than the Crown ever was, with regard to fulfilling the treaty terms.

A third hunter, Mr Ominayak, who had been hunting a moose on uncleared muskeg was also charged.[44] The Court looked to section 12 of the NRTA to determine that:

[i]t will be remembered that the NRTA modified the Treaty right to hunt. It did so by eliminating the right to hunt commercially but enlarged the geographical areas in which the Indian people might hunt in all seasons. The area was to include all unoccupied Crown land in the province together with any other lands to which the Indians may have a right of access. Lastly, the province was authorized to make laws for conservation.[45]

The Court went on to determine that 'reasonable regulations aimed at ensuring safety do not infringe aboriginal or treaty rights to hunt for food. Similarly these regulations do not infringe the hunting rights guaranteed by Treaty No. 8 as modified by the NRTA.'[46] Mr Badger and Mr Kiyawasew were found to be hunting on land that was visibly used; as they were they did not have a treaty right to use those lands. Their treaty rights were not infringed, the Supreme Court of Canada decided.[47]

Unilateral changes to the treaty right, as per the NRTA, resonate with the understanding that Canada's rights are superior to those of Indigenous peoples. Additionally, the notion of Crown sovereignty, in the case at least, displaced the notion of Indigenous sovereignty—which was not seriously entertained in the case.

---

[41] Ibid para 67. He was charged with shooting a moose outside the permitted hunting season contrary to s 27(1) of the Act. Wildlife Act, note 39, ss 15(1)(c), 26(1), 27(1).   [42] Ibid.
[43] Ibid.
[44] Mr Kiyawasew and Mr Ominayak both had shot moose. Both were charged under s 26(1) of the Act, with hunting without a licence. Ibid para 22.   [45] Ibid para 83.
[46] Ibid para 89.
[47] At ibid para 101, the Court found that: 'Mr. Badger and Mr. Kiyawasew were hunting on occupied land to which they had no right of access under Treaty No. 8 or the NRTA. Accordingly, ss. 26(1) and 27(1) of the Wildlife Act do not infringe their constitutional right to hunt for food.'

In 1999, the Supreme Court of Canada had the opportunity to render a decision with respect to the rights of Miq'maw people to fish under the Treaties signed in 1760–1761.[48] The Treaty itself contained a truck house clause which provided that:

And I do further engage that we will not traffick, barter or exchange any commodities in any manner but with such persons or the managers of such truckhouses as shall be appointed or established by His Majesty's Governor at [truckhouse location closest to the village in question] or elsewhere in Nova Scotia or Accadia.[49]

Mr Marshall was fishing for eels. He did not have a licence to do so. He sold them. He did not have a licence to do so. He caught them with a net during a closed season.[50] Mr Marshall argued that the 1760–1761 Treaties protected his right to fish and sell eels.[51]

The Court looked to section 35(1) to determine if the treaty right was an 'existing' one in order to arrive at its decision as to whether or not the right was protected. The majority determined that the rights described were rights which received section 35(1) protection under the *Badger* test.[52] The right protected in the Treaty, the Supreme Court of Canada decided, was not a literal right to a truck house but a right to 'continue to obtain necessaries'.[53]

The case is interesting in that Mr Marshall got an acquittal and had his treaty right recognized. It is also compelling that the honour of the Crown was heavily relied upon and that the deficiencies in the written treaty were addressed in terms of that honour. However, while recognizing Indigenous peoples' right, the right was limited to necessaries. Certainly it must be said that fishing and bringing your catch to a truck house established especially for your catch is an engagement in a commercial activity. Indigenous economic activities in the case are limited to familial provisioning. One could argue that this characterization primitives

---

[48] Peace and Friendship Treaties Between His Majesty the King and the LaHave Tribe of Indians 1760–1, <http://www.ainc-inac.gc.ca/al/hts/tgu/pubs/pft176061/pft176061-eng.asp>.

[49] *R v Marshall* [1999] SCJ 55, para 71, <http://www.quicklaw.ca> (a Supreme Court of Canada case). The Treaties and terms were written to gain the economic relationship and alliances with the Indigenous peoples. At para 32, the Court noted that '[a]s Governor Lawrence wrote to the Board of Trade on May 11, 1760, "the greatest advantage from this [trade] Article...is the friendship of these Indians"'.

[50] Ibid paras 62 and 65.

[51] At ibid para 7 Mr Marshall's position was characterized by the majority thusly: 'The appellant's position is that the truckhouse provision not only incorporated the alleged right to trade, but also the right to pursue traditional hunting, fishing and gathering activities in support of that trade.'

[52] The principle from *Badger*, by Cory J, is enumerated at ibid para 41:

[T]he honour of the Crown is always at stake in its dealings with Indian people. Interpretations of treaties and statutory provisions which have an impact upon treaty or aboriginal rights must be approached in a manner which maintains the integrity of the Crown. It is always assumed that the Crown intends to fulfil its promises. No appearance of "sharp dealing" will be sanctioned.

[53] Ibid para 56. This was equated with a 'moderate livelihood' as per Lambert JA, in *R v Van der Peet* (1993) 80 BCLR (2nd) 75 (the British Columbia Court of Appeal case), 126.

Indigenous economies and minimizes Indigenous rights. While the jurisdiction is (never stated) Indigenous jurisdiction the *allowable* self-determination is limited to economies of modesty. This stereotyped understanding of Indigenous economies denies the existence of acquisition, redistribution of wealth, and collective commercial activities and relegates Indigenous commerce to individualized and modest essentials.[54]

It is also interesting as interpretations of the case by other non-Indigenous fisherman caused panic in the fishing industry. So much so, that the Supreme Court of Canada issued a second judgment: *R v Marshall* (*Marshall II*).[55] Virtually unprecedented, many Indigenous rights advocates perceived the issuance of the second judgment as an effort to 'close the door' on treaty rights after the fact. An intervener to the Supreme Court of Canada decision (The West Nova Fisherman's Coalition) had, after the Supreme Court of Canada ruled in *Marshall I,* applied for rehearing of the appeal and a stay of the judgment pending that hearing.[56] Neither were granted but the Supreme Court of Canada did take the opportunity to expand upon (while evidently narrowing the terms of) their decision in *Marshall I.* The feeling of betrayal in many Indigenous rights advocates' minds came from the opportunity the Court took to provide ways and means for the provincial government to limit the treaty right. The judgment included the following roadmap:

- The Minister can always seek to justify the limitation on the treaty right because of the need to conserve the resource in question or for other compelling and substantial public objectives.[57]
- A 'closed season' can be used as a management tool; if it is used, it will have to be justified (as it is dealing with a treaty right).[58]
- Conservation has always been recognized to be a justification of paramount importance to limit the exercise of treaty and Aboriginal rights.[59]
- The Mi'kmaq Treaty right to participate in the largely unregulated commercial fishery of 1760 has evolved into a treaty right to participate in the largely regulated commercial fishery of the 1990s.[60]
- The paramount regulatory objective is the conservation of the resource. This responsibility is placed squarely on the Minister and not on the Aboriginal or non-Aboriginal users of the resource.[61]
- The Minister's authority extends to other compelling and substantial public objectives which may include economic and regional fairness, and recognition of the historical reliance upon, and participation in, the fishery by non-Aboriginal groups.[62]

[54] *R v Marshall*, note 49, para 58.
[55] *R v Marshall* [1999] SCJ 66 (a Supreme Court of Canada case) (*Marshall II*) <http://www.quicklaw.ca>.   [56] Ibid para 1.
[57] Ibid para 19.   [58] Ibid para 21.   [59] Ibid para 29.   [60] Ibid para 38.
[61] Ibid para 40b.   [62] Ibid para 40c.

Considered opinion may yield the understanding that the Supreme Court of Canada is providing legislators with the full knowledge of how to lawfully breach treaty rights. What do treaty rights mean if they are subject to legislative bodies that, potentially with the support of the Supreme Court of Canada's guidance, can eliminate them for reasons including regional fairness? Was regional fairness anticipated and aligned with the honour of the Crown? Indigenous sovereignty and jurisdiction that are subject to provincial and federal legislators' understanding of compelling public objectives surely face the same pressure that the Doctrine placed on Indigenous peoples trying to protect their traditional territories.

The ability to presume Indigenous usage patterns, non-commercialism, and the unilateral alteration of treaty rights are all Doctrinally informed. Unilateral legislative decisions altering treaties and limiting Indigenous rights are predicated on the same notions of supremacy and superiority of Canadian laws (and to a degree, of Canadian peoples). Unilaterally making determinations about Indigenous wealth, affluence, and commercialism and objectifying notions of Indigenous subsistence disregards a rich Indigenous history of trade, communal affluence, and economic self-determination. It also binds Indigenous economies to an antiquated and individualistic notion of impoverishment that does not reflect many Indigenous peoples' realities. The power to make presumptions (of non-commercialism, unquestioned adherence to unilateral legislative alterations of sacred treaties, and of non-conservatism or incapacity to make rules related to the same) is directly related to the Doctrinal ideology and stereotypes that facilitated false notions of Discovery and *terra nullius*.

4. Legislation

In the realm of legislating Indians, Canada has promulgated one of the ideological underpinnings of the Doctrine. The dogma that infidels have no rights is reflected in the codification related to hunting, oil and gas, Indian lands, and a number of other self-determining activities. That is not to say that Canada does not acknowledge Indigenous capacities in areas related to governance/self-governance. What is more likely to be observed is that Canada's statutory regime as it relates to Indigenous peoples is based on the notion of a 'comprehensive no'. The expansion of the 'comprehensive no' takes place, on a case by case (individual) basis. For example, section 12(1) of the 1952 Migratory Birds Convention Act[63] incorporated regulations that made it illegal for any person to 'kill, hunt, capture, injure, take or molest a migratory bird at any time except during an open season specified for that bird and that area...'.[64]

---

[63] Migratory Birds Convention Act 1952.

[64] The Regulation appeared at s 5(1)(a), Migratory Bird Regulations, PC 1958-1070, SOR/58-308. Section 12(1) itself provided for a fine between 10 and 300 dollars and / or an imprisonment term of 6 months or less.

The general legislation, in this instance, was applicable to all people in Canada. Whether or not it applied to Indians who had a protected right under treaty was the individualized question posed in *Sikyea v The Queen*.[65] In the 1964 Supreme Court of Canada decision, the fact that Mr Sikyea had a treaty right to hunt ducks under Treaty No 11 (whether in season or not) was not examined in any detail. The decision of the Court was made dependent upon an adjudication as to whether the duck was a wild duck or not (as wild ducks were included in the legislation).[66] Opting not to directly address the nature of the treaty right, the case came down to statutory interpretation and the 'comprehensive no'. No one was allowed to hunt wild ducks as the provisions of the Migratory Birds Convention Act did not allow for it. In this instance, no Indigenous right of sovereignty, jurisdiction, or even a negotiated treaty right survived the legislative 'comprehensive no'.

Section 88 of the Indian Act also impacted Indigenous peoples and is predicated on the assumed superiority of jurisdiction of both the federal and provincial governments. The section specifically addresses the impact of provincial powers on peoples defined as Indians under the Indian Act. Section 88 provides:

88. Subject to the terms of any treaty and any other Act of Parliament, all laws of general application from time to time in force in any province are applicable to and in respect of Indians in the province, except to the extent that those laws are inconsistent with this Act or the First Nations Fiscal and Statistical Management Act, or with any order, rule, regulation or law of a band made under those Acts, and except to the extent that those provincial laws make provision for any matter for which provision is made by or under those Acts.[67]

As we saw in the *Badger* decision, s 88 applies to people defined as Indians and provides that provincial laws of general application apply to Indians unless they conflict with an Aboriginal or treaty right. In terms of the interpretation of this section by the Canadian judiciary, the 'comprehensive no' again applies, with individual 'yeses' forming the exceptional cases (where an individual goes to court to disprove the blanket no). There have been a number of cases where section 88 and provincial authorities with respect to Aboriginal title have been ruled upon. In *Delgamuukw v British Columbia* it was determined that[68]

[S]. 88 extends the effect of provincial laws of general application which cannot apply to Indians and Indian lands because they touch on the Indianness at the core of s. 91(24).

---

[65] *Sikyea v The Queen* (1964) 50 DLR (2nd) 80 (a Supreme Court of Canada case).

[66] Ibid 83.

[67] Indian Act 1985 s 88. The section was added to the Indian Act in 1951. Section 87 (as it then was) provided:

87. Subject to the terms of any treaty and any other Act of Parliament, all laws of general application from time to time in force in any province are applicable to and in respect of Indians in the province, except to the extent that those laws are inconsistent with this Act or any order, rule, regulation, or by-law made thereunder, and except to the extent that those laws make provision for any matter for which provision is made by or under this Act.

Indian Act 1951, s 87.

[68] [1997] SCJ 108, para 182 (a Supreme Court of Canada case), <http://www.quicklaw.ca>.

For example, a provincial law which regulated hunting may very well touch on this core. Although such a law would not apply to aboriginal people proprio vigore, it would still apply through s. 88 of the Indian Act, being a law of general application.[69]

Most notably, former Chief Justice of the Supreme Court of Canada Antonio Lamer famously found in *Delgamuukw* that provinces cannot extinguish Aboriginal title[70] but that they could infringe Aboriginal title[71] in the application of section 88.

Broadly stated, the question is what meaning and trust is provided by section 91(24) when provincial laws of general application can be found to apply to Indians. Additionally, the 'comprehensive no' (rights, recognition) is extended to activities regulated by provinces. In order to garner a yes (recognition of a treaty or Aboriginal right) the question is individualized and individuals who have the means must come forward to test the blanket no. That Indigenous autonomies and jurisdictions which go to the root of Indianness receive notional protection prioritizes rights in view of their Canadian legal cognizability. Seemingly, then, Indigenous rights which are not categorized by Canada as Aboriginal or going to the heart of Indianness become rights without protection. Presumably, then, everyday activities which Indigenous people have historically engaged in, and do in a contemporary fashion engage in, which look like 'Canadian' or 'modern' activities will not be viewed as rights, and provincial laws of general application will presumptively regulate the activities. In this way, Indigeneity cannot be understood to have legally protected rights of modernity. Additionally, Indigenous jurisdictions and autonomies become part of the 'comprehensive no'—requiring individuals to come forward to assert a right to participate in the activity. This is directly tied to the Doctrine as activities engaged in which are part of Indigenous sovereign authorities can be legally relegated to an inferior position (with the superior position being occupied by federal and provincial declared authorities and sovereignty).

Contemporary Indian Act[72] provisions related to membership and governance are also rooted, at heart, in the Doctrine of Discovery. The capacity to make decisions about who/what is an Indian is a jurisdiction for which Canada has claimed responsibility for over 100 years.[73] While many would argue that the power to define who is an Indian is not the power to make decisions about identity and

[69] Ibid para 180. The case is discussed at length later in this chapter. Kent McNeil addresses the constitutionality of section 88 of the Indian Act and whether, with respect to rights protected under section 35(1) of the Constitution Act, an infringement in line with section 88 could be justified. A detailed discussion of the section and its impact on Aboriginal title is available in Kent McNeil's 'Aboriginal Title and Section 88 of the Indian Act' (2000) 34 Univ of British Columbia L Rev 159–94, referring to B Slattery, 'First Nations and the Constitution: A Question of Trust' (1992) 71 Canadian Bar Rev 261, 285.   [70] *Delgamuukw*, note 68, para 180.
[71] Ibid paras 160 and 165.   [72] Indian Act, note 67.
[73] Note the discussion in the previous chapter on historic versions of the Indian Act and An Act for the gradual enfranchisement of Indians (Chapter 4 note 89) within which the government of Canada legislatively empowered itself to make determinations about who/what is an Indian and who/what is not an Indian.

that the power to determine membership[74] has nothing whatsoever to do with the sovereign authority to make decisions about citizenship, there has been a colonial effect from the Canadian legal privileging of Indian status.

Furthermore, the Canadian imperial legal regime imposed the imperial Doctrinal racialized philosophy: Indians are incapable of making governmental decisions related to their members/citizens. As this imposed legislative administration was predicated on beliefs about Indigenous inferiority and Canadian supremacy, those beliefs, in some ways, extend to the present day manifestation of the Indian Act.

Canada's Department of Indian Affairs and Northern Development (which administers the Indian Act and other legislation that pertains specifically to peoples and nations defined as Indians and bands) has administrative responsibility for the implementation and operation of the Indian Act. Section 5 provides that the Department shall maintain an Indian register; every person entitled to be registered as an Indian is to be listed on the Register.[75] Section 6 contains a complex set of rules which, when applied, define Canadian legal membership standards. Canadian law was overhauled in 1985 in an attempt to make the legislation compliant with the equality provision of the Canadian Charter of Rights and Freedoms and ameliorate the profoundly destructive effects that disenfranchisement via the Act had on women, their children, and Indigenous communities.[76] Prior to that, a few cases brought before the Supreme Court of Canada addressed inequality of treatment for Indigenous peoples.[77] In particular, Indigenous women (and their children) who were disenfranchised by former versions of the Indian Act were able to apply for Indian membership under the terms of section 6.[78] The requirement that people who were disenfranchised by

---

[74] A power no longer exclusively belonging to Canada. Membership determination by First Nations was entrenched in the Indian Act 1985.

[75] Ibid s 5(1).

[76] Section 15 of the Canadian Charter of Rights and Freedoms, Part I of the Constitution Act, 1982, note 16. Section 15 provides for equal treatment before and under the law, and equal protection and benefit of the law without discrimination. Canada had, as mentioned in Chapter 4, a long legislative history of entrenched patriarchy which disallowed Indigenous women and their children membership under the Act. Section 6 was constructed in order to redress that inequality, thus bringing the section of the Indian Act in line with the equality provision of the Charter.

[77] *R v Drybones* (1969), [1970] SCR 282 (a Supreme Court of Canada case). For an example of the narrow interpretation of the Supreme Court of Canada see *Attorney-General of Canada v Lavell* [1974] SCR 1349 (a Supreme Court of Canada case).

[78] Many women's and Indigenous rights advocates argue that section 6 did not ameliorate the effects of involuntary enfranchisement housed in the Indian Act and that it merely postponed the effects and created a two-tier system within which some reinstated Indians would see Indian membership lapse after two generations. For a more detailed analysis of this discussion, see Megan Furi and Jill Wherrett, *Indian Status and Band Membership Issues* (Political and Social Affairs Division of the Government of Canada, Ottawa 1996 and Revised 2003), <http://www.parl.gc.ca/information/library/PRBpubs/bp410-e.htm>. In this article, the authors detail reinstatement under section 6(2) of the Act and state that it is subject to a 'second generation cut off rule' where 'status would be terminated after two successive generations of intermarriage between Indians and non-Indians'.

the government of Canada legislation have to apply for reinstatement as a member in accordance with government of Canada legislation that may have a built-in generational 'best before' date is, at least, the height of legislative arrogance and misanthropy. It also speaks to the implicit racialized Doctrinal understanding that the settler government possesses authorities and capacities superior to Indigenous governments to make decisions about membership determination (with related impacts on community, lands, territoriality, and services).

The same notions of superiority are built into the Act with respect to the Canadian legal capacity to determine band membership. Before 1985 if an individual had Indian status s/he also got band membership automatically. Section 10 of the Indian Act legislatively empowered nations to construct their own membership or citizenship codes.[79]

Furi and Wherret have written of this:

Prior to 1985, automatic entitlement to band membership usually accompanied entitlement to Indian status. The 1985 amendments recognized the rights of bands to determine their own membership. As a result, persons may possess Indian status, but not be members of a band. Section 10 enables First Nations to enact their own membership or citizenship codes, according to procedures set out in the Indian Act. Bands must follow two principles: the majority of the band's electors must consent to the band's taking control of membership, and to the set of membership rules (which must include a review mechanism); and the membership rules cannot deprive a person of previously acquired rights to membership. Once the band controls its membership list, Indian and Northern Affairs Canada (INAC) has no power to make additions or deletions, and no further responsibilities regarding the band list.

As of 28 June 1987, bands that chose to leave control of membership with the department were subject to the provision that a person who has Indian status also has a right to band membership. Membership lists for these bands are maintained by the department. These bands may still go on to take control of their own membership registration, but the rights of those individuals already registered and added to the band list are protected.[80]

The complexity of this situation should be evident on the face of it: Indian bands can now determine their own standards for membership (and can do so based on their traditional customs and laws) but must do so in accordance with settler notions of majority, consent, and governmental structure (Indian Act bands). However, with scant resources, economies increasingly pressured, and more than a century of imperial legalized division of families compounded in

---

[79] Section 10 provides:

10. (1) A band may assume control of its own membership if it establishes membership rules for itself in writing in accordance with this section and if, after the band has given appropriate notice of its intention to assume control of its own membership, a majority of the electors of the band gives its consent to the band's control of its own membership.

[80] Furi and Wherrett, note 78.

First Nations, the decisions to be made must be difficult ones. Lastly, requiring bands to make decisions in accordance with Canadian legislation and requiring that the methodology be provided to the Minister of the Department[81] connotes some notion of Doctrine based paternalism at least and derivative authority at worst.[82]

The Indian Act has been characterized as a set of 'cradle to grave' rules.[83] This is largely true. One particular category of Canadian legislation that is Doctrinally informed is in the section of the Indian Act that details Canadian legislative requirements with respect to the composition and some of the powers of band councils. The historic rationale and composition of the same is discussed in the previous chapter.[84] It is important to recognize that the authorities anticipated by the historic legislation have changed little and that municipal style governance structure and administrative and other categories still exist. It is also exceptionally important to acknowledge that the Act houses historic racialized notions of settler supremacy and Indigenous inferiority within its current incarnation that run counter to international, and even national, standards related to Indigenous rights. Notably, the antiquated section 74 of the Act which Canadian legislatively empowers the Minister to effectively 'erase' custom and traditional elections and enforce Indian Act formulated elections 'whenever he deems it advisable for the good government of a band...'.[85] This legislated authority can be argued to

---

[81]   Indian Act 1985, note 67, s 10(6).

[82]   A number of First Nations have brought actions against the government of Canada and against individuals who are seeking inclusion on membership lists. While it would be easy to simply state 'Indigenous Nations control their membership' the actuality—historic racism in the Act, gendered preference in the Act, the presumption of heterosexuality in the Act among others—is that many Indigenous citizens have difficulty obtaining membership for a myriad of reasons related to the historic discrimination in the Act. Compounded by the problems of legalized estrangement from their communities, scarce resources, and pressured economies in the Nations, and potentially the internalization of non-Indigenous standards of citizenship, many Indigenous citizens seeking inclusion on band membership lists or whom have been reinstated face an uphill battle. Cases that address this constructed fissure include: *Sawridge Band v Canada* [2004] 3 FCR 274 (a Federal Court of Appeal case), *McIvor v Canada* (Registrar, Indian and Northern Affairs) 306 DLR (4th) 193 (a British Columbia Court of Appeal case), and *Corbiere v Canada* (Minister of Indian and Northern Affairs), [1999] 2 SCR 203 (a Supreme Court of Canada case).

[83]   Indian Act 1985, note 67. This is particularly apt in that it houses rules related to guardianship and the money of infant children (ss 52–52.5) membership (s 6), descent of property (ss 42–44), wills (ss 45–47), and intestacy rules of property (ss 48–50.1).

[84]   Lindberg, Chapter 4, at 89. Current powers of the Council are enumerated at section 81(1).

[85]   Indian Act 1985, note 67, s 74(1). On 20 October 2009 the Minister of Indian Affairs informed the Barriere Lake Nation by mail that he was prepared to invoke the section. The government of Canada website states: 'If the community does not develop and ratify a leadership selection process by March 31, 2010, the Minister will exercise the powers conferred upon him by Section 74 of the Indian Act to ensure an election is held in accordance with the election provisions of the Indian Act and the Indian Band Election Regulations.' Indian and Northern Affairs Canada–Algonquins of Barriere Lake, <http://www.ainc-inac.gc.ca/ai/mr/is/brl-eng.asp>. The result of the application of this antiquated section would very likely be the overturn of a custom election result reached in the Barriere Lake First Nation. Many of the proponents of the traditional custom style of government point to a leaked memo within which the government of Canada advocated for the replacement of the traditional custom government with a Chief and council who

constitute erasure of the actual and traditional principles of good governance of a nation. Further, it privileges non-Indigenous standards of citizenship and governmental authority over Indigenous peoples. The attempt to legislatively entrench non-Indigenous standards of government and membership perpetuates the information held in the Doctrine that Indigenous legal orders, standards, and understandings are *less* than Canadian legal orders, standards, and understandings. They are not as cognizable by the Canadian government, but this does not mean that they are not applicable, accurate, and authoritative. In truth, what they are is less able to be manipulated. As standards which are housed within Indigenous nations, historians, and legal traditions, they are not able to be changed—if they can be changed—without community approval based upon community methodology for gaining and assessing approval.

It is with relation to Canadian legislation related to land and authorities for land that the most noticeable attack on Indigenous rights and titles occurs. Historically, the power to assume control of Indian lands was housed in the Indian Act. While treaties addressed the treaty rights to land and Aboriginal title and rights cases have delineated Aboriginal rights with respect to land, historically the notion that Canada had control over the administration of Indian lands was also built into the Indian Act.[86] Some Indigenous nations have found the application of Departmental administrative power arbitrary, to say the least.[87]

Contemporary provisions of the Indian Act also provide the Department with substantial administrative control (and some would argue arbitrary administrative authority) over Indian reserve lands. Section 18 of the current Act provides:

18. (1) Subject to this Act, reserves are held by Her Majesty for the use and benefit of the respective bands for which they were set apart, and subject to this Act and to the terms of

would be more receptive to 'improved collaboration'. Martin Lukacs, 'Minister's Memo Exposes Motives for Removing Algonquin Chief' (27 March 2009, Issue 60) *The Dominion*, <http://www.dominionpaper.ca/articles/2560>.

[86] See Lindberg, Chapter 4, note 89. An Act for the gradual enfranchisement of Indians, the better management of Indian affairs, and to extend the provisions of the Act 31st Victoria 1869, <http://www.ainc-inac.gc.ca/ai/arp/ls/pubs/a69c6/a69c6-eng.asp> outlined the requirement that no Indian or person marrying an Indian shall be deemed to be lawfully in possession of any land in such Townships or tracts, unless he or she has been or shall be located for the same by the order of the Superintendent General of Indian affairs.

[87] The Caughnawaga Indian Reserve Act 1934 applied The Indian Advancement Act 1886 to the Indigenous peoples at 'Caughnawaga'. As a result the reserve was divided into six sections. By an Order in Council (12 July 1906) (PC 1419) 'in the purported exercise of the powers conferred by section four of The Indian Advancement Act 1890, it was provided that the division of the Caughnawaga Indian Reserve into sections be done away with, and that the said reserve be comprised in one section'. The Act continues: 'and whereas it appears that there was no provision of The Indian Act or of any other statute authorizing the making of the last mentioned Order in Council, and that the same was and is, therefore, void and of no effect; and whereas it is expedient that anything duly done or suffered pursuant to the provisions of the said last mentioned Order in Council be validated, and that provision be made for again dividing the reserve into six sections…'. The end result was that His Majesty enacted the Caughnawaga Indian Reserve Act which validated the unlawfully made Order in Council.

any treaty or surrender, the Governor in Council may determine whether any purpose for which lands in a reserve are used or are to be used is for the use and benefit of the band.[88]

Additionally, in accordance with the Indian Act, possession of land in the reserve must be approved by the Minister of the Department;[89] the Minister can issue and recognize formerly issued Certificates of Possession,[90] location tickets,[91] and temporary possession.[92] The Canadian legislated Ministerial authority related to the administration of reserve lands is extensive.[93]

The legislative authority the Minister receives from the Indian Act is not only related to land rights of Indian peoples on reserve. The Indian Act empowers the government of Canada to consent to 'takings' of reserve land where a federal, provincial, or other authority is legislatively empowered to do so.[94] 'Taking' lands for public purposes is based on two Doctrinal premises: the reserve land is always subject to Crown underlying authority and Indian peoples are not 'the public' and therefore the public good does not have to take into account the rights, needs, and historic relationship that people defined as Indians have with their historic homelands.

There are many instances of Doctrine-based understandings housed in the legislation, but the presumption of superior authority of imperial governments arguably has no better examples than the sections of the Indian Act dealing with takings and surrender. Section 37 resonates with the intention and superiority that was reflected in the Royal Proclamation and in the historic Canadian legislative suite pertaining to Indian peoples requiring Crown consent prior to surrendering Indian lands prior to a sale or lease.[95] The seemingly odd contradiction of

---

[88] Indian Act 1985, note 67, s 18(1).   [89] Ibid s 20(1).   [90] Ibid s 20(2).
[91] Ibid s 20(3).
[92] Ibid s 20(4). In this instance, when a band with reserve land has allotted some of the land to an individual, the Minister is legislatively empowered to authorize the individual to temporarily occupy the land until s/he makes approves the allotment. Under section 20(5) the Minister can authorize a Certificate of Occupation whereby the individual (or devisees) can 'occupy the land in respect of which it is issued for a period of two years from the date thereof'.
[93] Ibid. They include the maintenance of a Reserve Land Register within which the above documentation is entered and tracked (s 21), approving compensation for improvements made to the land (s 23—in which the Minister can direct payment for the improvements by the new person in possession or the band), approval of transfer of possession (s 24), the correction or cancellation of Certificates of Possession or Occupation or Location Tickets (ss 25 and 26), and the issuance of permits allowing occupancy or residency on the reserve for one year (or longer with band approval) (s 28(2)).
[94] Indian Act 1985 s 35(1) reads in its entirety:

35. (1) Where by an Act of Parliament or a provincial legislature Her Majesty in right of a province, a municipal or local authority or a corporation is empowered to take or to use lands or any interest therein without the consent of the owner, the power may, with the consent of the Governor in Council and subject to any terms that may be prescribed by the Governor in Council, be exercised in relation to lands in a reserve or any interest therein.

[95] Ibid s 37(1). Indians may also surrender their lands directly to the Crown, and this is facilitated by section 38(1). This includes the rights and interests of the band and its members. Quite like the historic legislation, a valid surrender requires a majority vote (s 39(3)).

Canadian governmental recognition of some type of Indigenous land rights and a reluctance to even address notions of sovereignty is clearly evident in section 41, which provides:

41. An absolute surrender or a designation shall be deemed to confer all rights that are necessary to enable Her Majesty to carry out the terms of the surrender or designation.[96]

The notion of Canadian Departmental control of Indian lands (and monies)[97] is unacceptable to many and runs counter to the Indigenous legal understandings and laws related to the necessity of Indigenous guardianship and relationships with Indigenous traditional territories.[98]

   Canada has passed legislation that allows specific First Nations to opt in with respect to the power to manage Indian lands and make laws. The First Nations Land Management Act[99] legislatively provides for First Nations who were a party to the 1996 Framework Agreement on First Nation Land Management[100] to participate in a legislative regime related to land management. Under this legislation, First Nation powers include the power to manage First Nation land. The section detailing the powers provides that:

18. (1) A first nation has, after the coming into force of its land code and subject to the Framework Agreement and this Act, the power to manage first nation land and, in particular, may
   (a) exercise the powers, rights and privileges of an owner in relation to that land;
   (b) grant interests or rights in and licences in relation to that land;
   (c) manage the natural resources of that land; and
   (d) receive and use all moneys acquired by or on behalf of the first nation under its land code.[101]

The Act also details the power of the approving First Nations required capacities to: (a) acquire and hold property, (b) enter into contracts, (c) borrow money, (d) expend and invest money, and (e) be a party to legal proceedings.[102] The powers are exercisable by a Band Council or their designate.[103] The Act further acknowledges the cooperating First Nations capacity to make laws in accordance with

---

[96] Ibid s 41.   [97] Ibid ss 53–69.2.

[98] While the notion of surrendering reserve land to the Crown as a precursor to sale or lease is predicated to some degree on notions of superiority, it can also be said that, given the Crown role in the separation of Indigenous peoples from their lands historically, this protectionist role is an attempt to counterbalance the Crown's previous neglect of its duties.

[99] 1999, c. 24 (assented to 17 June 1999).

[100] Framework Agreement on First Nation Land Management (signed 1996) (Westbank, Musqueam, Lheidli T'enneh (Formerly Known As 'Lheitlit'en'), N'quatqua, Squamish, Siksika, Muskoday, Cowessess, Opaskwayak Cree, Nipissing, Mississaugas Of Scugog Island, Chippewas Of Mnjikaning, Chippewas Of Georgina Island, Saint Mary's, as represented by their Chiefs and all other first nations that have adhered to the Agreement And Her Majesty The Queen In Right Of Canada), <http://www.fafnlm.com/content/documents/Text%20of%20the%20Framework%20 Agreement%20on%20First%20Nation%20Land%20Management.pdf>.

[101] First Nation Lands Management Act 1999, note 99, s 18(1).   [102] Ibid s 18(2).

[103] Ibid ss 18(3) and 18(2).

its land code.[104] It is worth noting that the Act addresses the capacity of the First Nations to enforce their laws and make rules with respect to punishments.[105]

The Act includes provisions related to the alienation, expropriation, and exchange of land; First Nation land cannot be alienated except where exchanged for land in accordance with the Act and the Framework Agreement. Exchange of the land is still subject to Ministerial approval.[106]

Legislation pertaining to Indian lands is rife with imperialist notions of supremacy and rightful/righteous ownership. The administration of Indigenous peoples through successive incarnations of the Indian Act has, to some degree, introduced and normalized unilateral decision making by the Canadian government about Indian peoples. It constructs Indians as objects to be controlled and as subjects of foreign legislation (with past legislation outlawing religious gatherings, retention of lawyers without Crown approval, and permission to leave reserves without a pass). Legislation as it applies to Indigenous peoples has been interpreted in accordance with the 'comprehensive no'. There is power in this presumptive no as well: the power to assume the application of the 'comprehensive no', rather than examining the maybe. Perhaps we should even be addressing the presumptive 'comprehensive yes' in which Indigenous standards apply and Canadian law is presumed to break Indigenous laws. Universal applicability can no longer be presumed. Disproving that we broke Canadian laws is not enough if we are to unpack the Doctrinal legal history with any degree of accuracy, inclusion, and reciprocity.

What goes to the core of Indianness, more accurately of Indigeneity, must be determined by Indigenous legal orders, governmental orders, and standards. Cognizability of that fact must be constructed, interpreted, and understood by Canadian jurisdictions and bodies if we are to move beyond objectification of Indianness. If Indigenous peoples opt to participate in the Canadian judicial system, then cognizability must include Indigenous cognizability. Privileging

---

[104] Ibid. Such rights include: rights related to licences (s 20(1)(a)), the development, conservation, protection, management, use and possession of First Nation land (s 20(1)(b)), any matter arising out of or ancillary to the exercise of that power (s 20(1)(c)). First Nation laws, the Act provides, may include laws respecting the regulation, control, or prohibition of land use and development including zoning and subdivision control (s 20(2)(a)), subject to section 5, the creation, acquisition, and granting of interests or rights in and licences in relation to First Nation land and prohibitions in relation thereto (s 20(2)(b)), environmental assessment and environmental protection (20(2)(c)), the provision of local services in relation to First Nation land and the imposition of equitable user charges for those services (s 20(2)(d)), and the provision of services for the resolution of disputes in relation to first nation land (s 20(2)(d)).

[105] Ibid. Section 20(3) provides that: '[a] first nation law may provide for enforcement measures, consistent with federal laws, such as the power to inspect, search and seize and to order compulsory sampling, testing and the production of information'. Additionally, s 22(1) addresses the choices a First Nation may make with respect to offences (ie punishable on summary conviction and provide for the imposition of fines, imprisonment, restitution, community service, and any other means for achieving compliance).

[106] Ibid ss 27(1)(b) and 18(1). According to the Schedule attached to the legislation, 58 First Nations opted into the legislation.

Canadian understandings of Indianness needs to be stopped for a meaningful discussion to occur. The alternative to this is, of course, to rejuvenate our systems where Indigenous presumptions and cognizability (of citizenship standards, citizenship rules, relationships with land) are inherent to the process and substance.

5. Canadian case law

That notion of superiority of European sovereignty, title, law, and governance is still evident in the case law today. What is perhaps the most perplexing part of the discussion is that the legal conversations taking place in Canada seem, on the surface, to be so coherent and non-threatening to Indigenous rights. The problem is that the principles of supremacy buried in the Doctrine often seem to be archaic remnants. They are rarely discussed. When they are, we are forced to remember that the common law is based upon its legal precedents. We struggle to understand that the precedents are based upon historic policies, laws, and shared imperial understandings. It is difficult to see the layering of racialized philosophies and beliefs that informed those policies, laws, and shared imperial understandings. As a result, our vision of the Doctrine that was the basis for those philosophies and beliefs is obscured. Make no mistake, though. It's there.

A contemporary catalogue of Indigenist concerns with the Doctrinal influence on the Canadian judiciary's decisions related to rights and title might look something like this:

1. Canadian judicial decision making, in large part, addresses issues related to Indigenous peoples' rights to our lands and traditional territories in the third person.

2. Canada's judges examine Indigenous rights, particularly those related to land, through a colonial lens constructed with notions of settler dominance and original peoples' inferior rights.

3. Decisions at every conceivable level of the judiciary initially revealed intrinsic notions of cultural, linguistic, spiritual, economic, and moral superiority. Those notions have been entrenched in legal precedent, perpetuated without a cultural or racial audit, and continue to be put forward as law and legislation in Canada.

4. Modern cases examine Indigenous rights through this colonial lens. The findings related to Indigenous peoples' rights have us, at least, as unwitting and unfortunate unknowing peoples. At worst, we find ourselves and determinations related to our rights addressing the unwritten understandings of our humanity: Canada won, we lost.

5. A legal shorthand develops in which unproven assertions become commonly judicially accepted facts: Canadian sovereignty, our limited power to rule ourselves (internally), our inability to participate in activities that have a 'modern' bent.

6. Consultation and, sometimes (although increasingly less and less) accommodation begin to become discussed in instances which would have previously been negotiated as rights and title.

7. Worse than *terra nullius*, we are abandoned nations, judicially determined that because we were confined to reserves, because we were legislatively not entitled to live or travel where we liked, that we gave up our right to our land.

8. We find our obligations to our land, our relationships with our land cast as 'rights'. Housed within these casings, we find ourselves required to translate our understandings into something legally cognizable. If we do not do so, then, the 'characterization of the right' is something that is left to the judiciary.

9. A legal shorthand predicated on a legal history which found Indigenous peoples lacking in every conceivable manner becomes standardized and regularly alluded to with no full discussion or anti-colonial audit.

Modern Canadian case law related to Indigenous peoples owes much to the notions of superiority and the legacy of the Doctrine in judicial formulation of legal opinions with respect to the rights and titles of Indigenous peoples. A 1929 decision addressing the treaty rights of Indigenous peoples in what came to be known as the Province of Nova Scotia provided ample opportunity for the Nova Scotia County Court to expound upon the beliefs housed within the Doctrine of Discovery and make them Canadian law.[107]

The Judge, Patterson Co Ct J (Acting), wrote in his decision:

[T]he Indians were never regarded as an independent power. A civilized nation first discovering a country of uncivilized people or savages held such country as its own until such time as by treaty it was transferred to some other civilized nation. The savages' rights of sovereignty even of ownership were never recognized. Nova Scotia had passed to Great Britain not by gift or purchase from or even by conquest of the Indians but by treaty with France, which had acquired it by priority of discovery and ancient possession; and the Indians passed with it.[108]

The case dealt with the interpretation of a 1752 treaty between the 'Mick Macks' of Nova Scotia and His Majesty's representative (Governor Hopson).[109] The decision replicated the notion of the Doctrine of Discovery inherent within the colonial project by interpreting the Treaty in a manner informed by the same principles upon which the Doctrine itself was constructed. Instead of noting the actual terminology and content of the Peace and Friendship Treaty (which included, among other things: free liberty of hunting and fishing as usual, truck houses, bread, flour, and other provisions as necessary),[110] the Nova Scotia County

---

[107] The case was not followed in *R v McCoy* [1992] New Brunswick Judgment No 346 (a New Brunswick Queen's Bench Trial Division case) and was questioned in *R v Ellsworth* [1989] British Columbia Judgment No 2522 (a BC Provincial Court case). Resolved in 1929, the case served as law in Canada for 60 years.

[108] Patterson Co Ct J (Acting) in *R v Syliboy* [1929] 1 DLR 307 at 313, (1928) 50 CCC 389 at 396 (a Nova Scotia County Court case).　　　　　　　　　　　　　　　　[109] Ibid 307.

[110] Treaty between Enclosure in letter of Governor Hopson to the Right Honourable The Earl of Holdernesse, 6th of December 1752 Treaty or Articles of Peace and Friendship Renewed (between

Court delineated the discussion of Mi'kmaq economies in terms of 'rights' and 'rights acquisition' rather than in terms of the recognition and honouring of an Agreement or of the inherency of the rights. Even though the Treaty itself is most clearly a plea from His Majesty to the Mi'kmaq people not to attack them (with notions of burying the hatchet actually included in the draft), a Doctrine based characterization (addressing Indigenous people as savages and inferior and non-Indigenous peoples as sophisticated and superior in order to rationalize 'rightful' authority) was applied by the Court in interpreting the Grand Chief of the Mi'kmaq's right to hunt. Convicted under the province of Nova Scotia Lands and Forests Act[111] of having in his possession at Askilton in the County of Inverness on 4 November, last 15 green pelts, 14 muskrat, and one fox,[112] the Grand Chief argued his treaty right to hunt and trap.[113]

The Court found that the Treaty was not made with Mi'kmaq people as a whole but with 'a small body of that tribe living in the eastern part of Nova Scotia proper, with headquarters in and about Shubenacadie, and that any benefits under it accrued only to that body and their heirs'.[114] If this is so, then only a small body of Englishmen would have benefited from the Treaty; clearly this was not the case. The Treaty was applied to the nation as a whole and the interpretation clearly applied to the nation as a whole. The Court found that the Grand Chief could not 'claim any protection from it or any rights under [the treaty]'.[115]

When the Nishga Tribal Council sued the province of British Columbia for a declaration that their Aboriginal title to their traditional territory had never been extinguished, the Supreme Court of Canada had its first opportunity to emancipate itself from the notion of the Doctrine of Discovery as a source of Canadian

---

His Excellency Peregrine Thomas Hopson Esquire Captain General and Governor in Chief in and over His Majesty's Province of Nova Scotia or Acadie Vice Admiral of the same & Colonel of One of His Majesty's Regiments of Foot, and His Majesty's Council on behalf of His Majesty), <http://www.lennoxisland.com/portal/docs/fish_1752_treaty.doc> (1752 Treaty).

[111] Lands and Forests Act 1926 (Nova Scotia).

[112] *R v Syliboy*, note 108, 430 (307).

[113] Ibid. The relevant provision of the treaty provided:

4. It is agreed that the said Tribe of Indians shall not be hindered from, but have free liberty of Hunting and Fishing as usual and that if they shall think a Truck house needful at the River Chibenaccadie, or any other place of their resort they shall have the same built and proper Merchandize, lodged therein to be exchanged for what the Indians shall have to dispose of and that in the mean time the Indians shall have free liberty to being to Sale to Halifax or any other Settlement within this Province, Skins, feathers, fowl, fish or any other thing they shall have to sell, where they shall have liberty to dispose there of to the best Advantage.

[114] Ibid 432 (309).

[115] Ibid. At 436 (313), the Court addresses English common law conceptualizations of law and its relationship to land in the notion of Discovery. Discovery means that rights cannot be presumed to be held by the 'discovered'. This is established by the Court in its discussion of the Mi'kmaq rights in 'that they did not claim to be an independent nation owning or possessing their lands'. But the discovery rights of 'civilized' nations were presumed.

authority, sovereignty, and lawfulness.[116] The Supreme Court of Canada split on whether Aboriginal title continued to exist (and a seventh judge did not address the issue, instead deciding the case on a technicality).[117]

Justices Martland, Judson, and Richie intrinsically addressed 'discovery'— noting that the Nishga and their territory were not within the knowledge of the framers of the 1763 Royal Proclamation and were therefore outside the 'scope' of it.[118] However, the rationality of Indigenous sovereignty's existence was not extended to any situation where Indigenous peoples and their territories were known. Indigenous territory, these three Supreme Court of Canada judges held, automatically became a part of the Province of British Columbia when the Colony of British Columbia was established in 1858.[119] Upon entering the Canadian Confederation in 1871, Justices Martland, Judson, and Richie held, the fee transferred to the Province of BC.[120] This, in addition to Governor Douglas's proclamations and ordinances enacted between 1865 and 1870 revealed an intention to exercise absolute sovereignty, Justices Martland, Judson, and Richie found. This absolute intention was, by these members of the Court, equated with an absolute sovereignty and that any Aboriginal right/title was 'dependent upon the goodwill of the Sovereign'.[121] This absolute sovereignty was found to be inconsistent with any notion of Aboriginal title. This portion of the Court noted that section 91(24) of the (then) British North America Act was utilized to establish Indian reserves and that agreement was given on behalf of the Indians.[122]

On dissent, Justices Hall, Spence, and Laskin decried the notion of the erasure of Indian/Aboriginal rights absolutely upon 'conquest or discovery'.[123] This case, even though there was no clear majority on the point of the existence of Aboriginal rights and title, was the first in Canada to acknowledge the fallacy of the erasure of Indigenous sovereignty through intent. Something more was required. What 'something more' was still not conclusively decided by the Court. But, the understanding that 'the proposition that after conquest or discovery the native peoples have no rights at all except those subsequently granted or recognized by the conqueror or discoverer... is wholly wrong as the mass of authorities previously cited, including *Johnson v. McIntosh and Campbell v. Hall*, establishes'.[124] These three judges also looked to Viscount Haldane's statement in the *Amodu Tijani* case in finding that '[o]nce aboriginal title is established, it is presumed to continue until the contrary is proven'.[125]

---

[116] *Calder et al v Attorney-General of British Columbia* [1973] SCR 313 (a Supreme Court of Canada case). [117] Sovereign immunity from suit without a fiat.
[118] Ibid 323.   [119] Ibid 327.   [120] Ibid.   [121] Ibid 328.   [122] Ibid 336.
[123] Ibid 315. The dissenting judgment provided:

The proposition accepted by the Courts below that after conquest or discovery the native peoples have no rights at all except those subsequently granted or recognized by the conqueror or discoverer was wholly wrong. There is a wealth of jurisprudence affirming common law recognition of aboriginal rights to possession and enjoyment of lands of aboriginees precisely analogous to the Nishga situation.   [124] Ibid 416.
[125] Ibid 401.

It should be noted that there is a presumption in this judgment that the Nishga automatically came under British sovereignty. They were entitled to assert 'Indian title'[126]—but it should also be noted this title could (the three found) have been surrendered to the Crown, or exhausted by specific legislation concurrent with legislative authority.[127] The lack of input from the Indigenous nation itself must be addressed; Nishga understanding played little part in the decision.[128]

Intrinsically, the notion of the acceptability of erasure of Indigenous (title) may have changed the requirements, but the notion of Discovery, in which the discoverer had absolute dominion and administrative requirements to meet, was still in place.[129]

The Supreme Court of Canada took the opportunity to examine the nature of Aboriginal rights again in 1990. In *R v Sparrow*[130] the nation's highest court addressed the Aboriginal right to fish. Whether commercially or unrestricted were additional matters, but the Court took the opportunity to interpret section 35(1) of the Constitution Act.[131] Section 35, in its entirety, provides:

35. (1) The existing aboriginal and treaty rights of the aboriginal peoples of Canada are hereby recognized and affirmed.

(2) In this Act, 'aboriginal peoples of Canada' includes the Indian, Inuit and Métis peoples of Canada.

(3) For greater certainty, in subsection (1) 'treaty rights' includes rights that now exist by way of land claims agreements or may be so acquired.

(4) Notwithstanding any other provision of this Act, the aboriginal and treaty rights referred to in subsection (1) are guaranteed equally to male and female persons.[132]

The constitutional provision had been enacted in 1982, but the Supreme Court of Canada's decision in *Sparrow* was the first time the Court reviewed the provision

---

[126] Ibid 402.   [127] Ibid.

[128] Ibid 319. David Mackay is quoted on this page, stating: 'What we don't like about the Government is their saying this: "We will give you this much land." How can they give it when it is our own? We cannot understand it. They have never bought it from us or our forefathers. They have never fought our people and taken the land in that way, and yet they say now that they will give us so much land—our own land. These chiefs do not talk foolishly, they know the land is their own; our forefathers for generations and generations past had their land here all around us; chiefs have had their own hunting grounds, their salmon streams, and places where they got their berries; it has always been so. It is not only during the last four or five years that we have seen the land; we have always seen and owned it; it is no new thing, it has been ours for generations. If we had only seen it for twenty years and claimed it as our own, it would have been foolish, but it has been ours for thousands of years. If any strange person came here and saw the land for twenty years and claimed it, he would be foolish. We have always got our living from the land; we are not like white people who live in towns and have their stores and other business, getting their living in that way, but we have always depended on the land for our food and clothes; we get our salmon, berries, and furs from the land . . .'.

[129] Interestingly, Hall, Spence, and Laskin JJ examined the Marshall decisions extensively in *Johnson v McIntosh* 21 US 240 (1823) (starting at 380) and *Worcester v State of Georgia* 31 US 530 (1832) (starting at 383) in arriving at their decision. For a detailed discussion of these cases see Miller, Chapters 1 and 2 of this book.

[130] *R v Sparrow* [1990] 1 SCR 1075 (a Supreme Court of Canada case). <http://www.quicklaw.ca>.
[131] Constitution Act, note 16.   [132] Ibid s 35(1).

as it applied to an Aboriginal right. In this case, the right was put forward by a Musqueam fisherman as the right to fish. The Supreme Court of Canada characterized the issue as 'whether Parliament's power to regulate fishing is now limited by s. 35(1) of the Constitution Act 1982, and, more specifically, whether the net length restriction in the licence is inconsistent with that provision'.[133] The Regulations to the alleged impugned provincial Fisheries Act[134] also provided that the licences were for the purpose of obtaining food for that Indian and his family and for the band.[135]

The Court, as mentioned, took this opportunity to determine some of the specific meaning of the language of section 35(1) of the Canadian Constitution Act. In essence, not just the Aboriginal right to fish was examined, but all Aboriginal rights became subject to Canadian legal scrutiny.

'Existing', the Court found, clearly meant that the right has to be in existence in 1982 (when the Constitution Act was enacted). Rights extinguished before this time, the Court held, were not revived.[136] 'Existing aboriginal rights' the Court held, had to be 'interpreted flexibly so as to permit their evolution over time'.[137] The right to fish, the Supreme Court of Canada found, faced a 'progressive restriction'[138] over time. That the right is controlled 'in great detail by the regulations does not mean that the right is thereby extinguished....' wrote the Chief Justice and LaForest J in the judgment of the Court.[139] The Court continued, addressing the intention of the Crown and the role that intention plays in exercising Canadian sovereignty. In this case Canadian sovereignty is implicitly presumed without proof to be housed in the Crown as a result of 'discovery': 'The test of extinguishment to be adopted, in our opinion, is that the Sovereign's intention must be clear and plain if it is to extinguish an aboriginal right.'[140] The permits,

---

[133] *Sparrow*, note 130, 1083. The appellant Musqueam Indian band citizen was charged with fishing with a drift net longer than that permitted under the Band's Indian food fishing licence. The licence itself included a restriction on drift nets—they could be only 25 fathoms long. The appellant Musqueam Indian band citizen's net was 45 fathoms long.

[134] Ibid. Fisheries Act 1970 ss 34, 61(1) cited at paras 1 and 16.

[135] British Columbia Fishery (General) Regulations, SOR/84-248, s 27(1). In this section 'Indian food fish licence' means a licence issued by the Minister to an Indian or a band for the sole purpose of obtaining food for that Indian and his family or for the band.

[136] *Sparrow*, note 130, 1091.

[137] Ibid 1093. The Court went on to state: 'Clearly, then, an approach to the constitutional guarantee embodied in s 35(1) which would incorporate "frozen rights" must be rejected.' This has proven difficult for the Supreme Court of Canada to achieve. There is clearly a discomfort addressing modern exercise of ancient rights at the Supreme Court of Canada—with a demonstrated ability to reconcile the notion of rights with activities that, arguably, could be characterized as 'frozen' rights: activities such as hunting and fishing for sustenance and chopping down trees for traditional dwellings and spiritual ceremonies have been found to be existing treaty and Aboriginal rights by the Supreme Court of Canada. Discussion on this point and the cases that support the same will follow in this chapter. See *Marshall I*, note 49, *Marshall II*, note 55, and *R v Sioui* [1990] 1 SCR 1025 (a Supreme Court of Canada case).   [138] Ibid 1097.

[139] Ibid 1099.

[140] Ibid 1098, quoting *Attorney-General for Ontario v Bear Island Foundation* (1984) 49 OR (2nd) 353 (HC) (an Ontario High Court of Justice case).

the Court found, controlled the fisheries and did not define the rights nor exhibit a clear and plain intention to extinguish the Aboriginal right to fish.[141]

The Court then went on to address and define, for the first time in Canadian law, the meaning of 'recognized and affirmed' in section 35(1). The Court relied upon *Johnson v M'Intosh*[142] and the Royal Proclamation[143] to establish that:

[i]t is worth recalling that while British policy towards the native population was based on respect for their right to occupy their traditional lands, a proposition to which the Royal Proclamation of 1763 bears witness, there was from the outset never any doubt that sovereignty and legislative power, and indeed the underlying title, to such lands vested in the Crown; see *Johnson v M'Intosh* ... [and] the *Royal Proclamation* itself....[144]

The absolutism in the statement is strikingly clear and leaves little room for the conceptualization of correlate or shared sovereignty. Even further, Indigenous land rights are understood to sit on the rightful and superior title of the Crown. Finding its precision and spectacularly assured understanding of the rightfulness and legality of Canadian sovereignty, legislative power, and underlying title embedded in their understanding of Crown superiority, the Court does not examine the totalitarianism or universalism of non-Indigenous superiority housed in their decision. The Doctrine does not require that anyone with power examines the rationale or underlying tenets of supremacy that make the 'fact' of sovereignty, legislative power, and underlying title factual.

Armed with the understanding of the fact of Crown superiority, the Court does note that the recognition and affirmation found in section 35(1) do not give the Crown unfettered authority, indeed the terms 'incorporate the fiduciary relationship referred to earlier and so import some restraint on the exercise of sovereign power'.[145] The statement seems surprisingly mild given the earlier statement with regard to sovereignty until the Court reminds us that '[r]ights that are recognized and affirmed are not absolute'.[146]

That fiduciary duty,[147] embedded with notions of the honour of the Crown, is one which is viewed suspiciously; the non-Indigenous governments' objectives

---

[141] Ibid 1099.   [142] Ibid 1103 referring to *M'Intosh,* note 129.

[143] Royal Proclamation 1763, RSC, 1985, App II, No 1, 4–6.

[144] *Sparrow*, note 130, 1103. Addressing the government of Canada's policy with respect to Aboriginal title/claims, the Court stated:

Thus the Statement of the Government of Canada on Indian Policy (1969), although well meaning, contained the assertion (at p. 11) that 'aboriginal claims to land ... are so general and undefined that it is not realistic to think of them as specific claims capable of remedy except through a policy and program that will end injustice to the Indians as members of the Canadian community'.

[145] Ibid 1109.   [146] Ibid.

[147] Fiduciary duty with respect to Indigenous peoples was adjudicated in a 1984 decision of the Supreme Court of Canada. *Guerin v Canada* [1984] 2 SCR 335, a case in which the government of Canada approved a surrender of First Nation land at terms much less favourable than those approved by the First Nation, found that the government of Canada has a fiduciary duty to Aboriginal peoples. Dickson J for the majority found at para 83:

In my view, the nature of Indian title and the framework of the statutory scheme established for disposing of Indian land places upon the Crown an equitable obligation, enforceable by the courts,

may appear neutral but indeed may themselves constitute 'de facto threats to the existence of aboriginal rights and interests'.[148] While sympathetically stated, the notion of non-Indigenous governmental objectives as threats to the existence of Aboriginal rights was the terminology used to introduce the notion of the justification for infringement of those rights. In fact, what can be argued is that what ultimately is established by the Court is a template for the eradication of Aboriginal rights and the formula to ensure that the eradication is done Canadian lawfully. Any interference with a right is a *prima facie* infringement of s 35(1).[149] In the determination as to whether the right has been interfered with to the degree to constitute a *prima facie* infringement, the questions to be asked are whether the limitation on the right is unreasonable, whether the regulation imposes undue hardship, and whether the regulation denies the Aboriginal rights holders of their preferred means to exercise that right.[150]

If there is found to be an infringement, then the justification for the infringement begins. The Court found that '[t]his is the test that addresses the question of what constitutes legitimate regulation of a constitutional aboriginal right'.[151] The questions asked in this test for justification are whether there is a valid legislative objective,[152] whether the Crown was honourable in its dealings,[153] and whether there has been as little infringement as possible, whether fair compensation is available, and whether the Aboriginal group has been consulted regarding the implemented consultation measures.[154]

In essence, then, what occurs is that the Aboriginal party asserting/defending their Aboriginal right has to prove that the infringement is a *prima facie* infringement. At that point, if the infringement is proven, the onus shifts to the Crown.[155] The Crown then has to establish that the infringing regulation is justifiable.

The surface neutrality belies the value-laden judgments that are made in order to arrive at the decision as to whether a right continues to exist or has been extinguished. Initially, it should be asked whether the encapsulation of an Indigenous way of life into a wordbox (think: rights) has any relationship to the actuality of authorities and customs which Indigenous peoples correspond with and live lawfully in accordance with every day. There is also the quite frankly insulting proposition that activities which cannot be 'proven' to be existing cannot be exercised. In nations where written documentation was not used to record, as we had no 'perfect tool of empire' the standard of proof is an exceptionally difficult

---

to deal with the land for the benefit of the Indians. This obligation does not amount to a trust in the private law sense. It is rather a fiduciary duty. If however, the Crown breaches this fiduciary duty it will be liable to the Indians in the same way and to the same extent as if such a trust were in effect.

[148] *Sparrow*, note 130, 1110. One could wonder the same thing about seemingly neutral decisions of a judicial body. [149] Ibid 1111.

[150] Ibid 1112. The Court found that the onus for proving the infringement is on the individual or group who are challenging the legislation. Framing the justification in this way notionally requires the holders to intrinsically accept the right of the Crown (provincial or federal) as sovereign as only the Sovereign has the right to interfere with, legislate with regard to, the right.

[151] Ibid 1113.   [152] Ibid.   [153] Ibid 1114.   [154] Ibid 1119.
[155] Ibid 1121.

burden to meet. What can be understood to be 'existing' when the historical-legal paper trail (including the judgments of the Supreme Court) is so littered with false notions of Indigenous invisibility and inferiority, the underlying title of 'discovering nations', and the supremacy of settler sovereignty to Indigenous sovereignty?

Finally, the honour of the Crown is a really difficult concept upon which to found your understanding of the obligation of the government of Canada to Indigenous peoples. There is myth rooted in that as well.

Six years after *Sparrow,* the Supreme Court of Canada had another opportunity to examine and define Aboriginal rights. In *R v Van der Peet*[156] the Court reviewed section 35(1) of the Constitution Act again, this time in the context of a First Nation person's right to sell salmon. When she was charged with selling the salmon (the regulations governing food fishing licences—which she had—prohibited the sale of fish) Ms Van der Peet contended that the licensing scheme infringed her Aboriginal right to fish and that the regulations violated section 35(1).[157]

The majority decision was written by Lamer J and he phrased the issue as 'whether s. 35(1) recognizes and affirms the right of the Sto:lo [Nation, of which Ms. Van der Peet is a citizen] to sell fish...'.[158] He found that post-section 35(1) Aboriginal rights cannot be extinguished—they can only be regulated or infringed, and that any regulation or infringement must be justified under the *Sparrow* test.[159] Lamer J seems to understand that Aboriginal rights exist because Indigenous peoples were here first. Section 35(1) recognizes and affirms Aboriginal rights because *'when Europeans arrived in North America, aboriginal peoples were already here, living in communities on the land, and participating in distinctive cultures, as they had done for centuries'* (emphasis added).[160] While this seems promising, the notion of Crown supremacy in terms of sovereignty is clearly accepted and the measure by which reconciliation of interests can be achieved. Lamer writes of this, at para 31:

> More specifically, what s. 35(1) does is provide the constitutional framework through which the fact that aboriginals lived on the land in distinctive societies, with their own practices, traditions and cultures, is acknowledged and reconciled with the sovereignty of the Crown.[161]

By this telling, Indigenous peoples possess something not quite as formal as sovereignty, and instead have 'practices, traditions and cultures'. The case stands for the proposition that to be an Aboriginal right, a practice, custom, or tradition must be one which is integral to a distinctive culture.[162] This sounds like an achievable target, but for two things. The first is a problem of proof. Oral cultures may have difficulty proving the integral nature of an activity because

---

[156] *R v Van der Peet* [1996] 2 SCR 507 (a Supreme Court of Canada case).
[157] Ibid para 6.   [158] Ibid para 2.   [159] Ibid para 28.   [160] Ibid para 30.
[161] Ibid para 31.   [162] Ibid para 46.

of the requirement of proof of the continuity of exercise of the claimed activity from prior to contact to the current day.[163] Time dating them in this regard and requiring 'continuity', the Court says, avoids the problem of 'frozen rights'.[164] Criticism has also been made that this approach—time dating Indigenous activities at a 'pre-contact' period does exactly *that*: it freezes the rights so that proof of existing rights becomes more and more difficult to provide as the right becomes more contemporized.[165]

Finally, the Court asked the question: was the practice of exchanging fish for money or other goods an integral part of the specific distinctive culture of the Sto:lo prior to contact with Europeans?[166] The Supreme Court of Canada found that it was not. Given that the Sto:lo likely did not have money (and also as likely that they had all sorts of currency and exchanges in place prior to contact) the result is not that surprising.

One year later, the Court found itself dealing with another case in British Columbia. *Delgamuukw v British Columbia* was a claim brought forward by the hereditary chiefs of the Gitksan and Wet'suwet'en (individually and for their 'Houses').[167] The case allowed the Court to expand upon the implications of the constitutionalization of Aboriginal title. While the claim was originally for ownership and jurisdiction, the lower court transformed the claim into a claim of Aboriginal title.[168] This is related to the Doctrine notion that settlers had superior claim to land; Aboriginal nations could not be conceived of to actually own or have jurisdiction, the Court could only understand the claim if it was framed as Aboriginal title—something different, something less than actual ownership.

The influence of the Doctrine extended as well to the dates by which the Court would ascertain whether an Aboriginal right or Aboriginal title existed. With respect to Aboriginal rights, the time period to be examined to determine the existence of a right was the time of first contact. In terms of Aboriginal title, the

---

[163] Ibid para 59: 'The practices, customs and traditions which constitute aboriginal rights are those which have continuity with the practices, customs and traditions that existed prior to contact.'

[164] Ibid para 64. At para 73 the Court found that European arrival cannot be used to deprive Aboriginal peoples of a valid claim to an Aboriginal right.

[165] In 1996 as well the *R v Pamajewon* [1996] 2 SCR 821 decision of the Supreme Court of Canada (in which the First Nations leaders held bingos and operated gambling on reserve without regard to other jurisdictions' regulation) it was determined that 'high stakes' gambling was not the modern day equivalent of the gambling that had historically taken place in the nations. While the First Nations had characterized the right as a right to self-govern (and regulate economic activities), the Supreme Court of Canada characterized the right claimed as the right to participate in, and to regulate, gambling activities on their respective reserve lands (para 26).

[166] Ibid note 156, para 80.

[167] *Delgamuukw v British Columbia* [1997] 3 SCR 1010 (a Supreme Court of Canada case) <http://www.quicklaw.ca>.

[168] Ibid para 73. At para 74, the Supreme Court of Canada supported the decision, noting that if the First Nations had a concern about the prejudice of this ruling, they should have raised it—and they did not.

timeframe to be examined is the time at 'which the Crown asserted sovereignty over the land'.[169] This is significant. In order to prove that you have Aboriginal title you would need to prove that your nation or community had title at the time Crown sovereignty was asserted, necessitating recognition by your community or nation that it does not have that sovereignty. Further, the test for Aboriginal title requires the acceptance of Crown sovereignty at three junctures: (i) the land must have been occupied prior to sovereignty, (ii) if present occupation is relied on as proof of occupation pre-sovereignty, there must be a continuity between present and pre-sovereignty occupation, and (iii) at sovereignty, that occupation must have been exclusive.[170] The unstated, unspoken, assumed 'Crown' sovereignty is implicit to the Canadian legal conversation.

Regarding the notion of the supremacy of the Crown, Indigenous nations' inferior rights, and the presumed depleted sovereignty of the Indigenous nations, the Court wrote that:

Aboriginal title is a burden on the Crown's underlying title. However, the Crown did not gain this title until it asserted sovereignty over the land in question. Because it does not make sense to speak of a burden on the underlying title before that title existed, aboriginal title crystallized at the time sovereignty was asserted.[171]

Dr Borrows has written beautifully about this portion of the decision, musing, 'What alchemy transmutes the basis of Aboriginal possession into the golden bedrock of Crown title?'[172] The truth is likely simple: Aboriginal title did not appear. It is a casting of a lesser right in order to allow for the often illegal settlement of Indigenous territories and homelands without addressing the rightful owners/relations of the land. There could be no crystallization because Crown sovereignty could not replace Indigenous sovereignty just by virtue of non-Indigenous peoples settling in Indigenous territories and homelands. The Doctrine is rich in the decision, but *Delgamuukw* requires a specific Doctrinal magic: you must assume Indigenous inability, absence, and invisibility in order to imagine the crystallization of Crown sovereignty and superior title.

The case also marks the first time the Supreme Court of Canada extensively reviewed and expressed an opinion on the role of oral histories and oral legal histories in the interpretation of Aboriginal rights.

Lamer CJC referred to his decision in *Van der Peet* where 'I held that the ordinary rules of evidence must be approached and adapted in light of the evidentiary difficulties inherent in adjudicating aboriginal claims'.[173] He found that the 'laws of evidence must be adapted in order that this type of evidence [oral evidence] can be accommodated and placed on an equal footing with the types of historical evidence that courts are familiar with, which largely consists of historical

---

[169] Ibid para 142.   [170] Ibid para 143.   [171] Ibid para 145.
[172] John Borrows, 'Sovereignty's Alchemy: An Analysis of Delgamuukw v British Columbia' (1999) 37 Osgoode Hall LJ 538, 558.   [173] *Delgamuukw*, note 167, para 105.

documents'.[174] This is one space where the Supreme Court of Canada has made some positive ground. While it would be more accurate to address some of the oral traditions as legal orders and laws, the recognition of the shared space and equal consideration for evidence generated by both Canadian understandings of evidence and Indigenous understandings of evidence represents a step forward in the reconciliation of histories—perhaps some day room can also be made to accommodate Indigenous legal orders and legal philosophies as well.

Post-*Delgamuukw*, the Supreme Court of Canada seems to have seized upon Lamer CJC's (as he was then) statement in the decision that when impacting Aboriginal title[175] the Crown's fiduciary duty requires it to involve Aboriginal people when decisions are made involving their lands. Whether Aboriginal people have been consulted goes to the determination of justifiability of an infringement of Aboriginal title.[176] Lamer CJC, for the majority, addressed the issue of consultation thus:

There is always a duty of consultation ... The nature and scope of the duty of consultation will vary with the circumstances. In occasional cases, when the breach is less serious or relatively minor, it will be no more than a duty to discuss important decisions that will be taken with respect to lands held pursuant to aboriginal title.... In most cases, it will be significantly deeper than mere consultation. Some cases may even require the full consent of an aboriginal nation, particularly when provinces enact hunting and fishing regulations in relation to aboriginal lands.[177]

When the Haida people, who have claimed title to Haida Gwaii (and the waters surrounding it) for over a 100 years, launched their lawsuit objecting to the decisions to replace treefarm licences in their territory it was on the basis that they had an unresolved Aboriginal title claim to their traditional territories.[178] In *Haida Nation v British Columbia (Minister of Forests)* McLachlin J (writing the decision for the Court) expanded upon former Chief Justice Lamer's discussion of the duty to consult, determining that the duty to consult comes from the honour of the Crown and that it is part of a process of 'fair dealing' and reconciliation.[179]

---

[174] Ibid para 87.
[175] At ibid para 166 of the majority decision, Lamer J described Aboriginal title thus:

First, aboriginal title encompasses the right to exclusive use and occupation of land; second, aboriginal title encompasses the right to choose to what uses land can be put, subject to the ultimate limit that those uses cannot destroy the ability of the land to sustain future generations of aboriginal peoples; and third, that lands held pursuant to aboriginal title have an inescapable economic component.

[176] Ibid para 168.   [177] Ibid.
[178] *Haida Nation v British Columbia (Minister of Forests)* [2004] 3 SCR 511 (a Supreme Court of Canada case), paras 1, 4, and 5.
[179] Ibid para 32. At para 38 Chief Justice McLachlin wrote of this: 'consultation and accommodation before final claims resolution, while challenging, is not impossible, and indeed is an essential corollary to the honourable process of reconciliation that s. 35 demands. It preserves the Aboriginal interest pending claims resolution and fosters a relationship between the parties that makes possible negotiations.'

The duty does not extend to reaching an agreement, the duty is to consult (and 'if appropriate' to accommodate).[180] The case raises a number of interesting questions, chief among them this: if a determination is to be made about the proportionality of the duty to consult based upon the strength of the case and the seriousness of potential adverse effects,[181] should a 'pre-determination' such as this be made by the Crown (and allow them, in effect, to conduct a preemptive strike with respect to the justifiability of infringement)? Or, stated another way, did the Supreme Court of Canada provide a roadmap to the Crown to assist them with lawful infringements? One could argue that the case replaces the discussion of Aboriginal title with one of perceptions of potential Aboriginal title and that the case will be applied to preclude the bringing forward of Aboriginal title cases as the Crown is better able to avoid claims of infringement.

Canadian case law has constructed Aboriginal rights as a box. First, the word-boxes 'rights' and 'title' require a particular linguistic (if not legal) adherence in order that the topics discussed may be considered as ones which are Canadian legally cognizable. The rather steadfast construction of the box belies the permeability of the rights and their potential for erasure. The notion of 'existing' itself is an arbitrary one in which a right's correspondence with court constructed notions of Indigenous rights determine the right's legal cognizability.

That title, itself, may be exhausted through legislation is a Canadian legal fact which owes its existence to the limited notion of 'existence' and which breaks Indigenous laws of land relations. Judicial interpretations of the same, however informed and smartly constructed, cannot detach the section 35(1) limitation from its roots: 'existing' is arbitrary and the use of the term as a starting point for the determination of the possibility of rights' existence is predicated upon denial or erasure of a pre-1982 imperial existence. The clarity of the Crown's intention to extinguish can sometimes be arbitrary—even accidental—if you look to existing case law. However, it must be stated that many Indigenous nations and non-Indigenous peoples understand that there should be in place a presumption of colonial hostility and that Indigenous reality is often difficult to prove in the face of it given, as it was, that this imperial informed hostility is part of a continuum. Incidental impact on Aboriginal rights is an easily understood category (box). The ongoing impact of colonization on Indigenous peoples is not very well documented and the intricacies not very cognizable, given that they are to be observed and quantified by a body many would say is a participant in colonization.

There is absolutism that is also hard to measure: the presumed power of provinces and Canada to regulate and the presumption of legitimacy are hard to disengage from the notion of colonizing Indigenous peoples. Difficult to measure and not subject to quantification, colonial tools built from Doctrinal metal are hard to distinguish from colonial machinery. The implicit presumption of Canadian sovereignty is difficult for many to distinguish from allowed and

---

[180] Ibid para 10.   [181] Ibid para 29.

allowable infringement of Indigenous rights (neither of which intrinsically makes them lawful, one could argue).

All of which contributes to a problem of proof—not proof in the Canadian legal or judicial context—but proof of the colonial machinery moving the Canadian legal and judicial process (and forming its substance). As long as our notion of reconciliation involves reconciling Indigenous practices, traditions, and cultures with presumed Crown sovereignty, we are not really talking about reconciliation at all. As long as consultation is a legitimated opportunity of the assertion of power, we are not acknowledging our obligations as relations.

B. Changing Policy and Modern Day Agreements

Canadian constitutional, legal, and political policies related to Indigenous peoples have been and are largely still dependent upon the understanding that Indigenous peoples have a limited pool of rights because Canadians own Canada (and have an ongoing relationship with the 'original occupants' of the country now known as Canada).

It can be generally stated that the policy applicable and related to the Indigenous original inhabitants of Canada has often followed Canadian economic development or needs. For this reason, it can also be generally stated that Canadian policy with regard to Indigenous peoples often was dependent upon the nature of the role that Her Majesty's representatives perceived Indigenous peoples playing in the economy of Canada.

Canadian policy with regard to Indigenous peoples has changed over time to address different circumstances. While the notion of assimilation and civilization rooted in the Doctrine was part of an ad hoc, seemingly universally understood policy related to the perception of Indigenous deficiency, written policies detailing the understanding are mercilessly exiguous—particularly prior to 1900. What can be said is that formal policy was written in response to concerns raised about the obligations of the government of Canada or the provinces. For example, in 1934 the government of Alberta, responding to concerns about the welfare of Métis peoples in the province, developed a provincial policy towards Métis peoples.[182] The resultant report led to what became the Métis Population Betterment Act.[183]

---

[182] Initially called the Half-breed Commission, the provincial government panel travelled the province of Alberta to discuss and determine the state of Métis peoples' 'health, education, relief and general welfare of such population'. *Ewing Commission Report 1936,* Métis Settlements General Council website <http://historyonline.msgc.ca/images/1/117.pdf>. With many of the Métis peoples having accepted easily transferable scrip or having been left out of Treaties by Treaty Commissions travelling through the province in the late 1800s, there was a public concern about Métis peoples' levels of poverty.

[183] Province of Alberta, The Métis Population Betterment Act 1938.

As Métis peoples were not included in the section 91(24) designation of Indians, or lands reserved for Indians, Métis were externally labelled as a 'provincial concern'. Legislation followed which established Métis colonies on 'set aside Provincial lands'.[184] Ministerial powers over the lands in the 1942 Act were substantial, although the 1952 amendment to the Act[185] addressed the expanded powers of Métis governance through the recognition of Settlement Association and Local Boards.[186]

There followed a period where policy pertaining to Indigenous peoples was not perceived as a pressing concern. Until 1969 there was little reason for Canada to develop policy; Indigenous rights and Indigenous resistance were not as prevalent as they were soon to become.

In 1969 Indian Affairs Minister (and later Prime Minister) Jean Chretien tabled *The Statement of the Government of Canada on Indian Policy*[187] within which the government of Canada questioned the notion of what were to become comprehensive claims because '[t]hese are so general and undefined it is not realistic to think of them as specific claims capable of remedy except through a policy and program that will end injustice to Indians as members of the Canadian community'.[188] What this amounted to was a denial by Canada of Aboriginal title. The White Paper also recommended repeal of the Indian Act, that Indians become a provincial government responsibility, that the Department of Indian Affairs be wound up, and that title to Indian lands be transferred to Indian peoples.[189] The response to the White Paper was twofold: an Indian Association of Alberta leader, the late Dr Harold Cardinal, wrote The Red Paper (Citizens Plus) in response to the White Paper and it became a rallying cry for Indigenous people throughout their territories and across Canada. As well, in the face of united Indigenous response to the White Paper, Canada appointed a Claims Commissioner.[190]

Post-*Calder*, the policy towards claims recognition and resolution of course changed to address the findings of the Supreme Court of Canada. As a result, the government of Canada established the Office of Native Claims which was met

---

[184] Métis Population Betterment Act 1942 s 6.

[185] An Act to Amend the Métis Population Betterment Act 1952.

[186] The Métis Settlements in the province of Alberta now number 12 and a suite of legislation addressing authority for land, governance, and other facets of implementation was passed in 1990. For additional information see the Alberta legislation Métis Settlements Act 2004 (in which all matters related to the settlements, including governance and administration, are addressed), Métis Settlements Land Protection Act 1990 (in which alienation of the fee simple estate in the land can only be done with the approval of the Crown, the General Council, and a majority of the settlement members), and the Métis Settlements Accord Implementation Act 2000.

[187] Government of Canada, *Statement of the Government of Canada on Indian Policy* (The White Paper, 1969), <http://www.ainc-inac.gc.ca/ai/arp/ls/pubs/cp1969/cp1969-eng.asp#chp1>.

[188] Ibid s 5 (Claims and Treaties).

[189] Ibid s 2 (The New Policy).

[190] Emma Butt and Mary C Hurley, *Specific Claims In Canada* (Law and Government Division, Canada 2006), <http://www2.parl.gc.ca/content/LOP/ResearchPublications/prb0618-e.htm>.

by concern about the independence of the panel (in that it juggled obligation to Indigenous peoples/Indians and was involved in a dispute with them).[191]

As Canadian legal requirements changed, so did the nature of the modern day land claims. The first of these is the James Bay Northern Quebec Agreement. As a modern day treaty signed after *Calder*, but prior to the enactment of section 35(1) and the case law interpreting the section, many of the provisions already seem limiting and not particularly modern. The Agreement contains an extinguishment clause:

2.1 In consideration of the rights and benefits herein set forth in favour of the James Bay Crees and the Inuit of Quebec, the James Bay Crees and the Inuit of Quebec hereby cede, release, surrender and convey all their Native claims, rights, titles and interests, whatever they may be, in and to land in the territory and in Quebec, and Quebec and Canada accept such surrender.[192]

During this era of Indigenous rights discussion, it seems odd to consider the incorporation of corporations representing each community at a local government level as a particularly forward-looking means to address rights of Indigenous peoples.[193] However with no clear directives or policies in place to determine the ways and means to address claims, the negotiators did have some degree of choice (if not mandate) to creatively address outstanding claims at this juncture.[194] As a result, some of the language that narrows the capacity of Indigenous nations to make their own laws pertaining to specific territories does not appear in this document (while conflict with a non-Indigenous government law results in non-nation paramountcy).[195]

The government of Canada drafted and released a comprehensive claim policy in 1981[196] and this was revised in 1986.[197] Claims policy was further developed in 1982 with another policy paper on specific claims which provided that the government of Canada states it will recognize claims where it has a 'lawful obligation' or 'beyond lawful obligation' (ie failure to compensate for takings or fraud).[198]

---

[191] Ibid 2–3.

[192] The James Bay and Northern Quebec Agreement (JBNQA) 1975, <http://www.gcc.ca/pdf/LEG000000006.pdf>. [193] Ibid s 10.

[194] It is hard to critique a nation's determination about the best way to rule itself without knowledge of the tone or tenure of the negotiations or the understanding of what may have been conceded. For this reason, the discussion addresses the agreements only in terms of a comparative colonial point and makes no comment on their strength, viability, or concurrence with the particular Indigenous nations' standards. [195] JBNQA, note 192, s 129.

[196] Department of Indian Affairs and Northern Development, *In All Fairness: A Native Claims Policy—Comprehensive Claims* (Ottawa: Dept of Indian Affairs and Northern Development, 1981). Excerpts provided at: Patricia Sawchuk (ed), (1982) 2 The Canadian J of Native Studies 170–6.

[197] Department of Indian Affairs and Northern Development, *Comprehensive Land Claims Policy*, (Ottawa: Dept of Indian Affairs and Northern Development, 1986).

[198] Minister of Supply and Services, *Outstanding Business: A Native Claims Policy—Specific Claims* (Ottawa: Minister of Supply and Services, 1982). Excerpts provided by Patricia Sawchuk (ed) (1982), 2 The Canadian J of Native Studies, <http://www2.brandonu.ca/Library/cjns/2.2/Outstanding.pdf>.

With respect to specific claims, the process itself has been excruciatingly slow[199] and frustrating. As a result, a new Indian Claims Commission (ICC) was proposed to deal with specific claims.

The release of the *Sparrow* decision in 1990 changed the Canadian terrain with respect to legal discussions about Aboriginal rights. Discussions now had to take place beside section 35(1) and with *Sparrow* as a guidebook. Still, the legal arena could not speed up the processes or the political change.

In 1993, then, when the Nunavut Land Claims Agreement was signed off, it still contained a 'cede, release and surrender' clause that purported to extinguish the Inuit claim to land or waters anywhere 'within the sovereignty or jurisdiction of Canada...'.[200] Inuit-owned lands could be held in fee simple with or without mines and minerals[201] and the Agreement included a provision for a new Territory and its own Legislative Assembly.[202]

In British Columbia (where the land claims are largely comprehensive claims), the governmental response to the outstanding claims was to pass the 1996 British Columbia Treaty Commission Act, the purpose of which includes the facilitation of tripartite negotiations between First Nation government, the Canadian government, and the provincial government.[203]

The Royal Commission on Aboriginal Peoples was established in 1991 to address a very broad mandate. Specifically, tensions had erupted between Indigenous nations and Canada in some highly publicized protests and activities and the relationship was viewed as requiring examination and renewal. As well, the idea of the extinguishment of rights was detailed in an interim report issued by the Commission. Within that it was written:

[R]equiring Aboriginal peoples to extinguish [their Aboriginal] title in order to benefit from the protection of a modern treaty does not fit comfortably with the fact that the Crown is in a fiduciary relationship with Aboriginal peoples. Such a requirement, however well-intentioned, serves to exploit the very vulnerability and impoverished condition of Aboriginal peoples that treaties aim to redress.[204]

---

[199] Emma Butt and Mary C Hurley, *Specific Claims In Canada* (Ottawa: Law and Government Division, 2006) <http://www2.parl.gc.ca/content/LOP/ResearchPublications/prb0618-e.htm>. The authors note, with regard to specific claims, that from 1970 through 1981, of 250 claims submitted, 12 had been settled (note 8).

[200] Agreement Between The Inuit Of The Nunavut Settlement Area And Her Majesty The Queen In Right Of Canada 1993, s 2.7.1.(a), <http://www.nucj.ca/library/bar_ads_mat/Nunavut_Land_Claims_Agreement.pdf>.   [201] Ibid ss 19.2.1(a) and (b).

[202] Ibid s 4.1.1.

[203] British Columbia Treaty Commission Act 1996 s 5(1), <http://www.bclaws.ca/Recon/document/freeside/—%20t%20—/treaty%20commission%20act%20%20rsbc%201996%20%20c.%20461/00_96461_01.xml>.

[204] Royal Commission on Aboriginal Peoples, *Treaty Making in the Spirit of Co-Existence: An Alternative to Extinguishment* (Ottawa: Royal Commission on Aboriginal Peoples, 1995) 55. Cited within The Grand Council Of The Crees (Eeyou Istchee), 'The Systematic Dispossession of Aboriginal Peoples in Canada "Reciting The Symptoms, Ignoring The Cause: The Systematic Dispossession Of Aboriginal Peoples In Canada" A Response To The Government Of Canada's Third Periodic Report On The Implementation Of The International Covenant On Economic,

Chief Paulette summarizes the nature of the conflicting perspectives:

> In my language, there is no word for 'surrender'. There is no word. I cannot describe 'surrender' to you in my language, so how do you expect my people to [have] put their X on 'surrender'?[205]

The Commission also recommended an independent tribunal to replace the ICC (which has since ceased operation).[206]

In 1995, the government of Canada unveiled its policy on Inherent Right of Self-Government.[207] Under Part I, the policy outlines the requirement that the negotiations and agreements that come from the policy come from the section 35(1) recognition and must be within this framework. Aboriginal jurisdictions and authorities will operate 'within the framework of the Canadian Constitution'.[208] Some of the topics enumerated include the establishment of governing structures, internal constitutions, elections, leadership selection processes; membership; administration/enforcement of Aboriginal laws, including the establishment of Aboriginal courts or tribunals and the creation of offences of the type normally created by local or regional governments for contravention of their laws; property rights, including succession and estates; and land management (including: zoning; service fees; land tenure and access; and expropriation of Aboriginal land by Aboriginal governments for their own public purposes).[209] Hunting, fishing, and land management are also included as topics of negotiation.[210]

Several First Nations have negotiated self-government agreements with this policy operating as a guideline for topics of negotiation and the establishment of a mandate. The negotiations can take place with First Nations (some with and without existing treaty agreements). The negotiations do not operate to open the discussion or treaties, but to 'build on' the relationships established in the same.[211]

The notion that self-government negotiations and agreements must be predicated on Canadian constitutional understandings is not necessarily prohibitive

---

Social And Cultural Rights Submission Of The Grand Council Of The Crees (Eeyou Istchee) To The Committee On Economic Social And Cultural Rights' (1998), <http://www.gcc.ca/archive/article.php?id=67>.

[205] Royal Commission on Aboriginal Peoples, 'Looking Forward, Looking Back' *Report of the Royal Commission on Aboriginal Peoples* (Ottawa: RCAP, 1996), <http://www.uni.ca/library/rcap_look.html>. Statement of Chief Francois Paulette Treaty 8 Tribal Council Yellowknife, Northwest Territories, vol 2, Ch 2, 'Treaties', 3.8. Aboriginal Rights and Title: Sharing, Not Extinguishment, <http://www.collectionscanada.gc.ca/webarchives/20071211054857/http://www.ainc-inac.gc.ca/ch/rcap/sg/sh6_e.html>.

[206] Royal Commission on Aboriginal Peoples, ibid vol 2 *'Restructuring the Relationship'* Part Two, Chapter 4, 'Lands and Resources', 591. Recommendations 2.4.29–2.4.33.

[207] Indian and Northern Affairs Canada, 'The Government of Canada's Approach to Implementation of the Inherent Right and the Negotiation of Aboriginal Self-Government', <http://www.ainc-inac.gc.ca/al/ldc/ccl/pubs/sg/sg-eng.asp#Intro>. [208] Ibid.

[209] Ibid. In the application of laws, provincial and federal paramountcy will operate where 'overriding national or provincial importance' take precedence over Aboriginal laws.
[210] Ibid. [211] Ibid.

for many First Nations. However, the presumption that Indigenous guiding philosophies and constitutions do not operate equally alongside the Canadian constitution is of some concern. Paramountcy of Canadian and provincial laws in some instances may also be acceptable to some First Nations; however, the presumption that this is automatically the case is similarly reflective of the Doctrinal echo in modern negotiations related to Indigenous authorities. That a negotiation has to occur at all, instead of recognition of an Indigenous legal and governmental ordered reality can be considered a further re-entrenchment of the Doctrine in contemporary Canadian–First Nations legal relationships.

Following the *Delgamuukw* decision there was a measure of increased pressure on the government of Canada to deal with the outstanding claims of Indigenous peoples (and it can be argued that this was particularly the case for those claims of Indigenous peoples in British Columbia). When the Nisga'a Final Agreement Act[212] was passed in 2000, the recent case law, policy development, and the findings of the Commission must have informed the negotiating teams and all three levels of government when they sat at the table. The Act refers to 'modified' Aboriginal rights, including title.[213] The Act provides:

(2) For greater certainty, the aboriginal title of the Nisga'a Nation anywhere that it existed in Canada before the effective date of the Nisga'a Final Agreement is modified and continues as the estates in fee simple to those areas identified in that Agreement as Nisga'a Lands or Nisga'a Fee Simple Lands.[214]

No federal or provincial consent is required for the creation of estates or disposal of estates or interests to other persons.[215]

Canada's Specific Claims Tribunal Act came into effect on 16 October 2008.[216] First Nations are able to file a specific claim with the Tribunal on the basis of enumerated grounds, including Crown failure to fulfil an obligation

---

[212] Nisga'a Final Agreement Act 2000.   [213] Ibid s 7(1).

[214] Ibid s 7(2). In the House of Commons, Canada expanded on the meaning of 'modified' rights. See Nisga'a Final Agreement Bill Second Reading—Debate Adjourned. The Honourable Jack Austin moved the second reading of Bill C-9, to give effect to the Nisga'a Final Agreement. The Honourable Gildas L Molgat, Speaker. Hansard (Senate) vol 138, 2nd Session, 36th Parliament (16 December 1999):

The Nisga'a Final Agreement provides for a "modification of rights" approach. Using the modified aboriginal right approach, the Nisga'a aboriginal rights, including title, continue to exist, although only as modified, to have the attributes and geographic extent set out in the Nisga'a Final Agreement. This is accomplished through the agreement of all three parties and by the exercise of the legislative jurisdiction of the federal and provincial governments. As a result, whatever aboriginal rights the Nisga'a may have had at common law will be modified to become the rights set out in the Nisga'a Final Agreement. In this way, the certainty technique is based upon agreeing to rights rather than extinguishing them…'

[215] Nisga'a Final Agreement 1999 s 4.2, <http://www.ainc-inac.gc.ca/al/ldc/ccl/fagr/nsga/nis/nis-eng.pdf>.

[216] An Act to establish the Specific Claims Tribunal and to make consequential amendments to other Acts 2008.

to provide lands or other assets,[217] a breach of a legal obligation by the Crown related to the Indian Act or other legislation,[218] other breaches, illegality, and fraud. The Tribunal has the authority to award compensation only up to the amount of 150 million dollars.[219] It is hoped that the new Tribunals will be able to operate with more independence and expediency.

What can be clearly observed is that the negotiating process to address Indigenous lands recognition and authorities related to self-governance has been unsatisfactory to all involved. What can also be observed is that Canadian governmental changes to negotiation mandates/policy seem to change when law required the Canadian government to change them. The notion of a presumed surrender, excitingly, seems to be undergoing some change. Only time will tell what form that change will take. While imperial notions of paramountcy seem to have changed (given the observance of the recognition of Indigenous legal and governmental authorities in some regards), negotiations are still subject to a presumption of non-Indigenous governmental policy and laws as the framework under which discussion occurs. In nation to nation negotiations, paramountcy is not presumed.

A final note on modern day implementation of the Doctrine of Discovery: Canada continues to privilege business and corporate interests in and above Indigenous territories. The unlawful (in an Indigenous legal context, at least) taking of land was one means of applying the Doctrine in the 'New World'. In this even 'Newer World', the taking of natural resources from Indigenous territories through Canadian legal means and without Indigenous peoples' assent (as consultation is not consent) can be said to be just further positioning on the continuum of colonization.[220]

C. Conclusion

Canadian legislation, legal decisions, and negotiations related to land are often grounded upon antiquated theories about the rightfulness/righteousness of colonizer dominance and Indigenous submission. The philosophy of imperial domination fully informed colonial institutions: the conceptions and administration

---

[217] Ibid s 14(1)(a).   [218] Ibid s 14(1)(b).   [219] Ibid s 20(1)(a).

[220] In May of 2009, Canada's Indian Oil and Gas Act 1974 received Royal Assent; to bring 'federal legislation in line with similar legislation in the provinces, the new law will create a more transparent and efficient regime for oil and gas operations on reserve lands, thereby encouraging industry investment and economic development in First Nation communities'. Department of Indian and Northern Affairs Canada, 'Royal Assent Given to Legislation Modernizing the Indian Oil and Gas Act', <http://www.ainc-inac.gc.ca/ai/mr/nr/m-a2009/nr000000325-eng. asp>. The amendments will expand the power of the Governor in Council to make regulations related to exploration and production of oil and gas on First Nations land. Department of Indian and Northern Affairs Canada, 'Fact Sheet—Indian Oil and Gas Act Amendments' <http://www. ainc-inac.gc.ca/ai/mr/is/iogc-eng.asp>.

of governments, laws, and courts were built upon (and in many instances continue to reside upon) the bedrock of, at least, prejudiced beliefs about land ownership and ascendancy. Privileging empire and colonial religions, institutions and dogma, colonial institutions both ingested and emitted hypotheses, conjectures, and suppositions about Indigenous peoples and their authorities. These hypotheses, conjectures, and suppositions were largely unquestioned, absolutist, and mired in settler conceptualizations of paramountcy (of beliefs, philosophies, and laws). The law that led colonial peoples to Indigenous lands, law which was vitalized and perpetuated by both a failure to acknowledge Indigenous legal orders and the propensity to aggrandize colonial authorities, became the same law that was intrinsically granted authority over colonizers and the lands that they claimed as their own.

Perpetuation of the Doctrine of Discovery in the land now known as Canada could not have taken place without silence, collusion, and complicity. This is not to say that those who adhere to the Doctrinal precepts, principles, and (now) established laws relating to Indigenous lands and authorities subscribe to notions of dominance, racial supremacy, or universalism. What is does mean, however, is that the colonial silence and complicity occupies a space in every office where a law pertaining to Indigenous lands is drafted, in every courtroom where a decision is made about Indigenous lands, and at every negotiating table pertaining to Indigenous lands and authorities.[221]

It is not enough any more to cite the ancient laws or the Canadian laws that found their home on top of those ancient laws. Precedents constructed on notions of supremacy, Crown inherency, and paramountcy are simply not enough any more. Without a racial or cultural audit and without regard to Indigenous legal orders and notions of legal pluralism, we are all complicit if we do not speak up, question righteousness/rightfulness, and if we accept the presumption of settler legal dominance. We are all complicit if we do not address Indigenous governmental orders and authorities and if we unquestioningly presume colonial dominance in this realm.

We cannot continue to address the reality of Indigenous peoples' relationships with our land under legislation, precedents, or negotiations that are based upon the understanding that 'the Indians lost and therefore they get less'. It is not the case. It is not the law. It is not the truth. It is not the reality. We should not fear discussing this or finding otherwise. It is a different reality; many Indigenous

---

[221] This is not a condemnation of non-Indigenous laws or governance. It is not an indictment of Canadian legislators or judiciary. It calls upon all of us, as peoples in a shared territory, to acknowledge Indigenous legal and governmental orders, to question the notion of immediate Canadian sovereignty and the impossibility of cession of land by Indigenous peoples. It requires that Indigenous nations start or continue to bring sovereignty (a dirty word in many negotiations and court cases) to the table every time we talk about land. It may not, indeed, even be the word 'sovereignty'—but if we do not address our ongoing and lawful relationship without land, we too are complicit in the silence surrounding the Doctrine and settlement. This should not threaten anyone who subscribes to a notion of legislative and legal fairness.

peoples have been living that reality and have made overtures to share and discuss the same. Many non-Indigenous peoples share this reality. Some of the arguments which counter the recognition of this reality are based upon logistics, a lack of shared philosophies, and reliance upon the familiar—each of which has housed within it a notion of fearful 'taking'. As peoples who have experienced the takings and the fear, we have much to add to the discussion about the rightful sharing of land. We cannot continue to fear change if the change is based upon the understanding that Indigenous nations have the right to existences based upon their own philosophies, legal, and governmental orders.

Canada has this fear. Perhaps a contemporary example will assist. Canada is one of the nations, one of four (originally) which would not sign the United Nations Declaration on the Rights of Indigenous Peoples.[222] The Declaration itself acknowledges some components of some Indigenous realities. The Declaration Preamble provides:

Concerned that indigenous peoples have suffered from historic injustices as a result of, inter alia, their colonization and dispossession of their lands, territories and resources, thus preventing them from exercising, in particular, their right to development in accordance with their own needs and interests,

Recognizing the urgent need to respect and promote the inherent rights of indigenous peoples which derive from their political, economic and social structures and from their cultures, spiritual traditions, histories and philosophies, especially their rights to their lands, territories and resources,

Recognizing also the urgent need to respect and promote the rights of indigenous peoples affirmed in treaties, agreements and other constructive arrangements with States...[223]

The Declaration speaks of 'rights' and it is likely this reality that has inspired concern in the initial four nations that refused to sign the document. Nationality, self-determination, freedom discrimination, and the security of cultural and other practices are included in the document. It is a significant document for many reasons. For the purposes of this chapter, the recording and acknowledgement of injustice, colonization, and dispossession are exceptionally important.

Adoption of the Declaration by the General Assembly symbolizes many things for Indigenous peoples. Among them, and importantly, is the reconstruction of the international Indigenous legal norm. Acknowledging some treaties as having an international character, the Declaration shifts the discussion from domestic nations to international nations of Indigenous peoples. Additionally, the recognition of 'strengthen their distinct political, legal, economic, social and cultural institutions, while retaining their right to participate fully, if they so choose, in

---

[222] United Nations Declaration on the Rights of Indigenous Peoples, UN GAOR, 61st sess, GA Res 61/295, UN Doc A/RES/47/1 (2007), <http://www.un.org/esa/socdev/unpfii/en/drip.html>.
[223] Ibid.

the political, economic, social and cultural life of the State...'[224] may well prove to shift the terrain upon which Indigenous legal and governmental orders have been involuntarily or falsely placed since contact with settlers. The Declaration also provides that states shall provide mechanisms and redress for actions which dispossessed (or attempted to dispossess) Indigenous peoples of our lands, territories, and resources.[225] If applied with the same intent that I presume the drafters intended, then Indigenous relationships with our land, dispossession, and our authorities over the same are to be understood as internationally legally cognizable. Indigenous legal orders and governmental orders, in this context, normalized. Not universalized, but acknowledged as sharing space at the pluralist legal table.

The implications of this for Canada, one of a very small and increasingly smaller non-signatory nation minority, would appear to be ones which inspire fear. Why this is so is not hard to discern, but given that this is a United Nations organ document and is interpreted by many to be non-binding and creating no legal obligations,[226] Canada's reluctance to sign the same has been interpreted by many to be a signal of its dismissal of Indigenous rights as a whole. Whatever the rationale, not signing the Declaration has served, for many peoples, to perpetuate colonization as a modern ideology and activity. Acknowledging Canada's role in the attempted and actual colonization of Indigenous peoples would be a first step towards the reconciliation anticipated by the recent decisions of the Supreme Court of Canada.

---

[224] Ibid Article 5.   [225] Ibid Article 8.2(b).

[226] Megan Davis, 'The United Nations Declaration on the Rights of Indigenous Peoples', <http://ssrn.com/abstract=1392569>.

6

The Doctrine of Discovery in Australia

Aboriginal people in Australia claim to have the world's oldest living culture. There is evidence that Aboriginal people lived in Australia up to 100,000 years ago.[1] While anthropologists ponder the when, how, and why, Aboriginal people believe that they have inhabited their country since the beginning of time.[2] In this context, it is extraordinary that the doctrine of *terra nullius* would be used to assert Britain's claims to 'discovery' and to attempt to legitimize the assertion of British sovereignty over Australia.

A. First Contacts

First recorded contact between Europeans and Aboriginal and Torres Strait Islander people[3] in Australia was not with the British but, unsurprisingly, with the Dutch. Having risen as a superpower and establishing the Dutch East India Company in 1602 (based in Jakarta), the Dutch sailed constantly between Europe and the East Indies.

William Janszoon reached the Gulf of Carpentaria in the north-east of what the Dutch named New Holland in 1605. The first recorded landing of a European on Australian soil was that of Captain Dirk Hartog in October 1616 at what is now Cape Inscription on the western coast of Australia. He left an inscribed pewter plate that was found in 1697 by his countryman Willem de Vlamingh.

An expedition, sponsored by Anthony van Diemen and led by Abel Tasman, set out in 1642 to explore what lay to the south of the Dutch trading empire. He found what he dutifully called Van Diemen's Land, today known as Tasmania. In 10 months of exploring, Tasman had circumnavigated the Australian mainland without ever seeing it and, not surprisingly, van Diemen was unimpressed. But he set sail again in 1644 and he explored the Gulf of Carpentaria and

---

[1] Richard Broome, *Aboriginal Australians: Black Responses to White Dominance, 1788–2001* (Sydney: Allen and Unwin, 3rd edn, 2001); Robert Lawlor, *Voices of the First Day* (Rochester, VT: Inner Traditions, 1991).   [2] Broome, note 1; Lawlor, note 1.
[3] Aboriginal and Torres Strait Islander people are the two main Indigenous groups in Australia. It has become common to use the term 'Indigenous' when referring to both groups and 'Aboriginal' when referring to the Indigenous groups on mainland Australia.

Arnhem Land in the north of New Holland and sailed some way down the west coast. His observations of Aboriginal people were 'poor, naked people walking along beaches; without rice or many fruits, very poor and bad tempered people in many places'.[4]

William Dampier was the first British person to explore New Holland. He came to the north coast of Australia in 1688 and again in 1699. He had made a career of sailing around the Americas and then the Pacific. He gave a negative account of the Aboriginal people when he returned to Britain:

The Inhabitants of this Country are the miserablest People in the World. Setting aside their Humane Shape, they differ little from Brutes.[5]

Laced with the prejudices of its time, these observations contain the assumption of white superiority and black inferiority that was the prerequisite to asserting a claim over territory on the basis of 'discovery'.

Dampier also found the landscape devoid of any riches but took away about 40 samples of native flora. He would publish *A Voyage to New Holland* in 1703 giving the first published account of what would later become known as Australia.

B. Aboriginal Society and Practices[6]

At the time of European invasion, there were over 500 different tribal groups in pre-invasion society. Each lived in small groups of several families within their tribal area. They would meet at intervals in larger groups for ceremonies or trade. Some groups were patrilineal but many were matrilineal.

These groups were made of extended families. Some 'aunts' took on the role of mothers and were called the same name as 'mother'. Similarly some 'uncles' were fathers, and cousins were brothers and sisters. A person's relationship to others would dictate how to treat them and what a person's obligations were to them. It also determined whom you could and could not marry.

Within these different groups there was similarity and diversity. Australia is a vast continent. Groups living in the desert had a vastly different lifestyle to groups living in coastal areas. But in world views, governance structures and philosophy

---

[4] Vanessa Collingridge, *Documents of Australian History* (Scoresby, Victoria: Five Mile Press, 2008) 13.   [5] Ibid 11.

[6] This material that captures my father's knowledge about the traditional cultures of the Eualeyai and Kammillaroi nations has been published elsewhere—see Larissa Behrendt, *Aboriginal Dispute Resolution: A Step Towards Self-Determination and Community Autonomy* (Annandale: The Federation Press, 2005); Larissa Behrendt and Loretta Kelly, *Resolving Indigenous Disputes: Land Conflict and Beyond* (Annandale: The Federation Press, 2008). My father's papers are lodged in the NSW State Library and his recordings with Elders of the Eualayai and Kammillaroi nations are lodged with the Australian Institute of Aboriginal and Torres Strait Islander Studies in Canberra.

there were strong commonalities across the continent. All groups, for example, had a period of creation called the Dreaming. During this period the world was created by super beings. They created the land, humans, and animals.

These spirits gave ceremonies that explained the rules to live by. They then returned to the rocks and ground and water and sky. In some places, the spirit was a serpent, the Rainbow Serpent, who created the landscape as she travelled across the land. In my tribal area, the area inhabited by the Eualeyai in the northwest of New South Wales, this spirit was a serpent. The serpent lived underground and the places where he came up for air were springs and waterholes. This creation story has a similar theme across the continent even though there are regional differences in the specific telling of the story.

Aboriginal people were hunters and gatherers. Groups had similar technology, such as digging sticks and wooden hunting instruments but this varied between groups according to the climate. For instance, some groups used canoes and some did not. Some groups used fish bones to make tools and some did not.

Aboriginal people could cultivate plants like yams but chose not to and preferred to lead a semi-nomadic life. Groups knew all the food sources and inhabitants of their area and knew where all the water supplies could be found.

The relationship to the land is the same in all Aboriginal communities on mainland Australia. People had affiliations with tracts of country and had the right to hunt and feed in certain areas and to perform religious ceremonies in certain places. These custodians were also responsible for ensuring that the resources of a certain area were maintained.

Aboriginal people knew their relationship to others and the universe through their totems. People had three totems: a clan totem that linked a person to other people; a family totem that linked a person to the natural world (a person considered himself or herself to be descended from the family totem—they would not eat the meat of their totem and would have to ensure that animal's protection); and a spiritual totem that linked a person to the universe. Through these totems Aboriginal people realized that they were one with the land and all that moved upon it.

Aboriginal culture was oral. Attachment to the land was expressed through song, art, dance, and painting. People 'inherited' stories and songs and become their keepers, eventually passing them down to the next generations. Boundaries of tribal areas are fixed and explained in these cultural stories.

Through this story-telling, ancestral land was passed on to younger generations and they had responsibility to care for this country. Knowledge created an obligation to protect the land, respect the past, to not exploit the land's resources, to take the responsibility of passing the country on to future generations, and to maintain the religious ceremonies that needed to be performed there. In this way, ancestral land became personal so one was obliged to look after it. Other people's land had no meaning to someone who was a stranger to it and there were rarely conflicts over boundaries.

These ceremonies symbolize the attachment to the land and the commitment to protect it. Special religious significance is attached to the resting places of great ancestors. These are sacred sites that have importance for women as well as men. Thus the landscape was richly symbolic.

Mythical stories dictated appropriate modes of behaviour and set standards. In this way mythical beings were making laws. These collectively affirmed standards were enforced by applying social pressure to ensure conformity. Children were taught acceptable modes of behaviour through cultural stories and were taught by example rather than by the strict discipline used to rear European children.

Aboriginal nations were nomadic, hunter-gatherer societies that had complex laws and rules They did not, however, fit into European notions of what constituted a civilized society and there were none of the agrarian activities that Europeans believed were a necessary signal of a society that had its own laws.

C. Claiming Australia

Despite the increasing assertion of parliamentary sovereignty throughout the seventeenth century, the British Crown remained responsible for the conduct of Britain's foreign affairs. The Crown was able to determine the status and extent of overseas colonies like Australia. These broad terms left much to discretion. Colonies could be acquired through cession or conquest, treaty or agreement, or by the voluntary cession of the inhabitants.

The British Crown had assumed the authority to authorize individuals or companies to undertake colonization ventures and had, in accordance with the prerogative, given instructions to Captain James Cook to claim the continent of Australia. He planted the British flag in Botany Bay, an area that is approximately 30 kilometres from what is now the city of Sydney on 29 April 1770. He also carved details recording his arrival into a tree.

Ignoring previous contact with European powers, Cook proceeded with 'discovery' followed by annexation as the foundation for the exercise of British sovereignty over Australia. Aboriginal people were treated as lacking possession of the country thus giving Britain the authority under international law to lay claim to it.

Cook had been given instructions that laid out two courses of action for acquiring the continent. The letter given to the Captain on 30 July 1768 stated that, should he find the land inhabited, he was to 'endeavour by all proper means to cultivate a friendship and alliance with them' and was told to 'with the Consent of the Natives to take the possession of convenient situations in the country in the name of the King of Great Britain'.[7] He was also instructed: 'if you find the

---

[7] Collingridge, note 4, 16–17.

Country uninhabited Take Possession for His Majesty by setting up Proper Marks and Inscriptions as first discoverers and possessors'.[8]

Cook's actions—in planting a flag and carving a tree rather than in seeking to engage in any activity that might amount to gaining consent from 'the Natives'— indicate that he opted for the assertion of possession rather than of conquest.

After first landing at Botany Bay, Cook sailed north to what became known as Possession Island in the Torres Strait. There, on 22 August 1770, he once again asserted British authority over what he claimed was uninhabited land. His log records:

> At six possession was taken of this country in his Majesty's name and under his colours, fired several volleys of small arms on the occasion and cheer'd three times, which was answer'd from the ship.

Through these actions, Cook purported to take possession of the whole of the east coast of Australia for the British Crown.

On his return, he reported that Australia was sparsely populated. Joseph Banks, the naturalist who accompanied Cook on the voyage observed: 'This immense tract of land, considerably larger than all of Europe, is thinly inhabited.' He and Cook had seen only a small part of the coast and none of the interior. However, Banks hypothesized that the interior would be uninhabited because there would not be enough fish and the 'produce of the land' did not seem to be enough to support a population. They were of course wrong about this. The whole continent was populated and the pre-contact Aboriginal population has been estimated as being between 1 and 1.5 million people.[9]

Cook and his crew not only brought intelligence back of the sparse population but also the view that Aboriginal people in Australia were less technologically advanced than other Indigenous populations encountered by the British when building their Empire. They did not wear clothes. They had small, rudimentary huts and knew 'nothing of Cultivation'. From the accounts from Cook's voyage, Britain viewed Australia as almost empty. In a vast continent with a small, nomadic population, there was land available for possession.

In 1783, James Matra proposed placing the colony in New Holland and listed among its great advantages that it was 'peopled by only a few black inhabitants, who, in the rudest state of society, knew no other arts than were necessary to their mere animal existence'.

In subsequent years, legislative, executive, and judicial authority would confirm and reassert the assertion of sovereignty over Australia that Captain Cook's flag planting was supposed to symbolize. When doubts arose about Britain's claims or fears arose about the ambitions of other colonial powers, formal acts of annexation were undertaken in order to reassert Britain's claim to sovereignty

---

[8] Ibid.   [9] Broome, note 1.

over the continent. These were often followed by token or more substantial occupation to maintain and reassert British sovereignty.

D. Invasion

On 26 January 1788 the First Fleet, led by Captain Arthur Phillip, arrived back at the same spot. Finding no suitable source for fresh water, they travelled further north and disembarked at the site that is now the centre of Sydney. Upon landing, a simple ceremony took place in the form of unfurling the British flag. This was a symbolic way of reasserting the authority to possess the land. A toast was made to the new colony and gunfire was unleashed to consummate the arrival. A naval officer, Phillip Gidley King, who was later to become a governor of the colony, noted in his diary that these symbolic actions showed that New South Wales was 'taken for His Majesty'.

On 7 February, a military parade took place in the newly cleared land. Before an assembly of the new arrivals, the Governor read aloud his Commission. The Act of Parliament and the Letters Patent that established the courts were also announced. This was also an assertion of British authority, sovereignty, and jurisdiction.

The freemen and convicts who had survived the journey brought with them the principles of British constitutional law and this became the foundation for the legal system in Australia. They did not consist of a closely defined code of legal behaviour but were rather principles and broad guidelines that only operated as a result of government or parliamentary action.

In practice, the British Parliament left to government officials and Ministers of the Crown the flexibility to exercise 'royal authority' and decide which principles should operate to order the establishment and working of new colonies. This was true in Australia where the distance between the colonial power and the colony was so vast.

Executive actions and an act of the British Parliament paved the way for Britain's planned acquisition of the lands of Aboriginal people in Australia. Royal instructions were given to Governor Phillip that defined the territorial parameters of the new colony he was to establish and detailed, in general terms, the tasks he was to carry out.

The original instructions to Captain Phillip were designed by the Pitt government in 1786. It is clear that there was no anticipation of treaty making or agreements as part of their plan for the establishment of a new colony. Their plan stated:

The whole regulation and management of the settlement should be committed to the care of a discreet officer and provision should be made in all cases, both civil and military, by special instructions under the Great Seal or otherwise as may be thought proper.

Commissions were issued to the Governor and other officials and Letters Patent, issued under the Royal Prerogative, set out the powers and authority of the courts—civil and criminal—that were to operate in the colony of New South Wales. This became known as the First Charter of Justice for New South Wales.

These acts of the executive were reinforced by the Act of the British Parliament[10] that allowed for the derogation from existing criminal laws in Britain. Because the new colony was a penal colony, it was felt that trial by jury and other features of British criminal procedure should not operate.

Phllip was ordered to:

Immediately upon your landing, after taking measures for securing yourself and the people who accompany you as much as possible from any attacks or interruptions of the natives, proceed to the cultivation of the land.[11]

There was no need to negotiate or treat before using it.

From an Aboriginal point of view, it was a surprise that the British decided to stay. European ships sailing by were a rare but not uncommon experience and they always moved on. In the Aboriginal world view, it is inconceivable that people would not stay on their own land, but move on to land belonging to someone else. Oral histories from the Sydney region show that Aboriginal people had not expected British presence to be permanent. As it became clear that the British were staying, conflict and tensions with local Aboriginal tribes increased.[12]

E. Asserting the Doctrine of Discovery

Despite the earlier contact with other colonial powers, Britain had no rivals for the claim of dominion over the continent of Australia. This substantially decreased the impetus to enter into treaties or agreements with Aboriginal people and meant that the main assertion of British sovereignty was over the inhabitants, not to challenge the assertion of other colonial powers. However, Britain seemed to appreciate that its claim to possession of the whole continent was contestable.

The establishment of two penal colonies in Tasmania and the first attempt at one in Port Phillip, both in 1803, were attempts to ensure that any French ambitions were thwarted in these areas which, at this stage, were still part of the area claimed as New South Wales. In 1824, it was found that parts of the Torres Strait—namely Melville and Bathurst Islands—were not within the boundaries of the area proclaimed as part of New South Wales and so formal steps were taken to annex them. This was the same year that British settlements were established on the west coast of Australia.[13]

---

[10] 27 Geo, III, c 2 (1787).   [11] *Historical Records of New South Wales*, I(2): 87.
[12] Broome, note 2.
[13] Alex C Castles, *An Introduction to Australian Legal History* (Sydney: Law Book Company, 1970).

Likewise, official fears were expressed about France's possible intentions to assert its sovereignty over parts of the country even though there is bare evidence of any such ambition by the French. Under the doctrine of discovery, they would have had rights to some areas. So steps were taken to assert British sovereignty over the whole of the continent. Britain relied on the accepted protocol that claims to discovery had to be followed by annexation.

To this end, on 21 January 1827, Major Lockyer, who took charge of the British settlement in King George's Sound, southern Western Australia, proclaimed Britain's annexation of the whole continent. Just to make sure there were no questions, two years later Captain Fremantle, under authorization of the British Crown, again claimed 'all that part of New Holland which is not included within the territory of New South Wales'.[14]

Assertion of sovereignty over a colony also required occupation—or at least intention to possess, along with the capacity to exclude another aspiring colonial power from being able to assert title and right over the discovered territory. The British Crown appeared to have always acted on the assumption that the principles that applied to 'settled' colonies were applicable over New South Wales and later Australia.

While not needing to press its claim against other colonial powers, the British Crown did have occasion to assert its sole authority to deal with Indigenous people. In 1835, John Batman attempted to purchase a tract of land in the south-east of Australia in what is now Victoria directly from the Aboriginal people. The terms were that, in exchange for 600,000 acres of land, the Aboriginal people would receive blankets, looking glasses, tomahawks, beads, scissors, and other items and a 'Tribute of Rent Yearly'. His 'treaty' was signed by eight representatives of the Aboriginal nation. Batman pressed for recognition of this arrangement by the British authorities.[15]

The reaction of the colonial government was to issue a Proclamation asserting the full force of British sovereignty and power over the area. It declared: 'any bargain or contract made with the Aboriginal natives of New Holland...will be held to be null and void as against the rights of the Crown'. It also announced, 'in the most formal and public manner the right of the Crown of England to the Territory in question and the absolute nullity of any grant...made by any other party'.[16]

This is consistent to a limited extent with the jurisprudence developed by Chief Justice Marshall in the US Supreme Court. The principle that only the Crown could negotiate with Aboriginal people resonates with the finding in *Johnson v McIntosh*[17] that the 'discovery' of lands gave the discovering European power sovereignty and good title against all other European powers and gave them 'the sole right of acquiring the soil from the natives'.

[14] Ibid.   [15] Collingridge, note 4, 46.   [16] Castles, note 13, 20.
[17] *Johnson v McIntosh* 21 US (8 Wheat) 543 (1823).

However, the principle developed by Chief Justice Marshall that the 'Indians' retained the right of occupancy which the discovering nation could extinguish 'by purchase or by conquest' was not adopted into Australian law. Australian law also did not incorporate the principle established in *Cherokee Nation v Georgia*[18] that Aboriginal nations were to be considered a 'state', 'a distinct political society separated from others, capable of managing its own affairs and governing itself'. Chief Justice Marshall's concept of 'domestic dependant nations' would never be incorporated into Australia's law.

F. *Terra Nullius* as the Exercise of the Doctrine of Discovery

From the first stages of the assertion of sovereignty over Australia, the British made it clear that British laws operated over its newly acquired territory. It gave no recognition to the laws of Aboriginal people or recognition of their interests and rights to their land.

The concept of *terra nullius* was employed in practice many years before it formally became part of the Australian legal system. Aboriginal people had no legal standing to contest it. The earliest mention of the concept of *terra nullius* in the colonial laws was in a dispute that had nothing to do with Aboriginal people and their land. In 1819, a dispute arose between Governor Macquarie and a judge of the New South Wales Supreme Court, Barron Field, about the imposition of taxes—more specifically, whether the Governor had the ability to levy taxes or whether that had to be done through the Parliament. The Secretary for the Colonies, Earl Bathurst, referred the matter to the Attorney-General Samuel Shepherd and the Solicitor General Robert Gifford.

The matter was eventually resolved in favour of Field's view and Parliament, not the Crown, had the right to levy taxes. In conquered colonies, the issue of taxes was one that was left to the Crown's prerogative; in settled colonies, taxes were a matter for the Parliament. Shepherd and Gifford found that, 'the part of New South Wales possessed by His Majesty, not having been acquired by conquest or cession, but taken possession of by him as desert and uninhabited'.[19] While not concerning Aboriginal people, the decision had a direct bearing on them and their legal status. Under British law, Aboriginal people had no rights to their land.

The colonial law further acknowledged its reliance on the doctrine of *terra nullius* in 1822 when the issue arose as to whether the new Governor of New South Wales, Thomas Brisbane, had the authority to make laws by proclamation. In an opinion from the Colonial Office, it was reiterated that the power

---

[18] *Cherokee Nation v Georgia* 30 US (5 Pet) 1 (1831).
[19] Stuart Banner, *Possessing the Pacific: Land, Settlers and Indigenous People from Australia to Alaska* (Cambridge: Harvard University Press, 2007) 27.

was delegated to Parliament. There were only two situations where the Crown, through the Governor, could exercise direct power—where lands had been conquered or they had been voluntarily ceded. The Colonial Office determined that New South Wales did not fall into either of these categories because it was 'acquired neither by conquest nor cession, but by the mere occupation of a desert or uninhabited land'.[20]

Despite this reiteration of the doctrine of *terra nullius* and its consequence of acknowledging no rights flowing to Aboriginal people, there is some evidence that colonial officials were not entirely comfortable with the legitimacy and accuracy of the doctrine of *terra nullius* and the assumption that Aboriginal people had no rights to their lands. For example, in 1814, Governor Macquarie established a school for Aboriginal children and land that was to be occupied and farmed by Aboriginal people in Parramatta. In making the proclamation, he said that the grant was given to them because they had been excluded as 'the Natives from many of the natural advantages they have previously derived from the animal and other productions of this part of the Territory'.[21]

Stuart Banner in his book *Possessing the Pacific: Land, Settlers and Indigenous People from Australia to Alaska*[22] argues that while Governor Macquarie's point is clear, his words are carefully chosen, and that he believed that Aboriginal people were entitled to a form of compensation for the land they had lost and this implies that he knew they had some kind of property right in the land the British had occupied. It is evidence of the unease which the colonial government felt about the doctrine of *terra nullius*.[23]

The colonial Australian courts equally struggled with the extent to which they should recognize the laws of Aboriginal people. In 1829, the Supreme Court of New South Wales was asked in the case of *R v Ballard* to consider whether an Aboriginal person could be prosecuted for the alleged murder of another Aboriginal person.[24] Chief Justice Forbes and Justice Dowling said, in separate judgments, that it had always been the policy of the judiciary and government of New South Wales not to interfere in disputes between Aboriginal people.

The Chief Justice in his judgement noted:

I believe it has been the practice of the Courts of this country, since the colony was settled, never to interfere with or enter into the quarrels that have taken place between or amongst the natives themselves...But I am not aware that British laws have been applied to the aboriginal natives in transactions solely between themselves, whether contract, tort or crime...It may be a question admitting of doubt, whether any advantages could be gained, without previous preparation, by engrafting the institutions of our country, upon the natural system which savages have adopted for their own government...If their institutions, however barbarous or abhorrent from our notions of religion and civilisation, become matured into a system and produced all the effects upon their intercourse,

---

20 Ibid.   21 Ibid 31.   22 Ibid.   23 Ibid 31–2.
24 *R v Ballard*, Supreme Court of New South Wales, 13 June 1829, AILR vol 3, no 3, 1998.

that a less objectionable course of proceeding (in our judgement) could produce, then I know not upon what principle of municipal jurisdiction it would be right to interfere with them... with these general observations, I am of opinion that this man is not amenable to English law for the act he is supposed to have committed.

In his separate judgment, Justice Dowling said:

Until the aboriginal natives of this Country shall consent, either actually or by implication, to the interposition of our laws in the administration of justice for acts committed by themselves upon themselves, I know of no reason human, or divine, which ought to justify us in interfering with their institutions even if such interference were practicable.

While the language used by both jurists is racist by contemporary terms, they did recognize that Aboriginal people had their own systems of laws that governed relations amongst themselves. What was distinctive about the decision in this case was that it recognized a jurisdiction inherent in Aboriginal people for their own matters and left a space for it. However, this recognition did not last for long.

The 1836 case of *R v Murrell*[25] concerned another case where an Aboriginal person was charged with murder and his legal representative claimed that the colonial courts had no jurisdiction over him because Aboriginal people had their own laws that governed their relationships with each other.

Justice Burton delivered the opinion of the Court, which included Chief Justice Forbes and Justice Dowling. He said that Aboriginal people were:

...entitled to be regarded by civilised nations as a free and independent people, and are entitled to the possession of those rights which as such are valuable to them, yet the various tribes had not attained at the first settlement of the English people amongst them to such a position in point of numbers and civilisation, and to such a form of Government and laws, as to be entitled as so many sovereign states governed by law of their own.

Justice Burton questioned both the extent to which Aboriginal people could be said to have a system of laws and the extent to which they could be sovereign. He went on to add:

that the greatest possible inconvenience and scandal to this community would be consequent if it were to be holden by this Court that it has no jurisdiction in such a case as the present—to be holden in fact that crimes of murder and others of almost equal enormity may be committed by those people in our Streets without restraint so they be committed only upon one another! And that our laws are no sanctuary to them.

The issue of the jurisdiction of the Supreme Court of New South Wales was raised five years later in *R v Bonjon*.[26] It again was a case involving the murder of

---

[25] *R v Murrell*, Supreme Court of New South Wales, 11 April 1836, Sydney, AILR vol 3 no 3, 1998.
[26] *R v Bonjon*, Supreme Court of New South Wales (Willis J) 16 September 1841, Melbourne, AILR vol 3, 1998.

an Aboriginal person by anther Aboriginal. The defendant's lawyer argued that the Crown did not have jurisdiction over Aboriginal people since Aboriginal people have their own laws and punishments for crimes such as murder. The Crown prosecutor argued that it was lawful for a civilized country to occupy an uncivilized one and that the Crown brought the laws of England to the soil of New South Wales. Aboriginal people were protected by those laws, he argued, but also were bound to obey them.

In his decision, Justice Willis gave an overview of the history of the colonization of New South Wales and compared the way in which Aboriginal people in Australia had been treated with Indigenous people in other colonies. He gave an account of Captain Cook's arrival at Botany Bay and suggested that the population and social organization of Aboriginal people had been misjudged by the British. He noted that it was regretful that a treaty had not been made between the Crown and Aboriginal people.

Justice Willis wrote:

Whether the Sovereignty thus asserted within the limits defined by the Commission of His Excellency the Governor legally excludes the aborigines, according to the law of nations, as acknowledged and acted upon by the British Government, from the rightful sovereignty and occupancy of a reasonable portion of the soil, and destroys their existence as self-governing communities, so entirely as to place them, with regard to the prevalence of law among themselves, in the unqualified condition of British subjects or whether it has merely reduced them to the state of dependent allies, still retaining their own laws and usages, subject only to such restraints and qualified control as the safety of colonists and protection of the aborigines required, (subject to that right of right of pre-emption of their lands, which is undoubted) is the point upon which the present question mainly rests.

Justice Willis compared Australian jurisprudence to the overseas cases, particularly the judgments of Chief Justice Marshall of United States Supreme Court and his characterization of Indigenous people there as domestic dependent nations:

I am not aware of any express enactment or treaty subjecting the Aborigines of this colony to English colonial law, and I have shown that the Aborigines cannot be considered as Foreigners in a Kingdom which is their own. From these premises rapidly indeed collected, I am at present strongly led to infer that the Aborigines must be considered and dealt with, until some further provision be made, as distinct though dependent tribes governed among themselves by their own rude laws and customs. If this be so I strongly doubt the propriety of my assuming the exercise of jurisdiction in the case before me.

Justice Willis was aware that the Governor and Chief Justice did not approve of his judgment in the *Bonjon* case so he forwarded his judgment to the Law Officers of the Crown in London. They replied that the matter had already been decided in *Murrell's* case. Justice Willis was removed from office in 1843.

Australian courts would not, even if conceding a complex system of laws, give any space for the exercise of that jurisdiction until 1992.

G. Contesting *Terra Nullius*

While Australian legal history often describes the assertion of authority by the British on the basis of *terra nullius*—and therefore that no legal status was to be accorded to the nomadic Aboriginal people—this oversimplifies the original interaction between the colonizing power and those being colonized.

The number of Aboriginal people massacred as a result of frontier violence was contested. Historians Henry Reynolds and Lyndall Ryan have documented the frontier expansion that was both more violent than Australian history often acknowledges and more often resisted by Aboriginal people than is often recognized.[27] In parts of Australia, European expansion was impeded and even pushed back by the resistance of Aboriginal people.

Despite the resistance and guerrilla warfare that Aboriginal people engaged in, there was no attempt to enter into treaties or agreements with them. The colonial governments in Australia adopted the practice of granting lands or subsequently validating the lands taken over by squatters and endorsing the assertion of ownership over Aboriginal lands by official proclamation and annexation.

Australia is a large continent and the expansion process was a protracted one. The last recorded episodes of frontier conflict that resulted in the massacres of Aboriginal people occurred in the late 1930s in the north-west region of the country.[28] Despite this conflict, there was no attempt made by the British Crown or the colonial government to enter into treaties or agreements with Aboriginal people as a way of acquiring possession.

There were others who were vocal in their defence of the rights of Aboriginal people and in the view that their land was being taken from them unjustly. This came most strongly from missionaries and church organizations but also from journalists and writers.

In 1827, after the much publicized murders of settlers by Aboriginal people, the *Sydney Gazette* questioned whether these were not in fact justified as a response by Aboriginal people to British occupation of their land. The editorial stated:

Does the mere effecting of a settlement by no other right but that of the strongest and retaining possession owing to the physical weakness of the owners of the soil, for a period of forty years, does that divest them of their natural right to resist and expel the invaders, whenever they were in a situation to do so? We think not.[29]

---

[27] Henry Reynolds, *The Other Side of the Frontier: Aboriginal resistance to the European invasion of Australia* (Melbourne: Penguin, 1982); Henry Reynolds, *The Law of the Land* (Melbourne: Penguin, 1987); Henry Reynolds, *Frontier: Aborigines, Settlers and Land*, (Sydney: Allen & Unwin, 1987); Henry Reynolds, *Aboriginal Sovereignty: Reflections on Race, State and Nation* (Sydney: Allen & Unwin, 1996): Lyndall Ryan, *Aboriginal Tasmanians* (Sydney: Allen & Unwin, 1996).
[28] Bruce Elder, *Blood on the Wattle: Massacres and Maltreatment of Australian Aborigines since 1788* (Brookvale, NSW: National Book Distributors, 1992).
[29] Banner, note 19, 32.

In 1835, the *Sydney Herald* recorded the following in a similar vein:

It may be doubted that a people can be justified in forcibly possessing themselves of the territories of another people, who until then were its inoffensive, its undoubted, its ancient possessors.[30]

This point of view was repeated in the press often in the 1840s and 1850s.

The Quaker community were particularly vocal about the way in which Aboriginal people in Australia had been treated differently to Indigenous peoples in other colonies. A Quaker committee in London asked why the British purchased lands from the Indigenous people of other colonies but simply seized the land of Aboriginal Australians even though they considered they had rights to their traditional lands.

The influence of church-based groups was strong at this time. They were working to abolish slavery throughout the Empire and focusing generally on the welfare of Indigenous people in the colonies. Attacks on the concept of *terra nullius* and on assumptions about racial inferiority were part of a larger reform agenda.

Colonial officials were not without sympathy for these views either. The resignation of James Dredge from the post of assistant protector of Aborigines was tendered in protest at the treatment of Aboriginal people: 'they have been treated unjustly; their country has been taken from them, and with it their means of subsistence—while no equivalent has been substituted'.[31]

The Colonial Office itself expressed some sympathy towards the challenges to the doctrine of *terra nullius* and to the claims that Aboriginal people in Australia needed to be treated better. In 1837 a Select Committee of the House of Commons condemned the allocation of land to settlers without reference to:

the possessors or actual occupants … It might be presumed that the native inhabitants of any land have an incontrovertible right to their own soil: a plain and sacred right, however, which seems not to have been understood.

The Select Committee found that the property rights of Aboriginal people had been taken from them 'without the assertion of any other title than that of superior force'.[32]

There is some evidence that the colonial authorities were starting to soften in their stance on *terra nullius* and failure to recognise Aboriginal rights by the time they established the colony in South Australia. In 1835, the South Australian Colonisation Commission was instructed by the Colonial Office that it could not sell unexplored land to settlers because the new colony:

might embrace in its range numerous Tribes of People whose Proprietary Title to the Soil we have not the slightest ground for disputing. Before His Majesty can be advised to

---

[30] Ibid 33.   [31] Ibid.
[32] Paul Knaplund, *James Stephens and the British Colonial System, 1813–1847* (Madison: Wisconsin Press, 1953) 83–4; *British Parliamentary Papers: Anthropology: Aborigines*, 2:4, 5, 823; Banner, note 19, 35.

transfer to His Subjects, the property in any part of the Land of Australia, He must have at least some reasonable assurance that He is not about to sanction any act of injustice towards the Aboriginal Natives.[33]

While this may have seemed like a substantial change in policy, in practice, the South Australian Colonisation Commission was careful to acknowledge the appearance of respect for Aboriginal rights without actually doing so most usually by claiming that they would protect such rights 'where they are found to exist'.[34] No land was purchased from Aboriginal people and no treaties or agreements were entered into with the Aboriginal people about the use of their land or in recognition of their interests in their property.

H. Why no Treaty?

There has been much speculation as to why there was an absence of the treaty making that was more prevalent in North America and upon which New Zealand was asserted to have been acquired.

Some hypothesize that it was due to the fact that Aboriginal people were not the military force they were in other countries. Cook and Banks had both observed that they did not believe Aboriginal people to be 'a warlike people'. Cook described them as a 'timorous and inoffensive race, no ways inclinable to Cruelty'. In evidence to the committee that was tasked with choosing a location for a new penal colony, Banks said he was of the view that there would not be obstruction from 'the natives' to any settlement. He believed the Aboriginal people would 'speedily abandon the Country to the Newcomers'.[35]

Cook and his crew had also tried to trade with the Aboriginal people that they met but this proved to be unsuccessful. Aboriginal people showed no interest in the trinkets and goods that the British had brought with them. Cook observed that 'they had not so much as touch'd the things we had left in their hutts on purpose for them to take away'. The Aboriginal people 'set no Value on anything we gave them, nor would they ever part with any thing of their own for any one article we could offer them'. Banks concluded that there would be no means by which to purchase land from Aboriginal people because 'there was nothing we could offer that they would take'.[36] This assisted with the formation of the view that it would be pointless to try and enter into a treaty with Aboriginal people in order to acquire possession of Australia. This evidence suggested that it was going to be easier to conquer or settle the country rather than purchase it or negotiate for it and there was a clear view that Aboriginal people would not resist colonization.

The picture painted of Australia from the expedition was that it was a large continent with a small, peaceful, primitive hunter-gatherer society, uninterested

[33] Banner, note 19, 35.   [34] Ibid.   [35] Ibid 18.   [36] Ibid 19.

in trade and incapable of military resistance. This was a misleading view of the country but one that assisted in the decision that it would be an ideal location for a new penal colony.

Continuing to underpin the way in which the colonial powers dealt with Aboriginal people was the assumption that Aboriginal people were an inferior race. They were not only seen as inferior to Europeans because of the primitive culture, lack of intelligence, and their nakedness, they were seen as inferior to other Indigenous people whose lands had also become part of the British Empire.

Seen as being on the lowest level on the scale of civilization, Aboriginal people were often compared with monkeys and seen as the link between primates and modern man. Watkin Tench wrote in his diary: 'But how inferior they show when compared with the subtle African; the patient watchful American; or the elegant timid islander of the South Seas.'[37]

Aboriginal people were often compared unfavourably with the Māori, who had agricultural practices and were capable of being usefully employed. Methodist missionary, Reverend Joseph Orton, wrote in the 1830s:

It is the universal opinion of all who have seen them that it is impossible to find men and women sunk lower in the scale of human society. With regards to their manners and customs, they are little better than the beasts.[38]

The common consensus seemed to be that if the Aboriginal people of Australia were human at all, they were on the very lowest rungs of the evolutionary scale of civilization.

These were views not only prevalent during the early colonization of Australia. Views of European racial superiority and the inferiority of other races shaped thinking about Aboriginal people and their rights well into the twentieth century. They were certainly dominant in the 1880s and 1890s when a constitution for Australia was drafted. When it came into force in 1901, it was underpinned with the assumption that Aboriginal people, due to their inferiority and inability to cope with the onset of civilization, were a dying race.

All though this was to prove untrue and Aboriginal numbers started to increase by the 1930s, the legal framework for modern Australia had been set. Britain had used the doctrine of discovery to claim the continent and asserted that claim through executive and legislative action and judicial activity that relied upon the doctrine of *terra nullius*.

Against this background, the rights and sovereignty of Aboriginal people were for the most part ignored.

---

[37] Watkin Tench, *1788* (Melbourne: Text Publishing, Tim Flannery (ed), 2009).
[38] Banner, note 19, 23.

7

Asserting the Doctrine of
Discovery in Australia

The Doctrine of Discovery was employed by the British in their assertion of sovereignty over Australia but it was the doctrine of *terra nullius* that would be used to continue to support the legitimacy of the actions of the British Crown in claiming the continent. It would also shape the relationship between Indigenous people in Australia and the dominant legal system.

By the time Australia's modern legal system was being drafted at the end of the nineteenth century, Aboriginal people had been decimated by the impacts of colonization. Their numbers greatly reduced through violence, disease and poverty, the cultural fabric of communities had unravelled by dislocation, disruption to cultural practices, and the attempts to stop the speaking of Aboriginal languages.

Aboriginal people were not considered to be sovereign and were not considered to have any legal claim to their lands. By the time Australia's constitution came into force in 1901, it was assumed that Aboriginal people were a dying race. The framers of Australia's constitution did not reserve any place within the foundational document for the recognition of Aboriginal people nor for their laws or sovereignty.

A. Drafting the Australian Constitution

The framers of the Australian constitution believed that the decision making about rights protections—which ones we recognize and the extent to which we protect them—were matters for the Parliament. They discussed the inclusion of rights within the constitution itself and rejected this option, preferring instead to leave our founding document silent on these matters.

Reflecting dominant views at the time, the Australian constitution was influenced by the ideologies of white racial superiority. It is a document framed within the prejudices of a different era—of its own kind of xenophobia, sexism, and racism.

A non-discrimination clause was discussed in the process of drafting the constitution. George Williams in his book, *Human Rights under the Australian*

Constitution[1] notes that the Tasmanian Parliament proposed clause 110 that, in part, stated:

nor shall a state deprive any person of life, liberty, or property without due process of law, or deny to any person within its jurisdiction the equal protection of its laws.

This clause was rejected for two reasons:

- It was believed that entrenched rights provisions were unnecessary, and
- It was considered desirable to ensure that the Australian states would have the power to continue to enact laws that discriminated against people on the basis of their race.

This desire to enable legislation that discriminated on the basis of race was not just to ensure that the regulation of the lives of Aboriginal people could continue. It was seen as desirable to continue to control the movement of members of other races seen as inferior, particularly the Chinese who had been subjected to draconian legislative measures since the gold rushes decades before.

As testament of the new country's desire to use its legislative power for the promotion of white racial superiority, the first legislation passed through the new Australian Parliament were immigration laws that entrenched a 'white Australia' policy.

If one is aware of the intentions and the attitudes held by the drafters of the constitution then it comes as no surprise that it is a document that offers no protection against racial discrimination today. It was never intended to do so. Tolerance for discrimination on the basis of race and gender that was so prevalent in Australian society at the time the constitution was drafted has left a legacy in which our contemporary prejudices can find some comfort.

B. The Legacy of the Framers

The High Court case of *Kruger v The Commonwealth*[2] illustrates the legacy of the decision that the framers of the Australian constitution made to leave decision making about human rights to the legislature. It was the first case to be heard in the High Court that considered the legality of the formal government assimilation-based policy of removing Indigenous children from their families.

In *Kruger*, the plaintiffs had brought their case on the grounds of the violation of various rights by the effects of the Northern Territory Ordinance that allowed for the removal of Indigenous children from their families. The plaintiffs had claimed a series of human rights violations including the implied

---

[1] See George Williams, *Human Rights Under the Australian Constitution* (Melbourne: Oxford University Press, 2000).
[2] *Kruger v The Commonwealth* (1997) 190 CLR 1.

rights to due process before the law, equality before the law, freedom of movement, and the express right to freedom of religion contained in s 116 of the constitution.

They were unsuccessful on each count, a result that highlighted the general lack of rights protection in the Australian legal system. It also illustrates the way in which, through policies like child removal, there was a disproportionately high impact on Indigenous people as a result of those silences.

When the constitution was first drafted, it gave states the responsibility for matters relating to Aboriginal people. By the 1930s it was clear that Aboriginal people were not a dying race; their populations were slowly increasing. But they were living in segregated areas in abject poverty and these third world conditions became an increasing concern for many Australians and their governments. Even though there was no interest in recognizing and protecting Indigenous rights, there was a strong belief that the poverty and disadvantage in which Aboriginal people lived needed to end.

This concern fuelled a popular movement that gained momentum throughout the 1950s and 1960s and culminated in a referendum for a change to the constitution in 1967 that was passed with a 'yes' vote by over 90 per cent of all Australians. While the campaigns for the 'yes' vote focused on the need to give rights to Aboriginal people and to give them the same opportunities as everyone else, the actual changes to the constitution did not recognize or protect the rights of Indigenous people.

In reality, 1967 referendum did two things:

- It allowed for Indigenous people to be included in the census, and
- It allowed the federal parliament the power to make laws in relation to Indigenous people.

The notion of including Indigenous people in the census was, for those who advocated a 'yes' vote, more than just a body-counting exercise. It was thought that the inclusion of Indigenous people in the national population survey would create an imagined community and as such it would be a nation-building exercise, a symbolic coming together, a moment of inclusive nation-building.[3]

It is also clear from looking at the intentions of those who campaigned for the 'yes' vote that it was assumed that if power were given to the federal government to make laws in relation to Aboriginal and Torres Strait Islander people, it would use those powers for their benefit, not to disadvantage them. They believed that the changes to section 51(xxvi) (the 'races power') of the constitution to allow the federal government to make laws for Indigenous people was going to herald in an era of non-discrimination for Indigenous people.

It would turn out that the federal parliament could not be relied upon to act in a way that is beneficial to Indigenous people. There was an expectation that

---

[3] Marilyn Lake, *Faith: Faith Bandler, Gentle Activist* (Sydney: Allen & Unwin, 2002).

the granting of additional powers to the federal government to make laws for Indigenous people would see that power was used benevolently.

This has, however, not been the case. Legislation has been passed that takes away the rights of Aboriginal people, such as the *Native Title Amendment Act 1998 (Cth)*, and legislation that contains rights protections has been suspended from applying to Aboriginal people. For example, the *Racial Discrimination Act 1975 (Cth)* has been suspended to prevent its application only three times since it was passed and on each occasion this was so that it did not provide protection to Indigenous people.

One of those occasions was in a dispute over the development of a bridge in an area that the traditional owners felt was sacred. In order to resolve the matter, the federal government simply suspended heritage protection legislation from apply-ing to that area. The traditional owners challenged this. The case was *Kartinyeri v The Commonwealth* (the *Hindmarsh Island Bridge* case).[4]

Interestingly, the issue was raised as to whether the race power (s 51(xxvi)) of the constitution), which allows the federal government to make laws with regard to Indigenous people, could be used to deprive Indigenous people of their rights. The plaintiff had brought an action to prevent development over a site she asserted was sacred to her. The government sought to settle the matter by passing legislation, *the Hindmarsh Island Bridge Act 1997 (Cth)*, that repealed the application of heritage protection laws to the plaintiff. She argued, *inter alia*, that when Australians voted in the 1967 referendum to extend the federal race power to include the power to make laws concerning Aboriginal people it was with the understanding that the power would only be used to benefit Indigenous peoples.

Although the Court did not directly answer this issue, finding that the *Hindmarsh Island Bridge Act 1997 (Cth)* merely repealed existing legislation, it is interesting to note the arguments of the defence. On behalf of the federal govern-ment, the Solicitor General argued that there was nothing in s 51(xxvi) to prevent the government using the power to pass racially discriminatory laws, including Nazi style laws.[5] As abhorrent as that idea is—and as much as it appears to be the antithesis of our contemporary social values—there is much, when using ordi-nary rules of constitutional interpretation, to support this conclusion. One need only look at the intention of the drafters to see why it remains this way.

The case highlighted the way in which the expectation that the electorate might have had that the federal government would use their new powers only for the benefit of Aboriginal people had no influence in law. It reinforced the original intention of the framers of the constitution that the protection of rights was the responsibility of the legislature. And it highlighted that Aboriginal rights are not inherent. They are not seen to exist by the Australian legal system unless legis-lated for and, if they are so created, they are subject to the legislature's decision to repeal them.

---

[4] *Kartinyeri v Commonwealth* (1998) 195 CLR 337.   [5] See Williams, note 1.

This situation owes much to the doctrine of *terra nullius*. It is wholly consistent with the doctrine's failure to recognize the sovereignty and legal system of Aboriginal people. Even if courts did not refer directly to the doctrine, its shadows haunted Australian law.

C. Challenging the Status Quo

Despite the unfair playing field established by the Australian constitution, Aboriginal people still sought to assert their rights, particularly by reference to their inherent sovereignty or to common law principles that might assist with the recognition and protection of their rights. These attempts were largely unsuccessful.

For example, the Yolgnu sought to assert their rights to their traditional land in an attempt to prevent mining on it by taking their claims to court. In *Miliripum v Nabalco*[6] (also known as the *Gove land rights case*), Justice Blackburn, a single judge of the Northern Territory Supreme Court, determined that Australian common law did not recognize any interest of Aboriginal people to land and that the plaintiffs do not have rights that could be recognized as property rights. The failure to recognize Indigenous rights to land was directly linked to the adoption of the concept of *terra nullius* as a basis for justifying the British assertion of sovereignty over Australia.

Justice Blackburn was not unsympathetic to the situation of the Yolgnu. He admitted that they indeed had a complex system of laws and governance that had been overlooked, conveniently or otherwise, by the British, but he concluded that the doctrine of *terra nullius* was now so firmly entrenched into Australian law it could not be overturned, even if it was a legal fiction.

In 1976, an Aboriginal man was charged with murder.[7] He claimed that the Court had no jurisdiction over him to hear the matter because he was an Aboriginal person and a member of a sovereign people. Justice Rath followed the decision in *Murrell*'s case[8] and held that upon settlement there was only one sovereign and at that time Aboriginal people had become the subjects of the British Crown, entitled to its protection but also liable for breaches of it.

In the 1979 case of *Coe v Commonwealth*,[9] Coe attempted to raise questions about the legitimacy of the acquisition of Australia. He argued that Aboriginal people had sovereignty over Australia and that this continued after British invasion. He sought a declaration restraining the government from interfering with the Aboriginal possession of lands that they still held and an order for compensation for the lands they had lost.

[6] *Miliripum v Nabalco Pty Ltd and the Commonwealth* (1971) FLR 141.
[7] *R v Wedge* (1976) 1 NSWLR 581.
[8] *R v Murrell*, Supreme Court of New South Wales, 11 April 1836, Sydney, AILR vol 3, no 3, 1998. [9] *Coe v Commonwealth* (1979) 53 ALJR 403.

While the arguments of the Court centred on the statement of claim and whether it could be amended without considering the substantive questions, Justice Gibbs reiterated the view that the legitimacy of Australia's sovereignty could not be questioned in a domestic court. He said:

> If the amended statement of claim intends to suggest either that the legal foundation of the Commonwealth is insecure, or that the powers of the parliament are more limited than is provided in the Constitution, or that there is an Aboriginal nation which has sovereignty over Australia, it cannot be supported…The contention that there is in Australia an Aboriginal nation exercising sovereignty, even of a limited kind, is quite impossible to maintain.

The sovereignty of the Crown was not challenged by the plaintiffs in the *Mabo* case but the High Court's view that the issue of the legitimacy of the claim of sovereignty is non-justiciable in Australia's domestic courts was reiterated there. The position has been further affirmed in several subsequent cases.[10]

Given the tenacity with which the courts continued to reinforce the doctrine of *terra nullius*, it is easy to see why the decision in *Mabo v Queensland*[11] in 1992 to overturn it was so monumental.

D. The *Mabo* Case: Overturning the Doctrine of *Terra Nullius*

In 1982, Torres Strait Islanders from the Miriam people, of the Mer Islands or Murray Islands in the Torres Strait, began court action claiming that they had occupied them and the surrounding islands, seas, seabeds, and reefs since time immemorial; and that under their law individuals, family groups and the community as a whole had rights which had not been extinguished by Australia's or Queensland's sovereignty. They sought a declaration that their traditional rights to land, sea, seabeds, and reefs had not been extinguished. Importantly, in making their claim, they put the issue of their sovereignty to one side and only sought determination on the issue of their interests to land.

A decade later, the High Court delivered its judgment in the *Mabo* case[12] that by a majority found that the Murray Islanders hold Native title to their islands. The Court found that Australia was not unoccupied on settlement and that the Indigenous inhabitants had, and continue to have, legal rights to their traditional lands unless they have been validly extinguished.

The Court also overturned the doctrine of *terra nullius*.

---

[10] *Coe v Commonwealth (the Wiradjiuri claim)* (1993) 68 ALJR 110; *Walker v New South Wales* (1994) 182 CLR 45; *Wik Peoples v Queensland* (1996) 187 CLR 1.
[11] *Mabo v Queensland* (1992) 175 CLR 1, 107 ALR 1.   [12] Ibid.

Justice Brennan, who would later become Chief Justice, wrote the leading judgment:

The common law of this country would perpetuate injustice if it were to continue to embrace the enlarged notion of *terra nullius* and persist in characterising the indigenous inhabitants of Australian colonies as people too low in the scale of social organisation to be acknowledged as possessing rights and interests in land.

Native title is recognized and protected by the common law but does not originate from the common law. Native title arises from the customs and traditions of the Indigenous people whose rights are recognized. Justice Brennan noted:

Native title has its origins in and is given its content by the traditional customs observed by the Indigenous inhabitants of a territory. The nature and incidents of native title must be ascertained as a matter of fact by reference to those laws and customs.[13]

In this way, the Australian legal system recognizes and incorporates Aboriginal customary laws into its own structure.

To establish the content of Native title the customs and traditions of the Aboriginal people need to be proven. They have to demonstrate that their current customs and traditions give rise to an interest in the land that has existed continuously from the time of the colonial acquisition of sovereignty. This continuous connection does not necessarily need to include continuous physical presence on the land but may be demonstrated in other ways, such as through ongoing spiritual connections.

The Crown's ownership is subject to Native title and is not absolute. However the Crown as sovereign could extinguish Native title. The Crown must show a plain and clear intention to extinguish Native title and it can only be extinguished in a way that is lawful under the constitution and in accordance with state and federal legislation.

While the decision recognized that Indigenous Australians had and continue to have an organized society it explicitly declined to recognize the sovereign status of Indigenous Australians either at the time of colonization or currently. Justice Brennan stated that this would challenge Australia's sovereignty and any recognition would undermine the legitimacy of the High Court that gained its authority from the Australian Parliament whose sovereignty would be challenged.

Only Justice Toohey in *Mabo* considered the possibility of the federal government owing a fiduciary duty to native holders because of the vulnerability of their title. This is because the Crown has the power to act in a way that adversely impacts on Native title holders' property, and fiduciary responsibilities would protect them against abuse of this power. While fiduciary duties on the part of governments are recognized in other comparable jurisdictions such as Canada,

---

[13] *Mabo v Commonwealth* (1992) 175 CLR 58.

the Australian High Court has declined to follow Justice Toohey's reasoning in this respect.

Whilst overturning the doctrine of *terra nullius* and rejecting British claims to Australia on that basis, Justice Brennan found that Australia had been 'settled' and acknowledged that this status could only be challenged in an international court. The Indigenous perspective that characterizes this 'settlement' as an 'invasion' reflects the unsuccessful resolution of that assertion of British sovereignty. It is this grey area that leaves the legitimacy of the Australian state open to question.

In response to the judgment, and in anticipation of a plethora of claims to Native title by Indigenous people around Australia, the federal government established a legislative framework that defined Native title and a National Native Title Tribunal in an attempt to streamline claims.

The Native Title Act 1993 (Cth) established the National Native Title Tribunal for determining claims that could be mediated or conciliated and provided that the Federal Court would determine litigated claims. It defined Native title in section 223:

(1) The expression native title or native title rights and interests means the communal, group or individual rights and interests of Aboriginal peoples or Torres Strait Islanders in relation to land or waters, where:
  (a) the rights and interests are possessed under the traditional laws acknowledged, and the traditional customs observed, by the Aboriginal peoples or Torres Strait Islanders; and
  (b) the Aboriginal peoples or Torres Strait Islanders, by those laws and customs, have a connection with the land or waters; and
  (c) the rights and interests are recognised by the common law of Australia.

(2) Without limiting subsection (1), rights and interests in that subsection includes hunting, gathering, or fishing, rights and interests.

This legislative definition replaced the common law definition created by the High Court.

The federal government promised that, in addition to honouring Native title, it would develop a social justice package. However, the Keating government were voted out of office in 1996 before this was developed. They did, however, manage to establish the Indigenous Land Corporation (ILC) the year before.

The ILC was set up to administer a fund to buy land on behalf of Indigenous people in recognition of the fact that many Aboriginal people would, due to the impact and processes of colonization, be unable to prove that they maintained a Native title interest over their traditional land in the way the law described and defined it.

The social justice package was never delivered.

E. Legislative Recognition of Rights

While *Mabo* established Native title in the case brought by the people of the Murray Islands, it left open other questions that were subsequently settled by other court decisions:

- *Wik Peoples v Queensland*:[14] in 1996 the High Court held that Native title could still exist even if there were other interests in the land, such as a pastoral lease, so long as the exercise of Native title was not inconsistent with that other interest. If there was a conflict, Native title would be extinguished.
- *Yanner v Eaton*[15] established that Native title could extend, in some circumstances, to hunting and fishing rights.
- *Commonwealth v Yarmirr*[16] considered the extent to which Native title rights could extend to the sea and seabed up to and beyond the low water mark.

When the Howard government was elected into office in 1996 they adopted a hostile stance towards Indigenous rights. This hostility materialized into a derogation of Indigenous rights in many spheres including with respect to Native title. The government immediately proposed to amend the Native Title Act to make registration of claims more difficult and to increase the interests of miners and pastoralists. It made the registration of Native title claims more difficult for claimants and reduced the right of Native title holders to negotiate with respect to mining interests and limited Native title claimants' rights to information and comment with respect to other dealings related to their claims.

Prime Minister John Howard's rhetoric surrounding the passing of the Native Title Amendment Act 1998 (Cth) brought into focus the conflicting visions Australians have about our country. The federal government tried to gain popular support for its proposed legislative changes by portraying pastoral leases as small, family run farms. The Prime Minister continued to push an approach informed by the ideologies of white Australian nationalism and a psychological *terra nullius*, playing into 'settlement' myths of Australia's land being tamed by brave men who struggled to make a living off the land.

The Prime Minister stated:

Australia's farmers, of course, have always occupied a very special place in our heart.... They often endure the heart break of drought, the disappointment of bad international prices after a hard-worked season and quite frankly I find it impossible to imagine the Australia I love, without a strong and vibrant farming sector.[17]

---

[14] *Wik Peoples v Queensland* (1996) 187 CLR 96, 141 ALR 129.
[15] *Yanner v Eaton* (1999) 210 CLR 351, 166 ALR 258.
[16] *Commonwealth v Yarmirr* (2001) 184 ALR 113.
[17] 'The sooner we get this debate over the better for all of us' (1 December 1997), *The Age*.

This rhetoric sought to appeal to romanticized, nationalistic ideals that celebrated white settlement and ignored the impact on Aboriginal and Torres Strait Islander people. It treated the rights of Indigenous people in Australia as non-existent and ignored the fact that what the *Mabo* and *Wik* cases found was a legitimate property right held by Indigenous peoples. It brushed over the historical context in which dispossession took place. Howard employed a notion of formal equality in this debate:

… we have clung tenaciously to the principle that no group in the Australian community should have rights that are not enjoyed by another group.[18]

He also referred to the 'politics of guilt':

Australians of this generation should not be required to accept the guilt and blame for the past actions and policies over which they had no control.[19]

Howard's lack of historical context—massacres, dispossession, government policies of assimilation, and removal of children—enabled him to view the recognition of Native title interests in a vacuum. He seperated Native title from the historical events that facilitated and compounded the continual failure of Australian legal and political institutions to recognize it as a legitimate property right. He claimed that these wrongs were historic and should be treated as such; dispossession was claimed to be 'in the past' and therefore not the responsibility of Australians today. Yet, Native title was only recognized in 1992 and dispossession still continues today, facilitated by the passing of the Native Title Amendment Act, 1998 (Cth) whose enactment meant that 80 of the 115 claims then before the Native Title Tribunal in New South Wales (NSW) were dismissed.

These amendments received criticism from the United Nations Committee on the Elimination of All forms of Racial Discrimination. It found that several aspects of the amendments breached the International Convention on the Elimination of all Forms of Racial Discrimination in a number of respects, including the provisions with respect to the validation of non-Indigenous interests, deemed extinguishment of Native title, the expansion of pastoral interests, and the abolition and diminution of the right to negotiate.

Over more than a decade and a half of Native title cases, an increasingly conservative court has narrowed the definition of Native title and it is judges, not Aboriginal people, who have the largest role in recognizing the existence and defining the content of Native title.

In the *Yorta Yorta* case,[20] the Court found that the culture of the claimants had been eroded by the history of colonization and taken with it the Native title interests of the Yorta Yorta nation. The decision prompted Aboriginal people

---

[18] 'Racing Towards an election' (11 April 1998) *Sydney Morning Herald.*
[19] 'Mr. Howard unreconciled' (27 May 1997) *Sydney Morning Herald.*
[20] *Members of the Yorta Yorta Aboriginal Community v Victoria* (2002) HCA 58.

across Australia to realize the extent to which Australian courts and parliaments can recognize an Aboriginal right or interest but seek to override it through narrow judicial interpretations of facts and a Eurocentric gaze on Aboriginal history, experience, culture, and life.

F. Land Rights Legislation

The Native Title Act 1993 (Cth) was the result of a political response to the reinterpretation by the High Court of the common law that applied in Australia. There have, however, been other moments where legislation has provided recognition and protection of Aboriginal ownership to land as a result of political pressure and will.

Land rights legislation has been passed in some states, each with different features. The federal government passed the legislation that established a land rights regime in the Northern Territory.

The New South Wales Aboriginal Land Rights Act was passed in 1983 and is the most generous of all the land rights regimes established in Australia. The Act recognizes dispossession and dislocation of NSW Aboriginal people. It was intended as compensation for lost lands and for Aboriginal people to establish an economic base.

The beneficial intention of the NSW land rights regime is stated clearly in the preamble of the Act:

Land in the State of New South Wales was traditionally owned and occupied by Aborigines. Land is of spiritual, social, cultural and economic importance to Aborigines. It is fitting to acknowledge the importance which land has for Aborigines and the need of Aborigines for land. It is accepted that as a result of past Government decisions the amount of land set aside for Aborigines has been progressively reduced without compensation.

The Act sets up a state land council—the NSW Aboriginal Land Council—with regional representatives and 121 Local Aboriginal Land Councils, all of which are governed by Boards elected by the Aboriginal members. As the state's largest Aboriginal organization, and in the post-ATSIC era the largest elected representative body in Aboriginal Affairs, the New South Wales Aboriginal Land Council had, at the beginning of 2009, an asset base of over $2 billion in land holdings and over $680 million in cash assets.[21] With this asset base, it aims to protect the interests and further the aspirations of its members and the broader Aboriginal community through social housing, scholarship schemes, and community projects.

It has been a far more successful legislative model for the recognition of the dispossession of the rights of Aboriginal people than Native title. It is premised

[21] <http://www.alc.org.au/>.

on being a model that provides compensation for loss of land and other historical wrongs. But this more generous model, that also facilitates a form of representative governance, is still a legislative framework, still existing only at the benevolence of government, still vulnerable to abolition should the New South Wales government decide to repeal it.

G. Contemporary Aspirations for the Recognition of Sovereignty and the Protection of Indigenous Rights

The refusal of courts to consider the legitimacy of the assertion of British sovereignty has not stopped Aboriginal people from seeking a political solution to the protection of Aboriginal rights and the exercise of sovereignty. The clearest articulation from Indigenous people about what a comprehensive recognition and protection of their sovereignty and rights might look like was developed in 1995.

The consultation was undertaken by the Aboriginal and Torres Strait Islander Commission (ATSIC), a legislative national representative model that provided a voice for Aboriginal people at a national and regional level. It published a document, *Recognition, Rights and Reform: A Report to Government on Native Title Social Justice Measures*[22] as a response to the inquiry about further measures that the Australian government should consider to address the dispossession of Aboriginal and Torres Strait Islander peoples as part of the social justice package.

In preparing the report, ATSIC had consulted widely. As such, it became, and remains, the most accurate blueprint for reforms that reflect the views of Aboriginal and Torres Strait Islanders as to how best to achieve social justice. *Recognition, Rights and Reforms* responded to the Keating government's desire for constructive and realistic proposals to increase the participation of Indigenous peoples in Australia's economic life, to safeguard and develop Indigenous cultures, to help develop a positive community consensus, and to contribute to a lasting reconciliation.

The report noted that, at the time the social justice package was being considered, there were several other key initiatives that, in addition to the Native Title Act 1993 and establishment of the Indigenous Land Fund and the Indigenous Land Corporation, were concerned with achieving social justice for Aboriginal and Torres Strait Islander people, namely:

- a federal government Access and Equity Strategy;
- action taken to implement the government's response to the recommendations of the Royal Commission into Aboriginal Deaths in Custody;

---

[22] Aboriginal and Torres Strait Islander Commission, *Recognition, Rights and Reform: A Report to Government on Native Title Social Justice Measures* (Canberra: Australian Government Publishing Service, 1995).

- major reviews of policies and programmes in the key areas of Aboriginal and Torres Strait Islander employment, education, and health;
- the work of the Council for Aboriginal Reconciliation;
- the Centenary of Federation that was to occur in 2001; and
- the International Decade of the World's Indigenous People is commencing with a focus on the international recognition of indigenous rights.

These activities that coincided with the consultations and proposals for the social justice package highlighted the fact that there were several areas of action on Indigenous issues, particularly focused on Indigenous rights, that culminated to create a feeling that it was possible to achieve a new era of non-discrimination and recognition for Aboriginal and Torres Strait Islander people.

The recognition of fundamental rights and entitlements of Indigenous peoples was a central aspect of the proposals in *Recognition, Rights and Reforms*. The report noted that the ability to exercise and enjoy those rights—the normal citizenship or equality rights that Indigenous peoples share with all Australians, and the distinctive rights of Indigenous peoples—was critical to the achievement of social justice for Aboriginal and Torres Strait Islander people.

It identified several key areas where rights could be protected and made proposals in relation to each of them, namely:

- **Citizenship and Equality Rights** with particular issues identified as:
  - the enormous level of unmet need in Aboriginal and Torres Strait Islander communities for basic service delivery such as housing and infrastructure which results from a failure of governments responsible for delivering those services;
  - ensuring access and equity for Aboriginal and Torres Strait Islander people who are largely reliant on mainstream service delivery from all levels of government; and
  - ensuring an adequate and equitable range of service delivery in respect of remote and predominantly Aboriginal and Torres Strait Islander communities.
- **Indigenous Rights** where, with a view that the recognition of and support for self-determination is fundamental, further work was identified in the form of:
  - Autonomy Rights, which focus upon the right of Indigenous peoples to determine the way in which they live and control their social, economic, and political systems;
  - Identity Rights, which relate to the right to exist as distinct peoples with distinct cultures; and
  - Territory and Resource Rights, which encompass such things as land entitlements, the right to resources of that land, and the use of those resources.

Recognition, Rights and Reforms put forward a broad range of recommendations that covered the following areas:

- **The rights of Aboriginal and Torres Strait Islander peoples as citizens**, including:
  - ○ the reinforcement of access and equity provisions through legislation to ensure Indigenous people can better access their citizenship entitlements;
  - ○ an increased commitment to supporting international instruments which reinforce Indigenous rights; and
  - ○ support for measures to define, recognize and extend Indigenous rights including new initiatives in areas such as communal title and assertion of coextensive rights.

- **The recognition of the special status and rights of Indigenous Australians and the achievement of greater self-determination for Aboriginal and Torres Strait Islander peoples**, namely:
  - ○ the promotion and advancement of the constitutional reform agenda;
  - ○ Indigenous representation in Parliament with interim arrangements for speaking rights by the ATSIC Chairperson;
  - ○ the development of processes to start work on compensation issues;
  - ○ the promotion of regional agreements as a means of settling social justice issues on a regional basis commencing with pilot studies;
  - ○ recognition of a self-government option for Indigenous people within the framework of self-determination;
  - ○ support for initial work to develop a framework for a treaty and negotiation arrangements;
  - ○ legislative recognition of the Aboriginal and Torres Strait Islander flags; and
  - ○ increased support for Public Awareness initiatives.

- **Ensuring that Indigenous Australians are able to exercise their rights and share equitably in the provision of government programmes and services.**

- **The protection of the cultural integrity and heritage of Indigenous Australians**, including:
  - ○ legislative reforms to strengthen heritage protection legislation and protect Indigenous rights to cultural property;
  - ○ providing for greater involvement in environmental decision making;
  - ○ implementing the report of the Law Reform Commission on Aboriginal customary law; and
  - ○ support for extension of language programmes and broadcasting initiatives.

- **Measures to increase Aboriginal and Torres Strait Islander participation in Australia's economic life,** including:
  - ○ fostering closer links with industry;
  - ○ accessing the Community Development Employment Projects (CDEP) Scheme as an entitlement and removing anomalies;
  - ○ implementation of business training proposals of AEDP;
  - ○ fostering regional economic development; and
  - ○ further development of strategic business opportunities and resources for a stake in industry.

Other major proposals canvassed by the *Recognition, Rights and Reform* report were: major institutional and structural change, including constitutional reform and recognition, regional self-government and regional agreements, and the negotiation of a treaty or comparable document.

However, the election of the Howard government in 1996 meant that no action was taken on this agenda. His government subsequently abolished the Aboriginal and Torres Strait Islander Commission.

H. 'The Northern Territory Intervention': Continuing Legislative Power over Aboriginal People and their Rights

The federal government designed an 'intervention' into the Northern Territory in Australia, created in a 48-hour period and unveiled by Aboriginal Affairs Minister Mal Brough on 21 June 2007.

The package of legislation included many measures: widespread alcohol restrictions, quarantining welfare payments and linking them to school attendance, compulsory health checks to identify health problems and signs of abuse, forced acquisition of townships through compulsory leases, increased policing, introduction of market-based rents and normal tenancy arrangements, banning of pornography and auditing publicly funded computers, scrapping the permit system, and appointing managers to all prescribed communities.

While the promises of additional resources for policing, medical checks and housing were welcomed, other aspects of the policy approach raised concern:

- it was ideologically led and made no reference to the research or understandings about what actually works on the ground;
- in fact, the policy approach was in direct contradiction of what the research shows us works and what experts recommend as appropriate action;
- the rhetoric of doing what is in the best interests of Aboriginal people, or children, masked a list of other policy agendas—private ownership of land and welfare reform in particular—that were unrelated to effective approaches to

dealing with systemic problems of violence and abuse and instead sought to undermine community control over their land and resources; and

- the approach was paternalistic and top-down. It did not seek to include Aboriginal people in the outcomes.

The two aspects that caused the most concern were the quarantining of welfare and the requirements of leases over Aboriginal land in exchange for housing money.

1. Welfare quarantining

The quarantining of welfare payments was included as part of the intervention with the seductive rhetoric that it would be linked to school attendance. This played well with an electorate who probably assumed that poor attendance rates and poor educational outcomes for Aboriginal children were caused by the poor parenting of Aboriginal parents.

An evaluated trial of a scheme linking welfare payments to school attendance in Halls Creek found that the attitudes of parents of Aboriginal children were only one of the factors that affected school attendance. It pointed to the pivotal role that teachers and the school culture itself play in a community where children decide their own time use patterns at a very early age. The trial also showed that poor or good attendance did not necessarily run in families. In one family of five children, attendance ranged from 14 per cent to 88 per cent. It was also found that the housing situation in Halls Creek—where overcrowding is a critical problem—is unlikely to provide an environment where families can be 'school ready'.

There is no evidence that shows that linking welfare to behaviour change is effective. In fact, there is evidence to suggest that the imposition of such punitive measures in an already dysfunctional situation will exacerbate the stress in a household.

Evidence shows that improved attendance can be achieved by:

- breakfast and lunch programmes;
- programmes that bring the Aboriginal community, especially Elders, into the schools;
- Aboriginal teacher's aides and Aboriginal teachers;
- a curriculum that engages Aboriginal children; and
- programmes that marry programmes promoting self-esteem and confidence through engaging with culture with initiatives focusing on academic excellence.

These effective programmes and strategies show the importance of building a relationship between Aboriginal families and the school in order to target issues like school attendance. It also shows that there is much that the schools can also do to engage children with schooling. It suggests that, rather than simply punishing parents for their children's non-attendance, the government should be providing schools and teachers that meet the needs of the Aboriginal community.

It cost $88 million to make the initial administrative changes within the bureaucracy to facilitate the welfare quarantining yet not one additional dollar was spent in the intervention on any of the types of programmes that have been proven to engage Aboriginal children in schools in the first wave of the intervention.[23] There is data that shows that the Northern Territory spends 47c on the education of Indigenous children for every $1 spent on the education of non-Aboriginal students. Many Aboriginal communities in the Northern Territory do not have enough teachers, classrooms, or desks for all the children that reside in the community.

A punitive measure placed on families to ensure their children come to school is hypocritical from any government that neglects the same children by failing to provide adequate funding for a teacher and a classroom. Even if it did work to physically bring more children into a classroom, what is the quality of the education they will receive when there has been underinvestment in teachers and educational infrastructure?

But the problematic nature of the welfare quarantining policy does not stop there. Despite the rhetoric of linking the welfare payments to school attendance, when the policy was rolled out, it was not applied just to parents whose children did not attend school. It applied to anyone who lived in an Aboriginal community designated as a 'prescribed area' who was receiving a welfare payment—whether their children went to school or not, whether they even had children or not. People who had managed their money their whole lives suddenly found their income quarantined.

To achieve this, the federal government prevented the Racial Discrimination Act from applying, suspended protections and rights of appeal under the Northern Territory anti-discrimination legislation, and suspended the rights to appeal to the social security appeals tribunal. It took away the rights of the most marginalized within our community to complain about unfair treatment of, or unfair impact on, just about anyone.

Barbara Shaw lives in an Alice Springs town camp. She has her own children but often looks after others. She has supported her family all her adult life. She found, with no consultation, and no notice, that her income was suddenly restricted by quarantining. Barb is nobody's fool but she had problems navigating the system at first. She finds her ability to travel restricted because the store card she is issued with cannot be used in other states. She knows people who cannot travel for

---

[23] The government claimed that it started a school meal programme as part of the intervention. However, this was not like the community/school driven programmes but rather quarantined money from the income of parents who were subject to quarantining. This means that the families were supporting those programmes, not the government.

funerals (called 'sorry business') or cultural business because of these restrictions. She knows women who, like herself, could not afford Christmas presents because of the restrictive nature of the way the quarantining works. It is also impossible to buy white goods. Barb, who has always provided for her family, never neglected her children, and always focused on their education, resents that Centrelink, the government agency that distributes welfare payments, used to segregate the lines between those whose income was quarantined and those whose income was not. There were only black people in her line. She also resents the separate queues at the shops and has on more than one occasion been confronted by shop owners angry and frustrated with the card system. She cannot tell how much is on the card so sometimes she does not have enough for her purchases and has to take items back. Barb has taken her complaints about the welfare quarantining system to the United Nations since there is no forum within Australia that will hear her concerns.[24]

2. Housing policy

There are some stark differences between the treatment of housing in the community sector and Aboriginal community owned housing at the national level.

Housing in the community sector is the responsibility of the Minister for Housing, Tanya Plibersek. Aboriginal housing falls under the Minister for Indigenous Affairs, Jenny Macklin. Plibersek supports the establishment and use of the community housing sector to manage social housing. She has said that she wants to see the growth of the number of 'sophisticated not-for-profit housing organisations' that would operate alongside state-run housing providers. Plibersek has been supportive of what she thinks community-based housing organizations can provide and has observed that they are good at tenancy management, often have lower rates of rental arrears, and better track records at maintenance than state housing authorities.

By comparison, Macklin does not support Indigenous community housing providers. She has policies aimed at closing down the sector in favour of mainstream public housing. She does not have the same confidence in the Indigenous housing sector that Plibersek has in community housing. She seems to believe that they are poor managers and that maintenance is a problem. That is part of the thinking in why Aboriginal communities need to sign lease agreements in order to access housing money. Macklin has said, 'Lease arrangements are required to secure this major public investment in the communities and to make

---

[24] Barbara Shaw et al, *Request for Urgent Action under the International Convention on the Elimination of All Forms Racial Discrimination* (submission in relation to the Commonwealth Government of Australia, 28 January 2009, prepared by the author's legal representatives, see <http://www.jumbunna.uts.edu.au/research/submissions.html>). See also Alister Nicholson, Larissa Behrendt et al, *Will They be Heard?* (2009) at <http://rollbacktheintervention.wordpress.com/>.

sure that housing and management can be reformed to improve tenancy management, maintenance and repairs.'

Macklin is placing a lot of faith in mainstream housing providers to deliver for Aboriginal people. She has said that state and territory public housing authorities had a set of management systems in place that are desperately needed and lacking in remote communities and these communities will benefit from the 'strong regulatory framework provided by the State'. Strangely, the Housing Minister does not seem to share this view. Plibersek has recognized the failures of mainstream public housing authorities to deliver. Of the same system she has said, 'We are often not delivering opportunities for public housing tenants; 90% of stock is held by eight government providers; and our system is not transparent or accountable.'

Plibersek supports the transfer of the title of public housing *from* state and territory housing authorities *over to* the community housing sector so that they can provide housing. Macklin has a completely different attitude. She is insisting that the title of the land on which community housing is built must be transferred *from* the Aboriginal community *to* state housing authorities through a long-term lease (from 40 to 99 years). Housing will be delivered by government housing authorities (the same ones that Plibersek described as 'not transparent or accountable') and is contingent on communities leasing their land back and on responsibility for management of the housing being handed back to the public housing authority.

This is the housing policy to which Macklin has stuck tenaciously as part of the Northern Territory intervention and which it has rolled out in other states. More questions have been asked after the $800 million housing programme in the Northern Territory did not deliver one new house in 18 months.

Walpiri Elder, Harry Nelson Jakamarra, has said:

The Intervention housing program has not built any new houses at Yuendumu. We are just being blackmailed. If we don't hand over our land we can't get houses maintained, or any new houses built. We have never given away any Warlpiri land and we are not going to start now.[25]

Aboriginal people have asked why their rights to land have to be surrendered for access to housing money that other Australians can access without any such guarantee.

Richard Downs is a tall, striking but soft spoken Aboriginal leader from Ampilatwatja, a town three hours from Alice Springs. They were taken over with the five-year lease that came with the promise of new housing. The housing stock was transferred to Northern Territory Housing. No new houses were built and much needed repairs did not take place. By July 2009, the town was overflowing with raw sewerage. A plumber was supposed to be on his way but his truck broke

---

[25] <http://interventionwalkoff.wordpress.com/media-releases/>.

down, the community was told. They packed up and moved to a camp six kilo-metres from town. They fundraised to get a bore running and to build showers and toilets at their new site. They have become fierce critics of this aspect of the intervention.[26]

Richard Downs has said:

We are fed up with the federal government's Northern Territory intervention, controls and measures, visions and goals forced onto us from outside.... We had been waiting with patience to see where this intervention was heading, hoping there may be some humanity and compassion towards our Indigenous people, some respect to bring us back into the discussion process, to have a say in what is happening in our community. Instead our leaders and elders are treated with contempt, shown no respect, degraded, treated as lower-class outsiders.[27]

* * *

The irony of the situation for Aboriginal people in Australia is that, while tra-ditional systems of governance and dispute resolution have been undermined, marginalized, and ignored, there has also been a reluctance to support cohesive and coherent government structures that would provide Aboriginal people with new democratic, representative bodies.

There has also been a reluctance to devolve power and decision making to Indigenous people through representative bodies and community organizations despite evidence that shows that policy making is more effective in targeting areas of socio-economic need if Aboriginal people are given a central place in the development of policies that target their needs.

Aboriginal communities are capable of determining their own methods of dis-pute resolution but these have never been recognized. Between the models of governance and dispute resolution that existed in traditional Aboriginal culture and the imposed models of representation such as ATSIC that embody notions of representative democracy there is another alternative—the explorations of models of self-representation and dispute resolution that find a fluid merging of the distinctive characteristics of Aboriginal cultural governance structures and models of participatory democracy.

There has been a limited capacity on the part of Australian courts and law to recognize the laws of Aboriginal people. Despite the awareness of the develop-ment of jurisprudence in other jurisdictions, particularly the concept of domestic dependent nations in the United States, no such space was given to Aboriginal people.

---

[26] <http://interventionwalkoff.wordpress.com>.
[27] <http://rollbacktheintervention.wordpress.com/ampilatwatja-walk-off/>.

8

Asserting the Doctrine of Discovery in Aotearoa New Zealand: 1840–1960s

On the British stage of colonization, Aotearoa New Zealand often heralds itself as different, and thus better than other colonies in developing relationships with its Indigenous peoples (in particular, superior to its neighbour Australia). This is largely asserted in reference to the existence of relatively high intermarriage statistics, the urbanization of Māori, and a so-called treaty of cession, the Treaty of Waitangi, which constitutes a series of documents signed by a British Crown representative and more than 500 Māori chiefs in 1840.[1] However, close analysis of the events surrounding British assertion of sovereignty in Aotearoa New Zealand including the signing of the Treaty and its subsequent interpretation by the courts, and today, by Parliament, indicates a less than idyllic picture. This initial chapter explores how Britain sought annexation of Aotearoa via a treaty of cession steeped in a Discovery mindset. It argues that the ideology of Discovery, rather than cession, has been alive and well in Aotearoa New Zealand's legislature and courts since their colonial origin. Aotearoa New Zealand has been, and continues to be, caught in the colonial web of the Doctrine in a similar manner to other British colonized countries, including the United States, Canada, and Australia. In particular, this chapter traverses the early case law of *R v Symonds*,[2] *Wi Parata*,[3] and *Ninety-Mile Beach*.[4] First, it provides a background to the political and cultural make-up of the country. Second, it discusses the Treaty of Waitangi. Third, it explores historical legislation and early case law through to the 1960s.

---

[1] The Treaty of Waitangi Act 1975. To better understand the role of the Crown in New Zealand, see Noel Cox, 'The Treaty of Waitangi and the Relationship between Crown and Maori in New Zealand' (2002) 28 Brooklyn Journal of International Law 123. For a broad insight into how the legal system has sought to recognize, or not, Māori from 1840 to today see Jacinta Ruru, 'The Maori Encounter with Aotearoa New Zealand's Legal System' in Benjamin J Richardson, Shin Imai, and Kent McNeil (eds), *Indigenous Peoples and the Law: Comparative and Critical Perspectives* (Oxford: Hart Publishing, 2009) 111–33. Note that parts of this chapter develop work in Robert J Miller and Jacinta Ruru, 'An Indigenous Lens into Comparative Law: The Doctrine of Discovery in the United States and New Zealand' (2009) 111 West Virginia L Rev 849.

[2] *Regina v Symonds* [1847] NZPCC 387.

[3] *Wi Parata v Bishop of Wellington* [1877] 3 NZ Jur (NS) 72.

[4] *In Re Ninety-Mile Beach* [1963] NZLR 461.

A. Background

Before delving into the legal content of Discovery in Aotearoa New Zealand, it is imperative to provide a short geographical, cultural, and political glimpse of this southern hemisphere country. Aotearoa New Zealand constitutes of two large islands (the North Island and the South Island), a smaller third island (Stewart Island), and numerous other small islets. The majority of the population live on the North Island (and this was similarly true prior to the arrival of the Europeans). The lands were first discovered and peopled by the Māori tribes sometime on or after AD 800.[5] It is a mountainous landscape, densely forested with a comparatively cooler climate than the Pacific Islands. It swarmed with birds (many flightless) and teemed with fish (both freshwater and saltwater species). Grouped into distinct peoples, the Māori tribes became, literally, the people of the land (*tangata whenua*), living upon Papatuanuku, the earth mother, with Ranginui, the sky father, above. The common language (with regional dialectal differences) captured this interrelationship. For instance, *hapu* means 'sub-tribe' and 'to be pregnant'; *whanau* means 'family' and 'to give birth'; and *whenua* means 'land' and 'afterbirth'.[6] Of some 40 distinct *iwi* (tribes), and hundreds of *hapu*, each derived their identity from the mountains, rivers, and lakes.[7]

Aotearoa New Zealand is a unicameral country. Its appeal courts constitute (in order from the first court of appeal to the final court of appeal): the High Court, Court of Appeal, and since 2002, the Supreme Court (prior to 2002, the Privy Council Judicial Committee was New Zealand's highest court).[8] Under its constitutional system, Parliament is supreme and has no formal limits to its law-making power.[9] The Treaty of Waitangi is not part of the domestic law. Since the 1980s, the Treaty is commonly said to form part of its informal constitution along with the New Zealand Bill of Rights Act 1990 and the Constitution Act 1986. Therefore, for the judiciary or those acting under the law, the Treaty itself

---

[5] Ranginui Walker, *Ka Whawhai Tonu Matou: Struggle Without End* (Auckland: Penguin Books, 2nd edn, 2004) 24. Others put it at about AD 1200: Michael King, *The Penguin History of New Zealand* (Auckland: Penguin Books, 2003) 48.

[6] For an introduction to the Māori language see H W Williams, *Dictionary of the Maori Language* (Wellington: GP Publications, 1992) and H M Ngata, *English-Maori Dictionary* (Wellington: Learning Media, 1993).

[7] For an introduction to Māori mythology see Ross Calman and A W Reed, *Reed Book of Maori Mythology* (Wellington: Reed Books, 2nd edn, 2004).

[8] See Supreme Court Act 2003. Note that the Privy Council Judicial Committee consists of senior judges and was formerly the supreme court of appeal for the entire British Empire. It continues to hear appeals from some Commonwealth countries.

[9] To better understand New Zealand's constitutional system see Phillip Joseph, *Constitutional and Administrative Law in New Zealand* (Wellington: Thompson Brookers, 2nd edn, 2007); Matthew Palmer, 'Constitutional Realism About Constitutional Protection: Indigenous Rights Under a Judicialized and a Politicized Constitution' (2007) 29 Dalhousie LJ 1 (explaining New Zealand's constitutional system).

usually only becomes relevant if it has been expressly incorporated into statute. Even so, statutory incorporation of the Treaty has been a relatively recent phenomenon. It was once endorsed in the courts 'as a simple nullity'.[10] It was not until the 1970s, when Māori visibly took action to highlight Treaty breaches, that the Treaty began to gain mainstream recognition and, in turn, the attention of those in Parliament and the judiciary.[11]

At one level Aotearoa New Zealand's colonial experiences resonate strongly with Indigenous peoples' experiences in Canada, Australia, and the United States. British colonization undeniably affected who Māori were; disease and warfare decimated the population and legislation criminalized the Māori way of life.[12] But the tools for colonization and the recent remedies to overcome the disasters of colonization are in many ways unique to this South-West Pacific island country. There exists a single treaty of cession, the Treaty of Waitangi, and legal institutions with counterparts not found elsewhere in the world: the Māori Land Court and the Waitangi Tribunal.[13] Today, the Māori, as a significant and visible component of the population (currently constituting over 15 per cent of Aotearoa New Zealand's four million people),[14] are rebuilding their communities and ways of knowing. This chapter focuses on the pervading Doctrine of Discovery in early colonial Aotearoa New Zealand.

B. Claiming Sovereignty: Treaty of Waitangi 1840

In 1840, the British claimed sovereignty of the lands through a combination of the Doctrine of Discovery principles and the partially signed Treaty of Waitangi. Following the British explorer Captain James Cook's first visit to and circumnavigation of Aotearoa in 1779, European (consisting mostly of British and to a lesser extent French) explorers, whalers, and missionaries began arriving, bringing with them their own distinct world view, technology, goods, and animals.[15] In the 1830s Britain and France were seriously interested in claiming sovereignty of all, or parts, of New Zealand.[16] Britain strategically acknowledged

---

[10] *Wi Parata v Bishop of Wellington* [1877] 3 NZ Jur (NS) 72, 78.

[11] See Walker, note 5 and the following chapter in this book, Chapter 9.

[12] See Alan Ward, *A Show of Justice: Radical 'Amalgamation' in Nineteenth Century New Zealand* (Auckland: Auckland University Press, 1973).

[13] For reading on the Māori Land Court see Richard Boast, Andrew Erueti, Doug McPhail, and Norman F Smith, *Maori Land Law* (Wellington: Lexis Nexis, 2nd edn, 2004). For reading on the Waitangi Tribunal see Janine Hayward and Nicola R Wheen (eds), *The Waitangi Tribunal* (Wellington: Bridget Williams Books, 2004); Giselle Byrnes, *The Waitangi Tribunal and New Zealand History* (Auckland: Oxford University Press, 2004).

[14] Statistics New Zealand, <http://www.stats.govt.nz> (showing New Zealand's current population).

[15] See eg James Belich, *Making Peoples: A History of the New Zealanders from Polynesian Settlement to the End of the Nineteenth Century* (Auckland: Penguin Press, 1996).

[16] See eg Claudia Orange, *The Treaty of Waitangi* (Wellington: Allen & Unwin, 1987).

the independent sovereignty of some of the Māori tribes in 1835,[17] and then set about annexation. There is no clear date upon which New Zealand became a British colony. The entire process has been described as 'tortuous'[18] and involved several interrelated events relating to the signing of the Treaty of Waitangi in 1840.

But, first, the Declaration of Independence, signed in 1835, deserves mention. By the 1830s, the nature of Aotearoa New Zealand had changed drastically. Introduced diseases had had a devastating impact on Māori. Deaths resulting from intertribal warfare had increased exponentially as a result of access to musket guns. The 'unruly and unsanctioned behaviour of some settlers'[19] was getting out of hand. Pressure from colonizers seeking to acquire Māori lands was accumulating. The growing trade in preserved Māori heads was concerning British officials. The need for New Zealand built ships to sail registered with a flag was pressing. Eventually, in response to these many concerns, the Colonial Office in London appointed James Busby as British Resident in New Zealand. Busby was instructed by Governor Richard Bourke of New South Wales to introduce a settled form of government among Māori. Busby believed a collective Māori sovereignty was required to end intertribal warfare. On 20 March 1834, Busby invited 25 northern chiefs to gather at Waitangi to vote on a national flag. Some 18 months later, Busby called a second meeting at Waitangi, this time inviting 34 northern chiefs to sign the Declaration of the Independence of New Zealand. The thought that France might establish its own independent region in the north of the North Island spurred this action. The chiefs signed the Māori language version of the short Declaration on 28 October 1835. Clause 2 of the English version reads:

All sovereign power and authority within the territories of the United Tribes of New Zealand is hereby declared to reside entirely and exclusively in the hereditary chiefs and heads of tribes in their collective capacity, who also declare that they will not permit any legislative authority separate from themselves in their collective capacity to exist, nor any function of government to be exercised within the said territories, unless by persons appointed by them, and acting under the authority of laws regularly enacted by them in Congress assembled.

The British government recognized the Declaration. Busby continued to seek signatures from chiefs throughout the country until the late 1830s. By this time, some of the key players included the new Governor of New South Wales, George Gipps, and his appointment of William Hobson as Lieutenant Governor

---

[17] To read the Declaration of Independence and commentary, see Claudia Orange, *An Illustrated History of the Treaty of Waitangi* (Wellington: Bridget Williams Books, 2004) 13–16.

[18] David V Williams, 'The Foundation of Colonial Rule in New Zealand' (1988) New Zealand Univ L Rev 56.

[19] Te Puni Korkiri/Ministry of Maori Development, *He Tirohanga o Kawa ki to Tiriti o Waitangi. A Guide to the Principles of the Treaty of Waitangi as Expressed by the Courts and the Waitangi Tribunal* (Wellington: Te Puni Korkiri, 2001) 28.

(ratified 30 July 1839) and British consul to New Zealand (confirmed 13 August 1839).[20]

The specific events that really began the process of annexation itself began four years after the initial signing of the Declaration. First, the Letters Patent of 15 June 1839 amended the Commission of the Governor of New South Wales by enlarging this Australian colony to include 'any territory which is or may be acquired in sovereignty by Her Majesty…within that group of Islands in the Pacific Ocean, commonly called New Zealand…'.[21] The second event draws attention to the three Proclamations by Governor Gipps, published on 19 January 1840 proclaiming that: (1) the jurisdiction of the New South Wales Governor extended to New Zealand; (2) the oaths of office had been administered to Hobson as Lieutenant-Governor; and (3) no title to land in New Zealand purchased henceforth would be recognized unless derived from the Crown and that Commissioners would be appointed to investigate past purchases of land from Māori.[22] The initial signing of a 'treaty of cession' at Waitangi on 6 February 1840 constitutes the third event. The fourth event concerns Hobson's Proclamations of full British sovereignty over all of New Zealand on 21 May 1840. The fifth event is the ratification of Hobson's Proclamations by their publication in the *London Gazette* on 2 October 1840.[23]

These six interrelated events took place within a context wherein by the late 1830s, Britain officially sought to pursue sovereignty of New Zealand via means of cession if possible (treaty making was in vogue at that time for both British and French colonialists) or, if necessary, by asserting Discovery. On 14 August 1839, the British government issued instructions to Captain Hobson (confirmed by Governor Gipps as Lieutenant Governor in New Zealand stating:

[W]e acknowledge New Zealand as a Sovereign and independent State, so far at least as it is possible to make that acknowledgement in favour of a people composed of numerous, dispersed, and petty Tribes, who possess few political relations to each other, and are incompetent to act, or even to deliberate, in concert. But the admission of their rights, though inevitably qualified by this consideration, is binding on the faith of the British Crown. The Queen, in common with Her Majesty's immediate predecessor, disclaims, for herself and for her subjects, every pretension to seize on the islands of New Zealand, or to govern them as a part of the Dominion of Great Britain, unless the free and intelligent consent of the Natives, expressed according to their established usages, shall be first obtained.[24]

Hobson immediately sought further directions, claiming, in his letter to the Colonial Office 'that the development of the inhabitants of the North and South

---

[20] As explained in Orange, note 17.

[21] David V Williams, 'The Annexation of New Zealand to New South Wales in 1840: What of the Treaty of Waitangi' (1985) 2 Australian J of L and Society 41, 41–2 (citing A H McLintock, *Crown Colony Government in New Zealand* (Wellington: R E Owen, Govt. Print, 1958)).

[22] Williams, note 21 (citing 3 British Parliamentary Papers, *Colonies, New Zealand* Sessions 1835–42 (1970)).   [23] These events are set forth and explored in Williams, note 18.

[24] Waitangi Tribunal, *Ngai Tahu Report* vol 2 (Wai 27) (Wellington: GP Publications, 1997) 219.

Islands was essentially different and that with the wild savages in the Southern Islands, it appears scarcely possible to observe even the form of a Treaty'.[25] He suggested that he might be permitted to claim the south by right of Discovery.[26] The rationale for such a stance probably lay in the fact that the French had a foothold in parts of the South Island, notably at Akaroa on the Banks Peninsula. Lord Normanby, the Secretary of State for the Colonies, made his stance known in his reply of 15 August 1839. Normanby said 'that if, as Hobson supposed, South Island Māori were incapable from their ignorance of entering intelligently into the Treaty with the Crown then he might assert sovereignty on the grounds of discovery'.[27]

The British Crown presented the 'treaty of cession' in English and Māori for signing at Waitangi, a small settlement in the north of the North Island, in early February 1840.[28] Forty-three Māori chiefs, mostly from the northern tribe Nga Puhi, assented to the Māori version of the Treaty on 6 February 1840. Next, Hobson and his party travelled through the North Island seeking more signatures.[29] Hobson was spurred on to issue two proclamations of sovereignty when he became aware that the New Zealand Company settlement at the now named city of Wellington sought to establish its own form of government. The first was issued 'over the North Island "by right of cession" and the other over the South Island "by right of discovery" '.[30] The proclamations were made on 21 May 1840.[31] Meanwhile, Hobson had ordered Major Thomas Bunbury to proceed to the South Island to seek signatures to the Treaty of Waitangi.[32] On 30 May 1840, two Māori chiefs of the Ngai Tahu tribe signed the Treaty at Akaroa in the South Island.[33] Thereafter, Bunbury travelled down to the smaller southern Stewart Island, and landed at a part that was uninhabited. He duly proclaimed British sovereignty over Stewart Island based on Cook's Discovery.[34] Bunbury began his return journey, stopping at a very small offshore island, Ruapuku Island. There he successfully attained the signature of three Māori chiefs on 10 June 1840.[35] Two chiefs at the Māori village at Tairaroa, at the head of the Otago harbour, marked the third and final signature point in the South Island. Stopping at Cloudy Bay, on 17 June 1840, Bunbury formally proclaimed the British Queen's sovereignty over the South Island based on cession.[36]

---

[25] Ibid 215.   [26] Ibid.   [27] Ibid 215–16.

[28] For a good introduction to the signing of the Treaty of Waitangi see Orange, *An Illustrated History*, note 17; Orange, *The Treaty of Waitangi*, note 16.

[29] Orange, *The Treaty of Waitangi*, note 16, 60–91.

[30] Tipene O'Regan, 'The Ngai Tahu Claim' in I H Kawharu (ed), *Waitangi: Maori and Pakeha Perspectives of the Treaty of Waitangi* (Auckland: Oxford University Press, 1989) 234, 240. See also Walker, note 5, 97 (noting that Hobson 'proclaimed South Island on the basis that it was *terra nullius*, thereby ignoring the existence of the Ngai Tahu. Only the arrogance born of metropolitan society and the colonizing ethos of the British Empire was capable of such self-deception, which was hardly excused by the desire to beat the imminent arrival of the French at Akaroa').

[31] See Orange, *The Treaty of Waitangi*, note 16, 81.   [32] Ibid 73.   [33] Ibid 78.

[34] Ibid.   [35] Ibid 79.

[36] Ibid 80. For a more detailed account of these South Island signings see eg O'Regan, note 29; Waitangi Tribunal, note 23.

The Treaty of Waitangi is a short document, consisting of three articles expressed in an English version and a Māori version. The controversy today lies in the translation of the first two articles.[37] According to the English version, Māori ceded to the Crown absolutely and without reservation all the rights and powers of sovereignty (article 1), but retained full exclusive and undisturbed possession of their lands and estates, forests, fisheries, and other properties (article 2).[38] In contrast, in the Māori version, Māori ceded to the Crown governance only (article 1), and retained *tino rangatiratanga* (sovereignty) over their *taonga* (treasures).[39] Article 2 granted the Crown a preemptive right to purchase property from Māori, and article 3 granted Māori the same rights and privileges as British citizens living in Aotearoa New Zealand. Whereas the English version of the Treaty encapsulates the principles of the Doctrine of Discovery, the Māori version purports to be a blueprint for a different type of future bound more in respectful separation.

The bilingual treaty of cession was certainly a unique contractual agreement not replicated elsewhere.[40] Humanitarian interests, along with the need to control the unruly behaviour of some of the new settlers, and to keep at bay the interests of France and to a lesser extent the United States, contributed to the British desire for a signed treaty.[41] Māori chiefs signed for similarly numerous reasons. On its face, the Treaty looked as if it was asking little of Māori and offering them much in return. Māori expected to increase trade, to receive assistance in handling the new changes occurring in society, and 'not least, the possibility of manipulating British authority in inter-tribal rivalries'.[42]

---

[37] For an analysis of the textual problems with the Treaty see Bruce Biggs, 'Humpty-Dumpty and the Treaty of Waitangi' in I H Kawharu (ed) note 29, 300–12; R M Ross, 'Te Tiriti o Waitangi: Texts and Translations' (1972) 6 New Zealand J of History 129 (reprinted in Judith Binney (ed), *The Shaping of History: Essays from the New Zealand Journal of History* (Wellington: Bridget Williams Books, 2001)).

[38] Articles 1 and 2 of the English version of the Treaty of Waitangi. To view a copy of the Treaty, see Treaty of Waitangi Act 1975 sch 1.

[39] Articles 1 and 2 of the Māori version of the Treaty of Waitangi.

[40] See William Renwick, 'A Variation of a Theme' in William Renwick (ed), *Sovereignty and Indigenous Rights: The Treaty of Waitangi in International Contexts* (Wellington: Victoria University Press, 1991) 199, 207 (explaining that by the time the Treaties were signed on Vancouver Island, BC, Canada—a mere decade later—'British imperial policy was determined by strategic considerations not humanitarian intentions'). See also Caren Wickliffe, 'Te Timatanga: Maori Women's Access to Justice' (2005) 8(2) YB of NZ Jurisprudence Special Issue—Te Purenga 217, 229 (asserting that 'The Treaty of Waitangi is fundamentally different to treaties in the Americas ... [and] did not deal with the sovereign status of indigenous polities').

[41] In particular, see the instructions issued by the Permanent Under-Secretary of the Colonial Office responsible for British policy in New Zealand: Peter Adams, *The Fatal Necessity: British Intervention in New Zealand 1830–1847* (Auckland: Auckland University Press, 1977); Williams, 'Annexation' note 20.

[42] Orange, *The Treaty of Waitangi,* note 16, 58. Note that a colonial government was established in 1852. For more discussion see Peter Spiller, Jeremy Finn, and Richard Boast (eds), *A New Zealand Legal History* (Wellington: Brookers, 2nd edn, 2001).

However, it is argued here that while the English version of the Treaty may have provided a harmonious gloss of overt cession, the Treaty in fact simply encapsulated the Doctrine of Discovery mindset. These inconsistencies lead to the conclusion that the reality lies deeper in the covert Doctrine of Discovery-type actions pursued by the British colonials. For instance, there are the proclamations made before the drafting and initial signing of the Treaty. In addition, there is Hobson's instruction to seek signatures from South Island Māori followed by his proclamation of discovery over the South Island because those Māori are uncivilized. Moreover, not all Māori chiefs signed the Treaty therefore leaving large tracts of land outside the province of cession despite proclamations asserting cession over the whole country.[43] Even taking a liberal view of the English version of the Treaty, it is questionable whether it does more than implement the common law principle of Discovery.[44]

A year after it was signed, the Land Claims Ordinance 1841 was enacted. Section 2 of the Ordinance was to become the subject of several subsequent cases and is thus worthwhile repeating here:

Declared, enacted, and ordained that all unappropriated lands within the Colony of New Zealand, subject however to the rightful and necessary occupation and use thereof by the aboriginal inhabitants of the said Colony, are and remain Crown or domain lands of Her Majesty, Her heirs and successors, and that the sole and absolute right of pre-emption from the said aboriginal inhabitants vests in and can only be exercised by Her said Majesty, Her heirs and successors.

C. *Symonds* 1847

Following the signing of the Treaty of Waitangi, a colonial government was established.[45] The British began to make serious inroads into acquiring large

---

[43] See eg Ngaroma Tahana, 'Tikanga Maori Concepts and Arawa Rangatiratanga and Kaitiakitanga of Arawa Lakes' (2006) 2 Te Tai Haruru J of Maori Legal Writing 39; R P Boast, 'Recognising Multi-Textualsim: Rethinking New Zealand's Legal History' (2006) 37 Victoria Univ of Wellington L Rev 547.

[44] Thus I would dispute P G McHugh's claims that 'the Crown's acquisition of the sovereignty of New Zealand was premised at all times on the original sovereignty of the Maori chiefs' and '[t]he Crown thus recognized the original sovereignty of Maori over New Zealand. In moving towards the acquisition of sovereignty the Colonial office considered and rejected the possibility of an approach resembling Marshall's "doctrine of discovery" which would have allowed the Crown to issue constituent instruments without reference to Maori consent.' P G McHugh, *Aboriginal Societies and the Common Law: A History of Sovereignty, Status and Self-Determination* (Oxford: Oxford University Press, 2004) 166–7.

[45] For an excellent account that argues that this constituted the original breach of the Treaty see Hanna Wilberg, 'Facing up to the Original Breach of the Treaty' (2007) New Zealand L Rev 527. See also F M Brookfield, *Waitangi & Indigenous Rights: Revolution, Law & Legitimation* (Auckland: Auckland University Press, 2nd edn, 2006); Hanna Wilberg, 'Judicial Remedies for the Original Breach?' (2007) New Zealand L Rev 713.

tracts of land for British settlement.[46] At issue were those Europeans who had purchased land directly from Māori prior to 1840. Many individuals questioned whether the Māori held valid title to the land. The purchasers argued that the Māori did hold valid title because the British Crown had recognized the sovereignty of Māori in the Declaration of Independence and the Treaty of Waitangi. The purchasers said therefore Māori must be deemed to have had 'the power to alienate land like any other sovereign'.[47] The courts settled the issue in 1847 in the *R v Symonds*[48] case.

R v Symonds served to reinforce the sovereign rights of Britain in New Zealand. The facts of the case are similar to *Johnson v M'Intosh*, in which the US Supreme Court refused to recognize the validity in law of title to land purchased by individuals directly from the Indian owners.[49] The *Symonds* case involved a British individual who purchased land directly from Māori in accordance with a certificate issued by Governor Fitz Roy allowing him to do so.[50] The question that occupied the courts was whether the individual, Mr C Hunter McIntosh, had acquired legal title to the property. Both judges sitting on the case said no, and both did so by drawing on US jurisprudence.[51] This case is said to represent the foundational principles of the common law relating to Māori.[52] Additionally, it was the first case to explicitly rely on the Doctrine of Discovery ideology in New Zealand law. The most famous quote in the case is that stated by Justice Chapman:

Whatever may be the opinion of jurists as to the strength or weakness of the Native title, whatsoever may have been the past vague notions of the Natives of this country; whatever may be their present clearer and still growing conception of their own dominion over land, *it cannot be too solemnly asserted that it is entitled to be respected, and it cannot be extinguished (at least in times of peace) otherwise than by the free consent of the Native occupiers.* But for their protection, and for the sake of humanity, the Government is bound to maintain, and the Courts to assert, the *Queen's exclusive right to extinguish it.* It follows from what has been said, that in solemnly guaranteeing the Native title, and in securing what is called the Queen's pre-emptive right, *the Treaty of Waitangi,* confirmed by the Charter of the Colony, *does not assert either in doctrine or in practice any thing new and unsettled.*[53]

[46] See eg Richard Boast, *Buying the Land, Selling the Land: Governments and Maori Land in the North Island 1865–1921* (Wellington: Victoria University Press, 2008).

[47] McHugh, note 44, 168.   [48] [1847] NZPCC 387.

[49] *Johnson v M'Intosh* 21 US (8 Wheat) 543 (1823). For an outstanding discussion of the influence of US jurisprudence, including *Johnson v M'Intosh*, on Justice Chapman see Mark Hickford, '"Decidedly the Most Interesting Savages on the Globe": An Approach to the Intellectual History of Maori Property Rights, 1837–53' (Spring 2006) 27 History of Political Thought 122–67.   [50] *R v Symonds* [1847] NZPCC 387.

[51] Ibid.

[52] See eg Mark Hickford, 'Settling Some Very Important Principles of Colonial Law: Three "Forgotten" Cases of the 1840s' (2004) 35 Victoria Univ of Wellington L Rev 1.

[53] [1847] NZPCC 387, 390 (emphasis added). For a wider discussion of the early judgments by Justice Chapman see Shaunnagh Dorsett, 'Sworn on the Dirt of Graves: Sovereignty, Jurisdiction

The case held that the Queen had the *exclusive* right of preemption to purchase land from Māori as articulated in the Treaty of Waitangi. Justice Chapman observed that the 'intercourse of civilised nations'[54] (namely, Great Britain) with Indigenous communities (especially in North America) had led to established principles of law. This law, founded in the Doctrine of Discovery and encapsulated in the common law doctrine of Native title, stipulated that the Queen's preemptive right was exclusive. Thus, the doctrine stated that the Crown is the sole source of title for settlers. This was the exact same outcome as in *Johnson* which both judges in *Symonds* recognized. In fact, both judges in *Symonds* explicitly relied on several of the US Supreme Court Chief Justice John Marshall's judgments.[55]

Justice Chapman, in particular, had been following the US Supreme Court decisions. Chapman stated in an 1840 article, in reference to *Johnson* and *Worcester v Georgia*,[56] that:

discovery gave the Government by whose subjects or authority it was made, a title to the country and a sole right of acquiring land from the natives, *as against all European powers*....it must be clear, that the rights reserved to the native tribes could only be of modified character, but whether those rights were abridged or extensive—whether they were confined to a mere right of occupation, or amounted to something deserving the name of sovereignty, was a question which did not affect the relation between the discovering nation and civilised powers.[57]

In *Symonds*, Justice Chapman observed that in guaranteeing Native title and the Queen's preemptive right, 'the Treaty of Waitangi...does not assert either in doctrine or in practice any thing new and unsettled'.[58] While this observation could be disputed, especially on reading the Māori version,[59] the decision marked a covert application of the Doctrine of Discovery. Nonetheless the strength of this decision was not to be repeated in the courts for a long time. In fact, it was to take another 150 years before a court was to hold that Māori have proprietary interests in land despite a change in sovereignty.[60]

---

and the Judicial Abrogation of "Barbarous" Customs in New Zealand in the 1840s' (2009) 30 J of Legal History 175–97.

[54] Ibid 388.
[55] McHugh, note 44, 42 ('There is a strong congruence between the styles of reasoning in R v. Symonds and the Marshall cases').   [56] 31 US (6 Pet) 515 (1832).
[57] Hickford, note 52, 15 (citing Henry Chapman, 'The English, the French, and the New Zealanders' (4 April 1840) The New Zealand J 49). See also Mark Hickford, 'Making Territorial Rights of the Natives: Britain and New Zealand, 1830–1847' (DPhil Thesis, University of Oxford, 1999).
[58] *R v Symonds* [1847] NZPCC 387, 390 (per Chapman J); see also per Martin CJ at 395.
[59] See eg Eddie Durie, 'The Treaty in Maori History' in Renwick, note 40.
[60] *Attorney-General v Ngati Apa* [2003] 2 NZLR 643. But see *In re 'The Lundon and Whitaker Claims Act 1871'*, 2 NZ CA (1872). For commentary on the significance of *Symonds* and *In re Lundon* see John William Tate, 'Pre-*Wi Parata*: Early Native Title Cases in New Zealand' (2003) 12 Waikato L Rev 112.

D. Native Acts 1860s

The initial British Governors in Aotearoa New Zealand exerted a distinct colonialist policy based on the assumption that 'Maori were unusually intelligent (for blacks) and that intelligence translated into the desire to become British'.[61] Between 1840 and 1860, the tools for this evangelism—God, money, law and land—sought to convert Māori from 'savages' to 'civilisation' via assimilation by the '[m]ixing of the two peoples geographically'.[62] But the early evangelism had few complete successes. While many Māori did embrace Christianity, it was not at the exclusion of their own religion. Rather, 'Maori religion had always been open, able to incorporate new gods'.[63] Similarly, while many Māori tribes became commercialized (they dominated the food supply market from growing crops, to transporting and selling to the Pakeha), individualism did not flourish.[64]

By the late 1850s, however, the life of some tribes had been radically changed. Of significance, the British Crown had acquired most of the land in the South Island and the lower part of the North Island (constituting approximately 60 per cent of New Zealand's land mass and where approximately 10 per cent of Māori lived).[65] In most instances the tribes had been duped. First, there was controversy about the actual land included in the purchase agreements. Second, there was unrest in that the Crown had not set aside land for reserves for them as per the agreements.[66] Deeply disturbed by the correlation between selling land and loss of independence, the North Island tribes, who still retained some land, began turning against land sales. Importantly, the pan-tribal sentiment saw the emergence of the Māori King Movement.[67] Perturbed that land selling would come to an end, and that as a consequence the amalgamation of Māori would come to a halt, the British concluded that the 'law of nature' required help. The British declared war against some Māori tribes, but underestimated tribal resistance.[68] The New Zealand wars, which began in March 1860, did not abate until a decade later.[69] A tougher new evangelism emerged during this time with law becoming the central tool in destroying the Māori way of life.[70]

---

[61] James Belich, 'The Governors and the Maori (1840–72)' in Keith Sinclair (ed), *The Oxford Illustrated History of New Zealand* (Auckland: Oxford University Press, 2nd edn, 1996) 78.
[62] Ibid 80.   [63] Ibid 78.   [64] Ibid 80.   [65] Ibid 84.
[66] See eg Waitangi Tribunal, note 24, and O'Regan, note 30.
[67] For a discussion of Māori resistance movements, including the Māori King Movement see Lindsay Cox, *Kotahitangi: The Search for Maori Political* Unity (Auckland: Oxford University Press, 1993).
[68] See generally James Belich, *The New Zealand Wars and the Victorian Interpretation of Racial Conflict* (Auckland: Penguin, 1998).   [69] Ibid.
[70] See generally Richard Boast, 'The Law and the Maori' in Peter Spiller, Jeremy Finn, and Richard Boast (eds), *A New Zealand Legal History* (Wellington: Brookers, 2nd edn, 2001).

Large tracts of Māori land in the North Island were confiscated pursuant to legislation;[71] legislation stipulated that native schools could only receive funding if the curriculum was taught in the English language[72] (a policy which led to the near extinction of the Māori language and culture, and marginalized Māori 'by a deliberate policy of training for manual labour rather than the professions'[73]); and legislation ensured that any person practicing traditional Māori healing could became liable for conviction[74] (a policy which led to the loss of much traditional knowledge).[75]

At the heart of the new cultural genocide[76] crusade was the establishment of the Native Land Court. The Crown now waived its right of preemption (as endorsed in the Treaty of Waitangi and common law doctrine of Native title) in favour of permitting the Māori to freely alienate their land. However, Māori first had to obtain a certificate of title. The system sought to transform land communally held by *whanau* and *hapu* (Māori customary land) into individualized titles derived from the Crown (Māori freehold title).[77] The preamble to the Native Lands Act 1862 explained this system as follows:

whereas it would greatly promote the peaceful settlement of the Colony and the advancement and civilization of the Natives if their rights to land were ascertained defined and declared and if the ownership of such lands . . . were assimilated as nearly as possible to the ownership of land according to British law.[78]

A further significant statute was enacted in the 1860s: the Native Rights Act 1865. This Act made it clear that (1) Māori were deemed to be a natural-born subject of Her Majesty; (2) the courts had jurisdiction in all cases touching the persons and property (real or personal) of Māori; (3) Native title was to be determined according to the ancient custom or usage of Māori; and (4) any case concerning title to Native title was to be directed to the Native Land Court.[79]

The Doctrine of Discovery ideology was obviously permeating deeply into the colonial mindsets. This was not because the Crown sought to deny the existence

---

[71] See New Zealand Settlements Act 1863; Suppression of Rebellion Act 1863.

[72] See Native Schools Act 1858; Native Schools Act 1867; Native Schools Amendment Act 1871.

[73] Stephanie Milroy and Leah Whiu, 'Waikato Law School: An Experiment in Bicultural Legal Education' (2005) 8 YB of NZ Jurisprudence Special Issue—Te Purenga 173, 175.

[74] See Tohunga Suppression Act 1908.

[75] See Maui Solomon, 'The Wai 262 Claim: A Claim by Maori to Indigenous Flora and Fauna: Me o Ratou Taonga Katoa' in Michael Belgrave, Merata Kawharu, and David Williams (eds), *Waitangi Revisited: Perspectives on the Treaty of Waitangi* (Auckland: Oxford University Press, 2nd edn, 2005).

[76] For a discussion of this term see D Williams, 'Myths, National Origins, Common Law and the Waitangi Tribunal' (2004) 11 Murdoch U Electronic J <http://www.murdoch.edu.au/elaw/issues/v11n4/williams114_text.html>.

[77] See generally David Williams, *Te Kooti Tango Whenua: The Native Land Court 1864–1909* (Wellington: Huia Publishers, 1999).

[78] Native Lands Act 1862. See also Native Lands Act 1865.

[79] See Native Lands Act 1865 ss 2–5.

of Native title, but because it believed that it was civil to provide a route for it to become general land (land subject to individualized certificate of title). The legislation ensured 'Maori could participate in the new British prosperity only by selling or leasing their land'.[80] Or, as Hon Sewell, a Member of the House Representatives in 1870, reflected, the Act had two objectives. One objective was 'to bring the great bulk of the lands of the Northern Island which belonged to the Natives...within the reach of colonization'.[81] The other objective was:

the detribalisation of the Natives,—to destroy, if it were possible, the principles of communism which ran through the whole of their institutions, upon which their social system was based, and which stood as a barrier in the way of all attempts to amalgamate the Native race into our own social and political system.[82]

The Land Court was extraordinarily effective.[83] In the early years: a predatory horde of storekeepers, grog-sellers, surveyors, lawyers, land-agents, and money-lenders made advances to rival groups of Māori claimants and recouped the costs in land. Rightful Māori owners could not avoid litigation and expensive surveys if false claims were put forward, since Fenton (the Chief Judge), seeking to inflate the status of the Court, insisted that judgments be based only upon evidence presented before it.[84]

By the 1930s very little tribal land remained in Māori ownership (today it amounts to five per cent of Aotearoa New Zealand's total landmass). The Court's early work has been described as a 'veritable engine of destruction for any tribe's tenure of land',[85] and 'a scandal'.[86]

E. *Wi Parata* 1877

By the late 1870s, the now-named High Court, in line with the new evangelism, began to rewrite history. Of most significance, in 1877, the High Court, in *Wi Parata v. Bishop of Wellington*,[87] denied that Māori had sovereignty prior to 1840, and thus rejected the Treaty of Waitangi as a valid treaty.[88] In doing so, the Doctrine of Discovery came to the forefront of judicial reasoning.

The *Wi Parata* case concerned a chief seeking to gift land to the Crown so that the Crown would establish a native school on the land. In 1848, the chief of the

[80] Waitangi Tribunal, *Turanga Tangata, turanga Whenua: The Report on the Turanganui a Kiwa Claims* vol 2, Wai 814 (Wellington: Legislation Direct, 2004).
[81] Williams, note 76, 87–8 (quoting 29 August 1870, NZPD, vol 9, 361).   [82] Ibid.
[83] Ibid.   [84] Ward, note 12.
[85] I H Kawharu, *Maori Land Tenure: Studies of a Changing Institution* (Oxford: Clarendon Press, 1977) 15. See also B D Gilling, 'Engine of Destruction? An Introduction to the History of the Maori Land Court' (1994) 24 Victoria Univ of Wellington L Rev 115.
[86] M P K Sorrenson, 'The Purchase of Maori Lands, 1865–1892' (Masters thesis, The University of Auckland, 1955) 146 (citing *New Zealand Herald* (Auckland 2 March 1883) 4).
[87] [1877] 3 NZ Jur (NS) 72.   [88] Ibid.

Ngati Toa tribe sought to give tribal land at Witireia as an endowment for a school to be established there to educate the tribal children.[89] Accordingly, the chief entered into a verbal arrangement with the then Lord Bishop of New Zealand. In 1850, a Crown grant was made, without the knowledge or consent of the tribe, to the Lord Bishop. The grant stated that the land had been ceded from Ngati Toa for the school.[90] However, no school of any kind was ever established. The tribe sued seeking return of the land.[91] Chief Judge Prendergast relied on a new version of historical events and ruled in favour of the Crown grant by stating:

On the foundation of this colony, the aborigines were found without any kind of civil government, or any settled system of law. There is no doubt that during a series of years the British Government desired and endeavoured to recognize the independent nationality of New Zealand. But the thing neither existed nor at the time could be established. The Maori tribes were incapable of performing the duties, and therefore of assuming the rights, of a civilised community.[92]

Prendergast stressed that Britain had queried the capacity of Māori and pointed to the direction made by the British government to Captain Hobson, in stating that:

we acknowledge New Zealand as a sovereign and independent state, so far at least as it is possible to make that acknowledgement in favour of a people composed of numerous, dispersed, and petty tribes, who possess few political relations to each other, and are incompetent to act, or even to deliberate, in concert.[93]

Prendergast stated, in reference to this passage, that:

Such a qualification nullifies the proposition to which it is annexed. In fact, the Crown was compelled to assume in relation to the Maori tribes, and in relation to native land titles, these rights and duties which, jure gentium, vest in and devolve upon the first civilised occupier of a territory thinly peopled by barbarians without any form of law or civil government.[94]

Prendergast then reviewed the Land Claims Ordinance of 1841 and concluded that:

They express the well-known legal incidents of a settlement planted by a civilised Power in the midst of uncivilised tribes. It is enough to refer, once for all, to the American jurists, Kent and Story, who, together with Chief Justice Marshall, in the well-known case of *Johnson v. McIntosh*, have given the most complete exposition of this subject.[95]

He further stated at length that:

Had any body of law or custom, capable of being understood and administered by the Courts of a civilised country, been known to exist, the British Government would surely have provided for its recognition, since nothing could exceed the anxiety displayed to

---

[89] Ibid.   [90] Ibid.   [91] Ibid.   [92] Ibid 77.
[93] *Wi Parata v Bishop of Wellington* [1877] 3 NZ Jur (NS) 72.   [94] Ibid 77.
[95] Ibid.

infringe no just right of the aborigines. On the cession of territory by one civilised power to another, the rights of private property are invariably respected, and the old law of the country is administered, to such extent as may be necessary, by the Courts of the new sovereign. In this way British tribunals administer the old French law in Lower Canada, the Code Civil in the island of Mauritius, and Roman-Dutch law in Ceylon, in Guinea, and at the Cape. But in the case of primitive barbarians, the supreme executive Government must acquit itself, as best it may, of its obligation to respect native proprietary rights, and of necessity must be the sole arbiter of its own justice.[96]

These sentiments are a direct application of US case law. In particular, a very similar passage exists in *Cherokee Nation v Georgia*.[97] In reference to the Treaty of Waitangi, Prendergast stated that:

So far indeed as that instrument purported to cede the sovereignty—a matter with which we are not here directly concerned—it must be regarded as a simple nullity. No body politic existed capable of making cession of sovereignty, nor could the thing itself exist. So far as the proprietary rights of the natives are concerned, the so-called treaty merely affirms the rights and obligations which, jure gentium, vested in and devolved upon the Crown under the circumstances of the case.[98]

Prendergast was referring to American authorities and expressly likens 'the case of the Maoris' to 'that of the Indian tribes of North America'.[99] He concluded that 'the title of the Crown to the country was acquired, jure gentium, by discovery and priority of occupation, as a territory inhabited only by savages'.[100]

In reaching this conclusion, Prendergast was not hindered by any purported conflicting stance in a statute. In particular, he referenced section 3 of the Native Rights Act 1865 that read in part that the courts have the same jurisdiction 'in all cases touching the persons and property, whether real or personal, of the Maori people, and touching the title to land held under Maori custom and usage...' Prendergast reflected that the Act spoke 'as if some such body of customary law did in reality exist'.[101] He added: 'But a phrase in a statute cannot call what is non-existent into being.'[102] According to Prendergast, 'no such body of law existed'.[103]

This case is Aotearoa New Zealand's paramount Discovery case. It has played a significant role in New Zealand's legal history and was not conclusively overruled until 2003.

F. Privy Council Decisions Early 1900s

At the turn of the century the Privy Council had an opportunity to closely reflect on the *Wi Parata* decision and it did not like what it saw. In *Nireaha Tamaki v*

---

[96] Ibid 77–8.
[97] 30 US (5 Pet) 1 (1831). See McHugh, note 43, 172 (noting this similarity).
[98] *Wi Parata v Bishop of Wellington* 3 NZ Jur (NS) 72, 78.   [99] Ibid.   [100] Ibid.
[101] Ibid 79.   [102] Ibid.   [103] Ibid.

Baker,[104] decided in 1901, Lord Davey, in delivering the judgment for their Lordships, began: 'This is an appeal...in which questions of great moment affecting the status and civil rights of the aboriginal subjects of the Crown have been raised.'[105] The Crown argument, supported by the Court of Appeal, relied on the *Wi Parata* reasoning that there is no Māori customary law 'of which the Courts of law can take cognizance'. Lord Davey responded:

Their Lordships think that this argument goes too far, and that it is rather late in the day for such an argument to be addressed to a New Zealand Court. It does not seem possible to get rid of the express words of ss. 3 and 4 of the Native Rights Act, 1865, by saying (as the Chief Justice said in the case referred to) that 'a phrase in a statute "cannot call what is non-existent into being." It is the duty of the Courts to interpret the statute which plainly assumes the existence of a tenure of land under custom and usage which is either known to lawyers or discoverable by them by evidence'.[106]

Moreover, Lord Davey recognized that Chapman J, in deciding the *Symonds* case, had made some 'very pertinent' observations that Native title is entitled to be respected. But the final decision made by the Privy Council—in favour of the Māori applicant (and thus a reversal the Court of Appeal decision)—was dependent on statutory recognition of Native title and not the common law recognition of it.

However, astonishingly, Aotearoa New Zealand's domestic judiciary ignored the Privy Council's ruling that *Wi Parata* had gone too far.[107] As recognized by Robin Cooke, who became President of the Court of Appeal in 1986 and himself a Law Lord in 1996, this was 'the only recorded instance of a New Zealand Court's publicly avowing its disapproval of a superior tribunal'.[108]

In 1941, the Privy Council, in *Te Heuheu Tukino v Aotea District Maori Land Board*[109] heard a case concerning whether the Māori rights acquired in the Treaty of Waitangi were cognizable in the courts. The Privy Council answered no. It held: 'It is well settled that any rights purporting to be conferred by such a

---

[104] *Nireaha Tamaki v Baker* [1901] AC 561.   [105] Ibid 372.
[106] Ibid 382. For more discussion see Jim Evans, 'Reflections on *Nireaha Tamaki v Baker*' (2007) 2 Te Tai Haruru J of Maori Legal Writing 101.
[107] For example, see *Hohepa Wi Neera v Bishop of Wellington* [1902] 21 NZLR 655 (CA). For commentary see Mark Hickford, 'John Salmond and Native Title in New Zealand: Developing a Crown Theory on the Treaty of Waitangi, 1910–1920' (2007) 38 Victoria Univ of Wellington L Rev 853; John William Tate, 'Hohepa Wi Neera: Native Title and the Privy Council Challenge' (2004) 35(1) Victoria Univ of Wellington L Rev 73; David V Williams, '*Wi Parata* is Dead, Long Live *Wi Parata*' in Claire Charters and Andrew Erueti (eds), *Maori Property Rights and the Foreshore and Seabed: The Last Frontier* (Wellington: Victoria University Press, 2007) 31–58.
[108] Sir Robin Cooke, 'The Nineteenth Century Chief Justices' in Robin Cooke (ed), *Portrait of a Profession: The Centennial Book of the New Zealand Law Society* (Wellington: Reed, 1969) 36, 46. One of the more well-known cases to assert the *Wi Parata* precedent was *In Re Ninety Mile Beach* [1963] NZLR 461 (CA). See generally Richard Boast, 'In Re Ninety Mile Beach Revisited: The Native Land Court and the Foreshore in New Zealand Legal History' (1993) 23 Victoria Univ of Wellington L Rev 145.
[109] *Te Heuheu Tukino v Aotea District Maori Land Board* [1941] AC 308 (PC).

treaty of cession cannot be enforced in the Courts, except in so far as they have been incorporated in the municipal law.'[110] The Privy Council cited *Vajesingji Joravarsingji v Secretary of State for India*[111] as support for this finding. The Privy Council cited this decision at length and it is interesting to replicate here for its Discovery mindset:

When a territory is acquired by a sovereign state for the first time that is an act of state. It matters not how the acquisition has been brought about. It may be by conquest, it may be by cession following on treaty, it may be by occupation of territory hitherto unoccupied by a recognized ruler. In all cases the result is the same. Any inhabitant of the territory can make good in the municipal courts established by the new sovereign only such rights as that sovereign has, through his officers, recognized. Such rights as he had under the rule of predecessors avail him nothing. Nay more, even if in a treaty of cession it is stipulated that certain inhabitants should enjoy certain rights, that does not give a title to those inhabitants to enforce these stipulations in the municipal courts. The right to enforce remains only with the high contracting parties.[112]

Thus, according to the Privy Council, 'So far as the appellant invokes the assistance of the Court, it is clear that he cannot rest his claim on the Treaty of Watiangi…'.[113]

G. Cases and Policy in the 1960s

Commentators on New Zealand's Māori/Pakeha history often draw a distinction between pre and post-1970s and a similar approach is taken here. The next chapter considers the still permeating influence of the Doctrine of Discovery in New Zealand from the 1970s onwards. But it is pertinent to end this chapter with a brief discussion of some noteworthy court cases and policy documents that were released in the early 1960s. In 1962 and 1963, the Court of Appeal made two significant judgments which restricted Māori opportunities to pursue rights to riverbeds and the foreshore. Both decisions are laced with the Discovery ideology.

In the first case, *In Re Bed of Wanganui River*,[114] the Court of Appeal refused to accept a tribal interest in a riverbed, favouring instead a principle that endorsed individual ownership. The Court held that once a block of land fronting a non-tidal river has been investigated by the Māori Land Court and separate titles issued, the bed of the land adjoining the river becomes *ad medium filum* a part

---

[110] Ibid 596–7.   [111] [1924] LR, 51 Ind App 357.
[112] *Te Heuheu Tukino v Aotea District Maori Land Board* [1941] AC 308, 597—quoting from 360 of the *Vajesingji* case. For a critique of *Te Heuheu Tukino* see generally Alex Frame, 'Hoani Te Heuheu's Case in London 1940–1941: An Explosive Story' (2006) 22 New Zealand Univ L Rev 148.   [113] *Te Heuheu Tukino v Aotea District Maori Land Board* [1941] AC 308, 597.
[114] [1962] NZLR 600. For further discussion of this case see F M Jock Brookfield, 'The Waitangi Tribunal and the Whanganui river-bed' (2000) 1 New Zealand Univ L Rev 9.

of that block and the property of the respective owners of that block. In other words, the English common law principle of *ad medium filum* trumped Māori law. Gresson P read down the nature of Māori property law as not being capable of encapsulating individual or personal interests 'but was rather a right of occupancy and cultivation, somewhat analogous to a life interest as it is understood in English law'.[115] Gresson P espoused the superior nature of English law:[116]

in short, the Maoris (sic) held the land tribally and communally. For this somewhat *vague* tenure there was substituted a *defined* proprietary tenure of individuals or sets of individuals so that thereafter the land ceased to be held under a native title but became freehold land held under English tenure...

Turner J expressly denied the doctrine of Native title as is evident in this passage:[117]

Upon the signing of the Treaty of Waitangi, the title to all land in New Zealand passed by agreement of the Maoris (sic) to the Crown; but there remained an obligation upon the Crown to recognise and guarantee the full exclusive and undisturbed possession of all customary lands to those entitled by Maori custom. This obligation, however, was akin to a treaty obligation, and was not a right enforceable at the suit of any private persons as a matter of municipal law by virtue of the Treaty of Waitangi.

Turner J did not reference the *Wi Parata* decision to substantiate this point, but the reasoning is very similar to that earlier case. Likewise, Turner J did not reference the *Symonds* case which held a different view. The Doctrine of Discovery underlies the rationale in the passage quoted above.

In the second case, *In Re Ninety-Mile Beach*,[118] decided a year later, in 1963, the Court of Appeal held that 'once an application for the investigation of title to land having the sea as its boundary was determined, the Maori customary communal rights were then wholly extinguished'.[119] While the Court did not agree with the Crown's blunt argument that 'on the assumption of sovereignty the Crown by prerogative right became the owner of the foreshores of New Zealand', the Court did hold that:[120]

[j]ust as in the *Wanganui River* case this Court reached the conclusion that the transformation of the communal rights of the Maori people into individual ownership carried the title of the owner *ad medium filum* so I think in the present case we should hold that an investigation of a block of land abutting the sea was complete for all purposes.

North J said this about the Treaty of Waitangi:[121]

in my opinion it necessarily follows that on the assumption of British sovereignty—apart from the Treaty of Waitangi—the rights of the Maoris to their tribal lands depended wholly on the grace and favour of Her Majesty Queen Victoria, who had an absolute right

---

[115] Ibid 608.
[116] Ibid 609 (emphasis added). This type of language is repeated in the judgment, including for example the use of 'primitive peoples' in reference to Māori. Ibid 618 (per Cleary J).
[117] Ibid 623.   [118] [1963] NZLR 461. For further discussion see Boast note 107.
[119] Ibid 473 (per North J).   [120] Ibid.   [121] Ibid 468.

to disregard the Native title to any lands in New Zealand, whether above high-water mark or below high-water mark. But as we all know, the Crown did not act in a harsh way and from earliest times was careful to ensure the protection of Native interests and to fulfil the promises contained in the Treaty of Waitangi.

This passage reiterates *Wi Parata* type sentiments that the fate of Māori legal rights are at the whim of the government with no recognition of the doctrine of Native title guarantees. Gresson J, also part of this bench, reflected similarly on the Treaty:[122]

For the purposes of this case it is, I think, immaterial whether sovereignty was assumed by virtue of the Treaty of Waitangi in 1840, or by settlement or annexation before this date. In either event, after 1840, all titles had to be derived from the Crown, and it was for the Crown to determine the nature and incidents of the title which it would confer.

Gresson J went on to state:[123]

In the event, instead of exercising its prerogative right to extinguish Native title in any arbitrary fashion or contending that the Maoris' customary rights had been indirectly displaced by operation of the law, the Crown conscientiously set about transforming the communal rights of the Maoris into individual ownership through the machinery provided in the Native Lands Act of 1862, and the later Act of 1865.

Here, Gresson is assuming that the Crown has the right to extinguish Native title, which, it is true, the doctrine of Native title permits but only in certain circumstances such as via clear and plain legislation with compensation attached. The passage is indicative of the Doctrine of Discovery mindset.

These two Court of Appeal decisions closely followed the government's publication of its 1961 published *Report on Department of Maori Affairs* by J K Hunn (commonly referred to as the Hunn Report).[124] The main thrust of this report can be viewed in this reproduced paragraph:[125]

When the first Europeans arrived in New Zealand about A.D. 1800, the Maoris (sic) were in much the same condition as the Ancient Britons at the time of the Roman invasion in 55 B.C. In the short century and a half since then, many Maoris (sic) have overtaken the pakeha lead and adopted the 1960 pattern of living in every way. A few others, the slowest moving members of the race, have probably not yet passed the 1860 mark. There is at least a century of difference between the most advanced and the most retarded Maoris (sic) in their adjustment to modern life. The Maoris (sic) today could be broadly classified in three groups:

(a) A completely detribalized minority whose Maoritanga is only vestigial.

(b) The main body of Maoris (sic), pretty much at home in either society, who like to partake of both (an ambivalence, however, that causes psychological stress to some of them).

(c) Another minority complacently living a backward life in primitive conditions.

---

[122] Ibid 475.   [123] Ibid 478.
[124] J Hunn, *Report on Department of Maori Affairs, with Statistical Supplement* (Wellington: Government Printer, 1961).   [125] Ibid 15–16.

The object of policy should presumably be to eliminate Group C by raising it to Group B, and to leave it to the personal choice of Groups B members whether they stay there or join Group A—in other words, whether they remain 'integrated' or become 'assimilated'.

The Hunn Report had huge implications for law and policy relating to Māori.[126] Essentially, the vogue became to make no special rules for Māori; Māori were to be treated like Europeans living in New Zealand. For example, the Matrimonial Property Act 1963 made no distinction between general and Māori land thus enabling Māori land to become subject to *inter vivos* matrimonial property disputes. A poignant example was the Maori Affairs Amendment Act 1967. It amended the Maori Affairs Act 1953 by introducing new rules for wills and intestate succession to estates containing Māori freehold land. In regard to wills, it stated that Māori were no longer restricted in devising their interests in Māori freehold land to essentially blood relatives. Māori were to have the same testamentary freedom rights as Europeans.[127] In regard to intestate succession, it stated that persons entitled to succeed to a Māori person's estate shall be determined 'in the same manner as if the deceased person were a European'.[128] This marked a distinct change where for 100 years children had succeeded equally. The new law meant that the spouse would now succeed. This policy came under attack in the 1970s, and the *In Re Ninety Mile Beach* case was overruled in 2003. The *In Re Bed of the Wanganui River* case remains law although it has potential to be repealed in the future. These points are discussed in the next chapter.

H. Conclusion

While Aotearoa New Zealand may lay claim to good race relations, a close analysis of the events surrounding British assertion of sovereignty in this country indicate, as stated in the introduction to this chapter, a less than idyllic picture. The elements of the Doctrine of Discovery were alive and well in Aotearoa New Zealand in the colonial period of 1840–1960s. The next chapter brings this analysis into the contemporary era.

---

[126] See also I Prichard and H Waetford, *Report of Committee of Inquiry into the Laws Affecting Maori Land the Jurisdiction and Powers of the Maori Land Court* (Wellington: Department of Maori Affairs, 1965).

[127] Maori Affairs Act 1953 s 114 was repealed by Maori Affairs Amendment Act 1967 s 88(1).

[128] Maori Affairs Amendment Act 1967 s 76. For more information on this law see Jacinta Ruru, 'Implications for Maori: Historical Overview', in Nicola Peart, Margaret Briggs, and Mark Henaghan (eds), *Relationship Property on Death* (Wellington: Brookers, 2004) 445–65.

9

The Still Permeating Influence of the Doctrine of Discovery in Aotearoa/New Zealand: 1970s–2000s

This chapter shows how the legal principle of Discovery and its elements have continued to be used in Aotearoa New Zealand in contemporary times. The discussion is divided into three parts: case law, settlement, and constitution. The first part focuses on discussing the principal cases decided since the 1970s concerning Native title and Discovery. The second part case studies a series of natural resources—primarily national parks and the foreshore and seabed—to illustrate how the government's response to Māori claims in the new Treaty of Waitangi settlement era remains influenced by the Discovery doctrine. The third part centres on a continuing pressing live issue: the constitutional place of the Treaty of Waitangi. This part considers the judicial and government responses to the Treaty and in doing so portrays the persisting existence of Discovery elements despite a comparatively more reconciled existence.

This chapter focuses on contemporary post-1970s occurrences because a noticeable political and legal shift began to emerge at that time. For example, in 1975, the Labour government established the Waitangi Tribunal as a permanent commission of inquiry empowered to receive, report, and recommend on alleged Crown breaches of the principles of the Treaty of Waitangi post-1975.[1] Since 1985, it has had the specific jurisdiction to consider claims by Māori that they have been prejudicially affected by legislation, Crown policy or practice, or Crown action or omission on or after 6 February 1840.[2] The Tribunal generally can only make non-binding rather than binding recommendations to the Crown on redress for what it considers to be valid claims. These recommendations are made to assist the Crown in reaching a political settlement with Māori tribes. The Tribunal consists of up to 20 members, approximately half Māori, all with specialist knowledge and experience (often renowned historians). Moreover, in the

---

[1] Treaty of Waitangi Act 1975 s 6.
[2] Ibid, as amended by the Treaty of Waitangi Amendment Act 1985. For commentary see J Hayward and N R Wheen (eds), *The Waitangi Tribunal: Te Roopu Whakamana I te Tiriti o Waitangi* (Wellington: Bridget Williams Books, 2004); Alan Ward, *An Unsettled History: Treaty Claims in New Zealand Today* (Wellington: Bridget Williams Books, 1999).

mid-1980s, the Crown became committed to engaging with Māori in a 'fair and final' Treaty of Waitangi settlement process. The Office of Treaty Settlements is a separate unit within the Ministry of Justice and has the mandate to resolve historical Treaty claims (defined as claims arising from actions or omissions by or on behalf of the Crown or by or under legislation on or before 21 September 1992).[3] The settlements aim to provide the foundation for a new and continuing relationship between the Crown and the claimant group based on the Treaty of Waitangi principles. Settlements thus contain Crown apologies of wrongs done, financial and commercial redress, and redress recognizing the claimant group's spiritual, cultural, historical, or traditional associations with the natural environment.[4] This chapter draws on the work from the Waitangi Tribunal, the courts, and the settlement process to assess the continuing influence of the Discovery principles. While significant advancement has occurred in reconciliation between the Crown and Māori, the underlying tenet of Discovery remains evident. This chapter does not wish to undermine these reconciliation initiatives per se. Rather the purpose is to illustrate that, like it or not, components of Discovery continue to haunt legal and political reasoning.

A. Case Law Era

Since the 1970s, in several instances the courts began to curtail the Discovery elements evident in the legal system. As discussed in the previous chapter, Aotearoa New Zealand's now-named High Court, held in 1877, in the case of *Wi Parata v Bishop of Wellington,*[5] that the Treaty of Waitangi was a 'simple nullity' and that the common law doctrine of Native title was not applicable because Aotearoa New Zealand had been inhabited by 'barbarians' prior to the British Crown acquiring sovereignty of the country. The Privy Council, in 1941, in *Te Heuheu Tukino v Aotea District Maori Land Board,*[6] held that Māori could only refer to the Treaty of Waitangi in legal action in the courts where Parliament had incorporated the Treaty into statute. Moreover, in 1963, the Court of Appeal, in *In Re Ninety-Mile*

---

[3] See Office of Treaty Settlements, *Ka tika ā muri, ka tika ā mua: Healing the past, building a future: A Guide to Treaty of Waitangi Claims and Negotiations with the Crown* (Wellington: Office of Treaty Settlements, 1999). For an excellent overview see Catherine J I Magallanes, 'Reparations for Maori Grievances in Aotearoa New Zealand' in Federico Lenzerini (ed), *Reparations for Indigenous Peoples: International and Comparative Perspectives* (Oxford: Oxford University Press, 2008). See also Jessica Andrew, 'Adminstrative Review of the Treaty of Waitangi Settlement Process' (2008) 39 Victoria Univ of Wellington L Rev 225.

[4] For an insight into tribal governance entities see New Zealand Law Commission, *Waka Umanga: A Proposed Law for Maori Governance Entities*, Report 92 (NZLC, 2006) available online: <http://www.lawcom.govt.nz/>; the Waka Umanga (Maori Corporations) Bill 2007; M Gibbs, 'What Structures are Appropriate to Receive Treaty of Waitangi Settlement Assets?' (2004) 21 New Zealand Univ L Rev 197; R Joseph, 'Contemporary Maori Governance: New Era or New Error?' (2007) 22 New Zealand Univ L Rev 628.   [5] [1877] 3 NZ Jur (NS) 72.

[6] *Te Heuheu Tukino v Aotea District Maori Land Board* [1941] AC 308 (PC).

Beach,[7] held that 'once an application for the investigation of title to land having the sea as its boundary was determined, the Maori customary communal rights were then wholly extinguished'.[8] In contemporary times, the courts have begun to repeal these precedents as is discussed below.

1. *Te Weehi* 1986

In the 1980s, the High Court began to rectify the *Wi Parata* 1877 precedent and reintroduce a more apt application of the doctrine of Native title into Aotearoa New Zealand's common law. This commenced in the 1986 *Te Weehi*[9] case. Here the New Zealand High Court held that a Māori person had a right to take undersized shellfish, *paua* (abalone), even though it was in contravention of legislation, because no statute had plainly and clearly extinguished the customary right. Judge Williamson distinguished the earlier case law, which purported a *Wi Parata* type reasoning (namely the Court of Appeal's *In Re Ninety-Mile Beach*[10] decision), by holding that this case was 'not based upon ownership of land or upon an exclusive right to a foreshore or bank of a river'.[11]

Justice Williamson found in favour of Te Weehi, recognizing that the establishment of British sovereignty had not set aside the local laws and property rights of Māori, thus concluding that because there had been no plain and clear legislative extinguishment of the fishing right the right continues to exist: '[i]t is a right limited to the Ngai Tahu tribe and its authorised relatives for the personal food supply'.[12] In reaching this decision, Williamson J recognized the significance of the Treaty of Waitangi for New Zealand: 'obviously the rights which were to be protected by it arose by the traditional possession and use enjoyed by Maori tribes prior to 1840'.[13]

While *Te Weehi*, in 1986, reintroduced the doctrine, it did so in regard to native fishing rights, not title. Williamson J did not feel bound by the earlier *Wi Parata* type case law, distinguishing those cases from the one he was hearing on the right to take undersized paua because it was a 'non-territorial' claim; this case was 'not based upon ownership of land or upon an exclusive right to a foreshore or bank of a river'.[14] It was important for Williamson J to emphasize this aspect otherwise he would have been bound by higher court precedent. This case represents a significant attempt by the courts to curtail the Discovery ideology.

2. *Lands* case 1987

In 1987, the Court of Appeal handed down a landmark decision interpreting the principles of the Treaty of Waitangi: *New Zealand Maori Council v*

---

[7] [1963] NZLR 461. For further discussion see Richard Boast, 'In Re Ninety Mile Beach Revisited: The Native Land Court and the Foreshore in New Zealand Legal History' (1993) 23 Victoria Univ of Wellington L Rev 145–70.   [8] NZLR 473 (per North J).
[9] *Te Weehi v Regional Fisheries Officer* [1986] 1 NZLR 680 (HC).   [10] Note 7.
[11] *Te Weehi*, note 9, 692.   [12] Ibid 692.   [13] Ibid 686.   [14] Ibid 692.

Attorney-General.[15] Commonly referred to as the *Lands* case, the Court was asked to determine the significance of section 9 of the State-Owned Enterprises Act 1986: 'Nothing in this Act shall permit the Crown to act in a manner that is inconsistent with the principles of the Treaty of Waitangi.' This wording was unique—no other statute had ever confined those with statutory power to have some level of regard to the Treaty of Waitangi. At that time, the judicial mindset was still mostly steeped in the *Wi Parata* idea that the Treaty was 'a simple nullity'.[16] Māori took the opportunity afforded by the section to argue in the courts that the Crown had to act consistently with the Treaty in transferring its assets to state-owned business focused enterprises. They were successful.

All five justices (Cooke P, Richardson, Somers, Casey, and Bisson JJ) concurred to state that partnership, reasonableness, and good faith are the hallmarks of the expression 'the principles of the Treaty of Waitangi'. Cooke P specifically stated that the Treaty can no longer be treated as a 'dead letter'[17] and to do so 'would be unhappily and unacceptably reminiscent of an attitude, now past'.[18] Cooke P concluded: '[Treaty] principles require the Pakeha and Māori Treaty partners to act towards each other reasonably and with the utmost good faith. That duty is no light one. It is infinitely more than a formality.'[19] He stressed the importance of not freezing Treaty principles in time: 'What matters is the spirit.... The Treaty has to be seen as an embryo rather than a fully developed and integrated set of ideas.'[20] Richardson J observed that: 'the obligation of good faith is necessarily inherent in such a basic compact as the Treaty of Waitangi',[21] and Somers J likewise stated: 'Each party in my view owed to the other a duty of good faith.'[22] Casey J emphasized the importance of an 'on-going partnership',[23] and Bisson J described the Treaty principles as 'the foundation for the future relationship between the Crown and the Maori race'.[24] And, in a final paragraph inserted at the conclusion to the published unanimous judgment, Cooke P offered a reflection on how the Treaty partners were trying to work out the details of how Māori land claims could be safeguarded when land is transferred to a state enterprise. He stated, in what are the final lines to a 69-page Court of Appeal judgment, that '[t]he Court hopes that this momentous agreement will be a good augury for the future of the partnership. Ka pai.'[25]

The judgment thus marked a partial repeal of the *Wi Parata* precedent in regard to the 'simple nullity' status of the Treaty. However, it is important to recognize that the Court of Appeal assumed that the Crown had acquired legitimate sovereignty of the country, and so in part, continued to perpetuate a Discovery mindset.

---

15 [1987] 1 NZLR 641 (*Lands* case). To appreciate the importance of this case, see Jacinta Ruru (ed), *'In Good Faith' Symposium Proceedings marking the 20th anniversary of the* Lands *case* (Wellington: New Zealand Law Foundation, 2008).   16 Note 5, 78.
17 *Lands* case, note 15, 661.   18 Ibid 661.   19 Ibid 667.   20 Ibid 663.
21 Ibid 682.   22 Ibid 693.   23 Ibid 703.   24 Ibid 714.   25 Ibid 719.

3. *Muriwhenua Te Ika Whenua* and *McRitchie* 1990s

Subsequent case law in the 1990s reinforced the existence of the common law doctrine of Native title in Aotearoa New Zealand, but did not accept the arguments posed under it. The first of the three prominent cases is the 1990 Court of Appeal case *Te Runanga o Muriwhenua Inc v Attorney-General*.[26] This case concerned processes relating to a Crown proposed settlement of Māori commercial sea fishing rights. The Court made several observations in obiter dicta. For example, Cooke P made extensive reference to the Canadian case law, describing it as '[a]lthough more advanced than our own ... [which] is still evolving',[27] likely to provide 'major guidance'[28] for New Zealand. He added that New Zealand's courts should give just as much respect to the rights of New Zealand's Indigenous peoples as the Canadian Courts give to their Indigenous peoples.[29] President Cooke saw no reason to distinguish the Canadian jurisprudence on the basis of constitutional differences and emphasized the analogous approaches to the partnership and fiduciary obligations being developed in Canada under the doctrine of Native title and in New Zealand under the Treaty of Waitangi. This comparison enabled Cooke P to confidently conclude that '[i]n principle the extinction of customary title to land does not automatically mean the extinction of fishing rights'.[30]

Four years later, in 1994, the Court of Appeal concluded that neither under the doctrine of Native title nor under the Treaty of Waitangi do Māori have a right to generate electricity by the use of water power.[31] In this case, *Te Runanganui o Te Ika Whenua*, Cooke P referred to Canadian and Australian case law in devising the nature of Native title. He explained the doctrine:

On the acquisition of the territory, whether by settlement, cession or annexation, the colonising power acquires a radical or underlying title which goes with sovereignty. Where the colonising power has been the United Kingdom, that title vests in the Crown. But, at least in the absence of special circumstances displacing the principle, the radical title is subject to the existing native rights.[32]

Cooke P elaborated on the nature of Native title rights stating that first they are usually communal. Second, Native title rights cannot be extinguished (at least in times of peace) other than by the free consent of the native occupiers. Third, the rights can only be transferred to the Crown. Fourth, the transfer must be in strict compliance with the provisions of any relevant statutes. Fifth, it is likely to be in breach of fiduciary duty if an extinguishment occurs by less than fair conduct or on less than fair terms; and if extinguishment is deemed necessary then free consent may have to yield to compulsory acquisition for recognized specific public

---

[26] [1990] 2 NZLR 641.   [27] Ibid 645.   [28] Ibid 655.   [29] Ibid 655.
[30] Ibid 655.
[31] *Te Runanganui o Te Ika Whenua Inc Society v Attorney-General* [1994] 2 NZLR 20, 25.
[32] Ibid 23–4.

purposes but upon extinguishment proper compensation must be paid.[33] Cooke P then explained the scope of Native title in terms of a spectrum:

The nature and incidents of aboriginal title are matters of fact dependent on the evidence in any particular case.... At one extreme they may be treated as approaching the full rights of proprietorship of an estate in fee recognised at common law. At the other extreme they may be treated as at best a mere permissive and apparently arbitrarily revocable occupancy.[34]

The third of the three prominent cases was decided in 1990: *McRitchie v Taranaki Fish and Game Council*. Here, by majority, the Court of Appeal held that Māori cannot claim under the doctrine of Native title or under the Treaty a customary right to fish for introduced species.[35] Richardson P, for the majority, discussed the doctrine using the then leading Canadian and Australian cases—*R v Sparrow*[36] and *Mabo v Queensland (No 2)*[37]—for support that native rights 'are highly fact specific'. He explained the test as follows:

The existence of a right is determined by considering whether the particular tradition or custom claimed to be an aboriginal right was rooted in the aboriginal culture of the particular people in question and the nature and incidents of the right must be ascertained as a matter of fact.[38]

Despite these cases not accepting the arguments posed under the doctrine of Native title, they are historically significant simply because the courts accepted the *existence* of the Native title doctrine. This represented a marked change to the legal precedents evident in *Wi Parata* and the *In Re Ninety Mile Beach* cases.

4. *Ngati Apa* 2003

In 2003, the Court of Appeal, in *Attorney-General v Ngati Apa*,[39] finally reintroduced the full spectrum of the Native title doctrine and in doing so made significant strides towards displacing several Discovery elements. The factual situation of this case saw the Court accepting the possibility that Native title could encompass land that was either permanently or temporarily under saltwater. The unanimous decision contributed significantly to the removal of the full force of the Doctrine of Discovery.[40] All five judges overruled *Wi Parata*.

---

[33] Ibid 24.   [34] Ibid.

[35] *McRitchie v Taranaki Fish and Game Council* [1999] 2 NZLR 139. Note: Thomas J gave a strong dissent.   [36] [1990] 1 SCR 1075 (SCC).

[37] [1992] 175 CLR 1 (HCA).

[38] *McRitchie*, note 35, 147. Note: Thomas J, in dissent, interestingly found in favour of a Māori customary right to fish for introduced species by basing his decision entirely on New Zealand law—no reference was made to overseas decisions.   [39] [2003] 3 NZLR 643.

[40] See generally Jacinta Ruru, 'A Politically Fuelled Tsunami: The Foreshore/Seabed Controversy in Aotearoa/New Zealand' (2004) 113 J of Polynesian Society 57.

Significantly, the *Ngati Apa* decision explicitly foresaw the possibility of the doctrine of Native title by recognizing Indigenous peoples' exclusive ownership of the foreshore and seabed following a change in sovereignty. For example, Chief Justice Elias stated: 'Any property interest of the Crown in land over which it acquired sovereignty therefore depends on any pre-existing customary interest and its nature,'[41] and '[t]he content of such customary interest is a question of fact discoverable, if necessary, by evidence.'[42] Chief Justice Elias explained that '[a]s a matter of custom the burden on the Crown's radical title might be limited to use or occupation rights held as a matter of custom.'[43] The Chief Justice then quoted from a 1921 Privy Council decision, *Amodu Tijani v Secretary, Southern Nigeria*,[44] stating that Native title rights might 'be so complete as to reduce any radical right in the Sovereign to one which only extends to comparatively limited rights of administrative interference'.[45] Chief Justice Elias substantiated this possibility with reference to Canada by stating:

The Supreme Court of Canada has had occasion recently to consider the content of customary property interests in that country. It has recognised that, according to the custom on which such rights are based, they may extend from usufructory rights to *exclusive ownership* with incidents equivalent to those recognised by fee simple title.[46]

The other four justices discussed the common law doctrine of Native title in similar terms. For example, Justice Tipping began his judgment with the words 'When the common law of England came to New Zealand its arrival did not extinguish Maori customary title... title to it must be lawfully extinguished before it can be regarded as ceasing to exist.'[47] Justices Keith and Anderson, in a joint judgment, emphasized 'the onus of proving extinguishment lies on the Crown and the necessary purpose must be clear and plain'.[48] Finally, Gault P expressly recognized the uniqueness of New Zealand in the existence of the common law jurisdiction of Native title and the statutory jurisdiction of Māori customary land status, and stated that he prefers to 'reserve the question of whether it is a real distinction insofar as each is directed to interests of land in the nature of ownership'.[49]

Interestingly, the judges refer back to *Johnson*.[50] Chief Justice Elias quotes *Johnson*, recognizing that according to the Supreme Court of the United States, Native title rights 'were rights at common law, not simply moral claims against the Crown'.[51] Justices Keith and Anderson rely extensively on the early US jurisprudence, including citing at length from *Johnson*. For instance, in *Ngati Apa*,

---

[41] *Ngati Apa,* note 39, 655–6.   [42] Ibid 656.   [43] Ibid.
[44] [1921] 2 AC 399 (PC).   [45] *Ngati Apa,* note 39, 656.
[46] Ibid 656 (emphasis added). The Canadian case cited was *Delgamuukw v British Columbia,* [1997] 3 SCR 1010 (SCC).   [47] Ibid 693.
[48] Ibid 684.   [49] Ibid 673.   [50] *Johnson v M'Intosh* 21 US (8 Wheat) 543 (1823).
[51] *Ngati Apa,* note 39, 652.

Justices Keith and Anderson quoted the following from Chief Justice Marshall's opinion in *Johnson*:

While the different nations of Europe respected the right of the natives, as occupants, they asserted the ultimate dominion to be in themselves; and claimed and exercised, as a consequence of this ultimate dominion, a power to grant the soil, while yet in possession of the natives. These grants have been understood by all, to convey a title to the grantees, subject only to the Indian right of occupancy.[52]

The reasoning in *Ngati Apa* may be the best yet to be made by a judiciary, at least in the Commonwealth. It poignantly recognizes the interests of Indigenous peoples. For example, Chief Justice Elias stated:

[T]he common law as received in New Zealand was modified by recognised Maori customary property interests. If any such custom is shown to give interests in foreshore and seabed, there is no room for a contrary presumption derived from English common law. The common law of New Zealand is different.[53]

According to *Ngati Apa*, the common law of New Zealand is unique. Chief Justice Elias stressed this reality in stating:

In British territories with native populations, they introduced common law adapted to reflect local custom, including property rights. That approach was applied in New Zealand in 1840. The laws of England were applied in New Zealand only 'so far as applicable to the circumstances thereof'...from the beginning the common law of New Zealand as applied in the Courts differed from the common law of England because it reflected local circumstances.[54]

The Court did not proceed to answer whether specific tribes exclusively held land under salt water because the Court was reviewing the case on the issue of whether the Māori Land Court had jurisdiction to determine if the foreshore and seabed were Māori customary land (a land status rather than a Native title issue). All five judges held that the Māori Land Court did have the necessary jurisdiction to consider an application from Māori which asserted that specific areas of the foreshore and seabed were Māori customary land.[55] While Parliament enacted law that removed the possibility of Māori pursuing these claims in the courts, *Ngata Apa* remains undoubtedly Aotearoa New Zealand's most significant contemporary case. Importantly, it banished the *terra nullius* precedent evident in *Wi Parata* and the Discovery mindset prevalent in *In Re Ninety Mile Beach*.

---

[52] Ibid 680.   [53] Ibid 668.   [54] Ibid 562.

[55] Ibid. Note that in this decision there is extensive reliance on Canadian case law, and the Australian case *Mabo*, note 37. No post-*Mabo* Australian case was cited, including a case arguably on point, *Commonwealth v Yarmirr* [2001] 208 CLR 1. For a discussion on this see Jacinta Ruru, 'What Could Have Been: The Common Law Doctrine of Native Title in Land Under Salt Water in Australia and Aotearoa/New Zealand' (2006) 32(1) Monash Univ L Rev 116.

B. Settlement Statute Era

This part case studies a series of natural resources, specifically national parks and the foreshore and seabed, to illustrate how the government's response to Māori claims in the new settlement era remains influenced by the Discovery doctrine. Nonetheless, it is important at the outset to recognize that the government has made progress in settling with Māori. The two significant pan-tribal settlements concern commercial saltwater fisheries and Central North Island forests. The commercial fisheries settlement was negotiated in 1992 and dubbed the 'Sealord deal'. It included cash compensation, 50 per cent shareholding in Sealord Products Limited, 10 per cent of fish stocks introduced into the quota management system in 1986, and 20 per cent of all new stock brought into the system thereafter (now valued at around NZ$750 million).[56] The Central North Island forests settlement was negotiated in 2008 and dubbed the 'Treelord deal'. It included return of ownership to iwi of 170,000 hectares of forest valued at between NZ$170,000 million and NZ$190,000 million, and about NZ$248,000 million paid to the claimant tribes.[57] It is also thought that the tradeable carbon credits could be valued at between NZ$50 and NZ$70 million.[58]

In regard to legislated tribal settlements, more than 18 groups have received redress, amounting to a total value of more than NZ$921 million (with the largest cash compensation paid to single tribes being NZ$170 million).[59] Nonetheless, several parameters determine the scope of the negotiations: the Crown 'strongly prefers to negotiate claims with large natural groupings rather than individual whanau and hapu',[60] and it is attempting to settle all grievances within a tight budget and timeframe.[61]

Another confinement to these negotiations has been the Crown's unwillingness to consider vesting large tracts of land or natural resources in Māori. This is particularly evident in regard to national parks and the foreshore and seabed as is discussed below.

---

[56] See Treaty of Waitangi (Fisheries Claim) Settlement Act 1992 and Maori Fisheries Act 2004. For commentary on the settlement and legislation see Te Ohu Kaimoana's website at: <http://teohu.maori.nz/index.htm>.

[57] See Central North Island Forests Land Collective Settlement Act 2008.

[58] For newspaper coverage see: <http://www.stuff.co.nz/4505192a8153.html>.

[59] See Office of Treaty Settlements website at the settlement progress link: <http://www.ots.govt.nz/>.

[60] Office of Treaty Settlements, note 3, 32. Note: cross-claim boundary disputes are often at issue. For example, see cases such as: *NZ Maori Council v Attorney-General* [2007] NZCA 269 and *Te Runanga o Ngai Tahu v Waitangi Tribunal* High Court, Wellington C97/01, 2001; and see Waitangi Tribunal reports such as Waitangi Tribunal *The Report on the Impact of the Crown's Treaty Settlement Policy on Te Arawa Waka* (Wellington: Legislation Direct, 2007) and Waitangi Tribunal *Tamaki Makarau Settlement Process Report* (Wellington: Legislation Direct, 2007).

[61] See Maori Purposes Bill (No 55-1) cl 18 (tabled June 2006).

1. National parks

The Crown has an explicit policy that no large tracts of conservation land can be returned to Māori as part of Treaty of Waitangi settlements. While this policy is being fiercely debated by tribes in the North Island, the tribe that has the most amount of its traditional lands encased in the conservation estate—Ngai Tahu in the South Island—settled with the Crown in 1998. On the ownership front, Ngai Tahu were only able to secure a seven-day vestment of Aoraki/Mount Cook, the mountain that lies at the centrepiece of the Aoraki/Mount Cook National Park and is the country's tallest mountain. At the expiry of the seven days, Ngai Tahu must gift the mountain back to the nation.[62]

Comparatively more progress has been made on the management front, but nothing resembling co-management. Typical features include rights to representation on conservation boards and statutory acknowledgments of association. For example, pursuant to the Ngai Tahu Claims Settlement Act 1998, the Minister of Conservation, the Conservation Authority, and conservation boards in the bottom two thirds of the South Island must have particular regard to the advice of Te Runanga o Ngai Tahu in specific situations.[63] The Act declares certain mountaintops, lakes, and valleys as Topuni—a statutory label used to acknowledge 'Ngai Tahu values', meaning Ngai Tahu's cultural, spiritual, historic, and traditional association with specific areas.[64] The Act also recognizes the Ngai Tahu association with taonga species such as native birds, plants, animals, and fish.[65] However, similar legal rights do not exist for all other tribes.

The tribes in the North Island are all at various stages of seeking ownership of the four national parks that lie in the North Island: Tongariro, Taranaki, Urewera, and Wanganui. For example, in regard to the Tongariro National Park, while the Crown has become more accepting that it was initially an Indigenous place, it is uncertain whether the Crown will accept that it ought to return ownership to those tribes whose traditional area the park encases. In 1993, Aotearoa New Zealand became the first in the world to receive recognition under the revised World Heritage cultural landscapes criteria specifically recognizing the value of this land to Ngati Tuwharetoa.[66] The recently published management plan captures a new commitment to the tribes explicitly stating that management of the park must recognize and support the unique relationship Māori have with the park.[67] However, Ngati Tuwharetoa and Ngati Rangi remain mostly isolated from the management of the park. They have taken a claim to the Waitangi Tribunal asserting extensive Crown breaches of the Treaty of Waitangi in

---

[62] See Ngai Tahu Claims Settlement Act 1998 ss 13–18.   [63] Ibid s 273.
[64] Ibid ss 237–252.   [65] Ibid ss 287–296.
[66] See UNSECO World Heritage site at: <http://whc.unesco.org/en/list/421>.
[67] Department of Conservation, *Tongariro National Park Management Plan* (Wellington: Department of Conservation, 2006).

establishing the Park boundaries and subsequently managing it.[68] The Tribunal heard closing submissions in July 2007, and is due to make its recommendations in 2010. The tribes and the Crown will then enter direct negotiations aiming for reconciliation.[69] If the Tribunal accepts that iwi ownership of the park should comprise part of these negotiations, then the Crown's stance to not negotiate ownership will come under intense fire.[70] But because the Crown is deemed to be sovereign, and Parliament is supreme, tribes will have no redress in the courts if the Crown decides to remain steadfast to this Discovery-influenced policy.

2. Foreshore and seabed

While the Court of Appeal, in 2003, held that the Māori Land Court did have the necessary jurisdiction to consider an application from Māori which asserted that specific areas of the foreshore and seabed were Māori customary land,[71] Māori never had the opportunity to take a case to the Court. This was because the Labour-led government immediately announced its intention to enact clear and plain legislation asserting Crown ownership of the foreshore and seabed.[72] In response to the government's position, outlined in a report released in December 2003,[73] many Māori groups in protest of the policy lodged an urgent claim with the Waitangi Tribunal. At the Waitangi Tribunal, the Māori groups argued that the policy, if enacted, would constitute a serious breach of the Treaty of Waitangi principles and wider norms of domestic and international law.[74] The Tribunal agreed. It stated, in its March 2004 report, that the policy gave rise to serious prejudice toward the Māori groups by 'cutting off their access to the courts and effectively expropriating their property rights [by] put[ting] them in a class different from and inferior to all other citizens'.[75] Despite the Tribunal's strong recommendations for continued consultation between the government and Māori, the government rejected the report's central conclusions as based on 'dubious or incorrect assumptions'.[76] Furthermore, the government stressed the notion of

---

[68] For information about the claim see the Tribunal's website under the National Park Inquiry heading at: <http://www.waitangi-tribunal.govt.nz/inquiries/genericinquiries/nationalparkinquiry/>.

[69] See the work of the Office of Treaty Settlements at: <http://www.ots.govt.nz>.

[70] Other tribes are also challenging this policy. See eg the Tuhoe Negotiators Report 2009 in relation to the Urewera National Park at <http://www.tekotahiatuhoe.iwi.nz/doclibrary/.../ NegotiatorsReport-7.pdf>. In regard to the Wanganui National Park see Department of Conservation, *Conservation Management Strategy—Wanganui Conservancy* (Wellington: Department of Conservation, 2007) 33.   [71] *Ngati Apa*, note 39.

[72] Department of Prime Minister and Cabinet, *Summary of Foreshore and Seabed Framework* (Wellington: Department of Prime Minister and Cabinet, 2003), available at <http://www. beehive.govt.nz/foreshore/summary.php>.   [73] Ibid.

[74] See Waitangi Tribunal, *Report on the Crown's Foreshore and Seabed Policy* Wai 1071 (Wellington: Legislation Direct, 2004) xiv–xv, available at <http://www.waitangi-tribunal.govt. nz/scripts/reports/reports/1071/00AEFB80-5FE0-4D2E-AD9E-0F45E36B91AE.pdf>.

[75] Ibid.

[76] Michael Cullen, *Waitangi Tribunal Report Disappointing* (8 March 2004), available at <http:// www.beehive.govt.nz/node/19091> (describing Deputy Prime Minister Cullen's official speech).

parliamentary sovereignty—the idea that Aotearoa New Zealand's Parliament is supreme and is unhindered in its law-making abilities.

Section 3 of the Foreshore and Seabed Act 2004 states that its object is to:

preserve the public foreshore and seabed in perpetuity as the common heritage of all New Zealanders in a way that enables the protection by the Crown of the public foreshore and seabed on behalf of all the people of New Zealand, including the protection of the association of whanau, hapu, and iwi with areas of the public foreshore and seabed.[77]

This Act serves three purposes. First, the Act vests the land in Crown ownership: 'the full legal and beneficial ownership of the public foreshore and seabed is vested in the Crown, so that the public foreshore and seabed is held by the Crown as its absolute property'.[78] Second, it replaces the Māori Land Court's jurisdiction to issue land status orders with a new jurisdiction to issue customary rights orders. It also replaces the High Court's jurisdiction to hear and determine the common law doctrine of Native title with a new jurisdiction to determine territorial customary rights.[79]

The government's handling of the foreshore and seabed issue angered many Māori. Protests included a successful claim to the United Nations whereby the United Nations Committee on the Elimination of Racial Discrimination condemned the Act;[80] a political protest hikoi (march) of about twenty thousand Māori on Parliament grounds; and a resignation of a Māori Labour Cabinet Minister, Tarina Turia, followed by her re-election to the New Zealand Parliament as a representative of the newly formed Māori Party. The issue also sparked discussion about reforming New Zealand's constitutional order. This discussion has included debates over the proper location of the Treaty of Waitangi in New Zealand's constitution.[81]

---

[77] Foreshore and Seabed Act 2004 s 3.

[78] Ibid s 13(1). Note that s 13 defines the 'public foreshore and seabed' as meaning the foreshore and seabed but does not include any land that is, for the time being, subject to a specified freehold interest.

[79] Ibid at parts 3 and 4. For commentary on this Act and its background see generally F M (Jock) Brookfield, 'Maori Claims and the "Special" Juridical Nature of Foreshore and Seabed' (2005) New Zealand L Rev 179; Richard Boast, *Foreshore and Seabed* (Wellington: LexisNexis, 2005); Nin Tomas and Karensa Johnston, 'Ask That Taniwha Who Owns the Foreshore and Seabed of Aotearoa?' (2004) 1 Te Tai Haruru J of Maori Legal Writing 1; P G McHugh, 'Aboriginal Title in New Zealand: A Retrospect and Prospect' (2004) 2 New Zealand J of Public and Int'l L 139.

[80] See UN Office of the High Commissioner for Human Rights, Comm. on Elimination of Racial Discrimination (CERD), Decision 1 (66) NZ Foreshore and Seabed Act 2004, UN Doc CERD/C/DEC/NZL/1 (27 April 2005), available at: <http://www.unhcr.org/refworld/type,DECISION,,,42de62ef4,0.html>. See generally Claire Charters and Andrew Erueti, 'Report from the Inside: The CERD Committee's Review of the Foreshore and Seabed Act 2004' (2005) 36 Victoria Univ of Wellington L Rev 257.

[81] See generally B V Harris, 'The Treaty of Waitangi and the Constitutional Future of New Zealand' (2005) 2 New Zealand L Rev 189. See generally Colin James (ed), *Building the Constitution* (Wellington: Institute of Policy Studies, 2000); Matthew Palmer, 'Constitutional Realism About Constitutional Protection: Indigenous Rights Under a Judicialized and a Politicized Constitution' (2007) 29 Dalhousie LJ 1.

However, as part of the Māori Party's agreement to support the National-led government to commence its three-year term in Parliament in 2008, National agreed to review the Foreshore and Seabed Act. The review panel released its recommendations in 2009.[82] The government will most likely respond to the review report in early 2010. It seems likely that this Act will be repealed.

While national parks and the foreshore and seabed have been singled out here for discussion, they are not subject to unique government policy. For example, the government has also refused to consider iwi ownership of petroleum.[83] A pressing issue in the near future will be whether the Crown will acknowledge iwi ownership of freshwater.[84] Despite a clear trend illustrating the Crown's reluctance to acknowledge Māori ownership of large stretches of land or large components of natural resources, there are some exceptions. The notable exception is the Crown's acknowledgement of Te Runanga o Ngai Tahu ownership of all pounamu (meaning bowenite, nephrite, and serpentine—or more commonly referred to as greenstone or jade) found in its natural state.[85] However, even in regard to this exception, Ngai Tahu only gained recognition of their ownership via a settlement. Moreover, the starting point within that settlement was that the Crown was the original owner holding the authority to vest ownership in another. Accepting the existence of exceptions, the general conclusion remains that the Crown assumes ownership of natural resources and in doing so exudes a Discovery mindset.

C. Future Constitutional Era

Elements of the Discovery ideology are also paramount in debating the constitutional positioning of the Treaty of Waitangi. While the *Lands* case overruled the judicial reasoning that labelled the Treaty 'a simple nullity', the *Lands* case left untouched the precedent that holds that the Treaty can be enforced in the courts only where statutory incorporation has occurred. What then is the role of the Treaty in Aotearoa New Zealand's informal constitution?[86] This part

---

[82] Ministry of Justice, *Pākia ki uta, Pākia ki tai. Summary Report of the Ministerial Review Panel. Ministerial Review of the Foreshore and Seabed* (Wellington: Ministry of Justice, 2009). For more information including press releases and to view this report see <http://www.beehive.govt.nz/release/foreshore+and+seabed+act+review+received>.

[83] For information on the claim see Waitangi Tribunal, *The Petroleum Report* Wai 796 (Wellington: Legislation Direct, 2003). To view the government's response see media release by Hon Pete Hodgson 'Government's Response to the Waitangi Tribunal Petroleum Report' 21 November 2003 available at: <http://www.beehive.govt.nz/release/government+response+waitangi+tribunal039s+petroleum+report>.

[84] See discussion in Jacinta Ruru, *The Legal Voice of Maori in Freshwater Governance: A Literature Review* (Christchurch: Landcare Research, 2009).

[85] Ngai Tahu (Pounamu Vesting) Act 1997 s 3. Note that the Crown has enforced this provision—for the latest in a series of cases see *R v Saxton* [2009] 3 NZLR 29.

[86] For a brief introduction to this informal constitution, see Chapter 8, note 9 and accompanying text.

of this chapter reviews this issue for it is one that is currently gaining political momentum.[87] The views of the Waitangi Tribunal and the courts are canvassed.

1. A constitutional document?

In making recommendations on alleged Crown breaches of the Treaty of Waitangi, the Waitangi Tribunal has made several statements about the status of the Treaty of Waitangi. Early on, the Tribunal asserted a strong constitutional place for the Treaty of Waitangi. For example, in 1984 the Kaituna River Tribunal observed that:[88]

From being 'a simple nullity' the Treaty of Waitangi has become a document of importance approaching the status of a constitutional instrument so far as Maoris are concerned. It is not truly a constitutional instrument because conflict between an Act of Parliament or Regulation and the Treaty does not render the statute null and void. But it does expose the Crown to the risk of a claim that the statute in question is in conflict with the Treaty and to that extent it would seem prudent for those responsible for legislation to recognise the danger inherent in drafting statutes or regulations without measuring such instruments against the principles in the Treaty.

By 1988, the Tribunal had coined its most powerful and enduring classification of the Treaty as New Zealand's 'basic constitutional document'.[89] The phrase was explored in the 1991 Ngai Tahu Report. Here, the Ngai Tahu Tribunal stated, '[W]e believe that the Treaty of Waitangi should be seen as a basic constitutional document.'[90] However, the Ngai Tahu Tribunal disagreed with the counsel for the claimants that 'the power of Parliament will be curbed by its obligations to respect the terms of the Treaty'.[91] The Tribunal observed that there would 'appear to be formidable difficulties' in reaching that conclusion 'in the absence of further legislative action'.[92] The Tribunal concluded the point by stating '[T]his tribunal senses that the central importance of the Treaty in our constitutional arrangements is likely to receive growing recognition by the courts, the legislature and

[87] Note that several legal academics are currently arguing for a stronger constitutional role for the Treaty of Waitangi. See D V Williams, 'The Treaty of Waitangi—A "Bridle" on Parliamentary Sovereignty' (2007) 13(6) New Zealand Univ L Rev 596; Matthew S R Palmer, *The Treaty of Waitangi in New Zealand's Law and Constitution* (Wellington, Victoria University Press, 2008); Harris, note 81. For more discussion on the material here, see Jacinta Ruru, 'The Waitangi Tribunal' in Malcolm Mulholland and Veronica Tawhai (eds) *Weeping Waters. The Treaty of Waitangi and Constitutional Change* (Wellington: Huia Publishers, 2010) 127–142.
[88] Waitangi Tribunal, *Report of the Waitangi Tribunal on the Kaituna River Claim* Wai 4 (Wellington: Legislation Direct, 1984) 26.
[89] Waitangi Tribunal, *Report of the Waitangi Tribunal on the Muriwhenua Fishing Claim* Wai 22 (Wellington: Legislation Direct, 1988) 188.
[90] Waitangi Tribunal, *The Ngai Tahu Report* Wai 27 (Wellington: Legislation Direct, 1991) 224. Also expressed as such in the Waitangi Tribunal, *Report of the Waitangi Tribunal on Claims Concerning the Allocation of Radio Frequencies* Wai 26 (Wellington: Legislation Direct, 1990) and Waitangi Tribunal, *The Ngai Tahu Sea Fisheries Report* Wai 27 (Wellington: Legislation Direct, 1992).
[91] *The Ngai Tahu Report*, note 90, 224.   [92] Ibid.

the executive in the foreseeable future.'[93] Twenty years later that reflection has not borne reality.

In the 1980s and 1990s the courts made several strong statements about the status of the Treaty. In 1987, in *Huakina Development Trust v Waikato Valley Authority*,[94] Justice Chilwell stated that '[t]here is no doubt that the Treaty is part of the fabric of New Zealand society'.[95] Weeks later, in the *Lands* case, all the Court of Appeal justices reflected on the importance of the Treaty as, for example, providing 'the foundation for the future relationship between the Crown and the Maori race'.[96] In 1990, the President of the Court of Appeal Cooke spoke extrajudicially of the Treaty as 'simply the most important document in New Zealand's history'.[97] Similarly, in 1994, Lord Woolf of the Privy Council stated that the Treaty 'is of the greatest constitutional importance to New Zealand'.[98] More recently, Justice Baragwanath of the High Court has stated that the Crown's 'obligation to give due effect to the Treaty is a continuing one'.[99] However, judicial disquiet about the status of the Treaty is becoming evident. For example, while the High Court held in May 2007 that there was a possibility that the Treaty of Waitangi was equivalent to the Aboriginal peoples' protection granted in section 35 of the Canadian Constitution Act 1982 and therefore enforcing fiduciary obligations to protect Māori on the Crown,[100] the Court of Appeal overruled the decision. The Court of Appeal limited the scope of the Treaty of Waitangi stating 'If Gendall J [in the High Court] was saying that the Crown has a fiduciary duty in a private law sense that is enforceable against the Crown in equity, we respectfully disagree.'[101]

While the courts may be backtracking, in comparison, the Tribunal has consistently continued to emphasize the importance of the constitutional role of the Treaty. For example, in 1994, the Māori Electoral Option Tribunal recognized the Privy Council's articulation that the 'Treaty records an agreement executed by the Crown and Maori, which over 150 years later is of the greatest constitutional

[93] Ibid 226. [94] [1987] 2 NZLR 188. [95] Ibid 210.
[96] *Lands* case, note 15, 714.
[97] Sir R Cooke, 'Introduction' (1990) 14 New Zealand Univ L Rev 1.
[98] *New Zealand Maori Council v Attorney General* (PC) [1994] 1 NZLR 513, 516. See also discussions in *Attorney-General v New Zealand Maori Council (No 2)* [1991] 2 NZLR 147 (CA); *New Zealand Maori Council v Attorney-General* [1992] 2 NZLR 576 (CA); *New Zealand Maori Council v Attorney-General* [1994] 1 NZLR 513 (PC); *New Zealand Maori Council v Attorney-General* [1996] 3 NZLR 140 (CA).
[99] *Ngati Maru ki Hauraki Inc v Kruithof*, 11 June 2006, Baragwanath J, HC Hamilton CIV 2004-485-330 at para 50. See also *Takamore Trustees v Kapiti Coast District Council* [2003] 3 NZLR 496 (HC); *Carter Holt Harvey Ltd v Te Runanga o Tuwharetoa ki Kawerau* [2003] 2 NZLR 349 (HC).
[100] *New Zealand Maori Council v Attorney-General*, 4 May 2007, Gendall J, HC Wellington CIV-2007-485-95 at para 61.
[101] *New Zealand Maori Council v Attorney-General* [2008] 1 NZLR 318 (CA) (at 336).

importance to New Zealand'.[102] In 2001, the Napier Hospital Tribunal stated: '[T]he Treaty of Waitangi is the foundation document for modern constitutional government in New Zealand.'[103] In 2008, the Central North Island Claims Tribunal accepted 'that the Treaty and its principles have an enduring, if not an eternal, role in our legal system'.[104] Thus, does the Treaty restrain the right of the Crown to govern?

2. Reciprocity principle

The Tribunal has been consistent in its interpretation of the Treaty and its principles that the Crown's sovereignty (acquired via article 1 of the Treaty) is qualified by tino rangatiratanga (retained by Māori via article 2 of the Treaty). For example, the Orakei Claim Tribunal, in its 1987 report, stated that kawanatanga, as used in article 1 of the Māori version, 'is less than the supreme sovereignty of the English text and does not carry the English cultural assumptions that go with it, the unfettered authority of Parliament or the principles of common law administered by the Queen's Judges in the Queen's name'.[105] Moreover, the Ngai Tahu Tribunal, in its 1991 report, stated that tino rangatiratanga 'necessarily qualifies or limits the authority of the Crown to govern. In exercising its sovereignty it must respect, indeed guarantee, Maori rangatiratanga—mana Maori—in terms of article 2.'[106] Or as the Mohaka River Tribunal put it, the Crown is required to 'exercise its kawanatanga with due respect for tino rangatiratanga'.[107]

These reflections have been endorsed in subsequent Tribunal reports.[108] Throughout these reports, the Tribunal has referred to this qualification as the principle of reciprocity. While the Tribunal has emphasized that there is 'unity' and 'considerable overlap' amongst the Treaty principles and thus they must be read together,[109] this principle of reciprocity stands out as the '"over-arching principle" that guides the interpretation and application of other principles, such as partnership'.[110]

---

[102] Waitangi Tribunal, *Maori Electoral Option Report* Wai 413 (Wellington: Legislation Direct, 1994) para 3.2. The Tribunal is citing *New Zealand Maori Council v Attorney General* (unreported PC 14/93, 13 December 1993 at 3).

[103] Waitangi Tribunal, *The Napier Hospital and Health Services Report* Wai 692 (Wellington: Legislation Direct, 2001) 44.

[104] Waitangi Tribunal, *He Maunga Rongo. Report on the Central North Island Claims* Wai 1200 vol 4 (Wellington: Legislation Direct, 2008) 1235.

[105] Waitangi Tribunal, *Report of the Waitangi Tribunal on the Orakei Claim* Wai 9 (Wellington: Legislation Direct, 1987) 180 (cited in Waitangi Tribunal, *Te Raupatu o Tauranga Moana Report on the Tauranga Confiscation Claims* Wai 215 (Wellington: Legislation Direct, 2004) 20).

[106] *Ngai Tahu Report*, note 90, vol 3, 236–7 (cited in *Te Raupatu o Tauranga Moana*, note 105).

[107] Waitangi Tribunal, *The Mohaka Ki Ahuriri Report* Wai 201 (Wellington: Legislation Direct, 2004) 28.   [108] See for example *Te Raupatu o Tauranga Moana*, note 105.

[109] See for example Waitangi Tribunal, *The Tarawera Forest Report* Wai 411 (Wellington: Legislation Direct, 2003) 22.

[110] *Crown's Foreshore and Seabed Policy*, note 74, 130 and note 6, for a reference to other Tribunal reports that have endorsed this sentiment.

The most recent and comprehensive discussion of this principle lies in the Central North Island (CNI) Tribunal report, published in 2008. The CNI Tribunal reinforced the point made in previous Tribunal reports that it is a legitimate exercise of the Crown's governance role to (1) make national laws, and (2) make national laws that constrain the actions of members of society because article 1 endorsed the Crown as the 'only centralised body with the overview and capability necessary'[111] to enact laws for the benefit of all in society. The CNI Tribunal reinforced previous Tribunal assertions that the Crown must exercise its legitimate governance capabilities by exercising a 'careful balancing'[112] act that is consistent with its Treaty obligations. According to the Tribunal, the ' "test" is reasonableness, not perfection'.[113]

Thus, when would it be reasonable for the Crown to override article 2? The Turangi Township Tribunal set the standard test:

[I]f the Crown is ever to be justified in exercising its power to govern in a manner which is inconsistent with and overrides the fundamental rights guaranteed to Maori in article 2 it should be only in exceptional circumstances and as a last resort in the national interest.[114]

Other reports have developed this sentiment. For example, in the context of natural resources, the CNI Tribunal claimed that it might be reasonable for the Crown, having first conducted a careful balancing act, for the needs of other sectors of the community to trump its Treaty obligations to Māori. This might occur in five instances: (a) in exceptional circumstances such as war; (b) for peace and good order; (c) in matters involving the national interest; (d) in situations where the environment or certain natural resources are so endangered or depleted that they should be conserved or protected; and (e) where Māori interests in natural resources have been fully ascertained by the Crown and freely alienated.[115] Moreover, in several reports the Tribunal has stated in the context of the third instance and in regard to natural resources that the 'national interest in conservation is not a reason for negating Maori rights of property'.[116]

Should it be a source of concern that the Crown is restrained in its exercise of governance? The Tribunal thinks not. For instance, the Turangi Township Tribunal stated:

[T]he limited grant of sovereignty acquired by the Crown under the Treaty does not create a constitutional problem. Few, if any, western governments enjoy unqualified sovereign power. Apart from the legal constraints imposed by entrenched constitutions, where these exist, the powers of modern States are being increasingly constrained by international agreements.[117]

---

[111] *Central North Island Claims,* note 104, 1238.   [112] Ibid.   [113] Ibid.
[114] Waitangi Tribunal, *The Turangi Township Report* Wai 84 (Wellington: Legislation Direct, 1995).   [115] *Central North Island Claims,* note 104, 1239.
[116] Ibid 1240. See also, for example, the Waitangi Tribunal, *The Whanganui River Report* Wai 167 (Wellington: Legislation Direct, 1999) 330.
[117] *The Turangi Township Report,* note 114, 285.

Furthermore, the CNI Tribunal said that 'the concept of restrained governance is not a novel concept'.[118] This Tribunal reflected that the Crown is so constrained in many fields, including trade law and human rights. And, as the Waimumu Trust Tribunal asserted:[119]

We accept that the exercise of tino rangatiratanga is balanced by the Crown's legitimate exercise of its kawanatanga. This is the fundamental Treaty principle of reciprocity. Economic factors such as the availability of markets on the one hand, and the Crown's conservation policies on the other, are matters which will affect the choices available to claimants in the exercise of their tino rangatiratanga. It is critical that in situations where the claimants' choices are reduced almost to none that the Crown behave with scrupulous fairness.

In summary, the overall principle according to the Tribunal is that the Crown's sovereignty (kawanatanga) is qualified by tino rangatiratanga. While there are some exceptions to this rule, it is the rule. To visualize it, the CNI Tribunal endorsed the Muriwhenua Fishing Tribunal's assertion that 'the Crown has no right to determine for the tribes the wisest or best use of their fisheries resources for so long as the tribes regulate and enforce their own standards'.[120] But, is there wider judicial support for the Tribunal's stance?

D. Wider Judicial Support

The Tribunal has measurably advanced the discussion and understanding of the Treaty principles, and in particular the principle of reciprocity, in the conservation realm.[121] Specific consideration has been given to section 4 of the Conservation Act 1987 which reads: 'This Act shall so be interpreted and administered as to give effect to the principles of the Treaty of Waitangi.'

In summary, the Tribunal's position on section 4 is manifest in two ideas. First: the section 4 expression means that while the Crown has a right to govern, this right is qualified by the Māori right to exercise rangatiratanga. Although in exceptional circumstances the Crown may override this fundamental right of rangatiratanga, it may only do so as a last resort and if this is in the national interest. However, the 'national interest in conservation is not a reason for negating Māori rights of property'.[122] Second: if the resource in question is highly valued and of great spiritual and physical importance, then it is to be considered

---

[118] *Central North Island Claims,* note 104, 1239.
[119] Waitangi Tribunal, *The Waimumu Trust (SILNA) Report* Wai 1090 (Wellington: Legislation Direct, 2005) 85.   [120] *Central North Island Claims,* note 104, 1239.
[121] Note that a more detailed analysis of this part of the chapter appears in Jacinta Ruru, 'Managing Our Treasured Home: the Conservation Estate and the Principles of the Treaty of Waitangi' (2004) 8 New Zealand J of Envt'l L 243. For a detailed discussion of the Tribunal's reports concerning the environment see N R Wheen and J Ruru, 'The Environmental Reports' in *The Waitangi Tribunal* note 2.   [122] *The Whanganui River Report,* note 116, 330.

a taonga, and the Crown is under an affirmative obligation to ensure its protection to the fullest extent reasonably practicable.[123]

The Tribunal has progressed its first idea (that kawanatanga is generally subject to rangatiratanga) to a level where the courts, including the Court of Appeal, have not gone. The most significant case specific to section 4 is the Court of Appeal's *Ngai Tahu Maori Trust Board v Director-General of Conservation* decision.[124] Commonly referred to as the 'whale watch case', the Court recognized the Crown's right to govern and the Māori right to exercise tino rangatiratanga, but it did not consider how the two should operate together. Instead it focused on the first right, the Crown's governance right: 'The rights and interests of everyone in New Zealand, Maori and Pakeha and all others alike, must be subject to that overriding authority.'[125] Even though it emphasized kawanatanga, it skipped how kawanatanga, as an overriding authority, might relate to the right to exercise tino rangatiratanga. It simply focused on fiduciaries' duties, active protection, good faith, and so on—in other words, how the Treaty parties should operate towards one another. It did not turn on what a right of tino rangatiratanga encompassed nor how it could operate alongside a Crown right to govern.

The Waitangi Tribunal, in comparison, has emphasized that cession of sovereignty to the Crown by Māori was qualified by the retention of tino rangatiratanga: 'Maori ceded sovereignty to the Crown in exchange for the protection by the Crown of Maori rangatiratanga.'[126] The Tribunal has therefore been able to reach a level of comprehension between the rights, concluding that while the Crown has a right to govern, it must be proven to be in the national interest before governance is used to override an exercise of tino rangatiratanga.

Thus the Tribunal's jurisprudence provides evidence of a clear attempt to displace Discovery elements from Aotearoa New Zealand's legal system. However, the Tribunal and the Court of Appeal's understandings of the Treaty fail to mirror because the Tribunal says kawanatanga is subject to rangatiratanga, whereas the Court of Appeal assumes rangatiratanga is subject to kawanatanga. A future judicial re-examination of the Court of Appeal's decision may disrupt the Court's interpretation that other legislative provisions override Treaty principles. But this would only succeed if the courts developed the Tribunal reasoning and accepted that the national interest in conservation is not a reason for negating Māori rights of property. For example, it would have to hold that any inconsistency between a policy directive, such as conservation or preservation, should give way to a Treaty principle. It is certainly arguable that this should be the true interpretation of

---

[123] See Waitangi Tribunal, *Preliminary Report on the Te Arawa Representative Geothermal Resource Claims* Wai 153 (Wellington: Legislation Direct, 1993); Waitangi Tribunal, *Mohaka River Report* Wai 119 (Wellington: Legislation Direct, 1992).   [124] [1995] 3 NZLR 553 (CA).
[125] Ibid 558.
[126] Waitangi Tribunal, *Te Whanganui A Tara Me Ona Takiwa: Report on the Wellington District* Wai 145 (Wellington: Legislation Direct, 2003) 74. For another example, see *Mohaka Ki Ahuriri Report*, note 107, 21.

the strongly worded section 4 of the Conservation Act directive to give effect to the principles of the Treaty. However, the majority judgment in a later Court of Appeal decision, *McRitchie*,[127] does not suggest movement in this direction—in fact, it is silent on the implication of section 4. Moreover, the Waitangi Tribunal jurisprudence is of course not binding on the courts. Even though the courts have stated that the Tribunal's opinions 'are of great value to the Court',[128] and 'are entitled to considerable weight',[129] the courts are free to dismiss Tribunal statements. And, so, elements of the Discovery ideology remain paramount in the contemporary court precedents concerning the status of the Treaty and its role in fostering legal relationships between the Crown and Māori.

E. Conclusion

In conclusion to this chapter on the contemporary stance of the Doctrine of Discovery in Aotearoa New Zealand, a couple of points need to be made. First, even though the *Ngati Apa* decision was a bold decision and goes further than the courts in Australia and Canada have gone in accepting the possibility of Indigenous peoples' exclusive ownership of land under salt water, the decision is still premised on the notion that the British Crown legitimately acquired sovereignty of New Zealand. The Court does not canvass the possibility that sovereignty may still legitimately lie with some of the Māori tribes. Rather, it assumes a transfer in sovereignty has occurred and purports blanket rules as applying to all of New Zealand. Second, from the 1980s the New Zealand courts refer to Canadian and Australian case law, not US jurisprudence, even though New Zealand's jurisprudence on this point originated in extensive reference to Justice Marshall's decisions. Third, Parliament would not contemplate Indigenous ownership of the foreshore or seabed or other large tracts of land in, for example, national parks. In doing so, Parliament has blatantly resurrected the Doctrine of Discovery in New Zealand. While Parliament has acted in contravention of the common law Native title precedent, it is able to do so because it is supreme— New Zealand's courts have no power to restrict Parliament's behaviour. Even if this were not the situation, case law suggests that it would be unlikely for a court to revisit the Crown sovereignty issue. The Doctrine is thus still alive in Aotearoa New Zealand.

---

[127] *McRitchie*, note 35.   [128] *Lands* case, note 15, 662.
[129] *Moana Te Aira Te Uri Karaka Te Waero v The Minister of Conservation and Auckland City Council*, 19 February 2002, Harrison J, HC Auckland, M360-SW01 para 59.

10

Concluding Comparatively: Discovery in the English Colonies

Indigenous peoples first discovered the lands of Aotearoa New Zealand, Australia, Canada, and the United States. They made those lands their home. They were, and are, intricately linked to the land. Indigenous identity, world views, culture, and law all derive from these specific landscapes—our earth mother. When the Europeans arrived on the shores of these places, they found an old world of Indigenous lands. This book has focused on that European encounter, and especially on how the British sought to make these lands their home by asserting a fiction of first discovery. This final chapter draws on comparative law to summarize the discussion taking place in the preceding chapters to illustrate the combined permeating influence of the Doctrine of Discovery in the legal systems of Aotearoa New Zealand, Australia, Canada, and the United States.[1]

A. Comparative Law

Historically, comparative law, as a Western legal theory, has mostly produced a poor spectrum of results for Indigenous peoples. The results have ranged from worthless to destructive. Comparative law has its history in a colonial binary of ethnocentricity, meaning that comparisons have often taken place through evaluating other races and cultures by criteria specific to one's own culture. Lawyers, legal academics, judges, and legislatures have historically gazed at Indigenous peoples for the purposes of eliminating differences. This book is rife with these colonial instances. In all four countries, the European colonists pursued a mission to destroy the cultures, laws, and governments of Indigenous peoples. A campaign to 'civilize' these 'others' by making illegal the practising of all their ways of knowing was sought through the means of law. No comparative legal theorist would today desire 'a larking adventure in prospecting' among

---

[1] Note that this chapter draws on the framework developed in Robert J Miller and Jacinta Ruru, 'An Indigenous Lens into Comparative Law: The Doctrine of Discovery in the United States and New Zealand' (2009) 111 West Virginia L Rev 849.

'primitive' cultures.[2] The modern comparative law paradigm can provide a legitimate platform to conclude the work done in this book. As von Nessen has stated:

Comparative law accepts the important relationship between law, history and culture, and operates on the basis that each legal system is a unique mixture of the spirit of its people and is the product of a complex matrix of historical events which have produced a 'distinctive national character and ambience.'[3]

Moreover, Indigenous peoples have practised their own versions of comparative law for centuries: the sharing of knowledge and the adaptation of legal traditions through spending time with other tribal groups. Henderson emphasizes the importance for contemporary Indigenous scholarship to 'dialogue comparatively'.[4] He explains:

This methodology not only allows others to learn from the Indigenous experience, but also offers greater legitimacy for Indigenous peoples. The relevance of the 'Indigenous Humanities' to the postcolonial consciousness and law can provide teachings and lessons learned by Indigenous peoples around the world.[5]

John Borrows has recognized:

[o]ur intellectual, emotional, social, physical, and spiritual insights can simultaneously be compared, contrasted, rejected, embraced, and intermingled with those of others. In fact, this process has been operative since before the time that Indigenous peoples first encountered others on their shores.[6]

It is in this vein of respectfully coming together to share our experiences of the Doctrine of Discovery and our hope for a better future that we have been motivated here to conclude within a comparative framework.

Some recent legal texts have already sought to better understand the encounter between the common law legal system and the Indigenous peoples of North America and Australasia, including the work by Paul McHugh and Stuart Banner, although they do so from within a legal-historian lens and not specifically from within a comparative law theory.[7] Others have also completed impressive work,

---

[2] E Adamson Hoebel, *The Law of Primitive Man: A Study in Comparative Legal Dynamics* 3 (Cambridge: Harvard University Press, 1954).

[3] Paul von Nessen, *The Use of Comparative Law in Australia* (Pyrmont: Thomson Lawbook Co, 2006) 27–8.

[4] James (Sákéj) Youngblood Henderson, 'Postcolonial Indigenous Legal Consciousness' (2002) 1 Indigenous LJ 4 (citing L M Findlay, 'Always Indigenize! The Radical Humanities in the Postcolonial Canadian University' (2000) 31 Ariel 307).   [5] Ibid.

[6] John Borrows, *Recovering Canada: The Resurgence of Indigenous Law* (Toronto: University of Toronto Press, 2002) 147.

[7] Paul McHugh, *Aboriginal Societies and the Common Law: A History of Sovereignty, Status and Self-Determination* (Oxford: Oxford University Press, 2004); Stuart Banner, *Possessing the Pacific: Land, Settlers, and Indigenous People from Australia to Alaska* (Cambridge: Harvard University Press, 2007).

including the recent publications by Paul Keal,[8] Peter Russell,[9] and Christa Scholtz,[10] but these authors write from non-law perspectives, such as political science. The few legal academics that are explicitly situating their work on Indigenous legal systems, and within a comparative methodology, include Canadian law professors H Patrick Glenn and Kent McNeil, and Australian law professor Simon Young. Glenn's seminal book includes a chapter on Indigenous peoples—classified by Glenn as 'chthonic peoples'[11] and attempts to do something that we do not. The motivation for us to pursue comparative legal work in this chapter is not to describe who we are or the legal system dear to our hearts, but rather to examine how the Western legal system has developed and applied a property theory based in fiction to substantiate the continuing colonization of Indigenous peoples' land and resources.[12] McNeil and Young do something different from Glenn—their works focus on the judicial interpretations and applications of the doctrine of Native title.[13] Our work is thus in a similar vein to Young and McNeil—the difference being that in this book we have come together as Indigenous legal academics to focus specifically on the Doctrine of Discovery. This chapter represents some initial thoughts within the context of comparative law and the fiction of Discovery.

B. Comparative Analysis

The best way to compare and contrast Aotearoa New Zealand, Australia, Canada, and United States laws on Discovery is to analyse the 10 constituent elements of the Doctrine that were set out in Chapter 1.

1. First discovery

England relied on the principle of first discovery to allege land ownership and sovereign rights over the Indigenous peoples in Aotearoa New Zealand, Australia,

---

[8] Paul Keal, *European Conquest and the Rights of Indigenous Peoples: The Moral Backwardness of International Society* (Cambridge: Cambridge University Press, 2003).

[9] Peter H Russell, *Recognizing Aboriginal Title: The Mabo Case and Indigenous Resistance to English-Settler Colonialism* (Toronto: University of Toronto Press, 2005).

[10] Christa Scholtz, *Negotiating Claims: The Emergence of Indigenous Land Claim Negotiation Policies in Australia, Canada, New Zealand, and the United States* (Hoboken: Routledge, 2006).

[11] See generally H Patrick Glenn, *Legal Traditions of the World* (New York: Oxford University Press, 3rd edn, 2007) 58–92.

[12] In saying this, we think we echo John Wigmore's 1931 definition of comparative law as 'the tracing of an identical or similar idea or institution through all or many systems, with a view to discovering its differences and likenesses in various systems.... [I]n short, the evolution of the idea or institution, universally considered'. John H Wigmore, 'Comparative Law: Jottings on Comparative Legal Ideas and Institutions' (1931–32) 6 Tulane L Rev 48, 51.

[13] See Simon Young, *The Trouble with Tradition. Native title and cultural change* (Sydney: Federation Press, 2008), and Kent McNeil, 'Judicial Treatment of Indigenous Land Rights in the Common Law World' in Benjamin J Richardson, Shin Imai, and Kent McNeil (eds), *Indigenous Peoples and the Law. Comparative and Critical Perspectives* (Portland, OR: Hart Publishing, 2009).

Canada, and the United States. The Crown used this principle in its charters for exploration and colonization. For example, Henry VII directed John Cabot to 'discover...countries, regions, or provinces of the heathen and infidels...which before this time have been unknown to all Christians'.[14] Similarly, Elizabeth I directed Sir Walter Raleigh 'to discover...remote, heathen and barbarous lands, countries, and territories, not actually possessed by any Christian Prince, nor inhabited by Christian People...'.[15] James I also directed his subjects to establish a colony on lands 'which are not now actually possessed by any *Christian* prince or People...'.[16]

Specifically, in the United States, for instance, Richard Haylukt wrote in 1609 that James I's rights in America were by 'right of discovery'.[17] Furthermore, in 1638, Maryland enacted a law to control Indian land sales and based its legal authority on the Crown's 'right of first discovery' in which the King 'became lord and possessor' of Maryland.[18] Later, the English colonies used England's claim of 'first discovery, occupation, and possession'[19] to resist the Dutch colonies in the 'New World'.

After the American Revolution, state governments continued to expressly rely on first discovery to define their rights to the lands of Native people. From 1785 to 1786, for example, Alexander Hamilton represented New York in a land claim versus Massachusetts, which raised the issue of what state held the preemption power to buy certain Indian lands. In preparing his case, Hamilton created an extensive chart that documented the first discoveries and settlements in America of the English, French, and Dutch.[20] Moreover, Thomas Jefferson recognized that an American's first discovery of the Columbia River in 1792 gave the United States a claim under international law to the Columbia River and its watershed.[21] Additionally, in 1856, Congress enacted a law that Americans could claim deserted islands based on first discovery and occupation.[22] Plainly, the Crown, colonies, American states, and the United States all claimed rights based on first discovery.

Similarly, the British applied the first discovery principle in other British colonies including Canada, Australia, and New Zealand. In Canada, for example, in

---

[14] Patent of New England Granted by James I (3 Nov 1629) reprinted in W Keith Kavenagh (ed), 1 *Foundations of Colonial America: A Documentary History* 18.

[15] Letters Patent to Sir Humphrey Gilbert (1 June 1578), reprinted in W Keith Kavenagh (ed), 3 *Foundations of Colonial America: A Documentary History* (1973) 1694.   [16] Ibid 1698.

[17] Robert A Williams, Jr, *The American Indian in Western Legal Thought: The Discourses of Conquest* (New York: Oxford University Press, 1990) 161, 170, 177–8.

[18] Act for Trade with the Indians (1638), reprinted in reprinted in W Keith Kavenagh (ed), 2 *Foundations of Colonial America: A Documentary History* (1973) 1267.

[19] Williams, note 16, 161, 170, 177–8.

[20] Harold C Syrett and Jacob E Cooke (eds), XIV *The Papers of Alexander Hamilton* (New York: Columbia University Press, 1969) 702–15.

[21] Bernard DeVoto, *The Course of Empire* (Boston: Houghton Mifflin, 1952).

[22] Guano Islands Act of Aug. 18, 1856, ch 164, 11 Stat 119 (codified at 48 USC §§ 1411–19 (2000)).

a 1929 Nova Scotia case, the judge wrote:

... the Indians were never regarded as an independent power. A civilized nation first discovering a country of uncivilized people or savages held such country as its own until such time as by treaty it was transferred to some other civilized nation. The savages' rights of sovereignty even of ownership were never recognized. Nova Scotia had passed to Great Britain not by gift or purchase from or even by conquest of the Indians but by treaty with France, which had acquired it by priority of discovery and ancient possession; and the Indians passed with it.[23]

Symbolism played an important part in 'discovering' Australia. Behrendt writes in Chapter 6 of how Captain James Cook claimed Australia through the symbolic acts of, for example, planting the British flag on various stretches of soil. This was reinforced by symbolic actions undertaken during the establishment of the first colony in Sydney. These acts were designed to underscore the British claim to discovery and to thwart any attempts by the French to establish a presence in this part of the world.

In regard to New Zealand, even though a treaty of cession—the Treaty of Waitangi—was signed with some of the Māori tribes, the Discovery Doctrine pervaded the British motivations and subsequent negotiations with Māori. The British considered the lands of New Zealand as 'unsettled' until Britain claimed sovereignty. This is so because the British believed that they first discovered the lands and therefore had the sovereign right of the lands whether a treaty of cession was signed or not. The precedent was first discussed in the 1847 *Symonds*[24] case which drew heavily on US jurisprudence, in particular, *Johnson*.[25] The Court claimed that first discovery gave title against all other Europeans. Moreover, in *Wi Parata*,[26] Justice Prendergast expressly related this element to New Zealand. For example, he stated that the rights and duties under international law, *jure gentium*, 'vest in and devolve upon the first civilized occupier'.[27] The *jure gentium* or international law that he was referring to is the Doctrine of Discovery.

It is no surprise that this element of Discovery is similar in these four countries. It is an element of the international law that England utilized in colonizing our countries and that the colonists in North America and Australasia adopted to control their relationships with the Indigenous peoples.

2. Actual occupancy and current possession

The English Crown developed the principle that for European countries to turn a first discovery into a complete title, Europeans had to actually occupy and possess

---

[23] Patterson Co Ct J (Acting) in *R v Syliboy* [1929] 1 DLR 307, 313, (1928), 50 CCC 389 at 396 (a Nova Scotia County Court case). [24] *R v Symonds* [1847] NZPCC 387 (PC).
[25] *Johnson v M'Intosh*, 21 US (8 Wheat) 543 (1823).
[26] *Wi Parata v Bishop of Wellington* [1877] 3 NZ Jur (NS) 72. [27] Ibid 77.

the lands within a reasonable amount of time after first discovery. The Crown and the colonies actively applied that element of Discovery.

For instance, Miller writes in Chapter 2 that England and the United States relied on this element in arguments that raged for over four decades as they tried to prove that they had actually occupied the Oregon Country. They argued about the significance of the Lewis and Clark expedition, John Jacob Astor's fur post at Astoria, and the activities of the English fur companies, the Northwest Company and the Hudson's Bay Company.

Thomas Jefferson was undoubtedly motivated by this very element of Discovery when he directed Lewis and Clark to the mouth of the Columbia River. Subsequently, Jefferson was especially delighted when, in 1808, the American fur trader John Jacob Astor proposed to build the first permanent American establishment on the Pacific coast at the mouth of the Columbia River. Jefferson realized the significance of these actions under the international law of Discovery. He even argued in 1813 and 1816 that America's claim to the Oregon Country was based on permanent occupancy of the region after Astor's construction of Astoria in 1811. In the 1820s and 1830s, Congressman Caleb Cushing told the House of Representatives that America's title relied on 'the Law of Nations ... that priority of discovery, followed in a reasonable time by actual occupation, confers exclusive territorial jurisdiction and sovereignty'.[28]

In Chapter 5, Lindberg illustrated an interesting occupancy point whereby the Supreme Court of Canada, in 1996,[29] heard a case involving Treaty No 8 Indigenous citizens being charged with breaking provincial laws by hunting for food on privately owned land. One hunted near an occupied house, the other on a snow covered field. In both instances, the Court found that the lands could be understood to be occupied as they were clearly being put to a visible and incompatible (with hunting) use. As Lindberg wrote, the irony is startling in that the test for occupancy requires Indigenous peoples (who were presumed not to occupy lands in order for them to be declared unoccupied Crown lands) to assume that certain signs of non-Indigenous occupancy (a house, a bare field) equate with an understanding that the property is occupied and cannot be used to hunt.

While the British in Australia were confident of their claim to Discovery simply via occupation, in New Zealand the British were less sure. They were especially concerned about the French on the east coast of the South Island at Akaroa. In May 1840, the presence of the French motivated Captain Hobson to claim sovereignty of the South Island on the basis of Discovery rather than by treaty cession. This angered some of the French, including Captain Langlois, who continued to insist that '[t]he ownership and sovereignty of France over the South Island of New Zealand cannot be disputed. I have myself made treaties both for the land

---

[28] Cong. Globe, 25th Cong, 2d Sess 566 (1838).
[29] *R v Badger* [1996] SCJ 39 (a Supreme Court of Canada case).

and the cession of sovereignty...'.[30] Nonetheless, France tacitly acknowledged British sovereignty of New Zealand in 1840.

3. Preemption/European title

English and European colonists often claimed that they had gained the complete fee title to the lands of Indigenous peoples under first discovery. Yet they rarely meant that phrase in the literal sense, to mean the 'fee simple absolute' title (except of course with one exception). In regard to the United States, Miller has explained that all European colonists and countries realized that they had to buy the remaining legal rights of the Native people in America. What Europeans meant by claiming the 'fee title' was actually that they had acquired the power of preemption, the sole right to buy the lands from the Indigenous people. But, since Indigenous people were destined for extinction or assimilation, the European title of preemption only had to await that eventual destiny to morph into a complete fee title.

The English Crown and colonists used the power of preemption over American Indians from the beginning of their settlements in North America. All of the colonies enacted numerous laws to regulate the purchase and leasing of Indian lands because the colonies alleged they held the preemptive authority. In 1763, however, King George III attempted to reassert his preeminence in exercising the preemption power over Indian land purchases in the Royal Proclamation of 1763. The Articles Congress in 1783 and the new US government in 1790 also took absolute control over Indian land sales through preemption clauses in their governing documents, statutes, and treaties.

In 1792, Secretary of State Thomas Jefferson perfectly illustrated the definition of this element twice. First, he explained America's preemption right: 'our States, are inhabited by Indians holding justly the right of occupation, and leaving...to us only the claim of excluding other nations from among them, and of becoming ourselves the purchasers of such portions of land, from time to time, as they may choose to sell'.[31] Second, he explained the American preemption right over England and the Indian nations to the English ambassador when he stated to the ambassador that the United States had:

[a] right to preemption of their [Indian] lands; that is to say, the sole and exclusive right of purchasing from them whenever they should be willing to sell.... Did I suppose that the right of preemption prohibited any individual of another nation from purchasing lands which the Indians should be willing to sell? Certainly. We consider it as established by the usage of different nations into a kind of *Jus gentium* [international law] for America,

---

[30] A J Harrop, *England and New Zealand. From Tasman to the Taranaki War* (London: Methuen, 1926) 127.

[31] Letter from Thomas Jefferson to Messrs Carmichael & Short (14 October 1772), in Andrew A Lipscomb and Albert Ellery Bergh (eds), 13 *The Writings of Thomas Jefferson* (Washington DC: Thomas Jefferson Memorial Assoc, 1903) 416–17.

that a white nation settling down and declaring that such and such are their limits, makes an invasion of those limits by any other white nation an act of war, but gives no right of soil against the native possessors.[32]

In Canada, the right was enshrined in the Royal Proclamation whereby no private person could purchase Indian lands. However, as Lindberg explained in Chapter 4, the document essentially asserted protectionism but was in itself grounded in notions of superiority which it sought to protect Indigenous peoples from. In the 1887 case, *St Catharines Milling,* the Court declared:

Their possession, such as it was, can only be ascribed to the general provisions made by the royal proclamation in favour of all Indian tribes then living under the sovereignty and protection of the British Crown. That inference is, however, at variance with the terms of the instrument, which shew that the tenure of the Indians was a personal and usufructuary right, dependent upon the good will of the Sovereign.[33]

In New Zealand, the English expressly claimed this exact Discovery right. In article 2 of the Treaty of Waitangi, the British Crown negotiated for the right of preemption and the Māori expressly ceded this right to the Crown. In 1847, in the *Symonds* case, Justice Chapman reinforced the Queen's preemptive right in law, recognizing that the Queen acquired this right independent of the Treaty of Waitangi. The right of preemption was regarded as integral to the assertion of sovereignty. In the 1860s, the Crown waived its right of preemption in favour of establishing a court system empowered to regulate sales between Māori and settlers.[34] A new land status, Māori freehold land, was established. However, in regard to land that the Crown wanted to own but that Māori wished to retain, the common law developed to assert that the colonizing power acquired a radical title or underlying title that was subject to existing Māori rights in the land. Even though those rights are not supposed to be extinguished in times of peace other than by the free consent of the Māori occupiers, the Crown could, if it deemed it necessary, take such drastic action in specific circumstances to compulsorily acquire the land but must pay proper compensation. A modern day example of a breach of this common law rule was the enactment of the Foreshore and Seabed Act 2004. In this statute, the government purported ownership of the foreshore and seabed in return for almost no compensation. The government was able to do this because in New Zealand the government is supreme.

The obvious exception is Australia. Despite the British there being aware of the US jurisprudence, including *Johnson* and *Cherokee Nation*, the British did not accept continuing Aboriginal property interests in land following 'discovery'. It also did not accept as valid any land purchases between individual British

---

[32] Notes of a Conversation with George Hammond (3 June 1792), in 1 *The Writings of Thomas Jefferson*, 197 (New York: G P Putnam's Sons, Paul Leicester Ford (ed), 1892).

[33] *St Catharine's Milling and Lumber Company v The Queen* (1887) 13 SCR 577 (also reported: 4 Cart BNA 127) (a Supreme Court case), (54) 549. This case was later affirmed by the Privy Council.

[34] See eg Native Lands Act 1862, No 42.

and Aboriginal land owners. The British Crown simply asserted that through first discovery they had gained the complete fee title to the lands of Indigenous peoples—in a literal sense. While some doubt about this assertion began to mount in the courts in 1970s,[35] the fiction remained until the 1992 High Court case, *Mabo v Queensland (No 2).*[36]

4. Indian/Native title

Under European and American claims to preemption and title, it is no wonder that Indigenous peoples were considered by Euro-American legal systems to have lost the full ownership of their land. American Indians were considered to have only retained the right to occupy and use their lands. This right was still a valuable property right that could have endured forever if Natives never consented to sell their lands. However, under their restricted title, Natives could only sell to the government that held the power of preemption.

The English Crown and colonists used this principle against American Indians from the beginning. The Crown granted legal estates in lands in North America while almost totally ignoring Indian ownership. In the Royal Proclamation of 1763, however, George III demonstrated a more correct understanding of the restricted Indian title and that he would have to buy the remaining Indian property rights before he could acquire possession and use rights. The colonial governments also understood this principle. They all enacted numerous statutes that demonstrated the restricted Indian title and in which they authorized and ratified sales of Indian lands. Under Euro-American legal thinking and Discovery, Native peoples and their governments did not possess the right to sell their lands without the permission of the colonial governments. Thereafter, the new American state governments immediately imposed these same restrictions on the Indian nations.[37] The federal government also applied the idea of Indian title and restricted tribal real property rights. In 1810, the US Supreme Court defined some aspects of the limited rights possessed by the Indian nations when it held that the states could transfer their future titles in Indian lands even while the Tribes still possessed the lands.[38] In 1955, when the Court was faced with the question of Native land ownership in Alaska, it stated that the Tribe in question held only a limited right of occupancy: 'after the coming of the white man [the tribe held] what is sometimes termed original Indian title or permission from

[35] See *Miliripum v Nabalco Pty Ld and the Commonwealth* (1971) FLR 141 and *Coe v Commonwealth* (1979) 53 ALJR 403.

[36] *Mabo v Queensland (No 2)* (1992) 175 CLR 1.

[37] For example, a 1835 Tennessee Supreme Court case demonstrates the restrictions states imposed on Indian land holdings under the Discovery principle of Indian title and the resulting loss of economic value to Indians and their governments. *Tennessee v Forman* 16 Tenn (1 Yer) 256 (1835).

[38] *Fletcher v Peck*, 10 US (6 Cranch) 87, 138–9, 142–3 (1810) ('[T]he nature of the Indian title is not such as to be absolutely repugnant to [seisin] in fee on the part of the state').

the whites to occupy'.[39] Indian or Native title is obviously a limited form of real property ownership not equal to the fee simple title.

In Canada, in some provinces, there was an extensive history of treaty making that set about reserving small parcels of land for Aboriginal peoples. For example, in the Douglas Treaties a common term stated that:

[t]he conditions of our understanding of this sale is this, that our village sites and enclosed fields are to be kept for our own use, for the use of our children, and for those who may follow after us and the land shall be properly surveyed hereafter. It is understood, however, that the land itself, with these small exceptions, becomes the entire property of the white people for ever; it is also understood that we are at liberty to hunt over the unoccupied lands, and to carry on our fisheries as formerly.[40]

Contemporary case law continues to limit Native title. For example, the Supreme Court, in *Delgamuukw*, held that provinces cannot extinguish Aboriginal title but that they could infringe Aboriginal title.[41] The case established that presumed depleted sovereignty of the Indigenous nations; the Court wrote that:

Aboriginal title is a burden on the Crown's underlying title. However, the Crown did not gain this title until it asserted sovereignty over the land in question. Because it does not make sense to speak of a burden on the underlying title before that title existed, aboriginal title crystallized at the time sovereignty was asserted.[42]

In Australia, the course of history played out distinctly differently to that in North America. With the British claiming full fee simple title of the lands, there was no scope to acknowledge Native title. This legal position would not alter until the High Court handed down the decision in the *Mabo* case in 1992.

In stark contrast to Australia in particular, New Zealand, perhaps at the right end of a colonial recognition spectrum (with Australia at the far left end representing non-recognition), established a unique native land title system. For the first 20 years after the British Crown and Māori chiefs signed the Treaty of Waitangi, Māori could only sell, lease, or gift their land to the Crown in accordance with the right of preemption agreed to in the Treaty in 1840. In the 1860s, the colonial government waived its right of preemption in favour of Māori being able to freely alienate their land (similar to the opening of lands for colonial settlement in the United States pursuant to the Allotment Act of 1887). The catch to the Crown's decision to waive its right of preemption was that Māori first had to obtain a certificate of title from the newly established Māori Land Court to prove that they owned the land.[43] Once they had a certificate of title, they could sell, lease, or gift their land to whoever they wished. The system sought to transform

---

[39] *Tee-Hit-Ton Indians v United States* 348 US 272, 279 (1955).

[40] Douglas Treaties—Conveyance of Land to Hudson's Bay Company by Indian Tribes (1 May 1850) <http://www.ainc-inac.gc.ca/al/hts/tgu/pubs/trtydg/trtydg-eng.asp>.

[41] *Delgamuukw v British Columbia* [1997] SCJ 108 (a Supreme Court of Canada case) see paras 160 and 165.   [42] Ibid para 145.

[43] See Native Lands Act 1862 No 42 and Native Lands Act 1865 No LXXI.

land communally held by Māori families into individualized titles derived from the Crown. The early legislation was premised on encouraging as much alienation of Māori land as possible. Today, only a very small portion of Māori freehold land remains. New legislation now encourages the retention and development of that land by its Māori owners. Currently, nearly all transactions involving Māori freehold land need to be confirmed by the Māori Land Court, making it time-consuming and costly to even contemplate sale or lease.[44] Thus, 'Māori freehold' title, like 'Indian title' or 'Native title' in North America, is still considered today a limited ownership right.

5. Indigenous nations limited sovereign and commercial rights

The inherent sovereign powers of Indigenous nations and the rights of Indigenous peoples to free trade and diplomatic international relations were also limited by Discovery. After a first discovery by Euro-Americans, Indigenous nations were only supposed to deal with the European or American government that had discovered them. The Crown exerted this alleged authority in the charters it issued when it established governmental authority, jurisdiction, courts, and trade protocols in North America. All the colonies enacted numerous laws exercising exclusive control of the trade with Indians and tribes. The English colonies, in fact, objected to Dutch colonists trading with America Indians, and Dutch colonies in turn objected to Swedish colonists trading with Indians, all based on this element of Discovery.

The American states attempted to control Indian sovereign and commercial powers. The federal government also tried to take complete control of these activities because the Constitution granted it sole authority to engage in treaty making and commercial relations with the Indian nations. Additionally, Secretary of State Thomas Jefferson again demonstrated the correct understanding of this element in his 1792 conversation with the British ambassador. Jefferson explained the power the United States held over the Indian nations: 'A right of regulating the commerce between them and the whites. [Hammond asked do the English traders have to stay out? Jefferson said yes.]'[45]

President George Washington utilized this element. In 1795, at his urging, Congress created federal trading houses to totally control the Indian trade. Furthermore, in hundreds of treaties the federal government and tribes agreed that the United States would control the Indian trade and protect tribes in many ways. The Supreme Court came to interpret these provisions as creating a trust responsibility that requires the federal government to care for tribes in a ward/guardian relationship and that defines Indian tribes as 'domestic dependent nations.'[46]

---

[44] See Maori Land Act 1993/Te Ture Whenua Maori Act 1993, No 4.

[45] Thomas Jefferson, 'Notes of a Conversation with George Hammond', in Andrew A Lipscomb and Albert Ellery Bergh (eds), 7 *The Writings of Thomas Jefferson* (1903) 328–9.

[46] *Cherokee Nation v Georgia* 30 US (5 Pet) 1, 17 (1831).

In Canada, the Supreme Court has developed an Aboriginal rights test that describes Indigenous peoples as possessing something not quite as formal as sovereignty: practices, traditions, and cultures. Cases such as *Van der Peet*[47] stand for the proposition that to be an Aboriginal right, a practice, custom, or tradition must be one which is integral to a distinctive culture. As Lindberg states in Chapter 5, time dating Indigenous activities at a 'pre-contact' period freezes the rights so that proof of existing rights becomes more and more difficult to provide as the right becomes more contemporized. For example, contemporary Canadian case law continues to hold that the treaties protect subsistence level activities and not widespread commercial activities.[48]

In Australia, there has been no legal or political recognition of the sovereignty of Aboriginal people. Even the *Mabo* case, in finding that a Native title existed that was effectively defined by the laws and customs of Aboriginal people, avoided discussion of any implications for the recognition of the sovereignty of Aboriginal people. As a consequence, there has been no recognition of any jurisdiction vesting in Aboriginal people, even over areas where Native title has been established, and no building of Indigenous legal institutions like the tribal courts and governments established in the United States.

Similarly, in New Zealand, post the signing of the Treaty of Waitangi, the colonial government recognized no sovereign power held by Māori. It was not accepted that Māori retained any sovereignty, government, or commercial rights. Māori were simply to become British subjects as articulated in article 3 of the Treaty: 'In consideration thereof Her Majesty the Queen of England extends to the Natives of New Zealand Her royal protection and imparts to them all the Rights and Privileges of British Subjects.'[49] This approach meant that, in contrast to policies advanced in North America, in New Zealand there were no consistent efforts made to geographically isolate Māori by drawing lines to denote reserves. Māori were simply regarded as 'noble savages' who could be hastily Christianized and assimilated, thus leading to the demise of the separate Māori race.

6. Contiguity

This element granted Euro-Americans a Discovery and preemption claim over very large areas contiguous to their actual settlements in the 'New World'. Furthermore, contiguity held that the discovery of the mouth of a river created a claim over the entire drainage system of the river. The shapes of the Louisiana Territory, the western drainage system of the Mississippi River and the Oregon

---

[47] *R v Van der Peet*, [1996] 2 SCR 507 (a Supreme Court of Canada case).
[48] *R v Marshall* [1999] SCJ 55 (a Supreme Court of Canada case).
[49] Treaty of Waitangi, art 3, 6 February 1840, available at: <http://www.nzhistory.net.nz/category/tid/133>.

Country, and the drainage system of the Columbia River demonstrate the scope of this aspect of Discovery.

The English Crown and its colonial governments in North America used this Discovery element against other European and Indigenous governments. The royal charters claimed to grant property rights over vast areas of land, including islands and ocean surrounding colonial settlements. The charters granted rights as far as the head waters of many rivers and the contiguous lands. Thereafter, the colonies claimed their borders to the furthest degree possible based on contiguity. For example, the English colonies objected to Dutch colonies being established in America because they were within areas the English claimed based on contiguity.

Later, American states relied on this element when they cited the charters as setting their western borders at the Pacific Ocean. On the federal side, Thomas Jefferson demonstrated the use of contiguity in his research to determine the size of the Louisiana Territory. He relied on the drainage system of the Mississippi River and tried to determine the course and location of the tributaries of that river. Jefferson even hinted in his research that Louisiana gave the United States a claim as far as the Pacific. Notwithstanding his thoughts on this topic, there is no question that a House Committee claimed in 1804 that the Louisiana Territory stretched to the Pacific due to contiguity.[50]

Other American politicians also used contiguity to claim the Oregon Country. In 1819, Senator Thomas Hart Benton claimed American ownership due to '[c]ontiguity & continuity of settlement & possession'.[51] By the mid-1840s, President Polk and most Americans defined the Oregon Country as being the entire drainage system of the Columbia River, reaching far into present day British Columbia. American diplomats argued with England that the United States owned the entire Oregon Country on the ground of contiguity.

In Australia, the symbolic claiming of land was taken to have included large, unseen tracts of land. It was assumed that Captain Cook's claims in his 1770 expedition along the eastern coast of Australia included the inland that was not seen. Captain Phillip reasserted the British claim to the eastern part of the continent with his symbolic gestures that only took place where he decided to establish the colony that would become Sydney. Colonies were set up in what is now Victoria, Tasmania, and Queensland and it was also a matter of priority that a colony be established on the western coast of the continent to ensure that the British claim would be absolute and unchallenged.

In comparison, in New Zealand, the colonial government sought ownership of land via purchase from Māori or legislation permitting wide-scale confiscation. However, in regard to lakes and rivers, the owners of land abutting these waters,

---

[50] 13 Annals of Congress, 8th Cong, 1st Sess p 1124 (8 March 1804).
[51] 1 Thomas Hart Benton, *Thirty Years' View: or A History of the Working of the American Government for Thirty Years from 1820–1850* (1856, New York: Greenwood Press reprint 1968) 54.

for example, used the common law to justify exclusive rights to the lake's fisheries.[52] A similar trend has occurred in Canada.

7. *Terra nullius*

Discovery also defined lands that were not possessed or occupied by any person or nation, or that were not being used in a fashion that European legal systems approved, as being 'vacant' and available for first discovery claims.

The English Crown and colonists used *terra nullius* to claim the lands of American Indians. Thus, the Crown claimed the authority to grant rights in the 'deserts' and in the 'deserted', 'waste and desolate', 'hitherto uncultivated' lands 'which are not inhabited already' in America.[53] The colonists also relied on *terra nullius* because they thought, for example, that New Jersey was 'an uninhabited country found out by British subjects'.[54] For example, a 1765 history of New Jersey agreed and stated that English claims to New Jersey were based on first discovery, possession, and 'the well known *Jus Gentium*, Law of Nations, that whatever waste or uncultivated country is discovered, it is the right of that prince who had been at the charge of the discovery'.[55]

The United States used this element when arguing to England that the Pacific Northwest was a 'vacant territory'.[56] The US Supreme Court also relied on *terra nullius* in discussing Discovery.[57] Finally, in 1895, Senator Henry Cabot Lodge injected the idea of *terra nullius* into the 1895 Republican Party platform. The platform called for America to expand into 'all the waste places of the earth' and noted that Cuba was only 'sparsely settled'.[58]

Canadian case law has rarely dealt with the notion of *terra nullius* explicitly.[59] Nonetheless, the implicitly understood imperial construction of Indigenous primitivism remains affixed to Indigenous institutions, laws, and economic activities. As Lindberg has so eloquently put it in Chapters 4 and 5, doctrinal

---

[52] See Ben White, *Inland Waterways: Lakes: Rangahaua Whanui National Theme Q* (Wellington: Waitangi Tribunal, 1998), available at: <http://www.waitangitribunal.govt.nz/doclibrary/public/researchwhanui/theme/q/white/TITLEpp.pdf>.   [53] 1 *Foundations*, 22–3.

[54] *Arnold v Mundy*, 6 NJL 1, 83 (NJ Sup Ct 1821).

[55] Samuel Smith, *The History of the Colony of Nova-Caesaria or New Jersey: Containing an Account of its First Settlement, Progressive Improvements, the Original & Present Constitution & Other Events, to the Year 1721: With Some Particulars Since; And a Short View of Its Present State New Jersey* (1765, Trenton, NJ: William S Sharp, reprint 1890) 7–8.

[56] Robert Miller, *Native America, Discovered and Conquered: Thomas Jefferson, Lewis and Clark, and Manifest Destiny* (Westport, CN & London: Praeger Publishers, 2006) 153.

[57] *Martin v Waddell's Lessee*, 41 US (1 Pet) 367, 409 (1842). See also *United States v Rogers* 45 US (4 How) 567, 572 (1846).

[58] Julius W Pratt, 'John L. O'Sullivan and Manifest Destiny' (1933) 14 New York History 213, 234.

[59] L'Heureux-Dube J, in dissent in *R v Van der Peet* (1996) SCJ 77 (Supreme Court of Canada) at para 106 discusses the concept briefly. *Delgamuukw v British Columbia* (BCCA) (1993) BCJ 1395 (a case of the British Columbia Court of Appeal, which was overturned by the Supreme Court of Canada) referred to it briefly at para 659 in the context of defining the term and critically analysing it in relation to notions of primitivism.

understandings of Indigenous institutions, laws, and economic activities has mythologized Aboriginal peoples in Canada in some sort of undeveloped, individualistic, ideological *terra nullius*.

In Australia, the application of the doctrine of *terra nullius* has perhaps been the most insidious. Politically and judicially, the doctrine of *terra nullius* was reiterated through until the early 1990s with disastrous consequences for the Indigenous Australians. Interestingly, as Behrendt explained in Chapter 6, this hard stance was not consistently thought appropriate. Some brave judges held otherwise. For example, in an 1829 decision of the Supreme Court of New South Wales, one judge held '... I know of no reason human, or divine, which ought to justify us in interfering with their institutions even if such interference were practicable'.[60] In 1992, the High Court of Australia, in *Mabo*, finally overturned the doctrine of *terra nullius*. As discussed in Chapter 7, Justice Brennan, who wrote the leading judgment in the case, recognized that a continuing 'injustice' would eventuate if the common law were to continue to embrace *terra nullius*. The Court was not prepared to do this.

In contrast to Australia, the history of *terra nullius* in New Zealand has not been so clear-cut. In 2003, New Zealand's Court of Appeal stated that 'New Zealand was never thought to be terra nullius'.[61] However, the reasoning in the 1877 *Wi Parata* case is rife with *terra nullius* discourse. For example, the Court asserted that Māori had no form of civil government or any settled system of law, possessed few political relations to each other, and cited with approval Lord Normanby's August 1839 despatch to Captain Hobson that Māori were 'incompetent to act, or even to deliberate, in concert'.[62] In describing the Māori tribes as 'petty'[63] and as 'incapable of performing the duties, and therefore of assuming the rights, of a civilized community',[64] the Court essentially declared the country *terra nullius*. Moreover, the Crown's assumption of ownership of the foreshore and seabed in 2004 is perhaps an example of a revived *terra nullius* claim. In 2004, the government passed legislation claiming ownership of land under salt water without due regard to compensation for Māori because it believed, as was argued by Paul McHugh, that the foreshore and seabed occupies a 'special juridical space'.[65] McHugh advanced this reasoning in the Waitangi Tribunal. For example, he asserted that:

at common law, the Crown's sovereignty over the foreshore and seabed amounts to a 'bundle of rights' less than full ownership; therefore, the common law doctrine of aboriginal

---

[60] Justice Dowling (dissenting) in *R v Ballard* 1829 Supreme Court of New South Wales.
[61] *Attorney-General v Ngati Apa* [2003] 3 NZLR 643.
[62] *Wi Parata v Bishop of Wellington* (1877) 3 NZ Jur (NS) 72, 77.   [63] Ibid.
[64] Ibid.
[65] Waitangi Tribunal, *Report on the Crown's Foreshore and Seabed Policy* (Wellington: Waitangi Tribunal, 2004) 50 (quoting testimony of Paul McHugh), available at: <http://www.waitangi-tribunal.govt.nz>.

title, which has effect because of and at the moment of acquisition of sovereignty, cannot recognize customary rights that are greater than those of the sovereign.[66]

The Tribunal accepted this reasoning: 'the law cannot recognise for Indigenous people what it does not recognize for the sovereign power. It is a variant of the legal maxim: you cannot give what you do not have.'[67] In other words, the foreshore and seabed became *terra nullius*, only capable of Crown ownership.

8. Christianity

The religion of Europeans, English colonists, and American citizens was a significant aspect of Discovery. Under the Doctrine, non-Christian people did not have the same rights to land, property, sovereignty, and self-determination as Christians.

The English Crown and colonists in North America overtly used this element against American Indians. The Crown called on the Christian God's assistance and authority to colonize America, to claim Indian lands, and to expand the Christian flock by conversions. The colonies relied heavily on this element to justify their attempts to control Native people.[68]

The United States and the original 13 states also used religion to justify dominating Indian nations and trying to assimilate Indians into American society. The United States, for example, turned over the operation of many reservations and the education of Indian children to Christian denominations, and even granted tribal lands to churches. In contrast, Indian religious beliefs and ceremonies were officially ridiculed, suppressed, and outlawed for over 100 years.

In Canada, residential schools (affiliated with different Churches and supported by the Canadian government to varying degrees) were established on reserve to ensure that the tenets of the Doctrine were expanded and expounded to all Indian (and in some cases non-status Indians and Metis) students who attended them. Canada's indoctrination of Indigenous youth occurred through a rigorous programme which, in many cases, required students to speak only English, participate in foreign religious rites and activities, cut their hair, and participate in economic activities geared at 'civilizing' them. Generations of Indigenous children unlearned the principles of good parenting, Indigenous citizenship and culture—an impact which continues to affect Indigenous nations to this day. Indian Act provisions banning potlatch and sundance ceremonies made Indigenous spiritualities Canadian illegal and many of the ceremonies were reported to be lost or have gone underground.

[66] Ibid 52 (quoting testimony of Paul McHugh).
[67] Ibid 60. For a critique of this position see generally Jacinta Ruru, 'What Could Have Been? The Common Law Doctrine of Native Title in Land Under Salt Water in Australia & Aotearoa/New Zealand' (2006) 32 Monash Univ L Rev 116.
[68] See eg Amy E Den Ouden, *Beyond Conquest: Native Peoples and the Struggle for History in New England* (Lincoln, NE: University Nebraska Press, 2005).

In Australia, the need to civilize Aboriginal tribes was a convenient tool to assist with dispossession and the removal of Aboriginal people from their lands. It should be pointed out, however, that in the Australian context, while the Christianizing mission was used to promote the colonial agenda of expansion, religious groups were also some of the strongest advocates for the more compassionate and for the recognition of their rights.

Similarly, in New Zealand, a significant component of colonization involved the mandate to Christianize Māori, including the banning of Māori religious beliefs and ceremonies.[69]

9. Civilization

The assumed superiority of Euro-American cultures and civilizations was an important part of Discovery. Euro-Americans thought that God had directed them to bring civilized ways and education to Indigenous peoples and to exercise paternalism and guardianship powers over them.

From the beginning of North American explorations, the Crown and colonists justified the domination of American Indians and English legal rights on the assumption that they possessed the superior civilization and that Indians were savage barbarians. The American states and the United States also actively applied this Discovery element against American Indians. These governments attempted to destroy Indian people and their cultures, legal systems, and governments and make them into Euro-American clones. As one example, in 1895, the Republican Party platform stated the goal to expand America into 'all the waste places of the earth' because that would be a great gain 'for civilization and the advancement of the race'.[70]

The same ideology and actions were evident in Canada. For instance, in writing about the Indian Act, in Chapter 5, Lindberg asserted that the Canadian imperial legal regime imposed the imperial Doctrinal racialized philosophy: Indians are incapable of making governmental decisions related to their members/citizens. As this imposed legislative administration was predicated on beliefs about Indigenous inferiority and Canadian supremacy, those beliefs, in some ways, extend to the present day manifestation of the Indian Act.

In Australia, the prevalent ideologies that assumed white racial superiority had a strong role to play in the dispossession of Aboriginal people and the failure to recognize their laws, governance structures, and rights. Not only did it provide the basis for arguments that Aboriginal culture was too primitive and uncivilized to be able to establish that there were laws or governance structures that could be recognized, it also assisted in supporting the view that it was inevitable

---

[69] See Tohunga Suppression Act 1908, and Ani Mikaere, 'Cultural Invasion Continued: The Ongoing Colonisation of Tikanga Maori' (2005) 8(2) YB of NZ Jurisprudence Special Issue—Te Purenga 134.   [70] Pratt, note 58, 234.

that Aboriginal people, due to their inferiority, would eventually die out in the face of expanding European civilization. Aboriginal people in Australia were not just viewed detrimentally when compared to Europeans, there was also a view that, compared to other Indigenous peoples, Australia's Aboriginal population was seen as being, in Darwinian terms, on the lowest rung of the evolutionary ladder.

In New Zealand, this idea of civilization was inherent in many of the colonial actions. For instance, by the 1860s the colonial government had began to legislate against the use of Māori language, customs, and laws. The Māori Land Court was established with the express purpose to advance and civilize the Natives. The Court in the *Wi Parata* case justified not recognizing the Treaty of Waitangi or the doctrine of Native title because Māori were 'barbarians' and 'uncivilised'. Today, this reasoning is no longer accepted as precedent. In 2003, the Court of Appeal overruled *Wi Parata*.[71] No contemporary case law refers to Māori as uncivilized. Instead, the country is grappling with what it means if the government now accepts that all land in New Zealand was once owned by Māori. Currently, a comprehensive settlement process is taking place in New Zealand whereby the Crown is seeking to address and compensate for historical breaches of the Treaty of Waitangi.[72]

10. Conquest

This element asserts that Native lands and legal titles could be taken by military actions. The word was also used as a term of art to describe the rights Europeans gained automatically over Indigenous nations by making a first discovery. It was most overtly prevalent in the United States and New Zealand.

The Crown's grant of legal estates in America's Indian lands illustrates the implied use of this element. For example, in 1751 English officials expressly used this element when they claimed that Indian tribes had lost the ownership of their lands due to supporting the French in a losing war. The colony of Connecticut made a similar claim for over a century that it acquired title to Indian lands due to its victory in the Pequot War of 1637.

The US Articles of Confederation Congress also utilized the element of conquest after 1783–1784 when federal officials told tribes that they had lost the ownership of their lands due to fighting for the British in the Revolutionary War. Subsequently, this same Congress then expressly placed the element of conquest in the Northwest Ordinance of 1787, which stated that a 'just' war can take Indian title. In 1848, the US Congress then applied the Northwest Ordinance and the Discovery element of conquest to the Oregon Country.[73] The US Supreme Court

[71] *Ngati Apa*, note 51.
[72] See Government's Office of Treaty Settlements, available at: <http://www.ots.govt.nz>.
[73] See An Act to Establish the Territorial Government of Oregon, 9 Stat 323, 329 § 14 (1848).

defined this element in 1823,[74] and the federal courts have relied on it as part of Discovery ever since.

Similarly, in New Zealand, particularly in the 1860s and 1870s, the British unleashed war on North Island Māori to take land. Legislation was passed to legitimize the taking of Māori land even in instances of British military defeats.[75]

In Australia, there was strong resistance to the expansion of European colonies by Aboriginal people (and similarly in Canada). In Australia, while there were some early indications that members of the judiciary may have formed the view that Aboriginal people had an established and coherent system of laws that gave rise to a limited jurisdiction and were also sympathetic towards the position of Aboriginal people in light of their dispossession, it was firmly established within the colonial legal system by the 1830s that, as a consequence of British acquisition of Australia, Aboriginal people retained no legal rights to land or jurisdiction.

11. Summary

In sum, it is striking but not at all surprising how similar the use of the elements of Discovery is in the histories of Aotearoa New Zealand, Australia, Canada, and the United States. The comparative framework illustrates graphically just how deeply rooted the legal fictions of Discovery are in our legal systems. The Doctrine always has been, since European settlement, and is still today part of the property and constitutional law regimes of all four of our countries. While there are slight variations, the differences mostly arise from the different social and cultural contexts of the Indigenous peoples. For instance, even though there is a Treaty of Waitangi, Māori Land Court, and Waitangi Tribunal in New Zealand, the underlying tenor that the Parliament relies on to legitimize itself is the dialogue of covert Discovery, most recently evidenced in the Foreshore and Seabed Act 2004. Equally, notwithstanding hundreds of treaty promises by the United States to protect American Indian tribal property and Indian rights, and the US Declaration of Independence's statement that 'all men are created equal', American history demonstrates the exact opposite treatment of American Indian governments, Indian people, and their property rights by the United States. This is similarly true for what happened in Canada and Australia.

It is not surprising that the legal histories of Aotearoa New Zealand, Australia, Canada, and the United States in regard to their Indigenous peoples are so similar. This is a natural result of basing their conduct towards, and their claims against,

---

[74] *Johnson v M'Intosh*, 21 US (8 Wheat) 543 (1823) 589: 'The title by conquest is acquired and maintained by force.' See also *Tee-Hit-Ton Indians v United States* 348 US 272 (1955) 289–90: 'Every American schoolboy knows that the savage tribes of this continent were deprived of their ancestral ranges by force and that…it was not a sale but the conquerors' will that deprived them of their land.'   [75] See James Belich, *The New Zealand Wars* (Auckland: Penguin, 1998).

the Indigenous people on the Doctrine of Discovery. In fact, we are surprised to find any differences at all between the applications of Discovery in our countries. The numerous similarities are to be expected because all four of our countries share very similar colonization stories. If one understands the international law Doctrine of Discovery, it makes perfect sense that the English colonists in these countries have applied the same international legal principles against Indigenous peoples in the ways that they did.

Apparently, Europeans believed they possessed the only valid religions, civilizations, governments, laws, and cultures, and Providence must have intended that these people and their institutions should dominate Indigenous people in their countries. As a result, the governmental, property, and human rights of Indigenous peoples were almost totally disregarded as Discovery directed European colonial expansion in our countries. Even in modern times, these assumptions remain dangerous legal fictions.

In focusing on the Doctrine of Discovery, this book has reinforced what we already know: 'legal systems develop in close contact to others: new ideas may evolve within one line of tradition and then spread quickly, with great effect on other legal systems'.[76] The similarities are rife between Aotearoa New Zealand, Australia, Canada, and the United States—countries in the northern and southern hemispheres—in their treatment of their Indigenous peoples and their definitions of the legal rights of their Indigenous citizens. The common understanding is potent and illustrates the complexity that will be involved in any efforts to decolonize the legal systems in English colonies such as these countries.

C. Conclusion

The comparative law framework adopted in this concluding chapter illustrates the pervasiveness of the Doctrine of Discovery on an international scale and more relevantly in our countries. Moreover, Discovery is not just an esoteric and interesting relic of our histories. It continues to impact Indigenous peoples today in Australia, Canada, Aotearoa New Zealand, the United States, and many other countries around the world. For example, the Doctrine continues to play a very significant role in restricting the property, governmental, and self-determination rights of Indigenous peoples. The cultural, racial, and religious justifications that led to the development of Discovery raise serious doubts about the validity of the continued application of the Doctrine in modern day Indigenous affairs. And, in returning to the opening remarks in our Introductory chapter, this history

---

[76] Nils Jansen, 'Comparative Law and Comparative Knowledge' in Mathias Reimann and Reinhard Zimmermann (eds), *The Oxford Handbook of Comparative Law* (Oxford: Oxford University Press, 2006) 324, 339.

of English colonization and use of Discovery in the history and laws of our four countries is about the only explanation for why our four 'liberal' 'democratic' countries were the only ones in the world to vote against the Declaration on the Rights of Indigenous Peoples. The Doctrine of Discovery is a dangerous myth that must be acknowledged if ex-English colonies wish to realize respectful reconciled relationships with their Indigenous peoples.

Bibliography

AUSTRALIAN CHAPTERS

Aboriginal and Torres Strait Islander Commission, *Recognition, Rights and Reform: A Report to Government on Native Title Social Justice Measures* (Canberra: Australian Government Publishing Service, 1995).

Banner, Stuart, *Possessing the Pacific: Land, Settlers and Indigenous People from Australia to Alaska*. (Cambridge: Harvard University Press, 2007).

Behrendt, Larissa, *Aboriginal Dispute Resolution: A Step Towards Self-Determination and Community Autonomy* (Annandale: The Federation Press, 2005).

Behrendt, Larissa and Loretta Kelly *Resolving Indigenous Disputes: Land Conflict and Beyond* (Annandale: The Federation Press, 2008).

British Parliamentary Papers: Anthropology: Aborigines (Shannon: Irish University Press, 1968–1969).

Broome, Richard, *Aboriginal Australians: Black Responses to White Dominance, 1788–2001* (Sydney: Allen and Unwin, 3rd edn, 2001).

Castles, Alex C, *An Introduction to Australian Legal History* (Sydney: Law Book Company, 1970).

Collingridge, Vanessa, *Documents of Australian History* (Scoresby, Victoria: Five Mile Press, 2008).

Elder, Bruce, *Blood on the Wattle: Massacres and Maltreatment of Australian Aborigines Since 1788* (Brookvale, NSW: National Book Distributors, 1992).

Flannery, Tim (ed), *Watkin Tench, 1788* (Melbourne: Text Publishing, 2009).

Historical Records of New South Wales, Volume I.

Knaplund, Paul, *James Stephens and the British Colonial System, 1813–1847* (Madison: Wisconsin Press, 1953).

Lake, Marilyn, *Faith: Faith Bandler, Gentle Activist* (Sydney: Allen & Unwin, 2002).

Lawlor, Robert, *Voices of the First Day* (Rochester, VT: Inner Traditions, 1991).

Reynolds, Henry, *The Other Side of the Frontier: Aboriginal resistance to the European invasion of Australia* (Melbourne: Penguin, 1982).

Reynolds, Henry, *Frontier: Aborigines, Settlers and Land* (Sydney: Allen & Unwin, 1987).

Reynolds, Henry, *The Law of the Land* (Melbourne: Penguin, 1987).

Reynolds, Henry, *Aboriginal Sovereignty: Reflections on Race, State and Nation* (Sydney: Allen & Unwin, 1996).

Ryan, Lyndall, *Aboriginal Tasmanians* (Sydney: Allen & Unwin, 1996).

Sydney Morning Herald (11 April 1998 and 27 May 1997).

The Age (1 December 1997).

Williams, George, *Human Rights Under the Australian Constitution* (Melbourne: Oxford University Press, 2000).

CANADIAN CHAPTERS

Asch, Michael (ed), *Aboriginal and Treaty Rights in Canada: Essays on Law, Equality, and Respect* (Vancouver: UBC Press, 1997).

Borrows, John, 'Constitutional Law from a First Nation Perspective: Self-Government and the Royal Proclamation' (1994) 28 Univ of British Columbia L Rev 1.

Borrows, John, 'Sovereignty's Alchemy: An Analysis of Delgamuukw v British Columbia' (1999) 37:3 Osgoode Hall LJ 538.

Butt, Emma C and Mary C Hurley, *Specific Claims In Canada* (Ottawa: Law and Government Division, 2006).

Cardinal, Harold and Walter Hildebrandt, *Our Dream is That Our Peoples Will One Day Be Clearly Recognized as Nations* (Calgary: University of Calgary Press, 2006).

Christie, Gordon, 'Aboriginal Rights, Aboriginal Culture, and Protection' (1998) 36 Osgoode Hall LJ 447.

Department of Indian Affairs and Northern Development, *In All Fairness: A Native Claims Policy—Comprehensive Claims (Ottawa:* Department of Indian Affairs and Northern Development, 1981).

Department of Indian Affairs and Northern Development, *Comprehensive Land Claims Policy*, (Ottawa: Department of Indian Affairs and Northern Development, 1986).

Furi, Megan and Jill Wherrett, *Indian Status and Band Membership Issues* (Ottawa: Political and Social Affairs Division of the Government of Canada, 1996, revised 2003).

Hanke, Lewis, *Aristotle and the American Indians: A Study in Race Prejudice in the Modern World* (London: Hollis and Carter, 1959).

Harrisse, Henry, *John Cabot, The Discoverer Of North America And Sebastian, His Son A Chapter Of The Maritime History Of England Under The Tudors, 1496–1557* (London: Stevens, 1896).

Hildebrandt, Walter, Dorothy First Rider, Sarah Carter & the Treaty 7 Elders, and Tribal Council, *The True Spirit and Original Intent of Treaty 7* (Montreal: McGill-Queen's University Press, 1996).

Indian and Northern Affairs Canada, 'The Government of Canada's Approach to Implementation of the Inherent Right and the Negotiation of Aboriginal Self-Government.'

Macklem, Patrick, 'Normative Dimensions of an Aboriginal Right of Self-Government' (1995) 21 Queen's LJ 173.

Macklem, Patrick, 'What is International Human Rights Law? Three Applications of a Distributive Account' (2007) 52 McGill LJ 575.

McNeil, Kent, 'Aboriginal Title and Section 88 of the Indian Act' (2000) 34 Univ of British Columbia L Rev 159.

McNeil, Kent, 'Extinguishment of Aboriginal Title in Canada: Treaties, Legislation, and Judicial Discretion' (2001–02) 33 Ottawa L Rev 301.

McNeil, Kent, 'Section 91(24) Powers, the Inherent Right of Self-Government, and Canada's Fiduciary Obligations' (research paper prepared for the Office of the BC Regional Vice-Chief of the Assembly of First Nations 2002).

Miller, Robert J, *Native America, Discovered and Conquered: Thomas Jefferson, Lewis & Clark, and Manifest Destiny* (Westport, CT and London: Praeger Publishers, 2006).

Monture, Patricia, 'The Roles and Responsibilities of Aboriginal Women' (1992) 56 Sask L Rev 237.

Morris, Alexander, *The Treaties of Canada with the Indians of Manitoba and the North-West Territories, Including the Negotiations on Which They Were Based, and Other Information Relating Thereto* (Saskatoon: Fifth House Publishers, 1991).

Outstanding Business: A Native Claims Policy—Specific Claims (Ottawa: Minister of Supply and Services, 1982).

Price, Richard (ed), *The Spirit of the Alberta Indian Treaties* (Edmonton: University of Alberta Press, 1999).

Royal Commission on Aboriginal Peoples, *Treaty Making in the Spirit of Co-Existence: An Alternative To Extinguishment* (Ottawa: Royal Commission on Aboriginal Peoples, 1995).

Royal Commission on Aboriginal Peoples, *Report of the Royal Commission on Aboriginal Peoples: Looking Forward, Looking Back* (Ottawa: Canada Communication Group, Ottawa, 1996) Volume 1.

Sanders, Douglas, 'The Supreme Court of Canada and The "Legal And Political Struggle" Over Indigenous Rights' (1990) 22:3 Canadian Ethnic Studies 122.

Schoolcraft, Henry R, *The American Indians Their History, Condition And Prospects, From Original Notes And Manuscripts* (Buffalo: G H Derby, 1851).

Williams, Jr, Robert A, *The American Indian in Western Legal Thought: The Discourses of Conquest* (Oxford: Oxford University Press, 1990).

Williams, Jr, Robert A, 'Columbus's Legacy: The Rehnquist Court's Perpetuation of European Cultural Racism Against American Indian Tribes' (1992) 39 Fed B News & J 358.

Yukich, Kelly C, 'Aboriginal Rights in the Constitution and International Law' (1996) 30 University of British Columbia L Rev 235.

NEW ZEALAND CHAPTERS AND CONCLUDING CHAPTER

Adams, Peter, *The Fatal Necessity: British Intervention in New Zealand 1830–1847* (Auckland: Auckland University Press, 1977).

Andrew, Jessica, 'Administrative Review of the Treaty of Waitangi Settlement Process' (2008) 39 Victoria Univ of Wellington L Rev 225.

Banner, Stuart, *Possessing the Pacific: Land, Settlers, and Indigenous People from Australia to Alaska* (Cambridge: Harvard University Press, 2007).

Belich, James, 'The Governors and the Maori (1840–72)' in Keith Sinclair (ed), *The Oxford Illustrated History of New Zealand* (Auckland: Oxford University Press, 2nd edn, 1996).

Belich, James, *Making Peoples: A History of the New Zealanders from Polynesian Settlement to the End of the Nineteenth Century* (Auckland: Penguin Press, 1996).

Belich, James, *The New Zealand Wars* (Auckland: Penguin, 1998).

Boast, Richard, 'In Re Ninety Mile Beach Revisited: The Native Land Court and the Foreshore in New Zealand Legal History' (1993) 23 Victoria Univ of Wellington L Rev 145.

Boast, Richard, 'The Law and the Maori' in Peter Spiller, Jeremy Finn, and Richard Boast (eds), *A New Zealand Legal History* (Wellington: Brookers, 2nd edn, 2001).

Boast, Richard, *Foreshore and Seabed* (Wellington: LexisNexis, 2005).

Boast, Richard, 'Recognising Multi-Textualsim: Rethinking New Zealand's Legal History' (2006) 37 Victoria Univ of Wellington L Rev 547.

Boast, Richard, *Buying the Land, Selling the Land: Governments and Maori Land in the North Island 1865–1921* (Wellington: Victoria University Press, 2008).

Boast, Richard, with Andrew Erueti, Doug McPhail, and Norman F Smith, *Maori Land Law* (Wellington: Lexis Nexis, 2nd edn, 2004).

Borrows, John, *Recovering Canada: The Resurgence of Indigenous Law* (Toronto: University of Toronto Press, 2002).

Brookfield, F M Jock, 'The Waitangi Tribunal and the Whanganui river-bed' (2000) 1 New Zealand L Rev 9.

Brookfield, F M Jock, 'Maori Claims and the "Special" Juridical Nature of Foreshore and Seabed' (2005) New Zealand L Rev 179.

Brookfield, F M Jock, *Waitangi & Indigenous Rights. Revolution, Law & Legitimation* (Auckland: Auckland University Press, 2nd edn, 2006).

Byrnes, Giselle, *The Waitangi Tribunal and New Zealand History* (Auckland: Oxford University Press, 2004).

Calman, Ross and AW Reed, *Reed Book of Maori Mythology* (Wellington: Reed Books, 2nd edn, 2004).

Charters, Claire and Andrew Erueti, 'Report from the Inside: The CERD Committee's Review of the Foreshore and Seabed Act 2004' (2005) 36 Victoria Univ of Wellington L Rev 257.

Cooke, Robin (ed), *Portrait of a Profession: The Centennial Book of the New Zealand Law Society* (Wellington: Reed, 1969).

Cooke, Sir Robin, 'Introduction' (1990) 14 New Zealand Univ L Rev 1.

Cox, Lindsay, *Kotahitangi: The Search for Maori Political Unity* (Auckland: Oxford University Press, 1993).

Cox, Noel, 'The Treaty of Waitangi and the Relationship between Crown and Maori in New Zealand' (2002) 28 Brooklyn J of Int'l L 123.

Department of Conservation, *Tongariro National Park Management Plan* (Wellington: Department of Conservation, 2006).

Department of Conservation, *Conservation Management Strategy—Wanganui Conservancy* (Wellington: Department of Conservation, 2007).

Department of Prime Minister and Cabinet, *Summary of Foreshore and Seabed Framework* (Wellington: Department of Prime Minister and Cabinet, 2003).

Dorsett, Shaunnagh, 'Sworn on the Dirt of Graves: Sovereignty, Jurisdiction and the Judicial Abrogation of "Barbarous" Customs in New Zealand in the 1840s' (2009) 30 J of Legal History 175.

Evans, Jim, 'Reflections on Nireaha Tamaki v Baker' (2007) 2 Te Tai Haruru Journal of Maori Legal Writing 101.

Findlay, L M, 'Always Indigenize! The Radical Humanities in the Postcolonial Canadian University' (2000) 31 Ariel 307.

Frame, Alex, 'Hoani Te Heuheu's Case in London 1940–1941: An Explosive Story' (2006) 22 New Zealand Univ L Rev 148.

Gibbs, M, 'What Structures are Appropriate to Receive Treaty of Waitangi Settlement Assets?' (2004) 21 New Zealand Univ L Rev 197.

Gilling, B D, 'Engine of Destruction? An Introduction to the History of the Maori Land Court' (1994) 24 Victoria Univ of Wellington L Rev 115.

Glenn, H Patrick, *Legal Traditions of the World* (New York: Oxford University Press, 3rd edn, 2007).

Harris, B V, 'The Treaty of Waitangi and the Constitutional Future of New Zealand' (2005) 2 New Zealand L Rev 189.

Harrop, A J, *England and New Zealand: From Tasman to the Taranaki War* (London: Methuen, 1926).

Hayward, Janine and Nicola R Wheen (eds), *The Waitangi Tribunal. Te Roopu Whakamana I te Tiriti o Waitangi* (Wellington: Bridget Williams Books, 2004).

Henderson, James (Sákéj) Youngblood, 'Postcolonial Indigenous Legal Consciousness' (2002) 1 Indigenous LJ 4.

Hickford, Mark, 'Making Territorial Rights of the Natives: Britain and New Zealand, 1830–1847' (DPhil thesis, University of Oxford, 1999).

Hickford, Mark, 'Settling Some Very Important Principles of Colonial Law: Three 'Forgotten' Cases of the 1840s' (2004) 35 Victoria Univ of Wellington L Rev 1.

Hickford, Mark, ' "Decidedly the Most Interesting Savages on the Globe": An Approach to the Intellectual History of Maori Property Rights, 1837–53' (Spring 2006) 27 History of Political Thought 122.

Hickford, Mark, 'John Salmond and Native Title in New Zealand: Developing a Crown Theory on the Treaty of Waitangi, 1910–1920' (2007) 38 Victoria Univ of Wellington L Rev 853.

Hoebel, E Adamson, *The Law of Primitive Man: A Study in Comparative Legal Dynamics* (Cambridge: Harvard University Press, 1954).

Hunn, J, *Report on Department of Maori Affairs, with Statistical Supplement* (Wellington: Government Printer, 1961).

James, Colin (ed), *Building the Constitution* (Wellington: Institute of Policy Studies, 2000).

Jansen, Nils, 'Comparative Law and Comparative Knowledge' in Mathias Reimann and Reinhard Zimmermann (eds), *The Oxford Handbook of Comparative Law* (Oxford: Oxford University Press, 2006).

Joseph, R, 'Contemporary Maori Governance: New Era or New Error?' (2007) 22 New Zealand Univ L Rev 628.

Kawharu, I H, *Maori Land Tenure: Studies of a Changing Institution* (Oxford: Clarendon Press, 1977).

Keal, Paul, *European Conquest and the Rights of Indigenous Peoples: The Moral Backwardness of International Society* (Cambridge: Cambridge University Press, 2003).

King, Michael, *The Penguin History of New Zealand* (Auckland: Penguin Books, 2003).

McHugh, Paul, *Aboriginal Societies and the Common Law: A History of Sovereignty, Status and Self-Determination* (Oxford: Oxford University Press, 2004).

McHugh, Paul, 'Aboriginal Title in New Zealand: A Retrospect and Prospect' (2004) 2 New Zealand J of Public and Int'l Law 139.

McNeil, Kent, 'Judicial Treatment of Indigenous Land Rights in the Common Law World' in Benjamin J Richardson, Shin Imai and Kent McNeil (eds), *Indigenous Peoples and the Law: Comparative and Critical Perspectives* (Portland, OR: Hart Publishing, 2009).

Magallanes, Catherine J I, 'Reparations for Maori Grievances in Aotearoa New Zealand' in Federico Lenzerini (ed), *Reparations for Indigenous Peoples. International and Comparative Perspectives* (Oxford: Oxford University Press, 2008).

Mikaere, Ani, 'Cultural Invasion Continued: The Ongoing Colonisation of Tikanga Maori' (2005) 8 YB of NZ Jurisprudence Special Issue—Te Purenga 134.

Miller, Robert J and Jacinta Ruru, 'An Indigenous Lens into Comparative Law: The Doctrine of Discovery in the United States and New Zealand' (2009) 111 West Virginia L Rev 849.

Milroy, Stephanie and Leah Whiu, 'Waikato Law School: An Experiment in Bicultural Legal Education' (2005) 8 YB of NZ Jurisprudence Special Issue—Te Purenga 173.

Ministry of Justice, *Pākia ki uta, Pākia ki tai. Summary Report of the Ministerial Review Panel: Ministerial Review of the Foreshore and Seabed* (Wellington: Ministry of Justice, 2009).

Nessen, Paul von, *The Use of Comparative Law in Australia* (Pyrmont: Thomson Lawbook Co, 2006).

New Zealand Law Commission, *Waka Umanga: A Proposed Law for Maori Governance Entities*. Report 92 (NZLC, 2006).

Ngata, HM, *English-Maori Dictionary* (Wellington: Learning Media, 1993).

Office of Treaty Settlements, *Ka tika ā muri, ka tika ā mua. Healing the past, building a future. A Guide to Treaty of Waitangi Claims and Negotiations with the Crown* (Wellington: Office of Treaty Settlements, 1999).

Orange, Claudia, *The Treaty of Waitangi* (Wellington: Allen & Unwin, 1987).

Orange, Claudia, *An Illustrated History of the Treaty of Waitangi* (Wellington: Bridget Williams Books, 2004).

O'Regan, Tipene, 'The Ngai Tahu Claim' in I H Kawharu (ed), *Waitangi: Maori and Pakeha Perspectives of the Treaty of Waitangi* (Auckland: Oxford University Press, 1989).

Palmer, Matthew S R, 'Constitutional Realism about Constitutional Protection: Indigenous Rights Under a Judicialized and a Politicized Constitution' (2007) 29 Dalhousie LJ 1.

Palmer, Matthew S R, *The Treaty of Waitangi in New Zealand's Law and Constitution* (Wellington: Victoria University Press, 2008).

Phillip Joseph, *Constitutional and Administrative Law in New Zealand* (Wellington: Thompson Brookers, 2nd edn, 2007).

Prichard, I and H Waetford, *Report of Committee of Inquiry into the Laws Affecting Maori Land the Jurisdiction and Powers of the Maori Land Court* (Wellington: Department of Maori Affairs, 1965).

Renwick, William, 'A Variation of a Theme' in William Renwick (ed), *Sovereignty and Indigenous Rights: The Treaty of Waitangi in International Contexts* (Wellington: Victoria University Press, 1991).

Ross, R M, 'Te Tiriti o Waitangi. Texts and Translations' (1972) 6(2) New Zealand J of History 129 (reprinted in Judith Binney (ed), *The Shaping of History: Essays from the New Zealand Journal of History* (Wellington: Bridget Williams Books, 2001)).

Ruru, Jacinta, 'A Politically Fuelled Tsunami: The Foreshore/Seabed Controversy in Aotearoa/New Zealand' (2004) 113 J of Polynesian Society 57.

Ruru, Jacinta, 'Implications for Maori: Historical Overview', in Nicola Peart, Margaret Briggs, and Mark Henaghan (eds), *Relationship Property on Death* (Wellington: Brookers, 2004).

Ruru, Jacinta, 'Managing Our Treasured Home: the Conservation Estate and the Principles of the Treaty of Waitangi' (2004) 8 New Zealand J of Envt'l Law 243.

Ruru, Jacinta, 'What Could Have Been: The Common Law Doctrine of Native Title in Land Under Salt Water in Australia and Aotearoa/New Zealand' (2006) 32 Monash Univ L Rev 116.

Ruru, Jacinta (ed), *'In Good Faith' Symposium Proceedings marking the 20th anniversary of the* Lands *case* (Wellington: New Zealand Law Foundation, 2008).

Ruru, Jacinta, 'The Maori Encounter with Aotearoa New Zealand's Legal System' in Benjamin J Richardson, Shin Imai, and Kent McNeil (eds), *Indigenous Peoples and the Law: Comparative and Critical Perspectives* (Oxford: Hart Publishing, 2009).

Ruru, Jacinta, *The Legal Voice of Maori in Freshwater Governance: A Literature Review* (Christchurch: Landcare Research, 2009).

Russell, Peter H, *Recognizing Aboriginal Title: The Mabo Case and Indigenous Resistance to English-Settler Colonialism* (Toronto: University of Toronto Press, 2005).

Scholtz, Christa, *Negotiating Claims: The Emergence of Indigenous Land Claim Negotiation Policies in Australia, Canada, New Zealand, and the United States* (Hoboken: Routledge, 2006).

Solomon, Maui, 'The Wai 262 Claim: A Claim by Maori to Indigenous Flora and Fauna: Me o Ratou Taonga Katoa' in Michael Belgrave, Merata Kawharu, and David Williams (eds), *Waitangi Revisited: Perspectives on the Treaty of Waitangi* (Auckland: Oxford University Press, 2nd edn, 2005).

Sorrenson, M P K, 'The Purchase of Maori Lands, 1865–1892' (Masters thesis, The University of Auckland 1955).

Spiller, Peter, Jeremy Finn and Richard Boast (eds), *A New Zealand Legal History* (Wellington: Brookers, 2nd edn, 2001).

Tahana, Ngaroma, 'Tikanga Maori Concepts and Arawa Rangatiratanga and Kaitiakitanga of Arawa Lakes' (2006) 2 Te Tai Haruru J of Maori Legal Writing 39.

Tate, John William, 'Pre-*Wi Parata*: Early Native Title Cases in New Zealand' (2003) 12 Waikato L Rev 112.

Tate, John William, 'Hohepa Wi Neera: Native Title and the Privy Council Challenge' (2004) 35 Victoria Univ of Wellington L Rev 73.

Te Puni Korkiri/Ministry of Maori Development, *He Tirohanga o Kawa ki to Tiriti o Waitangi. A Guide to the Principles of the Treaty of Waitangi as Expressed by the Courts and the Waitangi Tribunal* (Wellington: Te Puni Korkiri, 2001).

Tomas, Nin and Karensa Johnston, 'Ask That Taniwha Who Owns the Foreshore and Seabed of Aotearoa?' (2004) 1 Te Tai Haruru J of Maori Legal Writing 1.

Waitangi Tribunal, *Report of the Waitangi Tribunal on the Kaituna River Claim* Wai 4 (Wellington: Legislation Direct, 1984).

Waitangi Tribunal, *Report of the Waitangi Tribunal on the Orakei Claim* Wai 9 (Wellington: Legislation Direct, 1987).

Waitangi Tribunal, *Report of the Waitangi Tribunal on the Muriwhenua Fishing Claim* Wai 22 (Wellington: Legislation Direct, 1988).

Waitangi Tribunal, *Report of the Waitangi Tribunal on Claims Concerning the Allocation of Radio Frequencies* Wai 26 (Wellington: Legislation Direct, 1990).

Waitangi Tribunal, *The Ngai Tahu Report* Wai 27 (Wellington: Legislation Direct, 1991).

Waitangi Tribunal, *The Ngai Tahu Sea Fisheries Report* Wai 27 (Wellington: Legislation Direct, 1992).

Waitangi Tribunal, *Mohaka River Report* Wai 119 (Wellington: Legislation Direct, 1992).

Waitangi Tribunal, *Preliminary Report on the Te Arawa Representative Geothermal Resource Claims* Wai 153 (Wellington: Legislation Direct, 1993).

Waitangi Tribunal, *Maori Electoral Option Report* Wai 413 (Wellington: Legislation Direct, 1994).

Waitangi Tribunal, *The Turangi Township Report* Wai 84 (Wellington: Legislation Direct, 1995).

Waitangi Tribunal, *Ngai Tahu Report* vol 2 (Wai 27) (Wellington: GP Publications, 1997).

Waitangi Tribunal, *The Whanganui River Report* Wai 167 (Wellington: Legislation Direct, 1999).

Waitangi Tribunal, *The Napier Hospital and Health Services Report* Wai 692 (Wellington: Legislation Direct, 2001).

Waitangi Tribunal, *Te Whanganui A Tara Me Ona Takiwa. Report on the Wellington District* Wai 145 (Wellington: Legislation Direct, 2003).

Waitangi Tribunal, *The Petroleum Report* Wai 796 (Wellington: Legislation Direct, 2003).

Waitangi Tribunal, *The Tarawera Forest Report* Wai 411 (Wellington: Legislation Direct, 2003).

Waitangi Tribunal, *Report on the Crown's Foreshore and Seabed Policy* Wai 1071 (Wellington: Legislation Direct, 2004).

Waitangi Tribunal, *Turanga Tangata, turanga Whenua: The Report on the Turanganui a Kiwa Claims* vol 2, Wai 814 (Wellington: Legislation Direct, 2004).

Waitangi Tribunal, *The Mohaka Ki Ahuriri Report* Wai 201 (Wellington: Legislation Direct, 2004).

Waitangi Tribunal, *Te Raupatu o Tauranga Moana Report on the Tauranga Confiscation Claims* Wai 215 (Wellington: Legislation Direct, 2004).

Waitangi Tribunal, *The Waimumu Trust (SILNA) Report* Wai 1090 (Wellington: Legislation Direct, 2005).

Waitangi Tribunal, *The Report on the Impact of the Crown's Treaty Settlement Policy on Te Arawa Waka* (Wellington: Legislation Direct, 2007).

Waitangi Tribunal, *Tamaki Makarau Settlement Process Report* (Wellington: Legislation Direct, 2007).

Waitangi Tribunal, *He Maunga Rongo. Report on the Central North Island Claims* Wai 1200 vol 4 (Wellington: Legislation Direct, 2008).

Walker, Ranginui, *Ka Whawhai Tonu Matou: Struggle Without End* (Auckland: Penguin Books, 2nd edn, 2004).

Ward, Alan, *A Show of Justice: Radical 'Amalgamation' in Nineteenth Century New Zealand* (Auckland: Auckland University Press, 1973).

Ward, Alan, *An Unsettled History: Treaty Claims in New Zealand Today* (Wellington: Bridget Williams Books, 1999).

Wheen N R and J Ruru, 'The Environmental Reports' in *The Waitangi Tribunal*.

White, Ben, *Inland Waterways: Lakes: Rangahaua Whanui National Theme Q* (Wellington: Waitangi Tribunal, 1998).

Wickliffe, Caren, 'Te Timatanga: Maori Women's Access to Justice' (2005) 8(2) YB of NZ Jurisprudence Special Issue—Te Purenga 217, 229.

Wigmore, John H, 'Comparative Law: Jottings on Comparative Legal Ideas and Institutions' (1931–32) 6 Tulane L Rev 48.

Wilberg, Hanna, 'Facing up to the Original Breach of the Treaty' (2007) New Zealand L Rev 527.

Wilberg, Hanna, 'Judicial Remedies for the Original Breach?' (2007) New Zealand L Rev 713.

Williams, David V, 'The Annexation of New Zealand to New South Wales in 1840: What of the Treaty of Waitangi' (1985) 2 Australian J of L and Society 41.

Williams, David V, 'The Foundation of Colonial Rule in New Zealand' (1988) New Zealand Univ L Rev 56.

Williams, David V, *Te Kooti Tango Whenua: The Native Land Court 1864–1909* (Wellington: Huia Publishers, 1999).

Williams, David V, 'Myths, National Origins, Common Law and the Waitangi Tribunal' (2004) 11 Murdoch U Electronic J

Williams, David V, 'Wi Parata is Dead, Long Live Wi Parata' in Claire Charters and Andrew Erueti (eds), *Maori Property Rights and the Foreshore and Seabed: The Last Frontier* (Wellington: Victoria University Press, 2007).

Williams, David V, 'The Treaty of Waitangi—A "Bridle" on Parliamentary Sovereignty' (2007) 13 New Zealand Univ L Rev 596.

Williams, H W, *Dictionary of the Maori Language* (Wellington: GP Publications, 1992).

Young, Simon, *The Trouble with Tradition. Native title and cultural change* (Sydney: Federation Press, 2008).

UNITED STATES CHAPTERS

Abbot, W W (ed), *Colonial Series: The Papers of George Washington* (Charlottesville, VA: University of Virginia Press, 1988) Volume IV.

Adams, Charles Francis (ed), *The Works of John Adams, Second President of the United States* (Boston: Little, Brown & Co, 1856) Volume X.

American State Papers: Documents, Legislative and Executive, of the Congress of the United States Volumes II–VI.

Ames, Susie M (ed), *County Court Records of Accomack-Northampton, Virginia 1632–1640* (Charlottesville: University Press of Virginia, 1954, reprint 1975).

Altholz, Josef Lewis (ed), *Selected Documents in Irish History* (Armonk, NY: M E Sharpe, Inc, 2000).

Anderson, Fred, *Crucible of War: The Seven Years' War and the Fate of Empire in British North America, 1754–1766* (New York: Alfred A Knopf, 2000).

Anderson, Terry L and Fred S McChesney, 'Raid or Trade? An Economic Model of Indian–White Relations' (1994) 37 J L Econ 39.

Annals of Congress, 8th Congress, 1st Session (8 March 1804).

Banner, Stuart, *Possessing the Pacific: Land, Settlers, and Indigenous People from Australia to Alaska* (Cambridge: Harvard University Press, 2007).

Barsh, Russell Lawrence and James Youngblood Henderson, *The Road: Indian Tribes and Political Liberty* (Berkeley, CA: University of California Press, 1980).

Beckham, Stephen Dow, *Ethnohistorical Context of Reserved Indian Fishing Rights: Pacific Northwest Treaties* (Portland, OR: Lewis & Clark College, 1984).

Beckham, Stephen Dow, *Lewis & Clark: From the Rockies to the Pacific* (Portland, OR: Graphic Arts Center, 2002).

Benton, Thomas Hart, *Thirty Years' View: or A History of the Working of the American Government for Thirty Years from 1820–1850* (1856, New York: Greenwood Press reprint 1968).

Berat, Lynn, *Walvis Bay: Decolonization and International Law* (New Haven: Yale University Press, 1990).

Billington, Ray Allen, *The Far Western Frontier, 1830–1860* (Evanston, IL: Harper & Row, 1956).

Blackstone, William, *Commentaries on the Law of England* (London: Dawsons of Pall Mall, 1966, reprint of 1765 edition).

Bourne, Edward Gaylord, 'Aspects of Oregon History Before 1840' (1906) VI Oregon Historical Quarterly 264.

Bowen, Catherine, *Miracle at Philadelphia* (Boston: Little, Brown, 1966).

Boyd, Julian P et al (eds), *The Papers of Thomas Jefferson* (Princeton: Princeton University Press, 1952) Volume VI.

Calloway, Colin G, *Crown and Calumet: British–Indian Relations, 1783–1815* (Norman: University of Oklahoma Press, 1987).

Calloway, Colin G (ed), *The World Turned Upside Down: Indian Voices from Early America* (Boston: St Martin's Press, 1994).

Cappon, Lester J (ed), *The Adams-Jefferson Letters* (Chapel Hill, NC: University of North Carolina Press, 1959) Volume II.

Carter, Clarence E (ed), *The Territorial Papers of the United States* (Washington DC: Gov't Printing Office, 1934) Volume 2.

Castles, Alex C, 'An Australian Legal History', in *Aboriginal Legal Issues, Commentary and Materials* (Holmes Beach, FL: Wm W Gaunt & Sons, H McRae et al (eds), 1991).

Chumbley, George Lewis, *Colonial Justice in Virginia* (Richmond: Diety Press, 1971).

Church and State Through the Centuries (New York: Biblo and Tannen, Sidney Z Ehler & John B Morrall (trans and eds), 1967)

Collier, John, *The Purposes and Operation of the Wheeler-Howard Indian Rights Bill, Hearings on H.R. 7902 Before the Senate and House Committees on Indian Affairs*, 73rd Congress, 2nd Session (1934) 15–18.

Colony Laws of North America Series, The (Wilmington: M Glazier, 1977).

Commager, Henry Steele, *Documents of American History* (New York: Appleton-Century-Crofts, 8th edn, 1968) Volume I.

Compilation of Messages and Papers of the Presidents, A (Washington DC: Bureau of National Literature, James D Richardson (ed), 1913) Volume 1.

Congressional Globe, 25th Congress, 2nd Session (May 1838).

Coulter, Robert T, 'The U.N. Declaration on the Rights of Indigenous Peoples: A Historic Change in International Law' (2009) 45 Idaho L Rev 6.

Cushing, John D (ed), *The Earliest Acts and Laws of the Colony of Rhode Island and Providence Plantations: 1647–1719* (Wilmington, DC: M Glazier, 1977).

Cushing, John D (ed), *Acts and Laws of New Hampshire 1680–1726* (Wilmington: M Glazier, 1978).

Cushing, John D (ed), *The First Laws of the State of Georgia* (Wilmington: M Glazier, 1981).

Cushing, John D (ed), *The First Laws of the State of Connecticut* (Wilmington: M Glazier, 1982).

Davenport, Frances G (ed), *European Treaties Bearing on the History of the United States and Its Dependencies to 1648* (Washington: Carnegie Institution of Washington, 1917).

Definitive Journals of Lewis & Clark, The (Lincoln: University of Nebraska Press, Gary E Moulton (ed), 1987) Volumes 1–13.

Deloria Jr, Vine, *God is Red: A Native View of Religion* (Golden, CO: Fulcrum Publishing, 2nd edn, 1994).

Deloria Jr, Vine and David E Wilkins, *Tribes, Treaties, & Constitutional Tribulations* (Austin: University of Texas Press, 1999).

DeVoto, Bernard, *The Course of Empire* (Boston: Houghton Mifflin, 1952).

DeVoto, Bernard (ed), *The Journals of Lewis and Clark* (Boston: Houghton Mifflin, 1953).

Dewey, Frank L, *Thomas Jefferson Lawyer* (Charlottesville: University Press of Virginia, 1986).

Early American Indian Documents: Treaties and Laws, 1607–1789 (Washington: University Publications of American, Alden T Vaughan and Barbara Graymont (eds), 1998) Volumes I–XXVI.

Ellis, Joseph J, *American Sphinx: The Character of Thomas Jefferson* (New York: Alfred A Knopf, 1998).

Erdmann, Carl, *The Origin of the Idea of Crusade* (Princeton: Princeton University Press, Marshall W Baldwin and Walter Goffart (trans), 1977).

Farrand Max, *The Framing of the Constitution* (New Haven: Yale University Press, 1913).

Farrand, Max (ed), *The Records of the Federal Convention of 1787* (New Haven: Yale University Press, 1937) Volume I.

Ferguson, Niall, *Colossus: The Price of America's Empire* (New York: Penguin Press, 2004).

Ferguson, Niall, *Empire: The Rise and Demise of the British World Order and the Lessons for Global Power* (New York: Basic Books, 2002).

Felix S Cohen's Handbook of Federal Indian Law (Charlottesville: Michie Company, Rennard Strickland et al (eds), 1982 edn).

Fitzpatrick, John C (ed), *The Writings of George Washington* (Washington DC: Gov't Printing Office, 1931).

Foner, Philip S (ed), *Basic Writings of Thomas Jefferson* (New York: Willey Book Co, 1944).

Ford, Paul (ed), *The Works of Thomas Jefferson* (New York: Putnam, 1905) Volume 10.

Ford, Worthington Chauncey (ed), *The Writings of John Quincy Adams 1816–1819* (New York: Macmillan Co, 1916; New York: Reprint, Greenwood Press, 1968) Volumes V–VI.

Foundations of Colonial America: A Documentary History (New York: Chelsea House, W Keith Kavenagh (ed), 1973) Volumes I–III.

Garrison, Tim Alan, *The Legal Ideology of Removal: The Southern Judiciary and the Sovereignty of Native American Nations* (Athens: University of Georgia Press, 2002).

Gibson, Charles (ed), *The Spanish Tradition in America* (New York: Harper & Row, 1968).

Goetzmann, William H, *Exploration and Empire: The Explorer and the Scientist in the Winning of the American West* (New York: Alfred A Knopf, 1966).

Golay, Michael, *The Tide of Empire: America's March to the Pacific* (New York: John Wiley & Sons Inc, 2003).

Hand, G J, *English Law in Ireland, 1290–1324* (Cambridge: Cambridge University Press, 1967).

Hanke, Lewis, *The Spanish Struggle for Justice in the Conquest of America* (Philadelphia: University of Pennsylvania Press, 1949).

Haynes, Sam W, *James K. Polk and the Expansionist Impulse* (New York: Longman, 1997).

Haynes, Sam W and Christopher Morris (eds), *Manifest Destiny and Empire: American Antebellum Expansionism* (College Station, TX: University of Texas Press, 1997).

Henderson, Ernest F (ed), *Select Historical Documents of the Middle Ages* (London: George Bell and Sons, 1910).

Heydte, Friedrich August Freiherr von der, 'Discovery, Symbolic Annexation and Virtual Effectiveness in International Law' (1935) 29 Am J Int'l L 448.

Horsman, Reginald, *Race and Manifest Destiny: The Origins of American Racial Anglo-Saxonism* (Cambridge: Harvard University Press, 1981).

House Document No 139, 20th Congress, 1st Session (11 February 1828).

House Report No 213, 19th Congress, 1st Session (1826).

Hulbert, Archer Butler (ed), *Overland to the Pacific: A Narrative-Documentary History of the Great Epochs of the Far West* (Denver: Denver Public Library, 1932–41).

Hull, Eleanor, *A History of Ireland* (Dublin: Phoenix Publishing Co, 1931) Volume I.

Hurtado, Albert L and Peter Iverson (eds), *Major Problems in American Indian History* (Toronto: Heath and Company, 1994).

Jackson, Donald (ed), *Letters of the Lewis and Clark Expedition with Related Documents 1783–1854* (Urbana, IL: University of Illinois Press, 2nd edn, 1978) Volumes I–II.

Jackson, Donald, *Thomas Jefferson & the Stony Mountains* (Urbana and Chicago: University of Illinois Press, 1981).

Jefferson, Thomas, 'The Limits and Bounds of Louisiana' in *Documents Relating to the Purchase & Exploration of Louisiana* (Boston: Houghton, Mifflin & Company, 1904).

Jones, Dorothy V, *License for Empire: Colonialism by Treaty in Early America* (Chicago: University of Chicago Press, 1982).

Journals of the Continental Congress (1786 and 1788) Volumes 33 and 34.

Kades, Eric, 'The Dark Side of Efficiency: *Johnson v. M'Intosh* and the Expropriation of American Indian Lands' (2000) 148 U Pa L Rev 1065.

Kappler, Charles J (ed), *Indian Affairs: Laws and Treaties* (Washington DC: Gov't Printing Office, 1904) Volume II.

Kennedy, Roger G, *Mr. Jefferson's Lost Cause: Land, Farmers, Slavery, and the Louisiana Purchase* (Oxford: Oxford University Press, 2003).

Kingsbury, Susan Myra (ed), *The Records of the Virginia Company of London* (Wilmington: Scholarly Resources, 1933).

Kurland, Phillip B and Ralph Lerner, *The Founder's Constitution* (Chicago: University of Chicago Press, 1987) Volume II.

Lamb, W Kaye (ed), *The Journals and Letters of Sir Alexander Mackenzie* (London: Cambridge University Press, 1970).

Laws of the Colonial and State Governments Relating to Indians and Indian Affairs, From 1633 to 1831 (Washington DC: Thompson and Homans, 1832; Stanfordville: Reprint, Earl M Coleman Enterprises Inc, 1979).

Leder, Lawrence H (ed), *The Livingston Indian Records, 1666–1723* (Gettysburg, PA: The Pennsylvania Historical Assoc, 1956; Stanfordville: Reprint, Earl M Coleman Publisher, 1979) 98.

Lipscomb, Andrew A and Albert Ellery Bergh (eds), *The Writings of Thomas Jefferson* (1903) Volumes I–XX.

Livermore, Shaw, *Early American Land Companies: Their Influence on Corporate Development* (New York: The Commonwealth Fund, 1939).

Lyons, Oren and John Mohawk (eds), *Exiled in the Land of the Free: Democracy, Indian Nations, and the U.S. Constitution* (Santa Fe, NM: Clear Light Publishers, 1992).

McLynn, Frank, *Wagons West: The Epic Story of America's Overland Trails* (New York: Grove Press, 2002).

Marshall, Thomas Maitland, *A History of the Western Boundary of the Louisiana Purchase, 1819–1841* (Berkeley: University California Press, 1914).

Merk, Frederick, *The Oregon Question: Essays in Anglo-American Diplomacy and Politics* (Cambridge: Belknap Press of Harvard University, 1967).

Miller, Robert J, 'American Indian Influence on the U.S. Constitution and Its Framers' (1993) 18 Am Indian L Rev 131.

Miller, Robert J, 'Economic Development in Indian Country: Will Capitalism or Socialism Succeed?' (2001) 80 Ore L Rev 757.

Miller, Robert J, 'Exercising Cultural Self-Determination: The Makah Indian Tribe Goes Whaling' (2001) 25 Am Indian L Rev 165.

Miller, Robert J, 'A New Perspective on the Indian Removal Period' (2002) 38 Tulsa LJ 181.

Miller, Robert J, *Native America, Discovered and Conquered: Thomas Jefferson Lewis and Clark, and Manifest Destiny* (Westport, CT and London: Praeger Publishers, 2006).

Miller, Robert J, 'Will others follow Episcopal Church's lead?' Indian Country Today, 12 August 2009, 5.

Morison, Samuel Eliot, *Admiral of the Ocean Sea* (Boston: Little, Brown & Co, 1942).

Morison, Samuel Eliot, *The European Discovery of America: The Southern Voyages* (New York: Oxford University Press, 1974) Volumes 1–2.

Muldoon, James (ed), *The Expansion of Europe* (Philadelphia: University of Pennsylvania Press, 1977).

Muldoon, James, *Popes, Lawyers and Infidels* (Philadelphia: University of Pennsylvania Press, 1979).

Nevins, Allan (ed), *The Diary of John Quincy Adams 1794–1845* (New York: Charles Scribner's Sons, 1951).

Newcomb, Steven T, *Pagans in the Promised Land: Decoding the Doctrine of Christian Discovery* (Golden, CO: Fulcrum Publishing, 2008).

Norgate, Kate, 'The Bull Laudabiliter' (January 1893) The English Historical Rev 18.

Nussbaum, Arthur, *A Concise History of The Law of Nations* (New York: Macmillan Co, 1947).

Onuf, Peter S, *Statehood and Union: A History of the Northwest Ordinance* (Bloomington: Indiana University Press, 1992).

Onuf, Peter S, *Jefferson's Empire: The Language of American Nationhood* (Charlottesville: University Press of Virginia, 2000).

Oregon Historical Quarterly Vols III (Sept 1902), XIX (Sept 1918), XX (Dec 1919).

Ouden, Amy E Den, *Beyond Conquest: Native Peoples and the Struggle for History in New England* (Lincoln: University Nebraska Press, 2005).

Pagden, Anthony, *Lords of all the World: Ideologies of Empire in Spain, Britain and France c. 1500–c. 1800* (New Haven: Yale University Press, 1995).

Pawlisch, Hans S, 'Sir John Davies, the Ancient Constitution and Civil Law' (1980) The Historical J 696.

Pawlisch, Hans S, *Sir John Davies and the Conquest of Ireland: A Study in Legal Imperialism* (Cambridge: Cambridge University Press, 1985).

Peterson, Merrill, *Thomas Jefferson and The New Nation* (New York: Oxford University Press, 1970).

Peyrouse, M De La, *A Voyage Round the World: Which was Performed in 1785, 1786, 1787, and 1788* (Edinburgh: J Moir, 1798).

Plumer, William, *Memorandum of Proceedings in the U.S. Senate, 1803–1897* (New York: Macmillan, Everett Somerville Brown (ed), 1923).

Pratt, Julius W, 'The Origin of "Manifest Destiny"' (4 July 1927) 32 The American Historical Rev 795.

Pratt, Julius W, 'John L. O'Sullivan and Manifest Destiny' (1933) 14 New York History 213.

Prestage, Edgar, *The Portuguese Pioneers* (London: A & C Black, 1966).

Prucha, Francis Paul, *The Great Father: The United States Government and the American Indians* (Lincoln: University of Nebraska Press, 1995).

Prucha, Francis Paul, *Documents of United States Indian Policy* (Lincoln: University of Nebraska Press, 3rd edn, 2000).

Purvis, Thomas L, *Colonial America to 1763* (New York: Facts on File, 1999).

Puy, Henry F De (ed), *A Bibliography of the English Colonial Treaties with the American Indians* (Mansfield: Martino Publishing, 1917, reprinted 1999).

Quinn, David Beers (ed), *The Voyages and Colonising Enterprises of Sir Humphrey Gilbert* (Liechtenstein: Kraus Reprint Ltd, 1967) Volume I.

Records of the Virginia Company of London: The Court Book, The (Washington DC: Gov't Printing Office, 1906).

Reynolds, Henry, *The Law of the Land* (New York: Viking Penguin, 1987).

Rhodehamel, John (ed), *George Washington Writings* (New York: Literary Classics of the US, 1997).

Robertson, Lindsay G, *Conquest by Law: How the Discovery of American Dispossessed Indigenous Peoples of Their Land* (Oxford: Oxford University Press, 2007).

Ronda, James P, *Lewis & Clark among the Indians* (Lincoln: University of Nebraska Press, 1984).

Ronda, James P, *Astoria & Empire* (Lincoln: University of Nebraska Press, 1990).

Ronda, James P (ed), *Thomas Jefferson and the Changing West* (St Louis: Missouri Historical Society Press, 1997).

Ronda, James P, *Finding The West: Explorations with Lewis and Clark* (Albuquerque: University of New Mexico Press, 2001).

Rossiter, Clinton (ed), *The Federalist Papers* (New York: New American Library, 1961).

Royce, Charles, *Indian Land Cessions in the US*, Bureau of American Ethnology, Eighteenth Annual Report, 1896–1897, part 2 (1899).

Rutland, Robert A (ed), *The Papers of George Mason* (Chapel Hill, NC: University of North Carolina Press, 1970) Volumes I–III.

Rutland, Robert A (ed), *The Papers of James Madison* (Charlottesville: University Press of Virginia, 1983).

Sanford, Charles (ed), *Reprint of Documents: Manifest Destiny and the Imperialism Question* (New York: John Wiley & Sons Inc, 1974).

Scott, E H (ed), *US Constitutional Convention, Journal of the Federal Convention* (Chicago: Albert Scott, 1893).

Seed, Patricia, *Ceremonies of Possession in Europe's Conquest of the New World, 1492–1640* (Cambridge: Cambridge University Press, 1995).

Seefeldt, Douglas, Jeffrey L Hantman, and Peter S Onuf (eds), *Across The Continent: Jefferson, Lewis & Clark, and the Making of America* (Charlottesville: University of Virginia Press, 2005).

Select Charters and Other Documents Illustrative of American History 1606–1775 (London: The MacMillan Company, William MacDonald (ed), 1906; Reprint, Littleton, Colorado, Rothman & Co, 1993).

Simsarian, James, 'The Acquisition of Legal Title to Terra Nullius' (March 1938) 53 Pol Sci Q 111.

Smith, Joseph Henry, *Appeals to the Privy Council from the American Plantations* (New York: Columbia University Press, 1950).

Smith, Samuel, *The History of the Colony of Nova-Caesaria or New Jersey: Containing an Account of its First Settlement, Progressive Improvements, the Original & Present Constitution & Other Events, to the Year 1721: With Some Particulars Since; And a Short View of Its Present State New Jersey* (1765, Trenton NJ: William S Sharp, reprint 1890).

Smyth, Albert Henry (ed), *The Writings of Benjamin Franklin* (New York: Macmillan Co, 1907).

Sosin, Jack M, *Whitehall and the Wilderness: The Middle West in British Colonial Policy, 1760–1775* (Lincoln: University of Nebraska Press, 1961).

Stephanson, Anders, *Manifest Destiny: American Expansion and the Empire of Right* (New York: Hill and Want, 1995).

Story, William W (ed), *The Miscellaneous Writings of Joseph Story* (Union, NJ: Reprint, Lawbook Exchange, 2000, 1852).

Syrett, Harold C and Jacob E Cooke (eds), *The Papers of Alexander Hamilton* (New York: Columbia University Press, 1962) Volume III.

Syrett, Harold C and Jacob E Cooke (eds), *The Papers of Alexander Hamilton* (New York: Columbia University Press, 1969) Volume XIV.

Thwaites, Rueben Gold (ed), *The Jesuit Relations and Allied Documents* (Cleveland: Burrows Bros Co, 1896).

Thwaites, Rueben Gold (ed), *Travels and Explorations of the Jesuit Missionaries in New France* (New York: Pageant Book Co, 1959).

Victoria, Franciscus de, *De Indis et de Iure Bellie Relectiones* (Washington: Carnegie Institution, Ernest Nys (ed) and John Pauley Bate (trans), 1917).

Wallace, Anthony F C, *Jefferson and the Indians* (Ann Arbor: University of Michigan Press, 1999).

Washburn, Wilcomb E (ed), *The American Indian and the United States: A Documentary History* (New York: Random House, 1973) Volume III.

Watson, Harry L, *Liberty and Power: The Politics of Jacksonian America* (New York: Farrar, Straus & Giroux, 1990).

Weeks, William Earl, *John Quincy Adams and American Global Empire* (Louisville, KY: The University Press of Kentucky, 1992).

Weeks, William Earl, *Building the Continental Empire: American Expansion from the Revolution to the Civil War* (Chicago: Ivan R Dee, 1996).

Weinberg, Albert K, *Manifest Destiny: A Study of Nationalist Expansionism in American History* (Gloucester, MA: Peter Smith, 1958).

Wheaton, Henry, *Elements of International Law* (Boston: Little, Brown, William B Lawrence (ed), 6th edn, 1855).

Wilcox, William B (ed), *The Papers of Benjamin Franklin* (New Haven: Yale University Press, 1959–2008) Volume V.

Wilkinson, Charles F, *American Indians, Time, and the Law* (New Haven: Yale University Press, 1987).

Williams, Jr, Robert A, *The American Indian in Western Legal Thought: The Discourses of Conquest* (New York: Oxford University Press, 1990).

Index

Printed and bound by CPI Group (UK) Ltd, Croydon, CR0 4YY